Uncertainty and Operations Research

Decision analysis based on uncertain data is natural in many real-world applications, and sometimes such an analysis is inevitable. In the past years, researchers have proposed many efficient operations research models and methods, which have been widely applied to real-life problems, such as finance, management, manufacturing, supply chain, transportation, among others. This book series aims to provide a global forum for advancing the analysis, understanding, development, and practice of uncertainty theory and operations research for solving economic, engineering, management, and social problems.

More information about this series at http://www.springer.com/series/11709

Hai Wang · Zeshui Xu

Theory and Approaches of Group Decision-Making with Uncertain Linguistic Expressions

Springer

Hai Wang
School of Information Engineering
Nanjing Audit University
Nanjing, Jiangsu, China

Zeshui Xu
Business School
Sichuan University
Chengdu, Sichuan, China

ISSN 2195-996X ISSN 2195-9978 (electronic)
Uncertainty and Operations Research
ISBN 978-981-13-3734-5 ISBN 978-981-13-3735-2 (eBook)
https://doi.org/10.1007/978-981-13-3735-2

Library of Congress Control Number: 2018964257

This Springer imprint is published by the registered company Springer Nature Singapore Pte Ltd.
The registered company address is: 152 Beach Road, #21-01/04 Gateway East, Singapore 189721, Singapore

Preface

Due to the complexity of problems in hand and the limitation of experts' cognition, uncertainties are generally inevitable in decision information. In the fuzzy linguistic approach, linguistic variables enable a manner to represent uncertain information which is close to human's cognition. It is necessary that, in the traditional way of computing with words, the experts have to represent decision information by means of certain terms. However, this is quite difficult when facing complex types of uncertainties. Uncertain linguistic expressions, which include more than one possible term in a direct or indirect way, are more consistent with people's language conventions. In order to enable the use of uncertain linguistic expressions in decision-making processes, some fundamental theories and approaches have been developed

On the basis of the existing models, this book introduces some linguistic models to represent two types of uncertain linguistic expressions which conform to natural language conventions, i.e., extended hesitant fuzzy linguistic term sets and linguistic terms with weakened hedges, and presents the related fundamental theories and approaches for group decision-making. Specifically, the book is organized by five parts as follows:

The first part is formed by Chap. 1. This chapter introduces the background of computing with words, the focused problems, and some related theory and techniques. A brief overview of this related area, such as the current developments of models of uncertain linguistic expressions, the group decision-making approaches, is also given in this chapter.

The second part is Chap. 2. This chapter presents the representational model of the virtual linguistic terms, extend the model of hesitant fuzzy linguistic term sets, and then introduces a new technique to model linguistic hedges. Computational models of these techniques, such as order relations, are also presented.

The third part goes through Chaps. 3–5. Chapters 3 and 4 focus on the group decision-making problems with the extended version of hesitant fuzzy linguistic term sets. Chapter 3 is under the framework of decision matrices, presents an information fusion based group decision-making approach and a two-phase group decision-making approach. Chapter 4 is based on the framework of preference relations, presents some new consistency measures, and then employs them to improve incomplete linguistic preference relations. Group decision-making problems and preference relations with hedges are focused in Chap. 5. A multigranular group decision-making approach is introduced and some theoretical aspects of the new preference relations are also discussed.

The fourth part includes Chaps. 6 and 7 where group decision-making problems with multiple types of uncertain linguistic expressions are considered. Two group decision-making approaches are introduced. The first one considers the aspiration levels taking the form of uncertain linguistic expressions and the second one presents descriptive measures for decision makers to understand the effects of uncertain parameters.

The last part includes Chap. 8. A hierarchical model is introduced for the evaluation of big data-based audit platforms. The model is solved in the case where the performances take the forms of multiple types of uncertain linguistic expressions, based on the uncertain linguistic expressions approach presented in Chap. 6.

This book can be used as a reference for engineers, technicians, and researchers who are working in the fields of intelligent computation, fuzzy mathematics, operations research, information science, management science and so on. It could also serve as a textbook for postgraduate and senior undergraduate students of the relevant professional institutions of higher learning.

The first author would like to thank Dr. Xiao-Jun Zeng at the University of Manchester for his insightful ideas and great suggestions. This work was supported in part by the National Natural Science Foundation of China under Grant 71571123 and Grant 71601092, and the Key University Science Research Project of Jiangsu Province (No. 16KJA520002, 18KJB413006) and the China Scholarship Council.

Nanjing, China
September 2018

Hai Wang
Zeshui Xu

Contents

Part I Introduction

1 Backgrounds and Literature Review 3
1.1 Linguistic Decision-Making in Qualitative Setting 3
1.2 Focused Problems 4
1.2.1 Novel CWW Models Based on ULEs 6
1.2.2 Preference Relations Based on ULEs 6
1.2.3 GDM Approaches Based on ULEs 7
1.2.4 Modelling Complex Problems Under Uncertainties 7
1.3 Recent Advances of the Focused Problems 8
1.3.1 Review of Modelling ULEs and Decision-Making Approaches 8
1.3.2 Review of Lingustic Hedges 14
1.3.3 Review of Group Decision-Making Approaches Under Uncertainty 15
1.3.4 A Summary of the Contributions and Limitations 20
1.4 Aims and Focuses of This Book 22
References 24

Part II Theory and Models of Uncertain Linguistic Expressions

2 Representational Models and Computational Foundations of Some Types of Uncertain Linguistic Expressions 35
2.1 Virtual Linguistic Model 35
2.1.1 Preliminaries 36
2.1.2 Syntax and Semantics of VLTs 37
2.1.3 Computational Model of VLTs 43
2.2 Extended Hesitant Fuzzy Linguistic Term Sets 44
2.2.1 Fuzzy Linguistic Approach and HFLTS 45
2.2.2 Representational Model of EHFLTSs 45

2.2.3 Basic Operations of EHFLTSs and Their Properties 46
2.2.4 A Partial Order of EHFLTSs 48
2.3 Total Orders of EHFLTSs 48
2.3.1 Existing Order Relations of EHFLTSs 49
2.3.2 Total Orders of EHFLTSs: A Generation Approach 50
2.4 Linguistic Terms with Weakened Hedges 55
2.4.1 Respresentational Model of LTWHs 56
2.4.2 Linguistic Computational Model Based on LTWHs 63
2.5 A Comparative Analysis on Similar Models of ULEs 66
2.5.1 Compared with the Existing Techniques of Modeling Hedges 66
2.5.2 LTWHs Versus ULTs and HFLTSs 67
2.5.3 Compared with Other Techniques 69
2.6 Concluding Remarks 70
References 70

Part III Group Decision-Making Based on a Single Type of Uncertain Linguistic Expressions

3 Group Decision-Making Based on EHFLTSs Under the Framework of Decision Matrix 75
3.1 A Framework of Multiple Groups Decision-Making 75
3.1.1 Mathematical Description of MGDM 76
3.1.2 Process of MGDM 77
3.2 A MGDM Approach Based on Information Fusion 79
3.2.1 Some Aggregation Operators of EHFLTSs 79
3.2.2 Properties of the Aggregation Operators 83
3.2.3 Implementation of the MGDM Processes 86
3.2.4 Applications 89
3.2.5 Comparative Analysis 90
3.3 A Two-Phase GDM Approach Based on Admissible Orders 92
3.3.1 Defining the EHFLOWA Operator Based on Admissible Orders 92
3.3.2 The Two-Phase GDM Approach 95
3.3.3 Application in Evaluations of Energy Technologies 97
3.3.4 Comparisons and Further Discussions 100
3.4 Conclusions 104
References 104

4 Preference Analysis and Applications Based on EHFLTSs 107
4.1 Some Consistency Measures of EHFLPRs 108
4.1.1 The Concept of EHFLPRs 108
4.1.2 Preference Relation Graphs 109

4.1.3 Additive Consistency for EHFLPRs 112
4.1.4 Selective Algorithm for Reducing EHFLPRs to LPRs Based on Additive Consistency 113
4.1.5 Weak Consistency for EHFLPRs 116
4.1.6 Broken Circle Algorithm for Reducing EHFLPRs to LPRs Based on Weak Consistency 117
4.1.7 Comparative Analyses 118
4.2 Improving Incomplete LPRs Based on Consistency Measures of EHFLPRs 122
4.2.1 Incomplete LPRs and Their Consistency Measures 123
4.2.2 An Interactive Algorithm to Reach Weak Consistency of Incomplete LPRs 124
4.2.3 A Consistency-Based Interactive Algorithm to Complete Incomplete LPRs 127
4.2.4 The Interactive Algorithm with Self-adaptive Evolution to Complete Incomplete LPRs 131
4.2.5 An Example Regarding the Evaluation of Energy Channels 134
4.2.6 Comparisions and Discussions 137
4.3 Conclusions 139
References 140

5 Preference Analysis and Group Decision-Making Based on LTWHs 141
5.1 Multi-granular Linguistic Decision-Making with LTWHs 141
5.1.1 The Framework of MGLDM Problems 141
5.1.2 Constructing Multi-granular Linguistic Model Based on Hedges 143
5.1.3 An Approach for MGLDM with LTWHs 144
5.1.4 An Application of Evaluating the Non-financial Performance of Banks 145
5.1.5 Compared with Similar MGLDM Approaches 147
5.2 Consistency Measures of Linguistic Preference Relations with Hedges 150
5.2.1 Some Basic Operations and Order Relations of LTWHs 151
5.2.2 Linguistic Preference Relations with Weakened Hedges . . . 152
5.2.3 Consistency Measures of LHPRs 154
5.2.4 Weak Consistency of LHPRs 156
5.2.5 Additive Consistency of LHPRs 158
5.2.6 Consistency Improving of LHPRs. 162
5.3 Conclusions 167
References 168

Part IV Group Decision-Making Based on Multiple Types of Uncertain Linguistic Expressions

6 An Aspiration-Based Approach with Multiple Types of Uncertain Linguistic Expressions 171
6.1 Utility Functions Based on Linguistic Aspiration Levels 171
6.1.1 Similarity Measure of ULEs 173
6.1.2 Linguistic Aspiration Levels and Utility Functions 174
6.2 An Approach for Multi-criteria Multi-groups and Multi-granular GDM 175
6.2.1 Framework of the Focused Problem 175
6.2.2 An Approach for M^3QDM Problems 176
6.3 Conclusions 180
References 180

7 Group Decision-Making with Multiple Types of Uncertain Linguistic Expressions: Stochastic Acceptability Analysis 183
7.1 Motivation of Considering Stochastic Acceptability Analysis 183
7.2 Probabilistic Representation of ULEs 185
7.3 Framework of the Stochastic Approach 186
7.3.1 Problem Description 186
7.3.2 Framework of the Stochastic Approach 187
7.4 Group Consensus 188
7.4.1 The Threshold of Acceptable Consensus of a Group of LDMs 188
7.4.2 Defining the Consensus Degree and Acceptable Consensus of a Group of PLDMs 190
7.4.3 Consensus Checking 191
7.4.4 Consensus Improving 193
7.5 Decision-Making with the Collective PLDM 195
7.6 Illustration and Comparisons 198
7.6.1 An Application of Personnel Selection 198
7.6.2 Comparative Analyses 201
7.7 Further Discussions 205
7.7.1 Complexity and Accuracy of the Simulation Algorithms 205
7.7.2 Suggestions About the Parameters 206
7.7.3 Further Extension 207
7.8 Conclusions 209
References 209

Part V Applications

8 Provider Selection of Big Data-Based Auditing Platforms with Uncertain Linguistic Expressions 213
8.1 The Hierarchical Model for BDAP Provider Selection 214
8.2 Solving the Model by the M^{3}GDM Approach 217
8.3 Comparisons and Further Discussions 219
8.3.1 Regarding the M^{3}QDM Approach 219
8.3.2 Regarding the Hierarchical Model. 221
8.4 Conclusions 221
References 222

Part I
Introduction

Part I

Introduction

Chapter 1
Backgrounds and Literature Review

The purpose of this chapter is to introduce the background of this book, make clear the focused problems, and then illustrate the outline and the organization of this book.

1.1 Linguistic Decision-Making in Qualitative Setting

Decision-making exists in many social, economic and management problems, such as investment decision-making, project evaluation, enterprise site selection, scientific achievement evaluation, to name but a few. In a decision-making problem, the decision maker has to evaluate the set of available alternatives in terms of a set of, usually contradictory, criteria. The essential of decision-making is to rank and select the alternatives based on the available information. In practice, due to the complexity of problems and the inevitable uncertainties of the decision information, it is usually infeasible for an individual expert to complete the whole work of evaluations. Thus the theory of group decision-making (GDM) was presented and developed based on social selection axioms. To model and manage the uncertainties in problems, the methodology of fuzzy sets was introduced to solve multiple criteria decision-making (MCDM) and GDM problems. Many fuzzy set-based approaches have been applied in fuzzy control, pattern recognition, medical diagnosis and some other fields.

In traditional fuzzy set-based approaches, uncertainties should be represented by specific membership functions. This results in the difficulty of information expressing. In fact, linguistic expressions are frequently considered to represent information with fuzzy uncertainty. Given a reference domain, theoretically, linguistic variables are the variables whose values take the form of natural or artificial linguistic expressions [145]. Although their values are not as accurate as those of traditional variables,

H. Wang and Z. Xu, *Theory and Approaches of Group Decision-Making with Uncertain Linguistic Expressions*, Uncertainty and Operations Research,
https://doi.org/10.1007/978-981-13-3735-2_1

linguistic variables are closer to natural languages and human recognition. For the representation of uncertain knowledge, the qualitative values of linguistic variables are easy to obtain. Thus, linguistic variables are a effective tool for modelling fuzzy and uncertain information.

However, there are some limitations in the traditional linguistic fuzzy approaches. Given a linguistic term set (LTS), these approaches require that experts have to select a certain term from the set. When facing complex uncertainty, the experts usually are not able to determine the most accurate term. Thus they might balance or hesitate among several possible terms. For instance, given the LTS $S = \{very\ low, low, mediu, high, very\ high\}$ for the evaluation of a big data-based audit platform (BDAP) with respect to the reliability of big data analyses, due to the limitation of available information and experts' knowledge, the linguistic opinions of an expert might be:

(1) between *medium* and *high*;
(2) at least *high*;
(3) *high* or *very high*;
(4) more or less *medium*.

These types of linguistic expressions are frequently emerged in real applications because the expert cannot determine the most suitable term. One feature of those is that they are not certain elements of the given LTS, but more than one term expressed in a direct or indirect manner. These expressions are thus called uncertain linguistic expressions (ULEs).

Till now, the investigations of ULEs lag behind the contributions which focus certain linguistic terms. In the above example, (1) can be modelled by means of uncertain linguistic terms (ULTs) [126]; (2) and (3) could be represented by hesitant fuzzy linguistic term sets (HFLTSs) [96] or their extended form. However, there is not only a linguistic term but also a linguistic hedge in (4). This book will pay attention to the theory and decision-making approaches of the last two types of ULEs and their mixed forms.

1.2 Focused Problems

Uncertainties are generally inevitable due to the limitation of cost of time and economics, or the nature of criteria. This drives the decision information to take the qualitative form. When the qualitative information is linguistic, ULEs are definitely an effective tool to represent the information. In this case, several aspects of ULEs, such as modelling and representing, information fusion, preference analysis, and GDM approaches, are vital to the practical problems in qualitative setting.

(1) **The theoretical aspect.**
The developments of models of ULEs could enrich the current fuzzy linguistic approach, enable experts to express their opinions by more types of natural linguistic expressions. Theoretically, experts could express their opinions by linguistic

expressions according to their language conventions if there are sufficient linguistic representational and computational models, no matter the expressions in their mind coincides with the syntactic rules of a specific model or not. This book tends to introduce some models for specific types of ULEs, their syntactic and semantic rules, and the associated computational foundations. Thus the range of values of linguistic variables are enlarged, and approaches for representing and operating qualitative information could be more flexible.

Preference analysis based on ULEs could enable experts to express their preferences by pairwise comparisons. The decision information in this case takes the form of preference relations or comparison matrices. If consistency measures and priority algorithms of preference relations based on specific types of ULEs are well developed, decision makers could understand the degree of consistency intuitively and obtain the relative importance degrees of objects. Therefore, the problems regarding preference relations of ULEs could be resolved elegantly.

GDM approaches based on ULEs enable decision makers to make rational decisions, and thus enrich the theory of decision-making under uncertainties. Especially, some approaches in this book facilitate decision makers to deal with multiple types of ULEs in one problem; some other approaches make decision makers to be convenient to understand how uncertainties influence final decisions.

(2) **The application aspect**.
Several decision-making approaches based on ULEs have been applied in economics, management, engineering and other fields. We herewith discuss the potential applications from the aspect of evaluation and selection of BDAPs, which is the major application problem of this book.

Big data, characterized by an immense volume and high velocity of data with varying and complex structures, have been demonstrated to be of the potential usefulness and capability of making informative, intelligent and felicitous decisions in various areas. Auditing data share the 5Vs (volume, variety, velocity, veracity and value) of big data. Thus, the profession of audit would benefit from the state-of-the-art big data techniques as well. Many researchers and auditors are optimistic about introducing big data techniques in auditing. As an important category of audit, governmental audit has been more and more important for Chinese government. In December 2015, Chinese government issued a new regulation to ensure the implementation of full audit coverage in the big data era. The intention of this regulation is to construct the mode of big data auditing, enhance the capability, efficiency and quality of auditing, and increase the scope and depth of auditing. Towards these targets, some articles of the regulation also pointed out that national auditing systems and platforms, namely BDAPs, should be built, associated with big data techniques, to enable and/or enhance the capability of analyzing and comparing data from multiple industries. One can expect that a series of BDAPs will emerge in a few years. To implement a BDAP, it is essential to evaluate and select from some outsourcing providers.

However, the audit in big data era is facing several challenges. A BDAP is considered for enhancing the capability and effectiveness of audit, thus it should not only exert the advantages of big data but also evade the possible risks caused by big data. In order to implement big data-based audit, the first task of auditors is to evaluate and select from available BDAPs. Whilst the evaluation and selection are very complicated and difficult because of the status of big data and auditing techniques. Some of the obstacles are: multiple fields and disciplines are involved; the criteria are complicated; multiple types of uncertainties are inevitable. In this case, enabling multiple types of ULEs would facilitate the procedures of evaluation and the representation of qualitative information, and then the corresponding GDM approaches would results in reasonable decisions based on the information.

Based on ULEs, this book focuses on three theoretical problems and an application problem. From the theoretical aspect, several novel models for computing with words (CWW) are introduced and some necessary theories are included. Associated with some existing models, a series of GDM approaches are also introduced. Finally, these contributions are applied in a practical problem.

1.2.1 Novel CWW Models Based on ULEs

CWW models are necessary so that linguistic expressions could be utilized to represent decision information. Generally, a CWW model includes two components: the representation model and computational model. The former defines the syntax and semantics of the involved linguistic expressions. Based on which, the use of this type of linguistic expressions coincides the framework of the classical linguistic fuzzy approach. The latter focuses on the necessary foundation of computing with these linguistic expressions, including the negation operator, order relations, and basic operations.

Some existing models of ULEs, such as ULTs and HFLTSs, represent uncertainty by means of their boundaries. However, in practice, our convention of thinking might be: a linguistic term, which is the most possible real value, is determined at first; due to the existence of uncertainty, other terms around the term could also be the real value. It is quite natural to consider a linguistic hedge to modify the term. In this case, the power and grade of the hedge implies the degree of uncertainty in the expert's mind. Therefore, this book introduces a novel CWW model based on the perspective of linguistic hedges, and enrich the range of values of a linguistic variable which could be considered by experts.

1.2.2 Preference Relations Based on ULEs

As a type of binary relations, preference relations are a frequently considered tool to express decision information indirectly. According to the forms of values, preference relations could be roughly classified into numerical preference relations (such as fuzzy preference relations) and linguistic preference relations (LPRs). In linguistic setting, LPRs depend on specific CWW models. To model the uncertainty in pairwise comparisons, the values of LPRs have been extended from single terms to ULTs and HFLTSs.

The investigations of preference relations mainly focus on the measure of consistency and the exploration of priority. Consistency measures are vital to check the logic consistency of a preference relation. Only the preference relations satisfying specific consistencies could be considered for decisions. Some traditional consistency measures, such as weak consistency and additive consistency, are defined based on transitivity. If uncertainties are involved, it is difficult to reach strict consistency. Acceptable consistencies are a compromising solution. Based on specific consistency, the priorities of preference relations can be explored accordingly. In sum, consistency measures are the primary target of the investigation of preference relations. When ULEs are introduced into the framework of preference relations, the definition of proper consistency measures are the essential work of decision-making with these expressions.

1.2.3 GDM Approaches Based on ULEs

GDM is a framework of decision making for complex problems in decision analysis. Roughly, due to the impact of several aspects, including scales and structures of groups, expressions of information, and preferences of decision makers, GDM approaches are usually different from each other. Most of the GDM approaches focus on the consensus of the group, and information fusion of the group. Although there are many contributions focusing on large sizes of groups, very few of them considers the inner structures of groups. In linguistic setting, there have been a lot of studies regarding ULTs and HFLTSs. However, most of them extend the traditional GDM approaches directly. Due to the existence of uncertainties, it would be very helpful to understand the connections between the degree of uncertainty and the resultant final decision. This could be achieved by means of descriptive measures which have not been well defined. Therefore, this book introduces a GDM framework based on the complex inner structures of groups, handles multiple terms in ULEs based on stochastic theory, analyzes the affects of parameters to final decisions, considers the linguistic aspirations levels and utilities of experts, and presents more general GDM approaches.

1.2.4 Modelling Complex Problems Under Uncertainties

As discussed above, the evaluation of a BDAP is a complex GDM problem in which several disciplines, such as data science, audit (especially, government audit), management, are involved. Several departments including big data R&D section, management section, audit section, and financial section should act together to complete the evaluation. Moreover, several aspects of big data techniques are under developing. There is a lack of mature industry standards. These result in the difficulties of evaluating alternatives with respect to big data related criteria. It is very hard for an expert to provide crisp and accurate values to measure an alternative. The provided information might be fuzzy, incomplete in the sense of a certain granular. Besides, there are many qualitative criteria in an evaluation model. Experts could only determine the performances of alternatives by their subjective perceptions, and could possibly express their opinions by linguistic expressions, such as ULEs, according to their individual linguistic conventions.

However, this can not be achieved by the traditional GDM techniques. The various types of uncertainties in the evaluation of a BDAP could not well handled by these approaches. The evaluation process requires experts from several different industries and disciplines. To avoid the possible unfair or unreasonable evaluations, each criterion should be evaluated by multiple experts with the similar knowledge and expertise. Moreover, the evaluation information could take multiple forms, such as numerical values and linguistic expressions. Especially, experts should be allowed to express their opinions in a flexible manner so that they could focus on the evaluations instead of representing their opinions in a predefined way. For qualitative criteria, multiple types of ULEs could be involved. Most of the current contributions focus on the use of HFLTSs. The developments of other types are quite limited.

1.3 Recent Advances of the Focused Problems

This section presents a brief overview on the focused fields, which includes the current status of modelling ULEs and the developments of GDM approaches.

1.3.1 Review of Modelling ULEs and Decision-Making Approaches

1.3.1.1 Decision-Making Based on HFLTSs

In some complex decision-making situations, a certain linguistic term may be not suitable to express the experts' linguistic opinions under uncertainty. The use of ULEs is a direct and precise manner to represent uncertain linguistic information. In the hesitant cases, if linguistic information takes the form of comparative linguistic expressions, the concept of HFLTSs is an effective solution. Based on the symbolic linguistic model, a context-free grammar and a transformation function are defined to represent the expressions and transform them into HFLTSs.

Definition 1.1 ([96]) Given a LTS $S = \{s_0, s_1, \ldots, s_\tau\}$, a HFLTS, denoted by h_S, is an ordered finite subset of the consecutive LTS S.

The set of all HFLTSs based on S is denoted as $\mathbf{H}_S$. The obvious and marked characteristics of HFLTSs can be summarized below [117]:

(1) HFLTSs are elicited by specific ULEs. The context-free grammar and the transformation function make the use of HFLTSs quite straightforward. The considered forms of comparative linguistic expressions are very natural and accord with our language conventions. HFLTSs extend the range of values that can be assigned to a linguistic variable.

(2) HFLTSs are proposed based on the symbolic linguistic model. As shown hereinabove, the involved LTS is a discrete set rather than a continuous set in the linguistic 2-tuple model or the virtual linguistic model. Based upon this condition, the finite and consecutive subset is then meaningful.

(3) Except for the possible terms, no other information is involved in HFLTSs. As being elicited by the specific types of comparative linguistic expressions, HFLTSs do not include any other information such as the priority of possible terms (as in the computation of fuzzy envelope), the probabilistic distribution of these terms (as in the distribution-based assessments [149], possibility distribution-based HFLTSs [122] and probabilistic linguistic term sets [91]), or the membership degree of the terms (as in discrete fuzzy numbers [111]). Certainly, these kinds of additional information, if available, should be taken into account in some special situations. But this information is not the inherent property of HFLTSs because it cannot be derived from comparative linguistic expressions.

These characteristics distinguish HFLTSs from other similar techniques that deal with complex linguistic information. Among these characteristics, some make HFLTSs be an outstanding tool whereas some limit the development of HFLTSs. Besides, some others are not strictly obeyed in the literature [117].

Handling HFLTSs is not easy because they are a subset of terms rather than a single term. To operate HFLTSs, some basic operations, such as complement, union and intersection, were defined by following the traditional operations in the set theory [96]. However, the union and complement of HFLTSs may not be a HFLTS. This limits the applicability of the operations. To compare two HFLTSs, the concept of envelopes was defined. Besides, utilizing the ordered weighted averaging (OWA) operator [138], the fuzzy envelope of a HFLTS was defined to present a fuzzy representation of the HFLTS [78]. The basic idea of the fuzzy envelope is that, taking the case of *between* s_i *and* s_j as an example, the possible terms in the middle position of a HFLTS are more important than those approaching the boundaries of the HFLTS. It is clear that this concept extends the major characteristics of HFLTSs. Figure 1.1 illustrates the HFLTS elicited by the comparative linguistic expression *between low and high*, its envelope and fuzzy envelope, respectively [117].

Since they were introduced, the theories and applications of HFLTSs have been developed very quickly. Generally, for computing with HFLTSs in decision-making, both of the following two distinct strategies are popular [117]: (as shown in Fig. 1.2)

(1) Computing with envelopes (or fuzzy envelopes). This strategy strictly follows the idea of Definition 1.1 and treats a HFLTS as an indivisible entirety. In this kind of processes, HFLTSs are transformed into their envelopes (or fuzzy envelopes) at first. Then the rest part of this kind of processes is somewhat like the linguistic

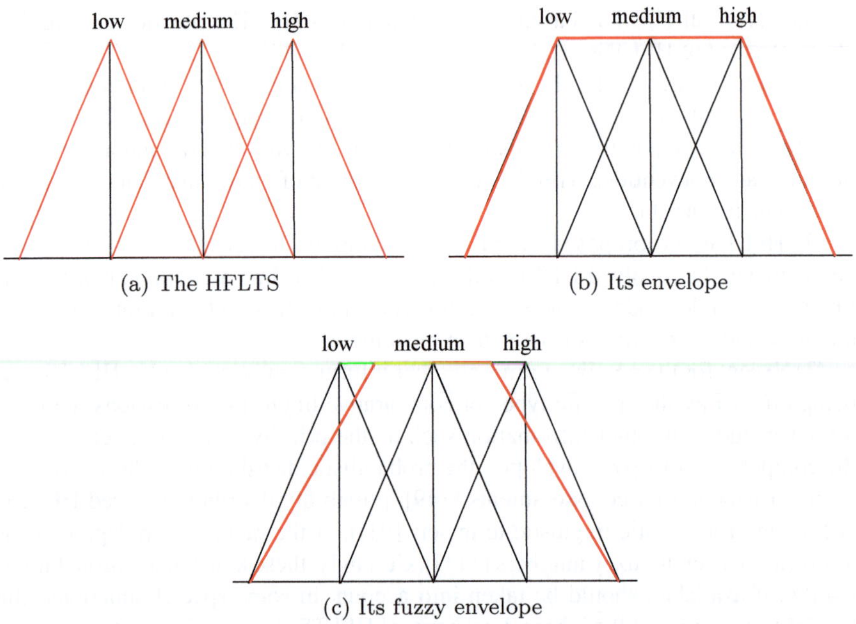

Fig. 1.1 The interpretations of comparative linguistic expression *between low and high*

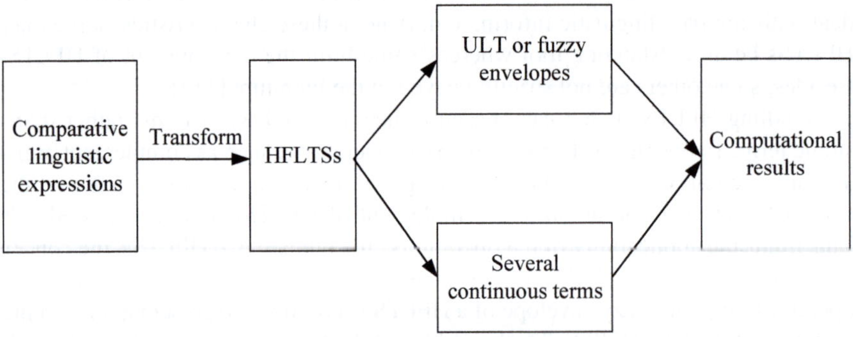

Fig. 1.2 The two computational strategies of operating HFLTSs

decision-making based on ULTs (or semantics). Roughly, in this sense, many existing approaches can be employed to handle HFLTSs after they are transformed into their envelopes (or fuzzy envelopes).

(2) Computing with possible terms. Bearing in mind the key idea and main motivation of hesitant fuzzy sets, this strategy tries to consider all possible terms included in a HFLTS. The linguistic 2-tuple model and the virtual linguistic model are frequently employed to implement the strategy. This strategy requires novel approaches to deal with multiple linguistic terms at the same time. For example, an additional

normalization step is usually included if the numbers of terms in the HFLTSs are distinct.

Till now, a number of contributions based on either of the two strategies have been published, focusing on basic operations, information aggregation, orders, information measures, preference relations, decision-making approaches and other applications.

(1) **Developments of HFLTSs based on computing with envelopes.**
The initial computational model proposed by Rodríguez et al. [96] is based on the basic operations in Definition 1.1 and the concept of envelopes. Two symbolic aggregation operators corresponding to the pessimistic and optimistic points of view were developed to fuse the set of envelopes of HFLTSs. The min-upper operator obtains the worst of the maximum linguistic terms, whereas the max-lower operator finds the best of the minimum linguistic terms. In [94], Rodríguez et al. improved the operators by means of the linguistic 2-tuple model. The operators for aggregating 2-tuples are employed to combine the boundary terms of HFLTSs. The aggregation idea of Chen and Hong [18] is based on the semantics of envelopes. In [70], a series of aggregation operators were developed based on the likelihood of each HFLTS being greater than the LTS S. The aggregation results are real numbers in the interval [0, 1].

Ordering any two HFLTSs can also be implemented by their envelopes. The partial order on $\mathbf{H}_S$ defined in [96] is based on the idea of the preference degree of two intervals derived by the envelopes. Similarly, the order relation in [70, 71] is based on the likelihood-based relation of intervals. A simple linear order can be found in [34], where a binary relation is defined to order the set of intervals.

Based on the envelopes of HFLTSs, some distance measures have been developed. The distance measure proposed by Beg and Rashid [6] is defined by the indices of terms of the envelopes. After representing all the HFLTSs in $\mathbf{H}_S$ by a graph, Falcø et al. [34] suggested defining the distance of the linguistic intervals by the geodesic distance in the graph. The idea of graph representation has been extended in [86] by the proposed lattice structure. Based on the lattice, two types of distances were defined. One was defined by the difference between the cardinality of union and the cardinality of intersection. The same idea can also be found in [29]. The other is equivalent to the geodesic distance between non-empty HFLTSs.

By introducing comparative linguistic expressions to LPRs, Liu et al. [81] defined the concept of hesitant fuzzy LPRs (HFLPRs). Associated with the proposed reciprocal condition, the proposed concept of HFLPRs is actually equivalent to the version proposed by Zhu and Xu [151]. In [81], the fuzzy envelope of each HFLTS in a HFLPR was derived at first. Then the fuzzy envelopes were transformed into linguistic 2-tuples according to a semantic transformation. Accordingly, techniques for linguistic 2-tuple preference relations can be employed. In addition, the process proposed in [29] can also deal with group consensus where decision information is collected by HFLPRs.

To facilitate the use of comparative linguistic expressions in decision-making, Rodríguez et al. [97] introduced a GDM model that extends and modifies the traditional LDM scheme. The model includes four steps: (1) definition of semantics, syntax and context-free grammar; (2) transformation into ULTs; (3) choice of aggregation operator; and (4) selection process. To aggregate the boundaries of ULTs, the operators based on linguistic 2-tuples are suggested. Thereafter a series of decision-making processes have been proposed for distinct situations. Rodríguez and Martínez [95] provided a group consensus model to check the consensus level and interact with the experts in the circumstance of HFLTSs. Some classical decision-making approaches, such as TOPSIS [6, 34], QUALIFEX [82], ELECTRE I [33], have been extended to suit the setting of HFLTSs. These approaches compute with either envelopes or fuzzy envelopes. Different from these, the semantics of envelopes and fuzzy envelopes have been employed for computation directly. Chang [16] proposed a reliability allocation method based on HFLTSs and minimal variance ordered weighted geometric weights, where HFLTSs are operated based on the semantics of their envelopes. In Zhang et al. heterogeneous information GDM processes [150], HFLTSs were transformed into their fuzzy envelopes.

(2) **Developments of HFLTSs based on computing with possible terms.**
To facilitate the second strategy, the definition of HFLTSs is often rewritten and extended, such as the definition in [76]. The extension has been utilized by most of the contributions of the second strategy.

Some basic operations for HFLTSs have been introduced to enable computing with possible terms. Wei et al. [118] revised the definition in [96] motivated by the intersection, union and complement of hesitant fuzzy sets. The union of two HFLTSs, in the sense of Wei et al. [118], is also a HFLTS. The arithmetical operations defined in [112, 151] require the same cardinalities of two HFLTSs, and the operations are actually made on each pair of possible terms in the same position. Recently, Gou et al. [43] developed some novel operations based on a pair of transformation functions. The transformation between HFLTSs and hesitant fuzzy elements are mathematically equivalent.

In the strategy of computing with possible terms, it is not so easy to define an order to compare any two HFLTSs. Several partial orders on $\mathbf{H}_S$ have been defined. A simple and frequently used order can be found in [77], where the partial order is motivated by the concept of expected values and variances in statistics. The order defined in [118] is to compute the averaging possibility degree of terms in one HFLTS being greater than those in another. Several other partial orders have been developed based on the same idea. For instance, the order in [115] is based on the degree that one HFLTS outranks another; the likelihood-based order in [107] is constructed by comparing any two possible terms which come from the two HFLTSs respectively. The order in [116] is similar to the traditional partial order defined for the set of n-dimensional vectors. The total orders defined in [113] can serve as total orders for HFLTSs.

Many operators have been proposed to fuse a collection of HFLTSs by the idea of computing with possible terms. Wei et al. [118] defined the linguistic weighted averaging operator and the linguistic OWA operator for HFLTSs based on the proposed convex combination operation. Thanks to the approximation step in the convex combination operation, the results of these two operators are also HFLTSs in the sense of Definition 1.1. However, the approximation results in loss of information. Zhang and Guo [146] improved these operators by employing the linguistic 2-tuple model and the concept of distribution-based assessments. Based on the virtual linguistic model, Gou et al. [44] defined the Bonferroni means operator for HFLTSs. Based on the predefined possibility distribution on possible terms, Wu and Xu [122] defined a new version of the linguistic weighted averaging operator and the linguistic OWA operator for HFLTSs. In order to aggregate HFLTSs based on unbalanced LTS, Dong et al. [30] defined some novel operators based on the linguistic 2-tuple model and the numerical scale model. The aggregation results were obtained by a mixed 0–1 linear programming model.

Several contributions focus on the distance and similarity measures of HFLTSs by different manners. Zhao et al. [24] presented some general processes to construct distance measures. Liao et al. [75] defined the distance of two HFLTSs by the averaging distance of any two possible terms. Then the distance of two collections of HFLTSs can be defined accordingly. If the collections of HFLTSs are presented with weights, then a class of weighted distance measures were developed in Xu et al. [136]. More general versions were then proposed in [77, 84]. Different from these contributions based on the L_p metric, the cosine distance measure proposed in [74] is from the geometric point of view. Similarity measures are usually defined directly according to the distance measures, as in [74, 75]. As an alternative, Hesamian and Shams [52] introduced the definition of similarity measure motivated by the classical similarity of fuzzy sets. A similarity-based order was also suggested.

Other information measures have also been developed. Farhadinia [38] defined the entropy of HFLTSs based on the existing distance and similarity measures. Later, Gou et al. [46] presented a systematic study on entropy and cross-entropy measures, associated with their relationship with similarity measures. The correlation coefficients of HFLTSs were defined in Liao et al. [76]. The group utility measure and individual regret measure were developed based on the generalized distance measure in Liao et al. [77]. Furthermore, a score function for measuring the hesitant degree of a HFLTS was defined in [119].

The concept of HFLPRs was initially defined by Zhu and Xu [151] based on the virtual linguistic model. The proposed HFLPRs are additive and reciprocal. In their proposal, a HFLPR should be normalized in advance. The consistency index of a HFLPR is then measured by its distance to the corresponding consistent normalized HFLPR. If the consistency of a HFLPR is unacceptable, then two optimization methods were proposed to improve the consistency index. Based on the linguistic 2-tuple model, Li et al. [72] developed an optimization model to estimate the range of consistency index of a HFLPR. Given a HFLPR, their model seeks for two reduced LPRs with the highest and lowest consistency indices respectively. The consistency measure defined in [120] is based on their suggested possibility distribution approach and the linguistic 2-tuple model. For consistency improving, their proposed algorithm adopts a local revision strategy to ensure the interpretability. Besides, a consensus reaching algorithm with a feedback system was also presented for GDM. The multiplicative consistency, as well as the consistency improving algorithm, was studied by Zhang and Wu [147]. Their idea was motivated by the multiplicative consistency of LPRs and the proposal of Zhu and Xu [151].

Based on the strategy of computing with possible terms, several classical decision-making processes have been extended. The TOPSIS-based approach was presented by Li et al. [73] associated with a distance-based method to weight the experts and an aggregation-based method to weight the criteria. The TOPSIS method developed in [74] is based on the cosine distance. Based on some information measures mentioned above, the traditional VIKOR method, TODIM method and QUALIFLEX method were also extended in [74, 77, 107, 119]. The outranking method was studied in [115, 116]. The alternative queuing method was applied in [45, 46]. Group consensus is a fundamental issue for GDM. Based on the assumption of possibility distribution, Wu and Xu [122] studied the consensus reaching algorithm to improve the groups decision matrices, an interactive version of consensus improving was discussed in their later contribution [121]. Other LDM problems have also been investigated, such as the multi-granular LDM with HFLTSs in [84] and the multidimensional analysis of preference in [137].

1.3.2 Review of Lingustic Hedges

The linguistic expressions involved in Sect. 1.3.1 take the form of multiple linguistic terms connected by conjunctions. This type of expressions coincide with natural linguistic convention. However, this is not the only manner in natural languages. In fact, experts may select a linguistic term which is the most possible to be the real value of a linguistic variable, and then choose a weakened hedge to modify the term based on the degree of uncertainty in his/her mind. Generally, linguistic hedges are a quite natural way to represent uncertainties and have been investigated for decades. However, the developments are quite limited, especially in the field of decision-making under uncertainties.

Basically, a linguistic hedge maps a fuzzy set to another fuzzy set [25]. The first model of linguistic hedges is the powering model proposed by Zadeh [144]. Each hedge corresponds to a specific value of the parameter of powering functions. This model has been widely used, such as in fuzzy classification [14, 17, 79], database query refinements [8], fuzzy modal logic [26] and etc. Another model is the shifting hedges [15]. A shifting hedge does not change the shape of membership function of an atomic term but shift it to a certain level.

Hedges can be classified into two categories, which are intensified hedges (such as very) and weakened hedges (such as more or less), according to their modified power. In the inclusive interpretation, a hedge modifies a linguistic term to its superset or subset; whereas in the non-inclusive interpretation, a hedge moves one term to another [56]. As it is widely known, hedges with the non-inclusive interpretation are commonly used in qualitative decision-making (QDM). But hedges with the inclusive interpretation, which just intensify or weaken the degree of a term, have not been considered in QDM.

In the perspective of MCDM in linguistic setting: (1) Linguistic hedges with non-inclusive interpretation have been investigated and applied in MCDM problems. (2) However, linguistic hedges with the other interpretation have not emerged in this area although there have been several techniques to model them. Most of this techniques focus on other applications such as fuzzy control [4, 19], algorithms refinements [41], approximate reasoning [93] fuzzy relation equations [5] and so on.

1.3.3 Review of Group Decision-Making Approaches Under Uncertainty

1.3.3.1 Group Decision-Making Based on Preference Relations

Preference relations are an important tool to evaluate alternatives. The advantage is to transform a global evaluation problem to several local pair-wise comparisons. Accordingly, the logical consistency of a preference relation should be checked by additional techniques. A preference relation is a binary relation, usually take the form of a matrix. Preference relations can be classified into multiple categories based on the representations of pair-wise comparisons. For instance, the 1–9 scales are utilized in the traditional analytical hierarchy process [99, 101], the 0.1–0.9 ratios are considered in fuzzy preference relations and interval-valued fuzzy preference relations [90, 127]. Intuitionistic fuzzy values and interval-valued intuitionistic fuzzy values are used in intuitionsitic fuzzy preference relations and interval-valued intuitionsitic fuzzy preference relations, respectively [130, 134]. In linguistic setting, preference relations have been extended to linguistic preference relations [47], uncertain linguistic preference relations [128], hesitant fuzzy linguistic preference relations [151], etc.

Consistency measures of preference relations have been attracted much attention and are usually defined by means of transitivity [48]. Two classical consistencies are the additive (or multiplicative) consistency and the weak consistency. The latter is usually considered as the lower limit that a preference relation has to satisfy. Besides, the degree of consistency is also frequently employed to ensure that a preference relation is with satisfactory consistency. For example, the consistency ratio is used to measure the consistency degree of a multiplicative preference relation being better than that of a randomly generated multiplicative preference relation [100]. Another widely used measure is the geometric consistency index [1].

Several approaches have been introduced for the case when the consistency of a preference relation is not satisfactory. There are two distinct strategies, i.e., the interactive strategy and the iterative strategy. The former seeks for the entries leading to terrible consistency degrees, feeds back to experts, and then waits for improvements [49, 50]. The latter revises some entries automatically, by iterative algorithms [133] or optimization models [28, 80], to improve the consistency degree of a given preference relation.

Incomplete preference relations have received great attention over the past decades. It is common that there must be $n(n-1)/2$ comparisons in a complete preference relation if n objects are involved in. However, the experts may provide preference relations with incomplete information because of: (1) the time pressure and the limitation of cost [22, 129], (2) the experts limited expertise of the problem and information processing capabilities [51, 129], and (3) the convenience and/or necessity to skip some direct critical comparisons [39, 135]. Generally, completions of incomplete preference relations can be done by two distinct strategies [109, 110]:

(1) Completing without the participation of the experts. This strategy makes use of mathematical techniques, such as iterative approaches and optimization approaches, to fill incomplete preference relations based on the hypothesis that the known entries possess high consistency level and are coincident with actual values of the expert's subjective preferences. That is why the objective functions of many optimization approaches are derived by minimizing the inconsistency degree. The advantage of the strategy is that it would not bring additional work to the experts once an incomplete preference relation is provided. However, if the incomplete preference relation is not consistent or acceptable consistent, some artificial approaches have to be put out to revise it. The revised version owns high consistent degree but may not coincide with the expert's actual opinions.

(2) Completing through interacting with the experts. This strategy completes an incomplete PR by absorbing new opinions from the experts to ensure that the derived preference relation is highly coincident with their actual preferences. It seems as if this strategy produces additional work for the experts and makes the speed of completion very slow. In fact, there are at least three reasons for this interactive strategy. First, this strategy can be started along with the procedure of giving original incomplete preference relations. It would make the original version more "accurate". Second, if incompleteness is caused by the first reason mentioned above, it may be necessary to ask the experts to improve the incomplete version to enhance reliabilities of the decision. Several military experts are asked to present their opinions concerning to what extent ones attribute is more important than another. Obviously, the most important issue is the correction and rationality of the obtained preference relations although some more work and time may be consumed. However, some of the attributes are qualitative and cannot be evaluated by objective data. Thus if some experts have hesitancy during the judgements, it would be helpful if there is an interactive system that can help completing the required assessments and elicit to figure out possible logical inconsistencies. Finally, algorithms based on this strategy can stop whenever no new information is provided even if not all missing entries are filled. In this case, the output of algorithms may be incomplete as well.

Most of the existing endeavours focus on the first strategy. The developments of incomplete preference relations mainly lie on the following two aspects. The first aspect is the consistency and the consensus measures of incomplete preference relations. Some studies discussed the additive consistency [39, 50, 80, 129] and multiplicative consistency [124] of incomplete fuzzy preference relations. The consensus measures are statistically analyzed by Chiclana et al. [23]. Whereas there may be contradictory even if a preference relation passes the consistent test successfully [59]. Therefore, serving as the minimum required condition of a consistent preference relation, Fedrizzi and Giove [39] investigated the weak consistency of incomplete fuzzy preference relations. On the other aspect, most of the studies focused on the missing information of the incomplete preference relations. Millet [85] discarded the incomplete information directly. Ebenbach and Moore [32] penalized negatively the experts providing incomplete preferences. However, the incomplete preference relation constructed by randomly deleting as much as 50% of the entries of a complete preference relation provides good results without compromising accuracy [13]. In addition, incomplete information is not equivalent to low quality information or inconsistent information. Thus, it is more desirable to manage incomplete information using the information provided by other experts [57], or only by his/her own assessments and consistency criteria. The latter has been a kind of techniques extensively applied in both individual decision-making and GDM. By the predefined consistencies, these techniques estimate the missing values of incomplete preference relations through two ways: iterative algorithms [3, 11, 12, 69] and optimization approaches [39, 42, 148].

Only a few studies have focused on the interactive strategy. Xu [131] and Chuu [24] proposed the interactive approaches for GDM to revise the experts' linguistic preference relations with relatively low degree of consistency. But they only considered the complete linguistic preference relations. Xu [132] dealt with the incomplete fuzzy preference relations in GDM, but the proposed interactive approach does not focus on the completing of incomplete fuzzy preference relations. The interactive model proposed by Herrera-Viedma et al. [49] included a feedback mechanism to give advice to the experts to revise their preference relations. However, in order to calculate the pre-defined consensus degrees and proximity measures, this model can only deal with the complete preference relations. Wu et al. [123] proposed an interactive model to build consensus among the group based on incomplete linguistic preference relations. Alonso et al. [2] developed a decision support system to aid the experts for completing the incomplete fuzzy preference relations. In fact, as the idea in [2], tolerances and deviations may exist when the experts express their preferences by incomplete linguistic preference relations, but there is not any procedure to check the existences and revise the tolerances.

In processes of GDM, individual preferences are usually fused by using aggregation operators. There are plenty of contributions in the field, such as the operators defined in [20, 21, 128]. Moreover, several GDM approaches have been developed to handle specific types of preference relations, such as the approaches based on multiplicative preference relations [68], fuzzy preference relations [50, 130], linguistic preference relations [125, 128], etc.

1.3.3.2 Decision-Making Based on Aspiration Levels

The concept of aspiration levels plays an important role in managerial decision-making. In the satisficing model [102], subjects seek an alternative or solution that meet aspiration levels, instead of maximizing the expected utility in the classical sense [10]. Ample and substantial empirical evidence indicates that individual preferences cannot be described by the conventional concave or convex utility functions [7, 10,

92]. The satisficing heuristic works as follows: if a solution (or a small set of solutions) can be found to satisfy the stated aspiration levels, then it is accepted; otherwise, the aspiration levels should be relaxed. If too many solutions are admitted by the aspiration levels, then they should be tightened [58]. Roughly, the consideration of aspiration levels would benefit to decrease the complexity of the problem in hand, because of the subject limitation of cognitive capabilities [9, 27].

Except for some specific concentrations of decision-making with single criterion utility function [7], most of the existing studies contribute to MCDM problems. Among them, most studies link aspiration levels to probabilities where risk choices are involved, some link them to reference points (mainly established from the perspective of prospect theory), and finally, others consider the fuzzy aspirations (in fuzzy or linguistic setting). The following is organized based on this taxonomy:

Stochastic MCDM, with the presence of aspiration levels, are usually solved by searching alternatives, which approach the aspiration levels at most. Frequently, this is implemented by the satisficing heuristic. The first interactive method, proposed in [83], selects the closest non-dominated alternative by obtaining feedback information and adjusting the aspiration levels. Thereafter, a number of solutions have been proposed based on this or similar ideas. For example, Nowaks methods [87, 88] for discrete stochastic MCDM are based on stochastic dominance rules. In a later paper [89], preference threshold is involved to lessen the interactive actions. When the size of alternatives is large, a quad tree-based method is developed by Sun and Steuer [103]. Apart from the development of MCDM solutions, Wang and Zionts [114] considered the robustness of solutions derived by interactive models, where a solution is robust if many aspiration levels map to it. Tsetlin and Winkler [108] developed a theoretical model which considers uncertain dependent aspiration levels and uncertain dependent performance levels. Their work demonstrates explicitly that it is vital to consider the dependence. Another theoretical model [9] is devoted to combining expected aspiration-based utility with loss and gain probabilities. Recently, Fantozzi and Spizzichino [37] formally described the connections between aspiration-based utility and aggregation-based extensions of capacities. Besides, there are also endeavors which seek for the alternative with the greatest degree of approaching to aspiration levels by optimization models. Yun et al. [143] utilized the genetic algorithm and a generalized data envelopment analysis to list the Pareto optimal solutions located close to aspiration levels. Associated with a case study, Feng and Lai [40] developed an integrated MCDM method with aspirations where the performance values take the form of numerical values, interval numbers, linguistic terms and uncertain linguistic terms. Instead of adjusting experts' aspiration levels, an optimization model was built to seek for the collective alternative ranking that is agreed by at least half of experts.

Most reference point-based methods are based on prospect theory where the value function divides outcomes into gains and losses. Fan et al. [35] proposed a prospect-theory-based MCDM solution where the performance values are either numeric values or interval numbers and the reference point is fixed by aspiration levels. In a similar contribution [36], three different types of aspirations are taken into account. The method proposed by Tan et al. [104] focuses on a class of stochastic MCDM problems. They model the psychological behavior of decision makers by means of a prospect stochastic dominance degree.

In the fuzzy environment, the aspiration level is neither a reference point nor a probabilistic distribution of choices, but a fuzzy set (like a linguistic term) defined in a domain. The employment of fuzzy set theory enables decision makers to specify imprecise and vague aspiration levels. Prior work of this field can be found in [53, 54]. Based on a bounded domain, their work presents solutions to obtain the probability of meeting fuzzy aspiration levels. The involved utility functions are monotonically increasing. Later, the fuzzy aspiration oriented model proposed in [141] handles three types of fuzzy preferences by the formulation of three types of fuzzy targets: fuzzy min, fuzzy max and fuzzy equal. Due to the vagueness of evaluating aesthetics, performing Kansei evaluation by fuzzy sets is much more efficient than using numerical data. Thereby several contributions, which focus on the Kansei evaluation, develop the theory and methods related to fuzzy aspiration levels. Yan et al. [139] first introduced three types of fuzzy aspiration levels to Kansei evaluation. The model has been improved by including the linguistic 2-tuple approach in [140]. The aggregation strategy in these two papers is criticized and improved in another development [55] where both vagueness and variation are included in the proposed uncertain Kansei profile. In a more recent study, Yan et al. [142] employed both stochastic dominance and fuzzy targets in order to avoid the potential subjectivity of CWW.

1.3.3.3 Group Decision-Making Based on Stochastic Analysis

The stochastic multi-criteria acceptability analysis (SMAA) is a family of MCDM methods for the problems with incomplete, imprecise, and uncertain information [61, 64]. When facing a problem with imperfect information, the SMAA method analyzes the space of feasible parameter values and computes some descriptive measures to support the decision makers to realize what kind of preferences and parameters could result in which actions, instead of seeking for techniques to determine the unknown parameters and imperfect information. Several variants and extensions have been proposed for various types of MCDM problems. Lahdelma [61] presented a general form, namely SMAA-2. The SMAA method in [66] considers the ordinal criteria. Lahdelma and Salminen[62] assumed that there are correlations among criteria and presented another version of SMAA. To increase the discrimination of alternatives, Lahdelma and Salminen [63] defined a new measure, i.e., cross-confident factor. The reference point-based SMAA was developed based on the prospect theory [67]. Based on Monte Carlo simulation, Tervonen and Lahdelma [106] presented the numerical calculation algorithms in SMAA. Recently, the uncertainty in SMAA methods were analyzed in [31]. For more recent developments of SMAA, please refer to [60, 105].

1.3.4 A Summary of the Contributions and Limitations

For decision-making with uncertain linguistic expressions, uncertain linguistic terms are the earliest tools and the corresponding contributions are relatively rich. HFLTSs are being developed very quickly although they have been proposed for only a few years. Under the framework of the linguistic fuzzy approach, theoretical foundations and decision-making approaches have been considered in many studies. From the quantitative aspect, the models of artificial linguistic expressions are richer than those of natural linguistic expressions. Each model has been more or less developed.

However, there are some limitations in the current developments of HFLTSs. The following aspects are important from the perspective of information representation and operation [117].

(1) More desirable computational strategies are required. The two strategies of operating HFLTSs are not perfect. The first strategy treats a comparative linguistic expression as an entity. This makes a HFLTS be a ULT, which drops the nature of HFLTSs. The second strategy highlights the feature of hesitation. However, the computational results are usually not HFLTSs any more. Therefore, novel strategies are much better if they could improve their interpretability and remain their outputs in the original range.

(2) Studies regarding HFLPRs are insufficient. Several studies focused on the consistency measures, such as additive consistency, weak consistency and multiplicative consistency, and the algorithms for consistency improving. But few of them proposed methods to explore priorities from HFLPRs with acceptable consistency. Moreover, the case where some entries of HFLPRs are missed has not been considered.

(3) Decision-making with HFLTSs requires more information fusion approaches. Most of the existing aggregation operators simply extend the idea of classical operators to cope with uncertain linguistic terms or extended HFLTSs. As stated in Rodríguez et al. [98], this kind of extensions, with a lack of theoretical or practical justification, make no sense. New aggregation approaches are welcome if they are driven by real world applications and/or if they present a new way to handle HFLTSs.

(4) HFLTSs could solve more complex applications if they are associated with other tools for granular computing, such as techniques for multi-granular linguistic decision-making. Although HFLTSs themselves are a tool for granular computing, the focus is different from other techniques. Multi-granular linguistic decision-making techniques are irreplaceable to represent the information granules of different reference domains. For example, we do not use the same LTS to both evaluate the grades of students with respect to a course and evaluate the research potential of students. In this case, unbalanced LTSs are frequently involved. Given a LTS, HFLTSs are suitable for the situation where the experts' granules of knowledge are coarser than the granule of the LTS. Some researchers started this scenario by introducing some rational information fusion techniques. More sophisticated decision-making approaches should be further investigated.

(5) Multiple types of uncertain linguistic information could be considered simultaneously. Due to the complexity of real problems, qualitative information may be represented by not only HFLTSs but also other types of complex linguistic expressions. Corresponding approaches should be developed to support decision-making based on multiple types of complex linguistic expressions. To do so, some basic issues, including basic operations, order relations and information measures, should be addressed at first.

(6) Novel models are necessary to represent more types of complex linguistic expressions. Although several types of complex linguistic expressions have been focused, current techniques do not cover all types of frequently used natural languages. For example, when evaluating an object, if we think that it may be *good*, but other terms around *good* are also possible, we may say that it is *more or less good* or it is *roughly good*. That is, to express the uncertainty of using a certain term, we may consider a linguistic hedge to modify the term instead of considering a linguistic interval. The hedges, *more or less* and *roughly*, do not modify the term to another, but modify the degree of certainty of using the term. It would be very interesting if some models could be proposed to incorporate this kind of linguistic expressions.

When considering the uncertainty involved in HFLTSs, the current developments suffer the following drawbacks:

(1) It is obvious that HFLTSs are the tool for representing the uncertainty of expressing performance values. Thus, it is rational to expect that the computational results should be uncertain. However, most of the existing approaches proposed certain indices for alternative ranking and/or selection. This means that at least a kind of defuzzification or averaging techniques has been used, and thus could lead to two limitations. Firstly, the final decision can not be explained intuitively, for example, from the view of probability. Secondly, it can be hardly to do the sensitive analysis.

(2) The weights of experts and/or criteria are expected to be specified exactly in many studies. In fact, experts may not want to express weights, especially weights of themselves, at all. This is caused by several reasons: they may expect that the weights would change over time; they could not assign any weights due to the time pressure or the difficulty of the problem; or they do not want to restrict themselves to some weights [61, 65]. Moreover, some decision-making approaches prefer to assign different weights to the same problem [107]. The use of exact weights may result in the difficulty of reaching group consensus. However, in most of the existing multiple criteria GDM approaches, if the weights are unknown or partially unknown, then some kinds of objective weighting methods, such as optimization models, are frequently considered to obtain an acceptable or optimal weight vector. In this case, the resultant decisions might be questionable or inadmissible if the decision maker does not accept the derived weight vector. Ideally, a robust decision should be supported by many different weight vectors.

These current developments have delivered great contributions to MCDM with aspiration levels. The merits of three categories of investigation are prominent. The probability-based methods and fuzzy aspiration-based methods have the advantage to model uncertainties of representing aspiration levels, whereas the reference point-based methods pay more attention to model the psychological behaviour of decision makers. The interactive methods seem to be a wonderful way to follow the idea of satisficing heuristic. Yet the optimization models can reduce the participation from experts.

However, there are some limitations in the existing fuzzy aspiration-based methods. Only single terms and uncertain linguistic terms are available in the methods. This would limit their applicability to complex problems in which the experts may prefer to express their opinions by various types of linguistic expressions due to their language custom and the degrees of uncertainties. Moreover, multi-granular linguistic information is inevitable in complex problems because one LTS may not be suitable for the entire evaluation criteria. But this has not been considered in the existing methods. All these identified limitations and omits are the issues to be addressed in the following sections.

1.4 Aims and Focuses of This Book

Based on the problems described in Sect. 1.2, the major aims of this book are: For the evaluation and selection of BDAPs, we introduce the fundamental theory and GDM approaches based on multiple types of ULEs, construct the rational and systematic methodology in linguistic setting. Especially,

(1) Theoretically, we introduce the foundation of the virtual linguistic model, extend the model of HFLTSs, present a new linguistic model which includes linguistic hedges as a tool to express uncertainties qualitatively, introduce consistency measures of preference relations based on specific types of ULEs, and then present a GDM framework based on the inner structure of groups.

(2) Technically, we introduce the definitions, improvements, and priority of preference relations based on the new linguistic models in (1), present GDM approaches based on information fusion and stochastic analysis, respectively, include descriptive measures for decision makers to understand the uncertainties, and introduce GDM approaches with multiple types of ULEs based on the linguistic aspiration levels of experts.

(3) For application, we introduce the hierarchical model for the evaluation of BDAPs, and then support the evaluation in real applications based on the proposed GDM approaches.

Corresponding to the aims, the content of this book could be specified as follows:

(1) Linguistic computational models:

- The syntactical and semantic rules of the virtual linguistic model based on a predefined LTS.
- The extended form of HFLTSs and the information fusion techniques, total orders of the form.
- The syntactical and semantic rules of linguistic terms with weakened hedges, and the associated basic operations and order relations.

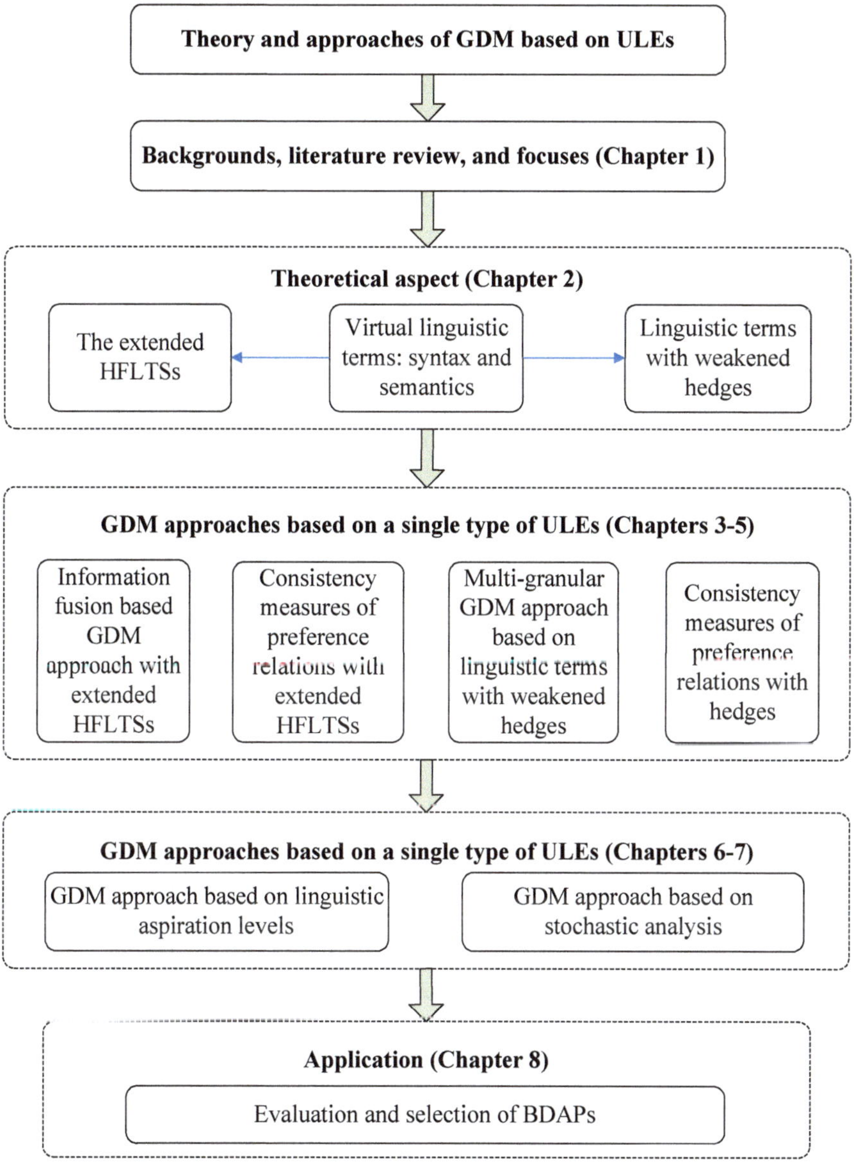

Fig. 1.3 The structure of this book

(2) Preference relations based on ULEs:

- The weak consistency and additive consistency of preference relations based on the extended HFLTSs, the improvement of their consistencies based on graph theory, and the regression of this type of preference relations to the traditional LPRs.

- The algorithms of improving incomplete LPRs according to specific consistency measures of the extended form of HFLTSs.
- The definition of consistency measures of linguistic preference relations with hedges by transitivity, the algorithms to check and improve the degree of consistency, and the relationships among several consistency measures.

(3) GDM approaches based on ULEs:

- A stochastic analysis based GDM approach based on multiple types of ULEs which includes the expected consistency index, consistency acceptability index, rank acceptability index, and an iterative GDM procedure for MCDM.
- A GDM framework for complex problems according to sizes of groups and inner structures of groups, and its implementation in the case of extended form of HFLTSs.
- A GDM approach in which the performances and aspiration levels could take the forms of multiple types of ULEs.
- The hierarchical model for the evaluation of BDAPs which is suitable for Chinese government audit, and a solution of the model based on the aspiration-based GDM approach.

The structure of the book is organized by five parts, as shown in Fig. 1.3. Specifically,

References

1. Aguaron, J., Moreno-Jiménez, J.M.: The geometric consistency index: approximated thresholds. Eur. J. Oper. Res. **147**(1), 137–145 (2003)
2. Alonso, S., Cabrerizo, F.J., Chiclana, F., Herrera, F., Herrera-Viedma, E.: An interactive decision support system based on consistency criteria. J. Mult. Valued Log. Soft Comput. **14**, 371–385 (2008)
3. Alonso, S., Chiclana, F., Herrera, F., Herrera-Viedma, E., Alcalá-Fdez, J., Porcel, C.: A consistency-based procedure to estimate missing pairwise preference values. Int. J. Intell. Syst. **23**(2), 155–175 (2008)
4. Ansari, M.M.T., Velusami, S.: DMLHFLC (Dual mode linguistic hedge fuzzy logic controller) for an isolated wind-diesel hybrid power system with BES (battery energy storage) unit. Energy **35**(9), 3827–3837 (2010)
5. Bartl, E., Belohlavek, R., Vychodil, V.: Bivalent and other solutions of fuzzy relational equations via linguistic hedges. Fuzzy Sets Syst. **187**(1), 103–112 (2012)
6. Beg, I., Rashid, T.: Topsis for hesitant fuzzy linguistic term sets. Int. J. Intell. Syst. **28**(12), 1162–1171 (2013)
7. Bordley, R.F., Kirkwood, C.W.: Multiattribute preference analysis with performance targets. Oper. Res. **52**(6), 823–835 (2004)
8. Bosc, P., Hadjali, A., Pivert, O.: Empty versus overabundant answers to flexible relational queries. Fuzzy Sets Syst. **159**(12), 1450–1467 (2008)
9. Brandstätter, E., Gigerenzer, G., Hertwig, R.: The priority heuristic: making choices without trade-offs. Psychol. Rev. **113**(2), 409–432 (2006)
10. Brown, D.B., Giorgi, E.D., Sim, M.: Aspirational preferences and their representation by risk measures. Manag. Sci. **58**(11), 2095–2113 (2012)

11. Büyüközkan, G., Çifçi, G.: A new incomplete preference relations based approach to quality function deployment. Inf. Sci. **206**, 30–41 (2012)
12. Cabrerizo, F.J., Pérez, I.J., Herrera-Viedma, E.: Managing the consensus in group decision making in an unbalanced fuzzy linguistic context with incomplete information. Knowl. Based Syst. **23**(2), 169–181 (2010)
13. Carmone, F.J., Kara, A., Zanakis, S.H.: A Monte Carlo investigation of incomplete pairwise comparison matrices in AHP. Eur. J. Oper. Res. **102**(3), 538–553 (1997)
14. Cetisli, B.: The effect of linguistic hedges on feature selection: part 2. Expert. Syst. Appl. **37**(8), 6102–6108 (2010)
15. Chandramohan, A., Rao, M.: Novel, useful, and effective definitions for fuzzy linguistic hedges. Discret. Dyn. Nat. Soc. **46**(546) (2006)
16. Chang, K.H.: A more general reliability allocation method using the hesitant fuzzy linguistic term set and minimal variance owga weights. Appl. Soft Comput. **56**, 589–596 (2017)
17. Chatterjee, A., Siarry, P.: Nonlinear inertia weight variation for dynamic adaptation in particle swarm optimization. Comput. Oper. Res. **33**(3), 859–871 (2006)
18. Chen, S.M., Hong, J.A.: Multicriteria linguistic decision making based on hesitant fuzzy linguistic term sets and the aggregation of fuzzy sets. Inf. Sci. **286**, 63–74 (2014)
19. Chen, C.Y., Hsieh, Y.T., Liu, B.D.: Circuit implementation of linguistic-hedge fuzzy logic controller in current-mode approach. IEEE Trans. Fuzzy Syst. **11**(5), 624–646 (2003)
20. Chiclana, F., Herrera, F., Herrera-Viedma, E., Martınez, L.: A note on the reciprocity in the aggregation of fuzzy preference relations using OWA operators. Fuzzy Sets Syst. **137**(1), 71–83 (2003)
21. Chiclana, F., Herrera-Viedma, E., Herrera, F., Alonso, S.: Induced ordered weighted geometric operators and their use in the aggregation of multiplicative preference relations. Int. J. Intell. Syst. **19**(3), 233–255 (2004)
22. Chiclana, F., Herrera-Viedma, E., Alonso, S., Herrera, F.: A note on the estimation of missing pairwise preference values: a uninorm consistency based method. Int. J. Uncertain. Fuzziness Knowl. Based Syst. **16**(supp02), 19–32 (2008)
23. Chiclana, F., GarcíA, J.T., Del Moral, M.J., Herrera-Viedma, E.: A statistical comparative study of different similarity measures of consensus in group decision making. Inf. Sci. **221**, 110–123 (2013)
24. Chuu, S.J.: Interactive group decision-making using a fuzzy linguistic approach for evaluating the flexibility in a supply chain. Eur. J. Oper. Res. **213**(1), 279–289 (2011)
25. De Cock, M., Kerre, E.E.: Fuzzy modifiers based on fuzzy relations. Inf. Sci. **160**(1), 173–199 (2004)
26. De Cock, M., Radzikowska, A.M., Kerre, E.E.: A fuzzy-rough approach to the representation of linguistic hedges. In: Technologies for Constructing Intelligent Systems 1, pp. 33–42. Springer (2002)
27. Diecidue, E., Van De Ven, J.: Aspiration level, probability of success and failure, and expected utility. Int. Econ. Rev. **49**(2), 683–700 (2008)
28. Dong, Y.C., Zhang, G.Q., Hong, W.C., Xu, Y.F.: Consensus models for AHP group decision making under row geometric mean prioritization method. Decis. Support. Syst. **49**(3), 281–289 (2010)
29. Dong, Y.C., Chen, X., Herrera, F.: Minimizing adjusted simple terms in the consensus reaching process with hesitant linguistic assessments in group decision making. Inf. Sci. **297**, 95–117 (2015)
30. Dong, Y.C., Li, C.C., Herrera, F.: Connecting the linguistic hierarchy and the numerical scale for the 2-tuple linguistic model and its use to deal with hesitant unbalanced linguistic information. Inf. Sci. **367**, 259–278 (2016)
31. Durbach, I.N., Calder, J.M.: Modelling uncertainty in stochastic multicriteria acceptability analysis. Omega **64**, 13–23 (2016)
32. Ebenbach, D.H., Moore, C.F.: Incomplete information, inferences, and individual differences: the case of environmental judgments. Organ. Behav. Hum. Decis. Process. **81**(1), 1–27 (2000)

33. Fahmi, A., Kahraman, C., Bilen, Ü.: ELECTRE I method using hesitant linguistic term sets: an application to supplier selection. Int. J. Comput. Intell. Syst. **9**(1), 153–167 (2016)
34. Falcó, E., García-Lapresta, J.L., Roselló, L.: Allowing agents to be imprecise: a proposal using multiple linguistic terms. Inf. Sci. **258**, 249–265 (2014)
35. Fan, Z.P., Zhang, X., Chen, F.D., Liu, Y.: Multiple attribute decision making considering aspiration-levels: a method based on prospect theory. Comput. Ind. Eng. **65**(2), 341–350 (2013a)
36. Fan, Z.P., Zhang, X., Zhao, Y.R., Chen, F.D.: Multiple attribute decision making with multiple formats of attribute aspirations: a method based on prospect theory. Int. J. Inf. Technol. Decis. Mak. **12**(04), 711–727 (2013b)
37. Fantozzi, F., Spizzichino, F.: Multi-attribute target-based utilities and extensions of fuzzy measures. Fuzzy Sets Syst. **259**, 29–43 (2015)
38. Farhadinia, B.: Multiple criteria decision-making methods with completely unknown weights in hesitant fuzzy linguistic term setting. Knowl. Based Syst. **93**, 135–144 (2016)
39. Fedrizzi, M., Giove, S.: Incomplete pairwise comparison and consistency optimization. Eur. J. Oper. Res. **183**(1), 303–313 (2007)
40. Feng, B., Lai, F.J.: Multi-attribute group decision making with aspirations: a case study. Omega **44**, 136–147 (2014)
41. Galea, M., Shen, Q.: Linguistic hedges for ant-generated rules, pp. 1973–1980. IEEE (2006)
42. Gong, Z.W.: Least-square method to priority of the fuzzy preference relations with incomplete information. Int. J. Approx. Reason. **47**(2), 258–264 (2008)
43. Gou, X.J., Xu, Z.S.: Novel basic operational laws for linguistic terms, hesitant fuzzy linguistic term sets and probabilistic linguistic term sets. Inf. Sci. **372**, 407–427 (2016a)
44. Gou, X.J., Xu, Z.S., Liao, H.C.: Multiple criteria decision making based on Bonferroni means with hesitant fuzzy linguistic information. Soft Comput. 1–15 (2016b)
45. Gou, X.J., Xu, Z.S., Liao, H.C.: Alternative queuing method for multiple criteria decision making with hybrid fuzzy and ranking information. Inf. Sci. **357**, 144–160 (2016c)
46. Gou, X.J., Xu, Z.S., Liao, H.C.: Hesitant fuzzy linguistic entropy and cross-entropy measures and alternative queuing method for multiple criteria decision making. Inf. Sci. **388**, 225–246 (2017)
47. Herrera, F., Herrera-Viedma, E.: Choice functions and mechanisms for linguistic preference relations. Eur. J. Oper. Res. **120**(1), 144–161 (2000)
48. Herrera-Viedma, E., Herrera, F., Chiclana, F., Luque, M.: Some issues on consistency of fuzzy preference relations. Eur. J. Oper. Res. **154**(1), 98–109 (2004)
49. Herrera-Viedma, E., Martínez, L., Mata, F., Chiclana, F.: A consensus support system model for group decision-making problems with multigranular linguistic preference relations. IEEE Trans. Fuzzy Syst. **13**(5), 644–658 (2005)
50. Herrera-Viedma, E., Chiclana, F., Herrera, F., Alonso, S.: Group decision-making model with incomplete fuzzy preference relations based on additive consistency. IEEE Trans. Syst. Man Cybern. Part B Cybern. **37**(1), 176–189 (2007)
51. Herrera-Viedma, E., Alonso, S., Chiclana, F., Herrera, F.: A consensus model for group decision making with incomplete fuzzy preference relations. IEEE Trans. Fuzzy Syst. **15**(5), 863–877 (2007)
52. Hesamian, G., Shams, M.: Measuring similarity and ordering based on hesitant fuzzy linguistic term sets. J. Intell. Fuzzy Syst. **28**(2), 983–990 (2015)
53. Huynh, V.N., Nakamori, Y., Ryoke, M., Ho, T.B.: Decision making under uncertainty with fuzzy targets. Fuzzy Optim. Decis. Mak. **6**(3), 255–278 (2007)
54. Huynh, V.N., Nakamori, Y., Lawry, J.: A probability-based approach to comparison of fuzzy numbers and applications to target-oriented decision making. IEEE Trans. Fuzzy Syst. **16**(2), 371–387 (2008)
55. Huynh, V.N., Yan, H., Nakamori, Y.: A target-based decision-making approach to consumer-oriented evaluation model for japanese traditional crafts. IEEE Trans. Eng. Manag. **57**(4), 575–588 (2010)

56. Kerre, E.E., De Cock, M.: Linguistic modifiers: an overview. Fuzzy Log. Soft Comput. **9**, 69–85 (1999)
57. Kim, J.K., Choi, S.H., Han, C.H., Kim, S.H.: An interactive procedure for multiple criteria group decision making with incomplete information. Comput. Ind. Eng. **35**(1–2), 295–298 (1998)
58. Köksalan, M., Wallenius, J., Zionts, S.: An early history of multiple criteria decision making. J. Multi Criteria Decis. Anal. **20**(1–2), 87–94 (2013)
59. Kwiesielewicz, M., Van Uden, E.: Inconsistent and contradictory judgements in pairwise comparison method in the AHP. Comput. Oper. Res. **31**(5), 713–719 (2004)
60. Lahdelma, R., Salminen, P.: Stochastic multicriteria acceptability analysis (SMAA). In: Trends in Multiple Criteria Decision Analysis, pp. 285–315. Springer (2010)
61. Lahdelma, R., Salminen, P.: SMAA-2: stochastic multicriteria acceptability analysis for group decision making. Oper. Res. **49**(3), 444–454 (2001)
62. Lahdelma, R., Salminen, P.: Stochastic multicriteria acceptability analysis using the data envelopment model. Eur. J. Oper. Res. **170**(1), 241–252 (2006a)
63. Lahdelma, R., Salminen, P.: Classifying efficient alternatives in SMAA using cross confidence factors. Eur. J. Oper. Res. **170**(1), 228–240 (2006b)
64. Lahdelma, R., Hokkanen, J., Salminen, P.: SMAA-stochastic multiobjective acceptability analysis. Eur. J. Oper. Res. **106**(1), 137–143 (1998)
65. Lahdelma, R., Salminen, P., Hokkanen, J.: Using multicriteria methods in environmental planning and management. Environ. Manag. **26**(6), 595–605 (2000)
66. Lahdelma, R., Miettinen, K., Salminen, P.: Ordinal criteria in stochastic multicriteria acceptability analysis (SMAA). Eur. J. Oper. Res. **147**(1), 117–127 (2003)
67. Lahdelma, R., Miettinen, K., Salminen, P.: Reference point approach for multiple decision makers. Eur. J. Oper. Res. **164**(3), 785–791 (2005)
68. Lai, V.S., Wong, B.K., Cheung, W.: Group decision making in a multiple criteria environment: a case using the AHP in software selection. Eur. J. Oper. Res. **137**(1), 134–144 (2002)
69. Lee, L.W.: Group decision making with incomplete fuzzy preference relations based on the additive consistency and the order consistency. Expert. Syst. Appl. **39**(14), 11666–11676 (2012)
70. Lee, L.W., Chen, S.M.: Fuzzy decision making based on likelihood-based comparison relations of hesitant fuzzy linguistic term sets and hesitant fuzzy linguistic operators. Inf. Sci. **294**, 513–529 (2015a)
71. Lee, L.W., Chen, S.M.: Fuzzy decision making and fuzzy group decision making based on likelihood-based comparison relations of hesitant fuzzy linguistic term sets1. J. Intell. Fuzzy Syst. **29**(3), 1119–1137 (2015b)
72. Li, C.C., Dong, Y.C., Herrera, F., Martínez, L.: An optimization-based approach to estimate the range of consistency in hesitant fuzzy linguistic preference relations, pp. 864–871. IEEE (2016)
73. Li, Z.M., Xu, J.P., Lev, B., Gang, J.: Multi-criteria group individual research output evaluation based on context-free grammar judgments with assessing attitude. Omega **57**, 282–293 (2015)
74. Liao, H.C., Xu, Z.S.: Approaches to manage hesitant fuzzy linguistic information based on the cosine distance and similarity measures for HFLTSs and their application in qualitative decision making. Expert. Syst. Appl. **42**(12), 5328–5336 (2015)
75. Liao, H.C., Xu, Z.S., Zeng, X.J.: Distance and similarity measures for hesitant fuzzy linguistic term sets and their application in multi-criteria decision making. Inf. Sci. **271**, 125–142 (2014)
76. Liao, H.C., Xu, Z.S., Zeng, X.J., Merigó, J.M.: Qualitative decision making with correlation coefficients of hesitant fuzzy linguistic term sets. Knowl. Based Syst. **76**, 127–138 (2015a)
77. Liao, H.C., Xu, Z.S., Zeng, X.J.: Hesitant fuzzy linguistic VIKOR method and its application in qualitative multiple criteria decision making. IEEE Trans. Fuzzy Syst. **23**(5), 1343–1355 (2015b)
78. Liu, H.B., Rodríguez, R.M.: A fuzzy envelope for hesitant fuzzy linguistic term set and its application to multicriteria decision making. Inf. Sci. **258**, 220–238 (2014)

79. Liu, B.D., Chen, C.Y., Tsao, J.Y.: Design of adaptive fuzzy logic controller based on linguistic-hedge concepts and genetic algorithms. IEEE Trans. Syst. Man Cybern. Part B Cybern. **31**(1), 32–53 (2001)
80. Liu, X.W., Pan, Y.W., Xu, Y.J., Yu, S.: Least square completion and inconsistency repair methods for additively consistent fuzzy preference relations. Fuzzy Sets Syst. **198**, 1–19 (2012)
81. Liu, H.B., Cai, J.F., Jiang, L.: On improving the additive consistency of the fuzzy preference relations based on comparative linguistic expressions. Int. J. Intell. Syst. **29**(6), 544–559 (2014)
82. Liu, H.C., You, J.X., Li, P., Su, Q.: Failure mode and effect analysis under uncertainty: an integrated multiple criteria decision making approach. IEEE Trans. Reliab. **65**(3), 1380–1392 (2016)
83. Lotfi, V., Stewart, T.J., Zionts, S.: An aspiration-level interactive model for multiple criteria decision making. Comput. Oper. Res. **19**(7), 671–681 (1992)
84. Meng, F.Y., Chen, X.H.: A hesitant fuzzy linguistic multi-granularity decision making model based on distance measures. J. Intell. Fuzzy Syst. **28**(4), 1519–1531 (2015)
85. Millet, I.: The effectiveness of alternative preference elicitation methods in the analytic hierarchy process. J. Multi Criteria Decis. Anal. **6**(1), 41–51 (1997)
86. Montserrat-Adell, J., Agell, N., Sánchez, M., Prats, F., Ruiz, F.J.: Modeling group assessments by means of hesitant fuzzy linguistic term sets. J. Appl. Log. **23**, 40–50 (2017)
87. Nowak, M.: Interactive approach in multicriteria analysis based on stochastic dominance. Control. Cybern. **33**(3), 463–476 (2004)
88. Nowak, M.: INSDECM-an interactive procedure for stochastic multicriteria decision problems. Eur. J. Oper. Res. **175**(3), 1413–1430 (2006)
89. Nowak, M.: Aspiration level approach in stochastic MCDM problems. Eur. J. Oper. Res. **177**(3), 1626–1640 (2007)
90. Orlovsky, S.: Decision-making with a fuzzy preference relation. Fuzzy Sets Syst. **1**(3), 155–167 (1978)
91. Pang, Q., Wang, H., Xu, Z.S.: Probabilistic linguistic term sets in multi-attribute group decision making. Inf. Sci. **369**, 128–143 (2016)
92. Payne, J.W.: It is whether you win or lose: the importance of the overall probabilities of winning or losing in risky choice. J. Risk Uncertain. **30**(1), 5–19 (2005)
93. Phuong, L.A., Khang, T.D.: Generalized modus tollens with linguistic modifiers for inverse approximate reasoning. Int. J. Comput. Intell. Syst. **7**(3), 556–564 (2014)
94. Rodríguez, R.M., Martínez, L., Herrera, F.: Eliciting comparative linguistic expressions in group decision making. In: 2013 Joint IFSA World Congress and NAFIPS Annual Meeting (IFSA/NAFIPS), pp. 771–776. IEEE (2013)
95. Rodríguez, R.M., Martínez, L.: A consensus model for group decision making with hesitant fuzzy linguistic information. In: 2015 10th International Conference on Intelligent Systems and Knowledge Engineering (ISKE), pp. 540–545. IEEE (2015)
96. Rodríguez, R.M., Martínez, L., Herrera, F.: Hesitant fuzzy linguistic term sets for decision making. IEEE Trans. Fuzzy Syst. **20**(1), 109–119 (2012)
97. Rodríguez, R.M., Martínez, L., Herrera, F.: A group decision making model dealing with comparative linguistic expressions based on hesitant fuzzy linguistic term sets. Inf. Sci. **241**, 28–42 (2013)
98. Rodríguez, R.M., Bedregal, B., Bustince, H., Dong, Y.C., Farhadinia, B., Kahraman, C., Martínez, L., Torra, V., Xu, Y.J., Xu, Z.S., et al.: A position and perspective analysis of hesitant fuzzy sets on information fusion in decision making. Towards high quality progress. Inf. Fusion **29**, 89–97 (2016)
99. Saaty, T.L.: A scaling method for priorities in hierarchical structures. J. Math. Psychol. **15**(3), 234–281 (1977)
100. Saaty, T.L.: Axiomatic foundation of the analytic hierarchy process. Manag. Sci. **32**(7), 841–855 (1986)

101. Saaty, T.L., Vargas, L.G.: Uncertainty and rank order in the analytic hierarchy process. Eur. J. Oper. Res. **32**(1), 107–117 (1987)
102. Simon, H.A.: Rational choice and the structure of the environment. Psychol. Rev. **63**(2), 129 (1956)
103. Sun, M., Steuer, R.E.: InterQuad: an interactive quad tree based procedure for solving the discrete alternative multiple criteria problem. Eur. J. Oper. Res. **89**(3), 462–472 (1996)
104. Tan, C.Q., Ip, W., Chen, X.H.: Stochastic multiple criteria decision making with aspiration level based on prospect stochastic dominance. Knowl. Based Syst. **70**, 231–241 (2014)
105. Tervonen, T., Figueira, J.R.: A survey on stochastic multicriteria acceptability analysis methods. J. Multi Criteria Decis. Anal. **15**(1–2), 1–14 (2008)
106. Tervonen, T., Lahdelma, R.: Implementing stochastic multicriteria acceptability analysis. Eur. J. Oper. Res. **178**(2), 500–513 (2007)
107. Tian, Z.P., Wang, J., Wang, J.Q., Zhang, H.Y.: A likelihood-based qualitative flexible approach with hesitant fuzzy linguistic information. Cogn. Comput. **8**(4), 670–683 (2016)
108. Tsetlin, I., Winkler, R.L.: Decision making with multiattribute performance targets: the impact of changes in performance and target distributions. Oper. Res. **55**(2), 226–233 (2007)
109. Ureña, R., Chiclana, F., Alonso, S., Morente-Molinera, J.A., Herrera-Viedma, E.: On incomplete fuzzy and multiplicative preference relations in multi-person decision making. Procedia Comput. Sci. **31**, 793–801 (2014)
110. Ureña, R., Chiclana, F., Morente-Molinera, J.A., Herrera-Viedma, E.: Managing incomplete preference relations in decision making: a review and future trends. Inf. Sci. **302**, 14–32 (2015)
111. Voxman, W.: Canonical representations of discrete fuzzy numbers. Fuzzy Sets Syst. **118**(3), 457–466 (2001)
112. Wang, H., Xu, Z.S.: Some consistency measures of extended hesitant fuzzy linguistic preference relations. Inf. Sci. **297**, 316–331 (2015)
113. Wang, H., Xu, Z.S.: Total orders of extended hesitant fuzzy linguistic term sets: definitions, generations and applications. Knowl. Based Syst. **107**, 142–154 (2016)
114. Wang, J.G., Zionts, S.: The aspiration level interactive method (AIM) reconsidered: robustness of solutions. Eur. J. Oper. Res. **175**(2), 948–958 (2006)
115. Wang, J.Q., Wang, J., Chen, Q.H., Zhang, H.Y., Chen, X.H.: An outranking approach for multi-criteria decision-making with hesitant fuzzy linguistic term sets. Inf. Sci. **280**, 338–351 (2014)
116. Wang, J., Wang, J.Q., Zhang, H.Y., Chen, X.H.: Multi-criteria decision-making based on hesitant fuzzy linguistic term sets: an outranking approach. Knowl. Based Syst. **86**, 224–236 (2015)
117. Wang, H., Xu, Z.S., Zeng, X.J.: Hesitant fuzzy linguistic term sets for linguistic decision making: current developments, issues and challenges. Inf. Fusion **43**, 1–12 (2018)
118. Wei, C.P., Zhao, N., Tang, X.J.: Operators and comparisons of hesitant fuzzy linguistic term sets. IEEE Trans. Fuzzy Syst. **22**(3), 575–585 (2014)
119. Wei, C.P., Ren, Z.L., Rodríguez, R.M.: A hesitant fuzzy linguistic todim method based on a score function. Int. J. Comput. Intell. Syst. **8**(4), 701–712 (2015)
120. Wu, Z.B., Xu, J.P.: Managing consistency and consensus in group decision making with hesitant fuzzy linguistic preference relations. Omega **65**, 28–40 (2016a)
121. Wu, Z.B., Xu, J.P.: An interactive consensus reaching model for decision making under hesitation linguistic environment. J. Intell. Fuzzy Syst. **31**(3), 1635–1644 (2016b)
122. Wu, Z.B., Xu, J.P.: Possibility distribution-based approach for MAGDM with hesitant fuzzy linguistic information. IEEE Trans. Cybern. **46**(3), 694–705 (2016c)
123. Wu, J., Chiclana, F., Herrera-Viedma, E.: Trust based consensus model for social network in an incomplete linguistic information context. Appl. Soft Comput. **35**, 827–839 (2015)
124. Xia, M.M., Xu, Z.S., Chen, J.: Algorithms for improving consistency or consensus of reciprocal [0, 1]-valued preference relations. Fuzzy Sets Syst. **216**, 108–133 (2013)
125. Xu, Z.S.: A method based on linguistic aggregation operators for group decision making with linguistic preference relations. Inf. Sci. **166**(1), 19–30 (2004a)

126. Xu, Z.S.: Uncertain linguistic aggregation operators based approach to multiple attribute group decision making under uncertain linguistic environment. Inf. Sci. **168**(1), 171–184 (2004b)
127. Xu, Z.S.: On compatibility of interval fuzzy preference relations. Fuzzy Optim. Decis. Mak. **3**(3), 217–225 (2004c)
128. Xu, Z.S.: An approach based on the uncertain LOWG and induced uncertain LOWG operators to group decision making with uncertain multiplicative linguistic preference relations. Decis. Support. Syst. **41**(2), 488–499 (2006a)
129. Xu, Z.S.: Incomplete linguistic preference relations and their fusion. Inf. Fusion **7**(3), 331–337 (2006b)
130. Xu, Z.S.: Intuitionistic preference relations and their application in group decision making. Inf. Sci. **177**(11), 2363–2379 (2007)
131. Xu, Z.S.: Group decision making based on multiple types of linguistic preference relations. Inf. Sci. **178**(2), 452–467 (2008)
132. Xu, Z.S.: An integrated model-based interactive approach to FMAGDM with incomplete preference information. Fuzzy Optim. Decis. Mak. **9**(3), 333–357 (2010)
133. Xu, Z.S., Wei, C.P.: A consistency improving method in the analytic hierarchy process. Eur. J. Oper. Res. **116**(2), 443–449 (1999)
134. Xu, Z.S., Yager, R.R.: Intuitionistic and interval-valued intutionistic fuzzy preference relations and their measures of similarity for the evaluation of agreement within a group. Fuzzy Optim. Decis. Mak. **8**(2), 123–139 (2009)
135. Xu, Y.J., Patnayakuni, R., Wang, H.M.: The ordinal consistency of a fuzzy preference relation. Inf. Sci. **224**, 152–164 (2013)
136. Xu, Y.J., Xu, A.W., Merigó, J.M., Wang, H.M.: Hesitant fuzzy linguistic ordered weighted distance operators for group decision making. J. Appl. Math. Comput. **49**(1–2), 285–308 (2015)
137. Xu, Y.J., Xu, A.W., Wang, H.M.: Hesitant fuzzy linguistic linear programming technique for multidimensional analysis of preference for multi-attribute group decision making. Int. J. Mach. Learn. Cybern. **7**(5), 845–855 (2016)
138. Yager, R.R.: On ordered weighted averaging aggregation operators in multicriteria decision making. IEEE Trans. Syst. Man Cybern. **18**(1), 183–190 (1988)
139. Yan, H.B., Huynh, V.N., Murai, T., Nakamori, Y.: Kansei evaluation based on prioritized multi-attribute fuzzy target-oriented decision analysis. Inf. Sci. **178**(21), 4080–4093 (2008)
140. Yan, H.B., Huynh, V.N., Nakamori, Y.: A group nonadditive multiattribute consumer-oriented kansei evaluation model with an application to traditional crafts. Ann. Oper. Res. **195**(1), 325–354 (2012)
141. Yan, H.B., Huynh, V.N., Ma, T.J., Nakamori, Y.: Non additive multi-attribute fuzzy target-oriented decision analysis. Inf. Sci. **240**, 21–44 (2013)
142. Yan, H.B., Ma, T.J., Sriboonchitta, S., Huynh, V.N.: A stochastic dominance based approach to consumer-oriented kansei evaluation with multiple priorities. Ann. Oper. Res. **256**(2), 329–357 (2017)
143. Yun, Y.B., Nakayama, H., Arakawa, M.: Multiple criteria decision making with generalized dea and an aspiration level method. Eur. J. Oper. Res. **158**(3), 697–706 (2004)
144. Zadeh, L.A.: A fuzzy-set-theoretic interpretation of linguistic hedges. J. Cybern. **2**(3), 4–34 (1972)
145. Zadeh, L.A.: The concept of a linguistic variable and its application to approximate reasoning-I. Inf. Sci. **8**(3), 199–249 (1975)
146. Zhang, Z., Guo, C.H.: New operations of hesitant fuzzy linguistic term sets with applications in multi-attribute group decision making. In: 2015 IEEE International Conference on Fuzzy Systems (FUZZ-IEEE), pp. 1–8. IEEE (2015)
147. Zhang, Z.M., Wu, C.: On the use of multiplicative consistency in hesitant fuzzy linguistic preference relations. Knowl. Based Syst. **72**, 13–27 (2014)
148. Zhang, G.Q., Dong, Y.C., Xu, Y.F.: Linear optimization modeling of consistency issues in group decision making based on fuzzy preference relations. Expert. Syst. Appl. **39**(3), 2415–2420 (2012)

149. Zhang, G.Q., Dong, Y.C., Xu, Y.F.: Consistency and consensus measures for linguistic preference relations based on distribution assessments. Inf. Fusion **17**, 46–55 (2014)
150. Zhang, X.L., Xu, Z.S., Wang, H.: Heterogeneous multiple criteria group decision making with incomplete weight information: a deviation modeling approach. Inf. Fusion **25**, 49–62 (2015)
151. Zhu, B., Xu, Z.S.: Consistency measures for hesitant fuzzy linguistic preference relations. IEEE Trans. Fuzzy Syst. **22**(1), 35–45 (2014)

References

Part II
Theory and Models of Uncertain Linguistic Expressions

Chapter 2
Representational Models and Computational Foundations of Some Types of Uncertain Linguistic Expressions

Based on the literature review in Chap. 1, we focus on some types of ULEs and introduce the corresponding models in this chapter. These models are based on the virtual linguistic model. Thus, we introduce a theoretical discussion on this model because it triggered off some debates due to the lack of syntactical and semantic rules.

2.1 Virtual Linguistic Model

Methodologies for CWW [42] are very useful for decision-making problems with qualitative criteria and thus have been widely studied and applied in many practical areas. CWW manipulates natural and artificial linguistic expressions which are less precise than numbers but much closer to human's brain mechanisms. All these linguistic expressions form the domain of possible values of a linguistic variable [41]. Till now, there are several famous linguistic decision-making models, such as the membership function-based model [8], the ordinal scales-based model [25, 38], the 2-tuple linguistic model [13] and the virtual linguistic model [31]. From a historical view, the virtual linguistic model can be considered as a variant of the 2-tuple linguistic model. Both of them are very popular as they compute linguistic expressions without loss of information.

When dealing with linguistic information by a certain computational model, the first and basic step is to choose LTSs with syntax and semantics [12]. Although the virtual linguistic model has been widely applied in information fusion-driven decision-making [20, 21], its lack of clear representation of syntax and semantics has triggered off some discussions [22]. Recently, Liao et al. [19] started the discussion with a special case. When the virtual linguistic terms (VLTs) are balanced

H. Wang and Z. Xu, *Theory and Approaches of Group Decision-Making with Uncertain Linguistic Expressions*, Uncertainty and Operations Research,
https://doi.org/10.1007/978-981-13-3735-2_2

and uniformly distributed in the considered domain, they constructed a simple yet meaningful mapping between the VLTs and their semantics graphically. To build a sound foundation of the virtual linguistic model, in this section, we mainly focus on the introduction of the syntax and semantics of VLTs in a general way [37].

2.1.1 Preliminaries

Given a nonempty domain U, a fuzzy set F on U is characterized by a membership function $\mu_F : U \to [0, 1]$. For each u of U, $\mu_F(u)$ represents the membership degree of u in F. Generally, a fuzzy set F can be denoted by:

$$F = \int_U \mu_F(u)/u \tag{2.1}$$

The class of all fuzzy sets on U is denoted by $\mathcal{F}(U)$. Furthermore, given $A, B \in \mathcal{F}(U)$, A is a subset of B, denoted by $A \subseteq B$, which holds if and only if $A(u) \leq B(u)(\forall u \in U)$.

A linguistic variable, whose values are words or sentences in a natural or artificial language, serves as an approximation of characterization of phenomena that is too complex or too ill-defined to be described by a conventional numerical variable. Fuzzy sets are used to represent the restrictions associated with the values of a linguistic variable. The definition of linguistic variable is as follows:

Definition 2.1 ([41]) A linguistic variable is characterized by a quintuple $(X, s(X), U, G, M)$, where X is the name of the variable; $S(X)$ (or simply S) denotes the term set of X with each term being a fuzzy variable denoted generically by s and ranging over the domain U which is associated with the base variable u ; G is a syntactic rule for generating the names, s, of values of X; and M is a semantic rule for associating with each s its meaning, $M(s)$, which is a fuzzy set of U.

As suggested by Zadeh [41], three denotations, i.e., the name s, its meaning (semantics) $M(s)$ and its restriction $R(s)$ will be used interchangeably to avoid a profusion of symbols.

An important facet of a linguistic variable is the following two rules:

(1) A syntactic rule, having the form of a grammar, to generate the names of the values of the variable.
(2) A semantic rule, to compute the meaning of each value.

If the number of terms in S is infinite, it is necessary to use an algorithm, rather than a table look-up procedure, to generate the elements of S and compute their semantics. When generating terms in S, linguistic modifiers play an important role. Given an atomic term, composite terms can be generated by modifying the atomic term to certain levels. Generally, given U, a fuzzy modifier FM on U, is a mapping such that [5]:

$$\begin{aligned} FM: \mathcal{F}(\mathcal{U}) &\rightarrow \mathcal{F}(\mathcal{U}) \\ s &\mapsto FM(s, \delta) \end{aligned} \tag{2.2}$$

where s is a given term and δ is a real number representing the degree of modification.

2.1.2 *Syntax and Semantics of VLTs*

The syntax and semantics of VLTs can be defined based on a given LTS [37]. Generally, a LTS with the semantics defined on the domain U can be denoted by

$$S^{(\tau)} = \{s_t | t = 0, 1, \ldots, \tau\} \tag{2.3}$$

where τ is a positive integer, the symbol s_t is used to represent both the name of the term and its semantics taking the form of a fuzzy set defined on the domain U. Each linguistic term $s_t \in S^{(\tau)}$ is called an original linguistic term and considered as an atomic term.

VLTs are generated by the proper linguistic modifiers based on the original linguistic terms. Roughly, we can generate a VLT by its closest original linguistic term. It is easy to generate a new VLT by a symbolic transformation as follows:

Definition 2.2 ([37]) Let S be a LTS defined by Eq. (2.3). For any $t \in \{0, 1, \ldots, \tau\}$, let

$$\delta \in \begin{cases} [0, 0.5), & t = 0 \\ [-0.5, 0], & t = \tau \\ [-0.5, 0.5), & else \end{cases} \tag{2.4}$$

then the pair (t, δ) generates a VLT s_α, where $\alpha = t + \delta$. The set of VLTs is denoted by $\bar{S} = \{s_\alpha | \alpha \in [0, \tau]\}$.

According to Definition 2.2, a VLT, s_α, is generated by an atomic term s_t and a real number δ satisfying $t = round(\alpha)$ and $\delta = \alpha - t$, where *round* is the classical round function. The original linguistic term can be viewed as a special VLT with $\delta = 0$.

Example 2.3 Given the following LTS (whose semantics are shown in Fig. 2.1)

$$\begin{aligned} S^{(8)} = \{&s_0 = extremely\ poor, s_1 = very\ poor, s_2 = poor, \\ &s_3 = slightly\ poor, s_4 = fair, s_5 = slightly\ good, \\ &s_6 = good, s_7 = very\ good, s_8 = extremely\ good\} \end{aligned}$$

let $t = 5$ and $\delta = 0.4$, a new VLT, named $s_{5.4}$, can be generated. Note that, different from original linguistic terms, it is hard to name a VLT by words or sentences exactly.

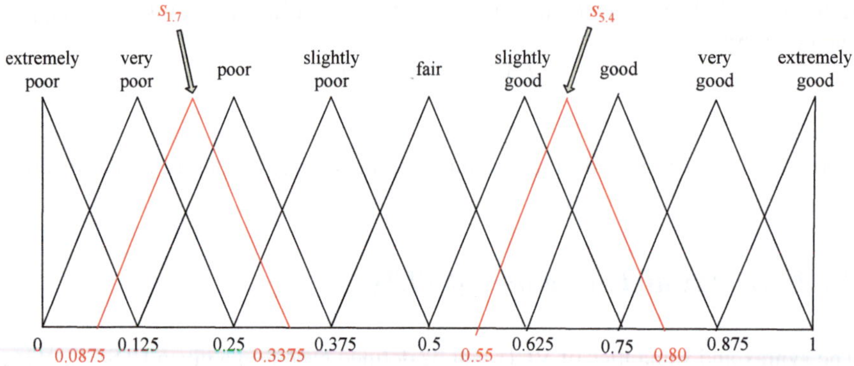

Fig. 2.1 Semantics of original linguistic terms and VLTs

Till now, only the symbolic has been generated for a VLT. Their meanings and semantics should be assigned. This will be completed by linguistic modifiers defined below:

Definition 2.4 ([37]) Let S be a LTS defined by Eq. (2.3). For any $\alpha \in [0, \tau]$, the semantics of the VLT s_α generated by Definition 2.2 is given by:

$$s_\alpha = FM(s_t, \delta) \tag{2.5}$$

where $t = round(\alpha)$, $\delta = \alpha - t$, $FM$is a linguistic modifier on U.

Similar to the 2-tuple linguistic model, the syntax and semantics of a VLT should be clarified by two parameters. However, there are some different details. In the syntactical aspect, a 2-tuple linguistic term is generated by a real number $\beta \in [0, \tau]$, whereas a VLT is generated by an original linguistic term and a real number δ. Moreover, in the semantic aspect, a 2-tuple linguistic term takes use of a real number β to represent its information, but we obtain the semantics of a VLT by means of a proper linguistic modifier. The use of linguistic modifiers is more complex than the semantic representation of 2-tuple terms, but we can fully use the semantics of original linguistic terms.

We can see that the semantics of s_α is defined by modifying its closest original linguistic term s_t to a certain level which is subject to another parameter δ. Especially, in the virtual linguistic model, each original linguistic term s_t keeps its original semantics defined in S. Based on Definition 2.4, a VLT s_α can be interpreted by the two parameters t and δ. In fact, t implies the original linguistic term s_t which is closest to s_α, and $|\delta|$ expresses the degree that s_α is close to s_t. Based on Definitions 2.2 and 2.4, an expert's evaluation can also be expressed by VLTs. In fact, if the expert can express his/her opinion by an original linguistic term accurately, then the original linguistic term is suitable; if there does not exist $s_t \in S$ for expressing the opinion accurately, then: (1) an original linguistic term s_t which is closest to the opinion, can be determined, (2) a number δ (described in Eq. 2.4) can be provided to measure the degree that the objective term s_α is close to s_t (More specifically, $|\delta|$ represents the degree of closeness, and $\delta > 0$ if s_α is greater than s_t, otherwise $\delta < 0$), and (3) a VLT s_α, where $\alpha = t + \delta$, can be used for the representation of the opinion.

Definition 2.4 only supplies a strategy to obtain the semantics of VLTs. The linguistic modifier should be determined according to the type of original terms distributed on the domain. The choice of linguistic modifiers is specified in the coming subsections, according to the graphical shapes of membership functions of original linguistic terms in S.

2.1.2.1 The Semantics of VLTs with Inclusive Interpretations

When linguistic terms are with inclusive interpretations, it is assumed that the semantic entailment always holds. Given $S^{(\tau)}$ defined on the domain U, the following condition is satisfied:

$$s_\tau \subseteq s_{\tau-1} \subseteq \cdots \subseteq s_0 \tag{2.6}$$

In this sense, one or more terms act as atomic terms and other terms are generated by means of modifiers. This kind of LTSs is often used in approximate reasoning [41]. Usually, the following order is assumed:

$$s_0 \leq s_1 \leq \cdots s_\tau \tag{2.7}$$

In Eq. (2.6), s_t represents the fuzzy sets corresponding to their semantics, whereas the symbols in Eq. (2.7) are just the names of linguistic terms.

Example 2.5 Given the domain $U = [0, 100]$ representing human's age, a linguistic term, denoted by s_1, named *old*, of the linguistic variable *Age* is defined by

$$s_1 = \int_{50}^{100} (1 + ((u - 50)/5)^2)^{-1}/u$$

Then two terms, s_0 = *more or less old* and s_2 = *very old* can be defined by

$$s_0 = \int_{50}^{100} (\mu_{s_1}(u))^{1/2}/u, \quad s_2 = \int_{50}^{100} (\mu_{s_1}(u))^2/u$$

Accordingly, a LTS, $S^{(2)} = \{s_0, s_1, s_2\}$, with inclusive interpretation is formed. The semantics of which are shown in Fig. 2.2.

Given a VLT in this context, its semantics can be specified based on the power modifier. Let $S^{(\tau)}$ be a LTS with inclusive interpretation. Suppose that the semantics of s_t is defined by $s_t = \int_U \mu_{s_t}(u)/u$, then the semantics of s_α is obtained by [37]:

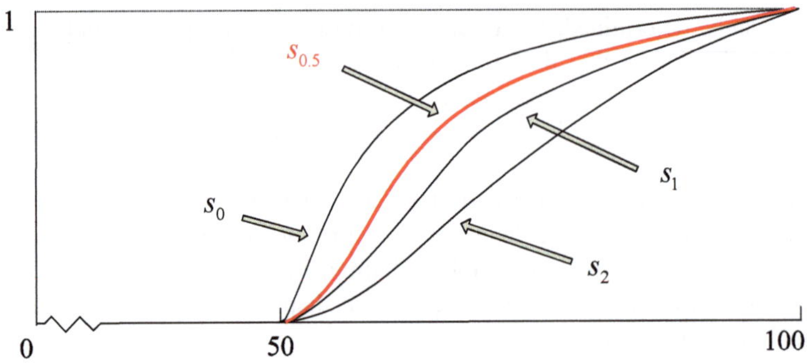

Fig. 2.2 An example of semantics of VLTs with inclusive interpretation

$$s_\alpha = FM(s_t, \delta) = \int_U (\mu_{s_t}(u))^{2^\delta}/u \tag{2.8}$$

where $t = round(\alpha)$, $\delta = \alpha - t$.

Example 2.6 Let $S^{(2)} = \{s_0, s_1, s_2\}$ be the LTS defined in Example 2.5, then the semantics of $s_{0.5}$ is (as shown in Fig. 2.2):

$$s_{0.5} = FM(s_1, -0.5) = \int_U (\mu_{s_t}(u))^{2^{-0.5}}/u = \int_{50}^{100} (1 + ((u - 50)/5)^2)^{-1/\sqrt{2}}/u$$

Motivated by the relationship between Eqs. (2.6) and (2.7), it is natural to define the orders of s_{α_1} and s_{α_2} according to the inclusive relation of their semantics. This results in the following theorem:

Theorem 2.7 ([37]) *Given two VLTs $s_{\alpha_1}, s_{\alpha_2} \in \bar{S}^{(\tau)}$ whose semantics are defined by Eq. (2.8), we have*

$$s_{\alpha_1} \le s_{\alpha_2} \Leftrightarrow \alpha_1 \le \alpha_2$$

2.1.2.2 The Semantics of VLTs with Non-inclusive Interpretations

The inclusion is not satisfied in LTSs with non-inclusive interpretations, as shown in Fig. 2.1. Most of the recent literature focuses on this kind of semantics. The predefined LTS is usually constructed by a few atomic terms and other terms are generated by shifting modifiers. Let's begin the semantics of VLTs in this context with a simply case. If original terms are uniformly distributed in the domain $U = [L, R]$, then the semantics of s_α can be defined by specifying Eq. (2.5) as follows [37]:

$$s_\alpha = \int_U \mu_{s_t}(u - \delta \cdot l/\tau)/u \tag{2.9}$$

where $l = R - L$ is the length of the domain U. Graphically, Eq. (2.9) shifts the membership function of s_t to a certain extent. As can be seen in most cases, trapezoidal fuzzy numbers are used to represent the piecewise linear membership functions. Thus, for any VLT $s_\alpha(\alpha \in [0, \tau])$, suppose $s_t = (a, b, c, d)(t = round(\alpha))$, then Eq. (2.9) can be rewritten as:

$$s_\alpha = (\max\{L, a + \delta \cdot l/\tau\}, b + \delta \cdot l/\tau, c + \delta \cdot l/\tau, \min\{R, d + \delta \cdot l/\tau\} \quad (2.10)$$

Example 2.8 Let $S^{(8)}$ be the LTS of Example 2.3, then $\tau = 8$, $U = [0, 1]$ and $l = 1$. Moreover, by using the notation of triangular fuzzy numbers, we have $s_2 = (1/8, 2/8, 3/8)$ and $s_5 = (4/8, 5/8, 6/8)$. According to Eq. (2.9), the semantics of VLTs $s_{1.7}$ and $s_{5.4}$ are (also can be found in Fig. 2.1):

$$s_{1.7} = \int_U \mu_{s_2}(u - (-0.3)/8)/u = (1/8 - 0.3/8, 2/8 - 0.3/8, 3/8 - 0.3/8)$$
$$s_{5.4} = \int_U \mu_{s_5}(u - (0.4)/8)/u = (4/8 + 0.4/8, 5/8 + 0.4/8, 6/8 + 0.4/8)$$

However, if original terms are non-uniformly distributed in the considered domain, it is hard to determine the semantics of VLTs by a simple shifting modifier. Given LTS $S^{(\tau)}$ in Eq. (2.3) with non-inclusive interpretation, $\forall s_\alpha(\alpha \in [0, \tau])$, two original terms s_t and $s_{t'}$ can be fixed by $t = round(\alpha)$ and

$$t' = \begin{cases} t - 1, & \delta < 0 \\ t, & \delta = 0 \\ t + 1, & \delta > 0 \end{cases}$$

Then Eq. (2.5) can be specified by a shifting modifier which shifts from s_t towards $s_{t'}$ to a certain extent. Different from Eq. (2.9), this step includes an affine transformation rather than simply translation. If the semantics of original terms can be expressed by trapezoidal fuzzy numbers, that is, $s_t = (a, b, c, d)$ and $s_{t'} = (a', b', c', d')$, then the semantics of s_α can be obtained by [37]:

$$s_\alpha = (\max\{L, \tilde{a}\}, \tilde{b}, \tilde{c}, \min\{R, \tilde{d}\}) \quad (2.11)$$

where $\tilde{a} = (1 - |\delta|)a + |\delta|a'$, $\tilde{b} = (1 - |\delta|)b + |\delta|b'$, $\tilde{c} = (1 - |\delta|)c + |\delta|c'$, $\tilde{d} = (1 - |\delta|)d + |\delta|d'$. More generally, suppose $s_t = \int_U \mu_{s_t}(u)/u$, $s_{t'} = \int_U \mu_{s_{t'}}(u)/u$, which are defined on a non-uniformly distributed domain U, then the semantics of s_α can be derived by three steps as shown in Fig. 2.3:

Step 1. Construct a transformation function f to transform the non-uniformly distributed domain U into a uniformly distributed version $\tilde{U}$. The semantics of original terms can be transformed simultaneously.

Step 2. Obtain the semantics of s_α on $\tilde{U}$ by Eq. (2.11).

Step 3. Transform the obtained function of semantics into the domain U by f^{-1}.

Example 2.9 Let $S^{(6)} = \{s_t | t = 0, 1, \ldots, 6\}$ be the non-uniformly distributed LTS defined on $U = [0, 1]$ [36]. The semantics of its original terms are shown in Fig. 2.4.

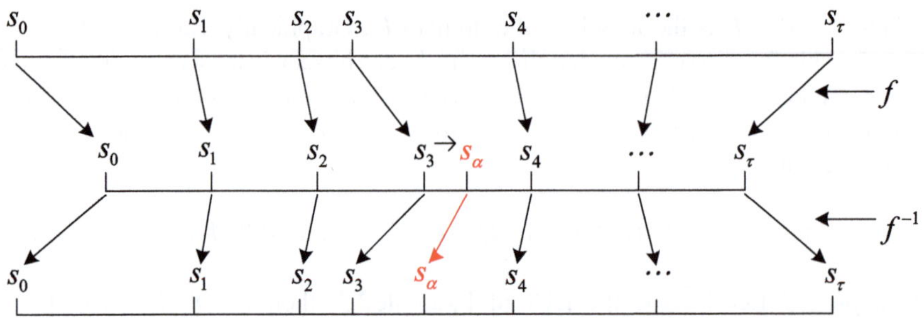

Fig. 2.3 The steps of obtaining the semantics of VLTs on non-uniform domain

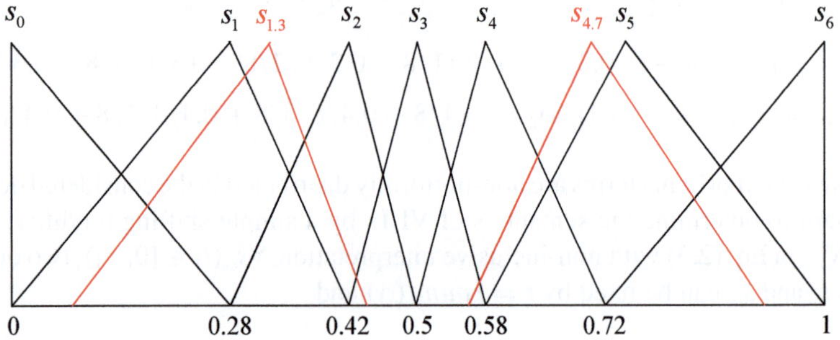

Fig. 2.4 Examples of the semantics of VLTs on non-uniform domain

According to Eq. (2.11), the semantics of $s_{1.3}$ can be derived by $s_1 = (0, 5/18, 5/12)$ and $s_2 = (5/18, 5/12/1/2)$ as follows:

$$\begin{aligned} s_{1.3} &= (0.7 \times 0 + 0.3 \times 5/18, 0.7 \times 5/18 + 0.3 \times 5/12, 0.7 \times 5/12 + 0.3 \times 1/2) \\ &= (0.08, 0.32, 0.44) \end{aligned}$$

Moreover, we can calculate the semantics by the idea of Fig. 2.3. We construct the transformation function $f : [0, 1] \to [0, 1]$, where

$$\tilde{u} = f(u) = \begin{cases} 3u/5, & 0 \le u < 5/18 \\ 6u/5 - 1/6, & 5/18 \le u < 5/12 \\ 2u - 1/2, & 5/12 \le u < 7/12 \\ 6u/5 - 1/30, & 7/12 \le u < 13/18 \\ 3u/5 + 2/5, & 13/18 \le u \le 1 \end{cases}$$

then the semantics of an original term s_t can be transformed into $\tilde{s}_t = \int_{[0,1]} \mu_{\tilde{s}_t}(\tilde{u})/\tilde{u}$. For instance, $\tilde{s}_5 = (4/6, 5/6, 1)$. Then according to Eq. (2.9), $\tilde{s}_{4.7} = (4/6 - 0.3/6, 5/6 - 0.3/6, 1 - 0.3/6)$. Using the inverse of f, the semantics of $s_{4.7}$ on the domain U is $s_{4.7} = (0.56, 0.78, 0.92)$.

2.1.3 Computational Model of VLTs

The computational model of VLTs plays an important role of fusing a collection of linguistic information and making decisions. One can reconstruct the computational models based on the semantics of VTLs. We have extended the original LTS to a continuous version $\bar{S}^{(\tau)} = \{s_\alpha | \alpha \in [0, \tau]\}$ based on the above-mentioned syntax and semantics. The computational model based on VLTs can be expressed as [37]:

$$(\bar{S}^{(\tau)})^n \xrightarrow{Ind} [0, \tau]^n \xrightarrow{C} [0, \tau] \rightarrow \bar{S}^{(\tau)}$$

where C is an aggregation operator, the function Ind returns the indices of the input VLTs:

$$Ind(s_\alpha) = \alpha \tag{2.12}$$

The first and third procedures correspond to the pair of transformation functions of the 2-tuple linguistic model. Some researchers have reported that the computational models of both the 2-tuple linguistic model and the virtual linguistic model are equivalent [9]. However, it should be noted that, in the virtual linguistic model, the above manipulation enables us to compute linguistic information according to the indices of VLTs, rather than computing through three discrete steps.

To operate with VLTs, the following issues should be figured out at first [37]:

(1) **Total order**. According to the discussion in Sect. 2.1.2, for any $s_\alpha, s_\beta \in \bar{S}^{(\tau)}$, it is rational to define the total order as:

$$s_\alpha \leq s_\beta \Leftrightarrow (s_{t_1} < s_{t_2}) \vee ((s_{t_1} = s_{t_2}) \wedge (\delta_1 \leq \delta_2)) \tag{2.13}$$

where $t_1 = round(\alpha)$, $\delta_1 = \alpha - t_1$, $t_2 = round(\beta)$, $\delta_2 = \beta - t_2$. Obviously, Eq. (2.13) is equivalent to [31]:

$$s_\alpha \leq s_\beta \Leftrightarrow \alpha \leq \beta \tag{2.14}$$

which means that the comparison of VLTs can be done by their indices. Thus, we have the following operations:

$$\max\{s_\alpha, s_\beta\} = s_\beta \Leftrightarrow s_\alpha \leq s_\beta, \quad \min\{s_\alpha, s_\beta\} = s_\alpha \Leftrightarrow s_\alpha \leq s_\beta$$

(2) **Negation operator**. Given $\bar{S}^{(\tau)}$, the negation operator neg is a mapping from $\bar{S}^{(\tau)}$ to a subset of $\bar{S}^{(\tau)}$ satisfying:

(i) neg is not empty and convex;
(ii) If $s_\alpha < s_\beta$, then $neg(s_\beta) < neg(s_\alpha)$, for any $s_\alpha, s_\beta \in \bar{S}^{(\tau)}$;
(iii) If $s_\beta \in neg(s_\alpha)$, then $s_\alpha \in neg(s_\beta)$, where $s_\alpha, s_\beta \in \bar{S}^{(\tau)}$.

If the linguistic terms are uniformly distributed, in other words, they are equally informative, then the negation neg becomes a simply case which has been widely used in the literature. In this case, $\forall s_\alpha \in \bar{S}^{(\tau)}$, its negation can be defined as:

$$neg(s_\alpha) = s_{\tau-\alpha} \tag{2.15}$$

(3) **Aggregation of LVTs**. We begin the aggregation with two VLTs. For any $s_\alpha, s_\beta \in \bar{S}^{(\tau)}$, their weights are w_1 and w_2 respectively, where $w_1 + w_2 = 1$, $w_1 \geq 0$, and $w_2 \geq 0$. Based on the semantics of VLTs, the weighted arithmetical averaging operator and the weighted geometric averaging operator can be defined as:

$$w_1 s_\alpha \oplus w_2 s_\beta = FM(s_{t_1}, \delta_1) \tag{2.16}$$

$$w_1 s_\alpha \otimes w_2 s_\beta = FM(s_{t_2}, \delta_2) \tag{2.17}$$

where $t_1 = round(w_1\alpha + w_2\beta)$, $\delta_1 = w_1\alpha + w_2\beta - t_1$, $t_2 = round(\alpha^{w_1} \cdot \beta^{w_2})$, $\delta_2 = \alpha^{w_1} \cdot \beta^{w_2} - t_2$, and FM is the fuzzy modifier specified in Sect. 2.1.2. It is clear that the operation is conducted by two steps. An original term s_{t_1} (or s_{t_2}) is determined at first. Then a modifier is used to move it to a VLT based on the parameter δ_1 (or δ_2). It should be noted that we use Eqs. (2.16) and (2.17) to illustrate the semantics of the results of aggregation. For application, they can be rewritten as:

$$w_1 s_\alpha \oplus w_2 s_\beta = s_{w_1\alpha + w_2\beta} \tag{2.18}$$

$$w_1 s_\alpha \otimes w_2 s_\beta = s_{\alpha^{w_1} \cdot \beta^{w_2}} \tag{2.19}$$

Equations (2.18)–(2.19) serve as the basic operation of VLTs as well. To aggregate $n (n \geq 2)$ VLTs, a series of aggregation operators based on these operations can be found in [31–33].

2.2 Extended Hesitant Fuzzy Linguistic Term Sets

As has been discussed in Sect. 1.3.1, the technique of HFLTSs extends classical CWW models, enables experts to consider multiple linguistic terms taking the form of comparative linguistic expressions. HFLTSs suffer from some limitations when they are used to represent groups' opinions. In GDM, individual evaluations can be represented by HFLTSs, but the group's evaluations can not be always represented by several consecutive terms. Suppose that three experts evaluate an object based on the LTS in Example 2.3, the first expert argue that it is *good*, the other two experts provide *between good and very good* and *at most fair*, respectively. Based on the union of HFLTSs, the opinions result in $\{s_0, s_1, s_2, s_3, s_4, s_6, s_7\}$. It is not a HFLTS. As a solution, one could synthesize the possible terms to obtain an averaging value by proper aggregation operators, such as [34]. This strategy is easy. But the original information is not sufficiently used. Alternatively, some models of artificial linguistic expressions, such as the evidential reasoning model [39], can be employed. However, these models usually require additional information, such as the probabilistic distribution and membership functions, which is not included in the provided expressions.

To deal with this situation, this section introduces a new model, i.e., extended hesitant fuzzy linguistic term set (EHFLTS). This model not only enhances the flexibility of QDM under uncertainty, but also focuses on a type of natural linguistic expressions.

2.2.1 *Fuzzy Linguistic Approach and HFLTS*

In the fuzzy linguistic approach, the LTS defined in Eq. (2.3) satisfies the following properties:

(1) Total order: $s_\alpha \leq s_\beta \Leftrightarrow \alpha \leq \beta$;
(2) Negation operator: $neg(s_\alpha) = s_{\tau-\alpha}$.

As shown in Sect. 2.1, lower indices are computed directly in the virtual linguistic model. In order to define some intuitive operation laws, Xu [32] revise Eq. (2.3) to the following form:

$$S^{(g)} = \{s_\alpha | \alpha = -g, \ldots, 0, \ldots, g\} \tag{2.20}$$

Accordingly, (2) is revised to $neg(s_\alpha) = s_{-\alpha}$. In thc virtual linguistic model, Eq. (2.20) can be extended to:

$$\bar{S}^{(g)} = \{s_\alpha | \alpha \in [-q, q]\} \tag{2.21}$$

where $q (q > g)$ is a sufficiently large positive integer.

The concept of HFLTSs, specified in Definition 1.1, was proposed by Rodríguez et al. [23] based on the idea of the fuzzy linguistic approach and hesitant fuzzy sets.

The basic operations are defined as follows:

Definition 2.10 ([23]) Let $\tilde{H}_S$, $\tilde{H}_S^1$ and $\tilde{H}_S^2$ be three HFLTSs based on LTS $S^{(g)}$,

(1) Complement: $\tilde{H}_S^c = S^{(g)} - \tilde{H}_S = \{s_\alpha | s_\alpha \in S^{(g)}, s_\alpha \notin \tilde{H}_S\}$;
(2) Union: $\tilde{H}_S^1 \cup \tilde{H}_S^2 = \{s_\alpha | s_\alpha \in \tilde{H}_S^1 \ or \ s_\alpha \in \tilde{H}_S^2\}$;
(3) Intersection: $\tilde{H}_S^1 \cap \tilde{H}_S^2 = \{s_\alpha | s_\alpha \in \tilde{H}_S^1 \ and \ s_\alpha \in \tilde{H}_S^2\}$.

Apparently, the union and complement of HFLTSs might not be HFLTSs.

2.2.2 *Representational Model of EHFLTSs*

In GDM problems, we may hesitate among several possible linguistic terms when considering the degree of an alternative satisfying a certain criterion. This terms might be consecutive or non-consecutive in the original LTS. Generally, we have the following definition:

Definition 2.11 ([26]) Let $S^{(g)}$ be a LTS. An ordered subset of linguistic terms of $S^{(g)}$ is called an EHFLTS, denoted as:

$$H_S(x) = \{s_\alpha | s_\alpha \in S^{(g)}\} \tag{2.22}$$

Given LTS $S^{(g)}$, $H_S(x) = \{\}$ and $H_S(x) = S^{(g)}$ are called the empty EHFLTS and full EHFLTS, respectively. It is clear that HFLTSs are the special case of EHFLTSs. For the convenience information processing, an ordered finite subset of virtual linguistic terms $\bar{S}^{(g)}$ is referred to as an EHFLTS as well.

Formally, let X be a fixed set, for $x \in X$, $H_S(x)$ can be represented as the following 2-tuple:

$$\{\langle x, h_S(x)\rangle | x \in X\} \tag{2.23}$$

where $h_S(x)$ is a set of p terms in $S^{(g)}$(or $\bar{S}^{(g)}$), that is

$$h_S(x) = \{s_{\alpha_1}, s_{\alpha_2}, \ldots, s_{\alpha_p}\} \tag{2.24}$$

Given x, $h_S(x)$ is abbreviated as h_S, which represents all possible linguistic terms. Some basic operations of EHFLTSs, such as the upper and lower bounds, envelopes, union, intersection, and complement, can be defined similar to those of HFLTSs.

In applications, EHFLTSs could be derived by two different ways. Firstly, according to Definition 2.10 and Eq. (2.24), we have the following theorem:

Theorem 2.12 ([26] Construction axiom) *The union of HFLTSs results in EHFLTS.*

Proof of Theorem 2.12 is omitted. We shall note that this construction axiom shows potential applications of the presented EHFLTSs. Individuals provide their evaluation information by HFLTSs. And then the group's evaluation is formed by the union of these HFLTSs, which results to an EHFLTS. Secondly, Eq. (2.24) represents a type of natural linguistic expressions taking the following form:

$$s_{\alpha_1} \textit{ or } s_{\alpha_2} \textit{ or } \cdots \textit{ or } s_{\alpha_p}.$$

2.2.3 *Basic Operations of EHFLTSs and Their Properties*

For the purpose of aggregation, we could define some arithmetic operations for EHFLTs as follows:

Definition 2.13 ([26]) Let h_S, h_S^1, and h_S^2 be three EHFLTSs based on $S^{(g)}$, $\lambda \geq 0$, then:

(1) $h_S^1 \oplus h_S^2 = \cup_{s_\alpha \in h_S^1, s_\beta \in h_S^2}\{s_\alpha \oplus s_\beta\} = \cup_{s_\alpha \in h_S^1, s_\beta \in h_S^2}\{s_{\alpha+\beta}\}$;

(2) $h_S^1 \otimes h_S^2 = \cup_{s_\alpha \in h_S^1, s_\beta \in h_S^2}\{s_\alpha \otimes s_\beta\} = \cup_{s_\alpha \in h_S^1, s_\beta \in h_S^2}\{s_{\alpha\beta}\}$;
(3) $\lambda h_S = \cup_{s_\alpha \in h_S}\{\lambda s_\alpha\} = \cup_{s_\alpha \in h_S}\{s_{\lambda\alpha}\}$;
(4) $(h_S)^\lambda = \cup_{s_\alpha \in h_S}\{(s_\alpha)^\lambda\} = \cup_{s_\alpha \in h_S}\{s_{\alpha^\lambda}\}$;
(5) $h_S^1 \vee h_S^2 = \cup_{s_\alpha \in h_S^1, s_\beta \in h_S^2}\{\max\{s_\alpha, s_\beta\}\}$;
(6) $h_S^1 \wedge h_S^2 = \cup_{s_\alpha \in h_S^1, s_\beta \in h_S^2}\{\min\{s_\alpha, s_\beta\}\}$.

Example 2.14 Let $S^{(8)}$ be the LTS in Example 2.3, $h_S^1 = \{s_0, s_2\}$, $h_S^2 = \{s_2, s_3, s_5\}$. We have $h_S^1 \oplus h_S^2 = \{s_0 \oplus s_2\} \cup \{s_0 \oplus s_3\} \cup \{s_0 \oplus s_5\} \cup \{s_2 \oplus s_2\} \cup \{s_2 \oplus s_3\} \cup \{s_2 \oplus s_5\} = \{s_2\} \cup \{s_3\} \cup \{s_4\} \cup \{s_4\} \cup \{s_5\} \cup \{s_7\} = \{s_2, s_3, s_4, s_5, s_7\}$.

Some mathematical properties of the operations are given in the sequel.

Theorem 2.15 ([26] Commutativity) *Let h_S^1 and h_S^2 be two EHFLTSs based on $S^{(g)}$, then*

(1) $h_S^1 \oplus h_S^2 = h_S^2 \oplus h_S^1$;
(2) $h_S^1 \otimes h_S^2 = h_S^2 \otimes h_S^1$;
(3) $h_S^1 \vee h_S^2 = h_S^2 \vee h_S^1$;
(4) $h_S^1 \wedge h_S^2 = h_S^2 \wedge h_S^1$.

Proof (1) $h_S^1 \oplus h_S^2 = \cup_{s_\alpha \in h_S^1, s_\beta \in h_S^2}\{s_{\alpha+\beta}\} = \cup_{s_\alpha \in h_S^1, s_\beta \in h_S^2}\{s_{\beta+\alpha}\} = h_S^2 \oplus h_S^1$;
(3) $h_S^1 \vee h_S^2 = \cup_{s_\alpha \in h_S^1, s_\beta \in h_S^2}\{\max\{s_\alpha, s_\beta\}\} = \cup_{s_\alpha \in h_S^1, s_\beta \in h_S^2}\{\max\{s_\beta, s_\alpha\}\} = h_S^2 \vee h_S^1$;
Similarly, we can prove (2) and (4). □

Theorem 2.16 ([26] Associativity) *Let h_S^1, h_S^2, and h_S^3 be three EHFLTSs based on $S^{(g)}$, then*

(1) $h_S^1 \oplus (h_S^2 \oplus h_S^3) = (h_S^1 \oplus h_S^2) \oplus h_S^3$;
(2) $h_S^1 \otimes (h_S^2 \otimes h_S^3) = (h_S^1 \otimes h_S^2) \otimes h_S^3$;
(3) $h_S^1 \vee (h_S^2 \vee h_S^3) = (h_S^1 \vee h_S^2) \vee h_S^3$;
(4) $h_S^1 \wedge (h_S^2 \wedge h_S^3) = (h_S^1 \wedge h_S^2) \wedge h_S^3$.

Proof (1) $h_S^1 \oplus (h_S^2 \oplus h_S^3) = h_S^1 \oplus (\cup_{s_\beta \in h_S^2, s_\gamma \in h_S^3}\{s_{\beta+\gamma}\}) = \cup_{s_\alpha \in h_S^1, s_\beta \in h_S^2, s_\gamma \in h_S^3}\{s_{\alpha+\beta+\gamma}\}$, $(h_S^1 \oplus h_S^2) \oplus h_S^3) = (\cup_{s_\alpha \in h_S^1, s_\beta \in h_S^2}\{s_{\alpha+\beta}\}) \oplus h_S^3 = \cup_{s_\alpha \in h_S^1, s_\beta \in h_S^2, s_\gamma \in h_S^3}\{s_{\alpha+\beta+\gamma}\}$.
Similarly, we can prove (2) (4). □

Theorem 2.17 ([26] Distributivity) *Let h_S^1, h_S^2, and h_S^3 be three EHFLTSs based on $S^{(g)}$, $\lambda \geq 0$, then*

(1) $\lambda(h_S^1 \oplus h_S^2) = \lambda h_S^1 \oplus \lambda h_S^2$;
(2) $(h_S^1 \otimes h_S^2)^\lambda = (h_S^1)^\lambda \otimes (h_S^2)^\lambda$.

Proof According to (3)–(4) of Definition 2.13, we have

$$s_\alpha \in h_S \Leftrightarrow \lambda s_\alpha \in \lambda h_S,\ (s_\alpha)^\lambda \in (h_S)^\lambda$$

(1) $\lambda(h_S^1 \oplus h_S^2) = \cup_{s_\alpha \in h_S^1, s_\beta \in h_S^2}\{\lambda(s_\alpha \oplus s_\beta)\} = \cup_{s_\alpha \in h_S^1, s_\beta \in h_S^2}\{\lambda s_\alpha \oplus \lambda s_\beta\}$, $\lambda h_S^1 \oplus \lambda h_S^2 = \cup_{\lambda s_\alpha \in \lambda h_S^1, \lambda s_\beta \in \lambda h_S^2}\{\lambda s_\alpha \oplus \lambda s_\beta\} = \cup_{s_\alpha \in h_S^1, s_\beta \in h_S^2}\{\lambda s_\alpha \oplus \lambda s_\beta\}$.
(2) Similar to the proof of (1). □

2.2.4 A Partial Order of EHFLTSs

Rodríguez et al. [23] utilized envelops of HFLTSs, ULTs, to compare information included in HFLTSs. However, as linguistic terms in EHFLTSs are not consecutive, envelops are not accurate for comparison. We introduce some concepts to define a simple version of partial order on the set of EHFLTSs. For more order relations, please refer to Sect. 2.3.

Definition 2.18 ([26]) Let h_S be an EHFLTS. $E(h_S) = (\oplus_{s_\alpha \in h_S} s_\alpha)/\#h_S$ is called the expected linguistic term of h_S, where $\#h_S$ is the number of linguistic terms in h_S.

Definition 2.19 ([26]) Let h_S be an EHFLTS, s_i and s_j be the smallest and biggest linguistic terms of h_S, respectively, then $D(h_S) = (j - i)/(2g + 1)$ is called the degree of hesitancy in h_S, where $2g + 1$ is the cardinality of LTS $S^{(g)}$.

The expected linguistic term reflects the averaging linguistic term of an EHFLTS, and the degree of hesitancy represents the degree of uncertainty in evaluation, $D(h_S) \in [0, 1]$. Using these definitions, we can compare two EHFLTSs by the following method.

Definition 2.20 ([26]) For any two EHFLTSs h_S^1 and h_S^2 based on $S^{(g)}$,

(1) If $E(h_S^1) < E(h_S^2)$, then h_S^1 is smaller than h_S^2, denoted by $h_S^1 < h_S^2$;
(2) If $E(h_S^1) = E(h_S^2)$: then (i) if $D(h_S^1) > D(h_S^2)$, then $h_S^1 < h_S^2$; (ii) if $D(h_S^1) = D(h_S^2)$, then h_S^1 and h_S^2 represent the same information, denoted by $h_S^1 \cong h_S^2$.

Note that, for two EHFLTSs, h_S^1 and h_S^2, if $h_S^1 = h_S^2$, then we mean the elements in h_S^1 and h_S^2 are absolutely the same; $h_S^1 \cong h_S^2$, we mean the expected linguistic terms and the degrees of hesitancy of the two are equal. Therefore, we have $h_S^1 = h_S^2 \Rightarrow h_S^1 \cong h_S^2$.

2.3 Total Orders of EHFLTSs

HFLTSs and EHFLTSs are helpful to model uncertain linguistic information in QDM problems. Unfortunately, we may need total orders (or linear orders) which allow comparing any possible EHFLTSs arising in the evaluations. For example, if the alternatives' overall performances are represented by EHFLTSs, or if some evaluation values are aggregated by the OWA operators, then the total orders play a vital role. However, the existing orders on the set of EHFLTSs are partial orders rather than total orders. If a partial order is adopted, then there may be ties between two different pieces of information. Falcó et al. [11] developed a total order for uncertain linguistic terms, which can be considered as a total order of HFLTSs as well.

This section is devoted to introducing total orders on the set of EHFLTSs by a general manner. The order relations could also serve as the orders on the set of HFLTSs.

2.3.1 Existing Order Relations of EHFLTSs

We will review the existing orders of EHFLTSs in this subsection. Some necessary concepts, such as weak and strict partial orders, total orders and aggregation functions, can be found in [2, 14].

Given LTS $S^{(g)}$ defined in Eq. (2.20), or $S^{(\tau)}$ defined in Eq. (2.3), two EHFLTSs are denoted as $h_S^1 = \{s_{\alpha_1}^1, s_{\alpha_2}^1, \ldots, s_{\alpha_m}^1\}$ and $h_S^2 = \{s_{\beta_1}^2, s_{\beta_2}^2, \ldots, s_{\beta_n}^2\}$. If h_S^1 and h_S^2 are reduced to HFLTS, they can be rewritten as $\tilde{h}_S^1 = \{s_\alpha^1, s_{\alpha+1}^1, \ldots, s_{\alpha+m}^1\}$ and $\tilde{h}_S^2 = \{s_\beta^2, s_{\beta+1}^2, \ldots, s_{\beta+n}^2\}$, respectively.

There are some total orders and partial orders of HFLTSs. The definition in Sect. 2.2.4 provides a partial order of EHFLTSs $\preceq_W$ as follows:

$$h_S^1 \preceq_W h_S^2 \Leftrightarrow E(h_S^1) < E(h_S^2) \vee (E(h_S^1) = E(h_S^2) \wedge D(h_S^1) \geq D(h_S^2)) \quad (2.25)$$

where the functions E and D are the expected linguistic term and the degree of hesitancy in Definitions 2.18–2.19. Liao et al. [20] defined the variance function of an EHFLTS $\sigma(h_S) = s_x$, where $x = \sqrt{\sum_{s_\alpha, s_\beta \in h_S} (\alpha - \beta)^2 / \# h_S}$. Associated with the score function, they proposed the following relation $\preceq_L$:

$$h_S^1 \preceq_L h_S^2 \Leftrightarrow E(h_S^1) < E(h_S^2) \vee (E(h_S^1) = E(h_S^2) \wedge \sigma(h_S^1) \geq \sigma(h_S^2)) \quad (2.26)$$

The binary relation $\preceq_L$ satisfies the following property:

Theorem 2.21 ([27]) *The relation $\preceq_L$ is a partial order of EHFLTSs but a total order of HFLTSs.*

Proof (1) Let $h_S^1 = \{s_1, s_2, s_3\}$, $h_S^2 = \{s_{1.184}, s_{2.816}\}$. We have $E(h_S^1) = E(h_S^2) = s_2$, $\sigma(h_S^1) = \sigma(h_S^2) = s_{0.816}$. However, $h_S^1 \neq h_S^2$. Thus, $\preceq_L$ is not a total order of EHFLTSs.

(2) According to Definitions 2.18–2.19, the order $\preceq_L$ is a total order if the following equations

$$\begin{cases} \alpha + \alpha + 1 + \cdots + \alpha + m = a \\ \sum_{\beta, \gamma \in \{\alpha, \alpha+1, \ldots, \alpha+m\}} (\beta - \gamma)^2 = b \end{cases}$$

have only one solution, where a HFLTS $h_S = \{s_\alpha, s_{\alpha+1}, \ldots, s_{\alpha+m}\}$ and $a \in [-q, q]$, $b \in [0, q]$. In fact, the second equation can be transformed into $m(m+1)^2(m+2)/12 = b$. It is clear that $\phi(m) = m(m+1)^2(m+2)$ is increasingly monotonic when $m > 0$. Thus, there exists only one solution for m and also only one α. □

Falcó et al. [11] presented an approach to order uncertain linguistic terms. Given two uncertain linguistic terms $[s_\alpha^1, s_{\alpha+m}^1]$ and $[s_\beta^2, s_{\beta+n}^2]$, the order $\preceq_F$:

$$[s_\alpha^1, s_{\alpha+m}^1] \preceq_F [s_\beta^2, s_{\beta+n}^2] \Leftrightarrow (2\alpha + m < 2\beta + n) \vee ((2\alpha + m = 2\beta + n) \wedge (m \geq n)) \quad (2.27)$$

Thus, we can define the order of two HFLTSs:

$$\tilde{h}_S^1 \preceq_F \tilde{h}_S^2 \Leftrightarrow [s_\alpha^1, s_{\alpha+m}^1] \preceq_F [s_\beta^2, s_{\beta+n}^2] \tag{2.28}$$

It is clear that the order $\preceq_F$ is a total order of HFLTSs [27].

2.3.2 Total Orders of EHFLTSs: A Generation Approach

We introduce a novel kind of total orders in this section by a generation approach [27].

To operate correctly, it should be ensured that the cardinalities of two EHFLTSs are equal. Let $h_S^1 = \{s_{\alpha_1}^1, s_{\alpha_2}^1, \ldots, s_{\alpha_m}^1\}$ and $h_S^2 = \{s_{\beta_1}^2, s_{\beta_2}^2, \ldots, s_{\beta_n}^2\}$ be two EHFLTSs based on $S^{(g)}$. We suppose $m < n$ without loss of generality. If $m < n$, then a normalization step might be used for computation, i.e., the R-normalization [19]. Let s^- and s^+ be the minimum and maximum terms in h_S^1, respectively, and $\xi (0 \leq \xi \leq 1)$ be an optimal parameter, then $n - m$ terms $\bar{s}$ are added to h_S^1, where

$$\bar{s} = \xi s^+ + (1 - \xi) s^- \tag{2.29}$$

It is clear that the parameter ξ, which should be provided by the decision makers, reflects their risk preferences. Especially, $\xi = 1$ and $\xi = 0$ correspond with the optimism and pessimism rules, respectively. The main advantage of this normalization is that it can take into account the risk preferences of the decision makers, but it needs to induce their risk preferences. In the rest of this section, the normalized result of h_S^1 is denoted by h_S^1 as well for simplification if no ambiguous meaning arises. If the cardinalities of EHFLTSs are normalized to n, then the set of all EHFLTSs based on $S^{(g)}$ can be denoted by $\mathcal{E}^n(S)$ as well.

Moreover, the operations in Definition 2.13 can be simplified as follows:

Definition 2.22 ([27]) Let h_S^1 and h_S^2 be two EHFLTSs based on $S^{(g)}$, $\#h_S^1 = \#h_S^2$, $\lambda_1 \in [0, 1]$, $\lambda_2 \in [0, 1]$, then

$$\lambda_1 h_S^1 \oplus \lambda_2 h_S^2 = \cup_{i=1}^{\#h_S^1} \{\lambda_1 s_{\alpha_i}^1 \oplus \lambda_2 s_{\beta_i}^2\} = \cup_{i=1}^{\#h_S^1} \{s_{\lambda_1 \alpha_i + \lambda_2 \beta_i}\} \tag{2.30}$$

where $s_{\alpha_i}^1$ and $s_{\beta_i}^2$ are the i-th elements of h_S^1 and h_S^2.

2.3.2.1 Admissible Orders of EHFLTSs

To ensure the admissibility of the derived total orders, we introduce a partial order of EHFLTSs similar to the classical partial order of vectors of dimension n.

Definition 2.23 ([27]) Given $h_S^1, h_S^2 \in \mathcal{E}^n(S)$, then

$$h_S^1 \preceq_V h_S^2 \Leftrightarrow s_{\alpha_i}^1 \leq s_{\beta_i}^2 \, (\forall i = 1, 2, \ldots, n) \tag{2.31}$$

Obviously, the relation $\preceq_V$ is a partial order. Thus, $(\mathcal{E}^n(S), \preceq_V)$ is a poset. Based on this poset, we define the total order on $\mathcal{E}^n(S)$ by a linear order that refines the above partial order.

Definition 2.24 ([27]) Given the poset $(\mathcal{E}^n(S), \preceq_V)$, if $\forall h_S^1, h_S^2 \in \mathcal{E}^n(S)$, the order $\preceq$ satisfies:

(1) $\preceq$ is a linear order on $\mathcal{E}^n(S)$;
(2) $h_S^1 \preceq_V h_S^2 \Rightarrow h_S^1 \preceq h_S^2$;
then $\preceq$ is called an admissible order on $\mathcal{E}^n(S)$.

Example 2.25 Motivated by the lexicographical order, we define a strict order on $\mathcal{E}^n(S)$ by

$$h_S^1 \prec_{Lex1} h_S^2 \Leftrightarrow (\exists m > 0)(((\forall i < m)(s_{\alpha_i}^1 = s_{\beta_i}^2)) \wedge (s_{\alpha_m}^1 < s_{\beta_m}^2)) \tag{2.32}$$

$$h_S^1 \prec_{Lex2} h_S^2 \Leftrightarrow (\exists m \le n)(((\forall i > m)(s_{\alpha_i}^1 = s_{\beta_i}^2)) \wedge (s_{\alpha_m}^1 < s_{\beta_m}^2)) \tag{2.33}$$

Then the following orders

$$h_S^1 \preceq_{Lex1} h_S^2 \Leftrightarrow (h_S^1 = h_S^2) \vee (h_S^1 \prec_{Lex1} h_S^2) \tag{2.34}$$

$$h_S^1 \preceq_{Lex2} h_S^2 \Leftrightarrow (h_S^1 = h_S^2) \vee (h_S^1 \prec_{Lex2} h_S^2) \tag{2.35}$$

are admissible orders on $\mathcal{E}^n(S)$. Given $h_S^1 = \{s_0, s_2, s_3\}$, $h_S^2 = \{s_0, s_1, s_4\}$, we have $h_S^2 \preceq_{Lex1} h_S^1$, $h_S^1 \preceq_{Lex2} h_S^2$.

Due to the presence of normalization of EHFLTSs, the order of two EHFLTSs is subject to the risk preferences of the decision makers.

Example 2.26 Let $h_S^1 = \{s_1, s_3\}$ and $h_S^2 = \{s_1, s_2, s_3\}$. Using R-normalization, if $\xi = 0$, then $h_S^1 = \{s_1, s_1, s_3\} \preceq_{Lex1} h_S^2$; if $\xi = 1$, then $h_S^2 \preceq_{Lex1} h_S^1 = \{s_1, s_3, s_3\}$; if $\xi = 0.5$, we have $h_S^1 = \{s_1, s_2, s_3\} = h_S^2$.

Because the admissible order $\preceq$ refines the partial order $\preceq_V$, the following property can be derived immediately:

Theorem 2.27 ([27]) *Let $\preceq$ be a admissible order on $\mathcal{E}^n(S)$. Then the greatest and smallest elements of $(\mathcal{E}^n(S), \preceq_V)$ are $\mathbf{1}_H = \{s_g\}$ and $\mathbf{0}_H = \{s_{-g}\}$, respectively.*

Admissible orders or partial orders can be generated by a set of specific mappings. For example, given n continuous mappings $f_i : (\bar{S}^{(g)})^n \to \bar{S}^{(g)}$ with $f_i(h_S) = s_{\alpha_i} (i = 1, 2, \ldots, n)$, the order $\prec_{Lex1}$ can be generated by $f_i (i = 1, 2, \ldots, n)$. Specifically, $h_S^1 \prec_{Lex1} h_S^2 \Leftrightarrow (\exists m > 0)(((\forall i < m)(f_i(h_S^1) = f_i(h_S^2))) \wedge (f_m(h_S^1) < f_m(h_S^2)))$. Generally, if the cardinalities of h_S^1 and h_S^2 (after normalization) are n, then there should be at least n mappings to generate the admissible order. In fact, we have the following conclusion:

Theorem 2.28 ([27]) *Let $\preceq$ be an admissible order on $\mathcal{E}^n(S)$. Then, it cannot be induced by $n-1$ continuous mappings $f_i : (\bar{S}^{(g)})^n \rightarrow \bar{S}^{(g)} (i = 1, 2, \ldots, n-1)$.*

Proof Because $h_S^1 \preceq h_S^2 \Leftrightarrow (h_S^1 = h_S^2) \vee (h_S^1 \prec h_S^2)$, it is enough if a strict order $\prec$ on $\mathcal{E}^n(S)$ should be induced by n continuous mappings. Suppose that there are $n-1$ continuous functions $f_i : (\bar{S}^{(g)})^n \rightarrow \bar{S}^{(g)} (i = 1, 2, \ldots, n-1)$ such that, for any $\forall h_S^1, h_S^2 \in \mathcal{E}^n(S)$, $h_S^1 \prec h_S^2$ if and only if there exists $m > 0$ such that $f_i(h_S^1) = f_i(h_S^2)(\forall i < m)$ and $f_m(h_S^1) < f_m(h_S^2)$, then $f_i(i = 1, 2, \ldots, n-1)$ is a continuous bijective mapping due to the linearity of $\prec$. It results to that $\bar{S}^n$ is isomorphic to $\bar{S}^{n-1}$ by continuous bijections. Using the function $I()$ in Eq. (2.12), we get that $[-q, q]^n$ can be isomorphic to $[-q, q]^{n-1}$ by continuous bijections. To show the contradiction clearly, let $n = 2$, it leads to the square $[-q, q]^2$ and the interval $[-q, q]$ are isomorphic by continuous bijections. This, obviously, contradicts the classical result of Brouwer [1]. □

According to Theorem 2.28, it is not surprising that most of the existing orders of EHFLTSs or HFLTSs are partial orders. We will concentrate on the generation of total orders in the coming subsection.

2.3.2.2 Generation of Admissible Orders

Motivated by [15], we present the following definition based on the admissible order $\preceq_{Lex1}$:

Definition 2.29 ([27]) Let $\preceq$ be an admissible order on $\mathcal{E}^n(S)$. The order $\preceq$ is called a generated admissible order if there exist n continuous mappings $f_i : (\bar{S}^{(g)})^n \rightarrow \bar{S}^{(g)}, i = 1, 2, \ldots, n$, such that $\forall h_S^1, h_S^2 \in \mathcal{E}^n(S)$:

$$h_S^1 \preceq h_S^2 \Leftrightarrow \{f_1(h_S^1), f_2(h_S^1), \ldots, f_n(h_S^1)\} \preceq_{Lex1} \{f_1(h_S^2), f_2(h_S^2), \ldots, f_n(h_S^2)\} \tag{2.36}$$

The mapping $(f_1, f_2, \ldots, f_n)$ is called a generating n-tuple of the order $\preceq$.

Example 2.30 Motivated by the concept of moment about the origin in statistics, we can construct an admissible order by improving the partial order $\preceq_L$. Given $h_S = \{s_{\alpha_1}, s_{\alpha_2}, \ldots, s_{\alpha_n}\}$, let $D_k(h_S) = s_{d_k}$, where $d_k = \sum_{j=1}^{n}(Ind(s_{\alpha_j}))^k, k = 1, 2, \ldots, n$. The relation $\preceq_{D_n}$ on $\mathcal{E}^n(S)$ defined by:

$$h_S^1 \preceq_{D_n} h_S^2 \Leftrightarrow (h_S^1 = h_S^2) \vee (h_S^1 \prec_{D_n} h_S^2) \tag{2.37}$$

is an admissible order, where

$$\begin{aligned} h_S^1 \prec_{D_n} h_S^2 \Leftrightarrow & (D_1(h_S^1) < D_1(h_S^2)) \vee (((D_1(h_S^1) < D_1(h_S^2)) \\ \wedge & (\exists m > 2)((\forall i < m)(D_i(h_S^1) = D_i(h_S^2))) \wedge (D_m(h_S^1) > D_m(h_S^2))) \end{aligned} \tag{2.38}$$

Obviously, according to the definition of $\preceq_{D_n}$, we have $h_S^1 = h_S^2$ if and only if $s_{\alpha_i}^1 = s_{\beta_i}^2 (\forall i = 1, 2, \ldots, n)$. The order $\preceq_{D_n}$ refines the partial order $\preceq_L$. If $n \geq 2$ and

$k = 2$, then the order $\preceq_{D_2}$ is order isomorphic to the order $\preceq_L$. Also notice that the order $\preceq_{D_n}$ works even if the cardinalities of h_S^1 and h_S^2 are not equal, and the normalization step is unnecessary. On the contrary, orders may be changed after normalization. For example, given $h_S^1 = \{s_1, s_3\}$, $h_S^2 = \{s_1, s_2, s_4\}$, we have $D_1(h_S^1) = s_2$, $D_1(h_S^2) = s_{7/3}$, thus $h_S^1 \preceq_{D_n} h_S^2$. But after R-normalization with $\xi = 1$, we get $D_1(h_S^1) = D_1(h_S^2) = s_{7/3}$, $D_2(h_S^2) = s_{19/3} < D_2(h_S^2) = s_7$, this leads to $h_S^2 \preceq_{D_n} h_S^1$.

Some properties of generating functions are presented in the following proposition:

Theorem 2.31 ([27]) *Let $\preceq$ be an admissible order on $\mathcal{E}^n(S)$ with the generating n-tuple $(f_1, f_2, \ldots, f_n)$. Then*

(1) $f_i(\{s_{-g}\}) < f_i(\{s_g\})$, $i = 1, 2, \ldots, n-1$;
(2) The functions $f_i (i = 1, 2, \ldots, n-1)$ are jointly strictly increasing on $\mathcal{E}^n(S)$ with respect to the order $\preceq_V$;
(3) If $\forall i = 1, 2, \ldots, n$, $f_i(h_S^1) = f_i(f_S^2)$, then $h_S^1 = h_S^2$;
(4) If the function f_n is increasing on $\mathcal{E}^n(S)$ with respect to the order $\preceq_V$, then $f_1 + f_2 + \cdots + f_n$ is strictly increasing.

Proof Let $h_S^1 = \{s^1_{\alpha_1}, s^1_{\alpha_2}, \ldots, s^1_{\alpha_n}\}$, $h_S^2 = \{s^2_{\beta_1}, s^2_{\beta_2}, \ldots, s^2_{\beta_n}\} \in \mathcal{E}^n(S)$. If $h_S^1 \preceq_V h_S^2$ and $h_S^1 \neq h_S^2$, we denote $h_S^1 \prec_V h_S^2$.

(1)–(2) Suppose $\{s^1_{\alpha_1}, s^1_{\alpha_2}, \ldots, s^1_{\alpha_n}\} \preceq_V \{s^2_{\beta_1}, s^2_{\beta_2}, \ldots, s^2_{\beta_n}\}$. As $(f_1, f_2, \ldots, f_n)$ is the generating n-tuple of the admissible order $\preceq$, $f_i(\{s^1_{\alpha_1}, s^1_{\alpha_2}, \ldots, s^1_{\alpha_n}\}) \leq f_i(\{s^2_{\beta_1}, s^2_{\beta_2}, \ldots, s^2_{\beta_n}\})$, $i - 1, 2, \ldots, n-1$. If there exists $i_0 \in \{1, 2, \ldots, n-1\}$ such that $f_{i_0}(\{s^1_{\alpha_1}, s^1_{\alpha_2}, \ldots, s^1_{\alpha_n}\}) \leq f_{i_0}(\{s^2_{\beta_1}, s^2_{\beta_2}, \ldots, s^2_{\beta_n}\})$, then the admissible order $\preceq$ can be generated without f_{i_0}. This is contradictory to Theorem 2.28. Thus, (2) is proven and (1) is obtained immediately by $\{s_{-g}\} \prec_V \{s_g\}$.

(3) It is true according to the definition of $\preceq_{Lex1}$ and Definition 2.24.

(4) For any $h_S^1 \prec_V h_S^2$, according to (2), we have $f_i(h_S^1) < f_i(h_S^2) (\forall i = 1, 2, \ldots, n-1)$. If f_n is increasing on $\mathcal{E}^n(S)$, i.e., $f_n(h_S^1) \leq f_n(h_S^2)$, then $(f_1 + f_2 + \cdots + f_n)(h_S^1) < (f_1 + f_2 + \cdots + f_n)(h_S^2)$. □

Notice that the converse of the property (3) may not hold in general. Let $n = 2$ and $f_1(\{s_{\alpha_1}, s_{\alpha_2}\}) = s_{\alpha_1}$, $f_2(\{s_{\alpha_1}, s_{\alpha_2}\}) = s_{-\alpha_1}$ for instance. Given $h_S^1 = \{s^1_{\alpha_1}, s^1_{\alpha_2}\}$, $h_S^1 = \{s^2_{\alpha_1}, s^2_{\alpha_2}\}$, it is obvious that $f_1(h_S^1) = f_1(h_S^2) \to s^1_{\alpha_1} = s^2_{\alpha_1}$ and $f_2(h_S^1) = f_2(h_S^2) \to s^1_{\alpha_2} = s^2_{\alpha_2}$. Thus, (3) is satisfied. However, the binary relation generated by the two functions, denoted by $\preceq_f$ is not an admissible order. In fact, if we consider $h_S^1 = \{s_0, s_1\}$ and $h_S^2 = \{s_0, s_2\}$, then $h_S^1 \preceq_V h_S^2$. But we have $f_1(h_S^1) = f_1(h_S^2)$, $f_2(h_S^2) = s_{-2} < s_{-1} = f_2(h_S^1)$, which means $h_S^2 \preceq_f h_S^1$. According to the statement (2) of Definition 2.24, $\preceq_f$ is not an admissible order.

2.3.2.3 Generating Total Orders by Aggregation Functions

According to Definition 2.29, we have the following theorem:

Theorem 2.32 ([27]) *Let $f_i : (\bar{S}^{(g)})^n \to \bar{S}^{(g)} (i = 1, 2, \ldots, n)$ be n continuous aggregation functions such that $\forall h_S^1, h_S^2 \in \mathcal{E}^n(S)$, $f_i(h_S^1) = f_i(f_S^2)(i = 1, 2, \ldots, n)$ hold if and only if $h_S^1 = h_S^2$. If we define the following relation $\preceq_{\{f_1,\ldots,f_n\}}$ on $\mathcal{E}^n(S)$:*

$$h_S^1 \preceq_{\{f_1,\ldots,f_n\}} h_S^2 \Leftrightarrow (h_S^1 = h_S^2) \vee (h_S^1 \prec_{\{f_1,\ldots,f_n\}} h_S^2) \tag{2.39}$$

where

$$\begin{gathered} h_S^1 \prec_{\{f_1,\ldots,f_n\}} h_S^2 \Leftrightarrow (\exists m > 0) \\ (((\forall i < m)(f_i(h_S^1) = f_i(h_S^2))) \wedge (f_m(h_S^1) < f_m(h_S^2))) \end{gathered} \tag{2.40}$$

then $\preceq_{\{f_1,\ldots,f_n\}}$ is an admissible order on $\mathcal{E}^n(S)$.

We hereby concentrate only on a special kind of aggregation functions for the generations of admissible orders of EHFLTSs. Given $\lambda = (\lambda_1, \lambda_2, \ldots, \lambda_n) \in [0, 1]^n$ with $\sum_{i=1}^n \lambda_i = 1$, the mapping $K_\lambda : (\bar{S}^{(g)})^n \to \bar{S}^{(g)}$ is defined by:

$$K_\lambda(s_{\alpha_1}, s_{\alpha_2}, \ldots, s_{\alpha_n}) = s_{\sum_{i=1}^n \lambda_i \alpha_i} \tag{2.41}$$

The mapping is similar to a weighted averaging function. Given n linearly independent weighting vector $\lambda_i = (\lambda_{i,1}, \lambda_{i2}, \ldots, \lambda_{in}), i = 1, 2, \ldots, n$, the relation $\preceq_{\lambda_1,\ldots,\lambda_n}$ on $\mathcal{E}^n(S)$ is defined by [27]:

$$h_S^1 \preceq_{\lambda_1,\ldots,\lambda_n} h_S^2 \Leftrightarrow (h_S^1 = h_S^2) \vee (h_S^1 \prec_{\lambda_1,\ldots,\lambda_n} h_S^2) \tag{2.42}$$

where

$$\begin{gathered} h_S^1 \prec_{\lambda_1,\ldots,\lambda_n} h_S^2 \Leftrightarrow (\exists m > 0)((\forall i < m)(K_{\lambda_i}(s_{\alpha_1}^1, s_{\alpha_2}^1, \ldots, s_{\alpha_n}^1) \\ = K_{\lambda_i}(s_{\beta_1}^1, s_{\beta_2}^1, \ldots, s_{\beta_n}^1))(K_{\lambda_m}(s_{\alpha_1}^1, s_{\alpha_2}^1, \ldots, s_{\alpha_n}^1) < K_{\lambda_m}(s_{\beta_1}^1, s_{\beta_2}^1, \ldots, s_{\beta_n}^1))) \end{gathered} \tag{2.43}$$

Then we have the following theorem:

Theorem 2.33 ([27]) *Let $\lambda_i = (\lambda_{i,1}, \lambda_{i2}, \ldots, \lambda_{in}) \in [0, 1]^n (i = 1, 2, \ldots, n)$ be n linearly independent vectors. Then the relation defined by Eq. (2.42) is an admissible order on $\mathcal{E}^n(S)$ generated by the n-tuple of aggregation functions $K_{\lambda_1}, K_{\lambda_2}, \ldots, K_{\lambda_n}$.*

Proof We first demonstrate that $\preceq_{\lambda_1,\ldots,\lambda_n}$ defines a linear order. In fact, given $h_S^1, h_S^2 \in \mathcal{E}^n(S)$, if $K_{\lambda_1}(h_S^1) = K_{\lambda_1}(h_S^2)$, then we have $\sum_{i=1}^n \lambda_{1i}\alpha_i = \sum_{i=1}^n \lambda_{1i}\beta_i$. Moreover, if $K_{\lambda_i}(h_S^1) = K_{\lambda_i}(h_S^2)$ holds for any $i = 1, 2, \ldots, n$, then we have the following equations:

$$\lambda_{j1}(\alpha_1 - \beta_1) + \lambda_{j2}(\lambda_2 - \beta_2) + \cdots + \lambda_{jn}(\alpha_n - \beta_n) = 0,\ j = 1, 2, \ldots, n \tag{2.44}$$

Because of the linearly independence of $\lambda_1, \lambda_2, \ldots, \lambda_n$, the system of Eq. (2.44) have only zero solution. This means $\alpha_1 - \beta_1 = \alpha_2 - \beta_2 = \cdots = \alpha_n - \beta_n = 0$. Thus, $K_{\lambda_i}(h_S^1) = K_{\lambda_i}(h_S^1)(i = 1, 2, \ldots, n) \Leftrightarrow h_S^1 = h_S^2$.

Finally, if $\{s_{\alpha_1}^1, s_{\alpha_2}^1, \ldots, s_{\alpha_n}^1\} \preceq_V \{s_{\beta_1}^2, s_{\beta_2}^2, \ldots, s_{\alpha_n}^1\}$, then $K_{\lambda_1}(h_S^1) \leq K_{\lambda_1}(h_S^2)$, which results in $h_S^1 \preceq_{\lambda_1,\ldots,\lambda_n} h_S^2$. □

If $n = 4$, then a similar result can be found in [6]. The main differences are: (1) We consider a general case ($n \geq 1$) but De Miguel et al. [6] fixed n to 4; and (2) We focus on linguistic setting rather than numerical setting.

Example 2.34 Let $\mathbf{v}^{(i)} = (v_1, v_2, \ldots, v_n)$ be a specific vector in which $v_i = 1$ and $v_j = 0 (j \neq i)$. The admissible orders $\preceq_{Lex1}$ and $\preceq_{Lex2}$ in Example 2.25 can be redefined by the orders $\preceq_{\lambda_1,\ldots,\lambda_n}$ and $\preceq_{\lambda_n,\ldots,\lambda_1}$, where $\lambda_i = \mathbf{v}^{(i)}(i = 1, 2, \ldots, n)$.

Generally, it is not surprising that the orders of two given EHFLTSs may not coincide if different admissible orders are considered. For instance, if $h_S^1 = \{s_0, s_1\}$, $h_S^2 = \{s_{-1}, s_2\}$, then $h_S^2 \preceq_{Lex1} h_S^1$ but $h_S^1 \preceq_{Lex2} h_S^2$. We clarify this fact by the following theorem:

Theorem 2.35 ([27]) *Let $h_S^1, h_S^2 \in \mathcal{E}^n(S)$ be two EHFLTSs which are not comparable by means of order $\preceq_V$. Then there exist two series of linearly independent vectors $\lambda_i = (\lambda_{i1}, \lambda_{i2}, \ldots, \lambda_{in})$ and $\eta_i = (\eta_{i1}, \eta_{i2}, \ldots, \eta_{in})$, $i = 1, 2, \ldots, n$, such that*

$$h_S^1 \preceq_{\lambda_1,\ldots,\lambda_n} h_S^2, \; h_S^1 \preceq_{\eta_1,\ldots,\eta_n} h_S^2 \tag{2.45}$$

Proof Suppose that $h_S^1, h_S^2 \in \mathcal{E}^n(S)$ are not comparable by means of $\preceq_V$, then there exist $i, j \in \{1, 2, \ldots, n\}$ such that $s_{\alpha_i}^1 < s_{\beta_i}^2$ and $s_{\alpha_j}^1 < s_{\beta_j}^2$. Then we let $\lambda_1 = \mathbf{v}^{(i)}$, $\lambda_i = \mathbf{v}^{(1)}$ and $\lambda_m = \mathbf{v}^{(m)}$ for $m \neq 1, m \neq i$. Similarly, $\eta_i = \mathbf{v}^{(j)}$, $\eta_j = \mathbf{v}^{(1)}$ and $\eta_l = \mathbf{v}^{(l)}$ for $l \neq 1, l \neq i$, where $\mathbf{v}^{(\cdot)}$ is the vector defined in Example 2.34. Then the result follows. □

Given a set of EHFLTSs, according to Theorem 2.35, we can make any of them to be the greatest one by constructing appropriate total orders. This fact implies the importance of total orders in GDM. This issue will be further discussed in Sect. 3.3.

2.4 Linguistic Terms with Weakened Hedges

When facing uncertainties, an expert often is not confident enough to use one certain linguistic term to represent his/her preference. ULTs, HFLTSs and EHFLTSs can be considered as the tools of modeling ULEs. However, according to our language conventions, an expert might be not able to describe the bounds of his/her opinions (as in the case of ULTs and HFLTSs) nor list all the possible terms (as in the case of EHFLTSs). In fact, when expressing the experts' opinions in QDM, linguistic hedges can be considered to modify the force expressed by a predefined linguistic term. If an expert is not sure to select one term, weakened hedges would be a natural way to express the uncertainty. This is usually implemented by using a hedge to modify the most possible term, like the expression *more or less good*. Note that, in this case, (1) hedges describe the degree of uncertainty qualitatively; (2) only the weakened hedges, such as *more or less* and *roughly*, could be considered to describe the uncertain degree; (3) according to Sect. 1.3.2, the focused hedges are inclusive hedges because they represent uncertain degrees rather than modify an original term to another.

To model the uncertainty implied by hedges in QDM, this section introduces a novel linguistic representational and computational model in which the linguistic expressions take the form of a weakened hedge and a linguistic term, which is named as linguistic term with weakened hedge (LTWH). Similar to ULTs, HFLTSs and EHFLTSs, LTWHs focus on natural linguistic expressions as well. However, LTWHs are not presented to extend or improve these techniques but represent another types of linguistic expressions. In practice, experts provide specific types of linguistic expressions according to their linguistic conventions. Thereby it is the decision makers' duty to select proper models to operate these expressions.

2.4.1 Respresentational Model of LTWHs

In this section, we will firstly introduce the syntax of LTWHs and then present the semantics by means of similarity relations defined in the domain. Similar to Sect. 2.1, we focus on the domain $U = [L, R]$.

2.4.1.1 The Syntax of LTWHs

we assume that a LTS on U, associated with semantics of each term, is defined by Eq. (2.3). The set of all weakened hedges considered in a QGM problem is denoted by [28]:

$$H^{(\varsigma)} = \{h_t | t = 1, 2, \ldots, \varsigma\} \tag{2.46}$$

where the hedge h_j has more weakening force than h_i if and only if $i < j$.

Generally, the set of weakened hedges for a specific QDM problem should be collected based on linguistic knowledge and the language custom of the involved experts by several steps: (1) Collect available weakened hedges; and (2) Order them according to their weakening power and then encode them. Especially, the hedges with the same or very approximate weakening power could be considered as the same one, i.e., encoded by the same h_t. In this book, we use these two hedges, i.e., $h_1 =$ *more or less* and $h_2 =$ *roughly*, in most of the examples because: (1) They are frequently used to represent uncertainties. In fact, some other weakened hedges, such as *rather* and *possibly*, can also be considered if necessary [24]; (2) It is straightforward that the weakening force of *roughly* is stronger than that of *more or less* [7]; (3) Using too many hedges may lead to the difficulty of distinguishing their semantics.

Definition 2.36 ([28]) Given LTS $S^{(\tau)}$ and a weakened hedge set (WHS) $H^{(\varsigma)}$ defined as before, a LTWH, denoted by a 2-tuple $l = \langle h_t, s_\alpha \rangle$, is generated by the following rule:

$$\begin{aligned} \langle weakened\ hedge \rangle &:= h_t,\ h_t \in H^{(\varsigma)} \\ \langle atomic\ term \rangle &:= s_\alpha,\ s_\alpha \in S^{(\tau)} \\ \langle LTWH \rangle &:= \langle weakened\ hedge \rangle \langle atomic\ term \rangle \end{aligned}$$

An atomic term s_α can be seen as a special case of LTWHs if the hedge *definitely* is used because *definitely* has no weakening force. That is, $s_\alpha = definitely\ s_\alpha$ for any $s_\alpha \in S^{(\tau)}$. Thus, we denote $h_0 = definitely$ and

$$\bar{H}^{(2)} = \{h_0 = definitely, h_1 = more\ or\ less, h_2 = roughly\} \tag{2.47}$$

Example 2.37 Given the LTS in Example 2.3 and the WHS in Eq. (2.47), some LTWHs could be:

$$\begin{aligned} l_1 &= \langle h_1, s_7 \rangle = more\ or\ less\ very\ good \\ l_2 &= \langle h_2, s_2 \rangle = roughly\ bad \\ l_3 &= \langle h_0, s_4 \rangle = (definitely)\ medium \end{aligned}$$

Note that, there are two hedges in l_1, i.e., *more or less* and *very*. However, they are totally different: (1) Semantically, the former is a weakened hedge whereas the latter is an intensified hedge; (2) the former is an inclusive hedge representing the degree of uncertainty, while the latter is a non-inclusive hedge which move *good* to a new term *very good*.

2.4.1.2 The Semantics of LTWHs

It is natural that the semantics of a LTWH $l = \langle h_t, s_\alpha \rangle$ is computed based on the known semantics of s_α. As the piecewise linear membership functions are usually used and linear triangular fuzzy numbers (TriFNs) are frequently considered to represent the vagueness of these linguistic assessments, Wang et al. [28] assumed that the semantics of each s_α is depicted by TriFNs. Formally, a TriFN tf can be depicted by a tri-tuple $tf = (a, b, c)$ such that $((\forall x \in U))$:

$$\mu_{tf}(x) = \begin{cases} (x-a)/(b-a), & \max\{L, a\} \le x \le b \\ (c-x)/(c-b), & b < x \le \min\{c, R\} \\ 0, & else \end{cases} \tag{2.48}$$

Frequently, the semantics of LTS $S^{(\tau)}$ is defined by: (1) insert $\tau - 1$ points, $x_1, x_2, \ldots, x_{\tau-1}$, into the domain U. The distances between any two adjacent points are generally different; (2) let $x_0 = L$, $x_\tau = R$; (3) let $x_i < x_j \Leftrightarrow i < j$. For convenience, let $\{x_{-i} | i = 1, 2, \ldots, \varsigma + 1\}$ and $\{x_{\tau+j} | j = 1, 2, \ldots, \varsigma + 1\}$ be two sets of virtual points satisfying (3), where ς is the number of hedges in Eq. (2.46). Based on the partition, the semantics of the term $s_\alpha (\alpha = 0, 1, \ldots, \tau)$ is represented by the TriFN $s_\alpha = (x_{\alpha-1}, s_\alpha, s_{\alpha+1})$. For instance, the semantics of the term s_0 in Fig. 2.1 is:

$$s_0 = (-0.125, 0, 0.125) = \begin{cases} (x + 0.125)/(0 + 0.125), & \max\{0, -0.125\} \le x \le 0 \\ (0.125 - x)/(0.125 - 0), & 0 < x \le \min\{0.125, 1\} \\ 0, & otherwise \end{cases} \tag{2.49}$$

It is clear that the domain U is divided into τ intervals. As can be seen in Eq. (2.48), the membership functions are linear in each interval. This implies that each interval can be regarded as uniformly distributed. Accordingly, the domain is said to be piecewise uniformly distributed. Especially, like the case of Fig. 2.1, if $|x_i - x_{i-1}| = |x_j - x_{j-1}| = \delta (\forall i, j = 1, 2, \ldots, \tau)$, and the two sets of virtual points satisfy $\{x_{-i} = L - i \cdot \delta | i = 1, 2, \ldots, \varsigma + 1\}$ and $\{x_{\tau+j} = R + j \cdot \delta | j = 1, 2, \ldots, \varsigma + 1\}$, where $\delta = (R - L)/\tau$, then the domain U is uniformly distributed. In sum, during this section, the domain is either (globally) uniformly distributed or piecewise uniformly distributed.

To derive the semantics of a LTWH, we conduct the analysis in this section based on the following premises [28]:

(1) Given $s_\alpha \in S^{(\tau)}$, the following semantic entailment holds:

$$\langle h_1, s_\alpha \rangle \subseteq \langle h_2, s_\alpha \rangle \subseteq \cdots \subseteq \langle h_\varsigma, s_\alpha \rangle \tag{2.50}$$

That is, for any $x \in U$,

$$\mu_{\langle h_1, s_\alpha \rangle}(x) \le \mu_{\langle h_2, s_\alpha \rangle}(x) \le \cdots \le \mu_{\langle h_\varsigma, s_\alpha \rangle}(x) \tag{2.51}$$

(2) For any $t \in \{1, 2, \ldots, \varsigma - 1\}$, the gap of weakening force between h_t and h_{t+1} are equal. In this case, the semantics of LTWHs can be defined recursively, i.e., $\langle h_{t+1}, s_\alpha \rangle = \langle h_t, \langle h_1, s_\alpha \rangle \rangle$ for any $s_\alpha \in S^{(\tau)}$, $t \in \{1, 2, \ldots, \varsigma - 1\}$.

In fact, there may exist a hedge whose weakening power is between h_t and h_{t+1}. We ignore this hedge and consider only h_t and h_{t+1} to avoid unnecessary difficulty of both using and representing this hedge. That is, we reduce the number of available hedges subjectively to ease the application of decision makers.

Based on these premises, it is enough to compute the semantics of $\langle h_1, s_\alpha \rangle$ ($s_\alpha \in S^{(\tau)}$). Motivated by De Cock and Kerre [5], one could analyze the similarity between any $x, y \in U$ at first. It is intuitive that x is $\langle h_1, s_\alpha \rangle$ if and only if x is similar to some y which are s_α. If the LTS is uniformly distributed in U, then the similar relation can be defined according to $|x - y|$. However, if this is not the case, the positive correlation between the similarity relation and the value of $|x - y|$ may be false. Given a LTS with semantics, the similarity between x and y could be defined by recognizing the density of domain. Generally, a similarity measure can be defined by a mapping $Sim : U \times U \rightarrow [0, 1]$ satisfying the following properties:

(1) $0 \leq Sim(x, y) \leq 1$;
(2) If $x = y$, then $Sim(x, y) = 1$;
(3) $Sim(x, y) > Sim(x, y')$ for any $x < y < y'$;

where $x, y, y' \in U$. Now we firstly focus on the case of uniformly distributed domains.

As shown in Fig. 2.1, if $x = 0.1$, $y = 0.2$, then $Sim(x, y)$ should be greater than 0 because they both are *very low* to a certain degree; if $z = 0.5$, then $Sim(x, z)$ should be equal to 0 because they do not belong to a term with a positive degree at the same time. Based on this nature, we may define the similarity measure by the following definition:

Definition 2.38 ([28]) Let U be a uniformly distributed domain. For any $x, y \in U$, the similarity between x and y is defined by:

$$Sim(x, y) = \begin{cases} 1 - |x - y|/\delta, & |x - y| < \delta \\ 0, & otherwise \end{cases} \tag{2.52}$$

It is obvious that Definition 2.38 satisfies the required properties of a similarity measure mentioned above. Take Fig. 2.1 as an example. If $x = 0.1$, then $\mu_{s_2}(x) = 0$, but $\mu_{\langle h_1, s_2 \rangle}(x)$ should be greater than 0 because x is similar to some point, such as 0.2, which is s_2. Thus, given $x \in U$, $\mu_{\langle h_1, s_\alpha \rangle}(x)$ could be defined by the semantics $\mu_{s_\alpha}(x)$ and the similarity defined in the domain. Based upon the idea of upper approximation of rough fuzzy sets [10], we have the following definition:

Definition 2.39 ([28]) Let $S^{(\tau)}$ be the LTS defined in a uniformly distributed U. For any $x \in U$,

$$\mu_{\langle h_1, s_\alpha \rangle}(x) = \sup_{y \in U} \mathcal{T}(Sim(x, y), \mu_{s_\alpha}(y)) \tag{2.53}$$

where the function Sim is the similarity measure defined in Definition 2.38, $\mathcal{T}$ is a triangular norm.

Example 2.40 Let $S^{(6)}$ be the LTS defined in the uniformly distributed domain $[0, 1]$ and $s_3 = (0.3333, 0.5, 0.6667)$, $\mathcal{T}(x, y) = \min\{x, y\}$. If $x = 0.3$, then we have $\mu_{s_3}(0.3) = 0$,

$$\mu_{\langle h_1, s_3 \rangle}(0.3) = \sup_{y \in U} \min\{Sim(0.3, y), \mu_{s_3}(y)\} = 0.4$$

The computational process can be shown visually in Fig. 2.5. Moreover, the semantics of $\langle h_1, s_3 \rangle$ can be found in Fig. 2.6.

Liang and Mendel [18] suggested characterizing a type-2 fuzzy set by a pair of upper and lower membership functions, each of which is a membership function of a

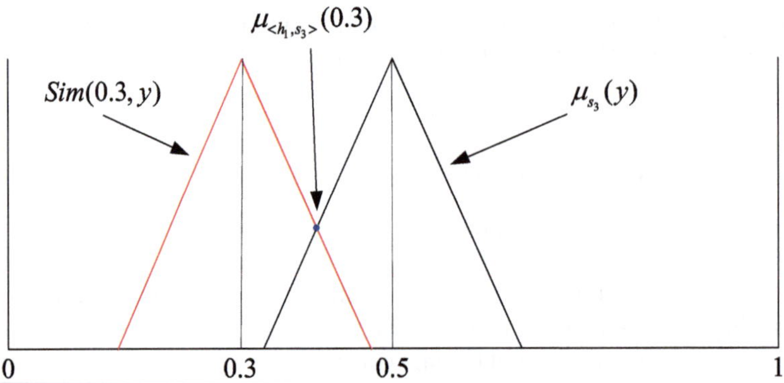

Fig. 2.5 An example of the derivation of the semantics of *more or less medium*

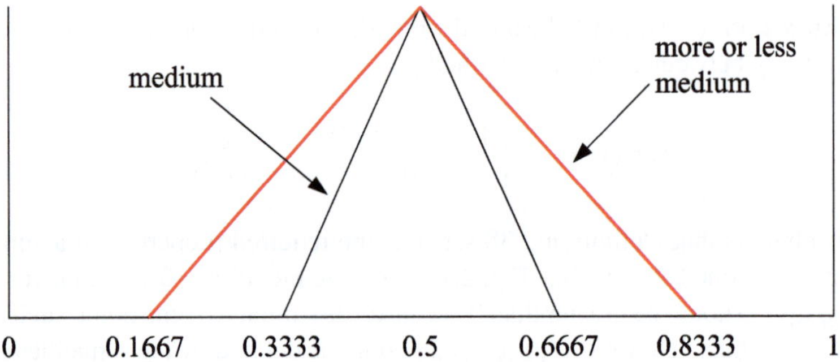

Fig. 2.6 The semantics of *medium* and *more or less medium*

type-1 fuzzy set. The bounded area between the two functions represents the footprint of uncertainties. As shown in Fig. 2.6, an atomic term and a LTWH form a specific type-2 fuzzy set and the semantics of the LTWH acts as the type-2 upper membership function. In our case, thanks to the similarity measure which is defined objectively based on the distribution of the domain, the uncertainty of using a linguistic term is fixed if the hedge is given. Therefore, we can model the uncertainty implied by a hedge using only the upper membership function. Type-2 fuzzy sets are not necessary in this case.

It is interesting to notice that, as shown in Fig. 2.6, the semantics of a LTWH can be represented by a TriFN if the atomic term is represented by a TriFN. In fact, we have $s_3 = (0.3333, 0.5, 0.6667)$ and $\langle h_1, s_\alpha \rangle = (0.1667, 0.5, 0.8333)$. Generally, we have the following theorem:

Theorem 2.41 ([28]) *Given LTS $S^{(\tau)}$ defined in the uniformly distributed domain U and $T(x, y) = \min\{x, y\}$, for any $s_\alpha = (x_{\alpha-1}, x_\alpha, x_{\alpha+1}) \in S^{(\tau)}$, we have*

$$\langle h_1, s_\alpha \rangle = (x_{\alpha-2}, x_\alpha, x_{\alpha+2}) \tag{2.54}$$

Proof For any $x \in U$,

(1) If $x \leq \max\{L, x_{\alpha-2}\}$, then $\forall y \in U$, $\min\{Sim(x, y), \mu_{s_\alpha}(y)\} = 0$. According to Definition 2.39, $\mu_{\langle h_1, s_\alpha\rangle}(x) = 0$.

(2) If $\max\{L, x_{\alpha-2}\} < x \leq \max\{L, x_{\alpha-1}\}$, like the case in Fig. 2.5, then we have

$$\begin{aligned}\mu_{\langle h_1, s_\alpha\rangle}(x) &= \sup_{y\in U}\min\{Sim(x, y), \mu_{s_\alpha}(y)\}\\ &= \sup_{y\in[x-\delta,x+\delta]}\min\{1-(y-x)/\delta, (y-x_{\alpha-1})/(x_\alpha - x_{\alpha-1})\}\\ &= (x - x_{\alpha-2})/2\delta\end{aligned}$$

(3) If $\max\{L, x_{\alpha-1}\} < x \leq x_\alpha$, then

$$\begin{aligned}\mu_{\langle h_1, s_\alpha\rangle}(x) =& \sup_{y\in[x-\delta,x+\delta]}\min\{1-|x-y|/\delta, \mu_{s_\alpha}(y)\}\\ =& \max\{\sup_{y\in[x_{\alpha-1},x]}\min\{1-(x-y)/\delta, (y-x_{\alpha-1})/\delta\},\\ &\sup_{y\in[x,x_\alpha]}\min\{1-(y-x)/\delta, (y-x_{\alpha-1})/\delta\},\\ &\sup_{y\in[x_\alpha,x+\delta]}\min\{1-(y-x)/\delta, (x_{\alpha+1}+y)/\delta\}\}\\ =& \sup_{y\in[x,x_\alpha]}\min\{1-(y-x)/\delta, (y-x_{\alpha-1})/\delta\}\\ =& (x - x_{\alpha-2})/2\delta\end{aligned}$$

Similar to (1), if $x \geq \min\{R, x_{\alpha+2}\}$, we have $\mu_{\langle h_1, s_\alpha\rangle}(x) = 0$; Similar to (2)-(3), we can get $\mu_{\langle h_1, s_\alpha\rangle}(x) = (x_{\alpha+2} - x)/2\delta$ if $x_\alpha \leq x \leq \min\{R, x_{\alpha+2}\}$. Associated with Definition 2.39 and Eq. (2.48), the proof is complete. □

Repeating the procedure of the above proof, one can obtain $\langle h_1, \langle h_1, s_\alpha\rangle\rangle = (x_{\alpha-3}, x_\alpha, x_{\alpha+3})$. Based on the second premise, we can draw the following conclusion immediately:

Theorem 2.42 ([28]) *Let $S^{(\mathcal{T})}$ be the LTS defined in uniformly distributed domain U, $\mathcal{T}(x, y) = \min\{x, y\}$. For any $s_\alpha = (x_{\alpha-1}, x_\alpha, x_{\alpha+1}) \in S^{(\mathcal{T})}$ and $h_t \in H^{(\varsigma)}$, we have*

$$\langle h_t, s_\alpha\rangle = (x_{\alpha-t-1}, x_\alpha, x_{\alpha+t+1}) \tag{2.55}$$

Now, we begin to consider the case of piecewise uniformly distributed domains. This case is frequently considered as well in many studies, such as [35, 36, 40]. For instance, the first part of Fig. 2.7 shows the LTS defined in [36]. In this case, the complicated issue of defining the semantics of a LTWH is to obtain the similarity between any two objects in the domain. To address it, a piecewise linear function could be employed to transform the piecewise uniformly distributed domain into a uniformly distributed one. Then the conclusions in the above subsection can be used directly. Formally, The derivation of semantics of the LTWH based on piecewise uniformly distributed domain can be divided into the following three steps:

Step 1. Employ the following piecewise linear function $f : [L, R] \to [0, 1]$ such that

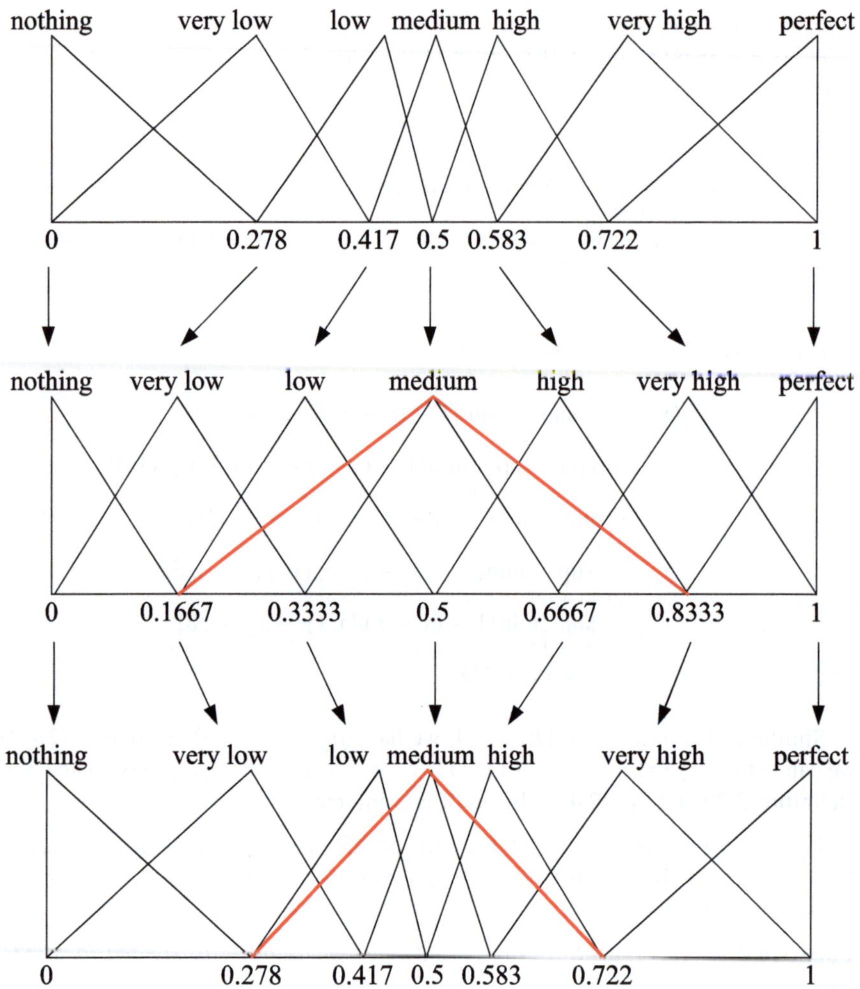

Fig. 2.7 An example of deriving semantics of LTWHs based on piecewise uniformly distributed domain

$$f(x) = \frac{x - ((\alpha - 1)x_\alpha - \alpha x_{\alpha-1})}{\tau(x_\alpha - x_{\alpha-1})}, x \in [x_{\alpha-1}, x_\alpha] \tag{2.56}$$

to map each interval $[x_{\alpha-1}, x_\alpha]$ into $[(\alpha - 1)/\tau, \alpha/\tau]$, where $\alpha = 1, 2, \ldots, \tau$. Thus the domain U is transferred to another uniformly distributed domain [0, 1]. The linguistic term $s_\alpha = (s_{\alpha-1}, s_\alpha, s_{\alpha+1})$ corresponds to linguistic term $\tilde{s}_\alpha = ((\alpha - 1)/\tau, \alpha/\tau, (\alpha + 1)/\tau), \alpha = 0, 1, \ldots, \tau$.

Step 2. Calculate the semantics of the new LTWH $\langle h_1, \tilde{s}_\alpha \rangle$. According to Theorem 2.42, we have $\langle h_1, \tilde{s}_\alpha \rangle = ((\alpha - 2)/\tau, \alpha/\tau, (\alpha + 2)/\tau), \alpha = 0, 1, \ldots, \tau$.

Step 3. Calculate the semantics of the LTWH $\langle h_1, s_\alpha \rangle$ by mapping the TriFN derived in Step 2 into another TriFN in the domain U, using the inverse function f^{-1}. Apparently, the result coincides with the one of Theorem 2.41, i.e., $\langle h_1, s_\alpha \rangle = (x_{\alpha-2}, x_\alpha, x_{\alpha+2})$.

The steps can be illustrated by the following example.

Example 2.43 Let $S^{(6)}$ be the LTS shown in the first part of Fig. 2.7 and $s_3 = (0.417, 0.5, 0.583)$ be the linguistic term *medium*. According to the Eq. (2.56), we get a new linguistic term $\tilde{s}_3 = (0.3333, 0.5, 0.6667)$ defined in the uniformly distributed domain $[0, 1]$. Because of Theorem 2.42, we have $\langle h_1, \tilde{s}_3 \rangle = (0.1667, 0.5, 0.8333)$, as shown in the second part of Fig. 2.7. Then the TriFN can be mapped into $(0.278, 0.5, 0.722)$. Thus we obtain the semantics of the LTWH (i.e., *more or less medium*):

$$\langle h_1, s_3 \rangle = (0.278, 0.5, 0.722)$$

Associated with the second premise, Theorem 2.42 can be extended to a general form which is summarized in the next theorem.

Theorem 2.44 ([28] The semantic rule) *Let* $S^{(\tau)} = \{s_\alpha = (x_{\alpha-1}, x_\alpha, x_{\alpha+1}) | \alpha = 0, 1, \ldots, \tau\}$ *be the LTS defined in the domain* U, $\mathcal{T}(x, y) = \min\{x, y\}$. *For any* $s_\alpha \in S^{(\tau)}$, $h_t \in H^{(\varsigma)}$, *we have*

$$\langle h_t, s_\alpha \rangle = (x_{\alpha-t-1}, x_\alpha, x_{\alpha+t+1}). \tag{2.57}$$

2.4.2 Linguistic Computational Model Based on LTWHs

To enable computing with LTWHs in decision-making, we shall focus our attention on several concepts in advance, which are the negation, order relations and basic computational laws.. The set of all LTWHs based on the sets $S^{(\tau)}$ and $H^{(\varsigma)}$ is denoted by $\mathcal{L}$ in the rest of this book, i.e., $\mathcal{L} = \{l = \langle h_t, s_\alpha \rangle | h_t \in H^{(\varsigma)}, s_\alpha \in S^{(\tau)}\}$.

2.4.2.1 Negation Operator of LTWHs

The negation operator of a LTWH can be defined by the corresponding negation operator of its atomic linguistic term.

Definition 2.45 ([28]) Given $\langle h_t, s_\alpha \rangle \in \mathcal{L}$, its negation operator, denoted by $Neg(\langle h_t, s_\alpha \rangle)$, is the mapping $Neg : \mathcal{L} \to \mathcal{L}$ defined by

$$Neg(\langle h_t, s_\alpha \rangle) = \langle h_t, neg(s_\alpha) \rangle \tag{2.58}$$

where neg is the negation operation defined along with $S^{(\tau)}$.

To ensure that the negation of a LTWH is also a LTWH, it is necessary to let the function *neg* be a one-one mapping. Based on the classical and rational version of function *neg* in Eqs. (2.15) and (2.58) can be rewritten as [28] :

$$Neg(\langle h_t, s_\alpha \rangle) = \langle h_t, s_{\tau-\alpha} \rangle \tag{2.59}$$

It should be mentioned that the function *neg* may be not a one-one mapping if the reference domain is extremely non-uniformly distributed. In this case, the generalized version of negation should be defined according to the semantics of linguistic terms. See [24] for more details.

2.4.2.2 Order Relation of LTWHs

To compare any two given LTWHs, the order relation on the set $\mathcal{L}$ should be defined. Inspired by the classical total order on $S^{(\tau)}$ defined in Eq. (2.14), we introduce the following partial order ($\forall \langle h_{t_1}, s_{\alpha_1} \rangle, \langle h_{t_2}, s_{\alpha_2} \rangle \in \mathcal{L}$) [28] :

$$\langle h_{t_1}, s_{\alpha_1} \rangle \preceq_V \langle h_{t_2}, s_{\alpha_2} \rangle \Leftrightarrow (t_1 = t_2) \wedge (s_{\alpha_1} \leq s_{\alpha_2}) \tag{2.60}$$

The partial set (poset) defined by $\mathcal{L}$ and $\preceq_V$ is denoted by $(\mathcal{L}, \preceq_V)$. In practical applications, the partial order $\preceq_V$ may be not enough. Total orders are necessary to make sure any two LTWHs are comparable. For example, given $\langle h_{t_1}, s_{\alpha_1} \rangle, \langle h_{t_2}, s_{\alpha_2} \rangle \in \mathcal{L}$, the relation $\preceq_{Lex}$ defined by [28]:

$$\langle h_{t_1}, s_{\alpha_1} \rangle \preceq_{Lex} \langle h_{t_2}, s_{\alpha_2} \rangle \Leftrightarrow (s_{\alpha_1} < s_{\alpha_2}) \vee ((s_{\alpha_1} = s_{\alpha_2}) \wedge (t_1 \geq t_2)) \tag{2.61}$$

is a total order on $\mathcal{L}$ and refines partial order $\preceq_V$. However, take the LTS in Example 2.3 for example, we obtain $\langle h_1, s_4 \rangle \preceq_{Lex} \langle h_0, s_4 \rangle$, which means that *medium* is better than *more or less medium*. Thus the order $\preceq_{Lex}$ is based on the strategy of risk aversion. Because of the uncertainty involved in the linguistic hedges, it is inevitable to consider risk preference when distinguishing two LTWHs. We may need total orders based on other strategies if the decision maker is risk neutral or risk loving. In the following definition, we introduce a general framework to develop admissible orders for specific applications.

Definition 2.46 ([28]) Given the poset $(\mathcal{L}, \preceq_V)$, if the order $\preceq$ defined on $\mathcal{L}$ satisfies:

(1) $\preceq$ is a total order on $\mathcal{L}$;
(2) for any $\langle h_{t_1}, s_{\alpha_1} \rangle, \langle h_{t_2}, s_{\alpha_2} \rangle \in \mathcal{L}$, $\langle h_{t_1}, s_{\alpha_1} \rangle \preceq_V \langle h_{t_2}, s_{\alpha_2} \rangle \rightarrow \langle h_{t_1}, s_{\alpha_1} \rangle \preceq \langle h_{t_2}, s_{\alpha_2} \rangle$;
Then $\preceq$ is called an admissible order.

In fact, an admissible order is a total order which refines the partial order $\preceq_V$. Hence, the order $\preceq_{Lex}$ is an admissible order.

2.4.2.3 Basic Operational Laws of LTWHs

Based on a total order $\preceq$ defined in $\mathcal{L}$, two operations could be defined as follows:

Definition 2.47 ([28]) Given $\langle h_{t_1}, s_{\alpha_1}\rangle, \langle h_{t_2}, s_{\alpha_2}\rangle \in \mathcal{L}$ and $\langle h_{t_1}, s_{\alpha_1}\rangle \preceq \langle h_{t_2}, s_{\alpha_2}\rangle$,
(1) Maximum operation: $\langle h_{t_1}, s_{\alpha_1}\rangle \cup \langle h_{t_2}, s_{\alpha_2}\rangle = \langle h_{t_2}, s_{\alpha_2}\rangle$;
(2) Minimum operation: $\langle h_{t_1}, s_{\alpha_1}\rangle \cap \langle h_{t_2}, s_{\alpha_2}\rangle = \langle h_{t_1}, s_{\alpha_1}\rangle$.

When aggregating a collection of LTWHs, the weight of each LTWH may be taken into account. In this case, we have to operate both linguistic information and the associated weights. Operations which are more accurate than the maximum and minimum operations should be developed. In order to reach reasonable accuracy and acceptable interpretability, this kind of operations can be achieved by two procedures as follows:

$$\mathcal{L}^n \xrightarrow{F} \tilde{F}(\mathbf{R}) \xrightarrow{app} \mathcal{L} \tag{2.62}$$

where F is an aggregation operator, $\tilde{F}(\mathbf{R})$ is the fuzzy set representing the intermediate aggregation result, the function app transfers the intermediate result into a LTWH in $\mathcal{L}$. Specifically, these procedures can be implemented based on the virtual linguistic model and the function $round$.

Definition 2.48 ([28]) Given $l_1 = \langle h_{t_1}, s_{\alpha_1}\rangle, l_2 = \langle h_{t_2}, s_{\alpha_2}\rangle \in \mathcal{L}$, their weights are w_1 and w_2, respectively, where $w_1, w_2 \in [0, 1]$. Then the weighted averaging of l_1 and l_2, denoted by $w_1 l_1 \oplus w_2 l_2$, is derived by the following two steps:

(1) Aggregation: $w_1 l_1 \oplus w_2 l_2 = \langle h_{w_1 t_1 + w_2 t_2}, s_{w_1\alpha_1 + w_2\alpha_2}\rangle$;
(2) Approximation: $w_1 l_1 \oplus w_2 l_2 = \langle h_t, s_\alpha\rangle$, where $t = round(w_1 t_1 + w_2 t_2)$, $\alpha = round(w_1\alpha_1 + w_2\alpha_2)$.

According to Definition 2.48, the first step obtains the accurate aggregation results based on the idea of the virtual linguistic model, but leads to the lack of interpretability. The second step ensures that the result is in $\mathcal{L}$ and thus is interpretable. It is clear that the approximation may result in loss of information. As will be seen in the next example, the two steps could provide satisfactory results in many cases. For simplicity, we can rewrite them as follows [28]:

$$\begin{aligned} w_1 l_1 \oplus w_2 l_2 &= w_1\langle h_{t_1}, s_{\alpha_1}\rangle \oplus w_2\langle h_{t_2}, s_{\alpha_2}\rangle \\ &= \langle h_{round(w_1 t_1 + w_2 t_2)}, s_{round(w_1\alpha_1 + w_2\alpha_2)}\rangle \end{aligned} \tag{2.63}$$

However, if the approximate result is not enough and only the ranking of objects is necessary for some special cases, then the aggregation result in the first step can be used and considered as virtual linguistic terms with virtual hedges. The second step can be ignored. In these cases, the total order $\preceq$ defined in the above section works as well.

Example 2.49 Given the WHS $\bar{H}^{(2)}$ defined by Eq. (2.47) and LTS $S^{(8)}$ defined by Fig. 2.1, two linguistic expressions *roughly low* and *definitely very high* are denoted by $l_1 = \langle h_2, s_2 \rangle$ and $l_2 = \langle h_0, s_6 \rangle$. Their weights are denoted by w_1 and w_2. If $w_1 = 0.8$, $w_2 = 0.2$, then

$$round(0.8 \times 2 + 0.2 \times 0) = 2, \; round(0.8 \times 0.2 + 0.2 \times 6) = 2.8,$$
$$w_1 l_1 \oplus w_2 l_2 = 0.8 \langle h_2, s_2 \rangle \oplus 0.2 \langle h_0, s_6 \rangle = \langle h_2, s_3 \rangle.$$

The aggregating result is close to l_1. Similarly, if $w_1 = w_2 = 0.5$, then $w_1 l_1 \oplus w_2 l_2 = \langle h_1, s_4 \rangle$, which can be considered as the mean of l_1 and l_2; if $w_1 = 0.1$ and $w_2 = 0.9$, then $w_1 l_1 \oplus w_2 l_2 = \langle h_0, s_6 \rangle$, which results to the same value of l_2.

Any specific operator can be defined according the problems in hand. For instance, the most commonly used operator, i.e., the weighted averaging operator, can be defined based on Definition 2.48. Given a set of n LTWHs $\{l_i = \langle h_{t_i}, s_{\alpha_i} \rangle \in \mathcal{L} | i = 1, 2, \ldots, n\}$ with the weighting vector $\mathbf{w} = (w_1, w_2, \ldots, w_n)$ having $\sum_{i=1}^{n} w_i = 1$ and $w_i \geq 0 (i = 1, 2, \ldots, n)$, the weighted averaging operator of LTWHs (LTWHWA) is mapping $LTWHWA : \mathcal{L}^n \to \mathcal{L}$ such that

$$LTWHWA_{\mathbf{w}}(l_1, l_2, \ldots, l_n) = w_1 l_1 \oplus w_2 l_2 \oplus \cdots \oplus w_n l_n = \langle h_t, s_\alpha \rangle \quad (2.64)$$

where $t = round(\sum_{i=1}^{n} w_i t_i)$, $\alpha = round(\sum_{i=1}^{n} w_i \alpha_i)$.

2.5 A Comparative Analysis on Similar Models of ULEs

In order to show the characteristic of the proposed CWW model, this section will conduct the comparisons with some existing studies of modelling hedges and some similar linguistic models which consider ULEs.

2.5.1 *Compared with the Existing Techniques of Modeling Hedges*

We will recall the main idea of several techniques at first. The shifting hedge suggested by Lakoff [16] does not change the shape of membership function of an atomic term but shift it to a certain level. As shown in Fig. 2.1, the intensified hedge *very* modifies the term *high* to a new term *very high*. The powering hedge [41] would be the most widely acknowledged kind of hedges. Given the linguistic term s_α, the semantics of $\langle h_t, s_\alpha \rangle$ is defined by $(\mu_{s_\alpha}(x))^\gamma$, where γ is determined according to the weakening power of h_t. For weakened hedges, γ is fixed in [0, 1]. For example, Cordón et al. [4] let $\gamma = 1/2$ and $\gamma = 2$ to represent *more or less* s_α and *very* s_α, respectively, in a fuzzy rule-based classification system. Accordingly, the surface rule structure is changed by incorporating hedges. Later, Casillas et al. [3] improved the work of Cordón et al. [4] by tuning both surface rule structure and deep rule structure, where the deep rule structure is tuned by adjusting the parameters of membership functions of linguistic terms. De Cock and Kerre [5] presented the first approach to model hedges by fuzzy relations. Recently, Lewis and Lawry [17] represented linguistic hedges based on the label semantics framework. The approach is defined with both unmodified prototypes and differing prototypes. The result of the former is similar to the powering hedge and the latter changes the core of the atomic term.

We can see that the proposed model in Sect. 2.4 is not the first model to model hedges but the first one to model uncertainty of using single terms in QDM. Others focus on general definition of hedges, natural language processing or artificial intelligence. Accordingly, only weakened hedges are focused on. Instead of concentrating on specific hedges, Wang et al. [28] presented a general representational and computational framework to enable computing with a set of hedges satisfying the two premises in Sect. 2.4. The powering hedges are usually criticized because they are arbitrary and semantically ungrounded. The model in this section, the fuzzy relation-based model and the label semantic model have a clear semantic grounding. The label semantic model highly depends on the threshold and its computational process is much more complex than that of the proposed model. The model in this section and the fuzzy relation-based model utilize piece-wise linear membership functions for representing semantics and thus the application is simple. Theoretically, the model in this section could be a special case of the fuzzy relation-based model because of the specification of domain and similarity relations [5]. But, thanks to Theorem 2.44, the proposed computational model is much easier than others.

2.5.2 LTWHs Versus ULTs and HFLTSs

Let $S^{(\tau)}$ be a LTS defined by Eq. (2.3) and $H^{(\varsigma)}$ be the WHS defined by Eq. (2.46). Given $s_{\alpha-1}, s_\alpha, s_{\alpha+1} \in S^{(\tau)}$ and $h_1 \in H^{(\varsigma)}$, three distinct linguistic expressions with similar semantics can be constructed, which are the ULT $l^{(I)} = [s_{\alpha-1}, s_{\alpha+1}]$, the HFLTS $l^{(H)} = \{s_{\alpha-1}, s_\alpha, s_{\alpha+1}\}$ and the LTWH $l^{(L)} = \langle h_1, s_\alpha \rangle$. For any $x \in U$, we have $\mu_{l^{(I)}}(x) \geq 0 \Leftrightarrow \mu_{l^{(H)}}(x) \geq 0 \Leftrightarrow \mu_{l^{(H)}} \geq 0$. Thus it is sufficient to compare these techniques by the three linguistic expressions. Table 2.1 summarizes their syntactic and semantic rules.

The second column of Table 2.1 lists the forms of linguistic expression which are adopted to elicit the three types of linguistic values. ULTs are introduced for the case when the linguistic argument does not match any of the atomic terms but located between two distinct terms [30]. HFLTSs are developed to suit the case when experts are thinking of several terms at the same time [23], and thus can be represented by several consecutive terms in a LTS. As can be seen in Table 2.1, three forms of linguistic expression can be considered for eliciting HFLTSs. It seems that the syntactic rules of ULTs and HFLTSs are similar, but they are totally different. ULTs are on the basis of the virtual linguistic model. Thus when considering

Table 2.1 Comparisons among ULTs, HFLTSs and LTWHs

Technique	Syntax	Semantics
ULT ($[s_{\alpha-1}, s_{\alpha+1}]$)	Between $\cdots$ and $\cdots$	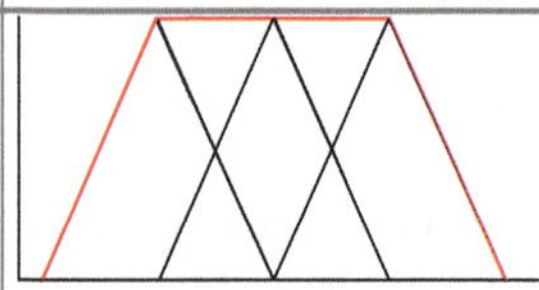
HFLTS ($\{s_{\alpha-1}, s_{\alpha}, s_{\alpha+1}\}$)	Greater than $\cdots$; Lower than $\cdots$ Between $\cdots$ and $\cdots$	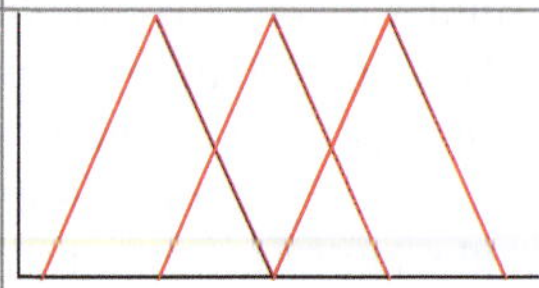
LTWH ($\langle h_1, s_{\alpha}\rangle$)	Weakened hedge + atomic term	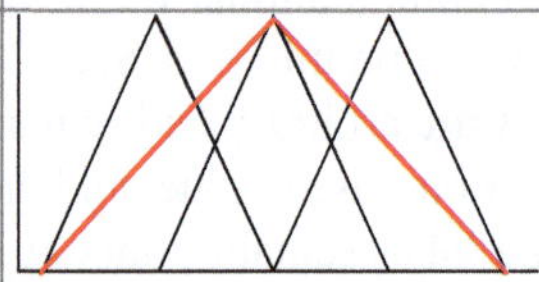

$[s_{\alpha-1}, s_{\alpha+1}]$, any VLTs in the interval are included. Whereas in HFLTSs, such as $\{s_{\alpha-1}, s_{\alpha}, s_{\alpha+1}\}$, only the listed atomic terms in the predefined LTS are involved. Different from ULTs and HFLTSs, LTWHs begin with only one atomic term, and employ a weakened hedge to express the uncertainty around the term. For instance, when we say something is *more or less* s_{α}, the fact is that s_{α} is the most possible term. The possibility of the object being s_{α} is greater than it is $s_{\alpha-1}$ or $s_{\alpha+1}$. From this point of view, we would like to emphasize that the purpose of introducing LTWHs is neither to serve as a substitute of the existing tools nor to be a better technique. LTWHs are proposed to represent another way of human thinking. And this way is very natural but has not been systematically studied.

The third column in Table 2.1 shows the semantics of the techniques. It can be derived from the corresponding syntactic rules. Clearly, the semantics are quite different. But it is not necessary to highlight the difference unless one is going to compute with their semantics.

There are also some relationships among the computational models of the three techniques. Their ideas of the order relation and negation operations are similar to each other. But other operations, especially the aggregation operators, are totally different. The operations of ULTs are defined based on the operation of virtual linguistic model, whose details can be found in [30]. The operations of HFLTSs are more complex than those of ULTs. One strategy is to compute based on their envelopes, i.e., ULTs. Thus, HFLTSs are transformed into ULTs for computing. Another strategy is to compute by using each component term in the HFLTS. This strategy is closer to the idea of hesitation. However, the aggregation results may be not HFLTSs but

Table 2.2 The main features of the comparable techniques of modeling uncertain linguistic information

Technique	Necessary information	Computational strategy	Computational result
ULT	Two terms, as the interval boundary	Compute with its boundary	ULT
HFLTS	A list of several consecutive terms	Compute with its envelope or each term	ULT or EHFLTS
EHFLTS	A list of several terms	Compute with each possible term	EHFLTS
LTWH	A term and a weakened hedge	Compute with the term and the hedge	LTWH
PpLT	A proportion of two terms	Compute with terms and probabilities	PpLT
LDA	A probabilistic distribution of several terms	Compute with terms and probabilities	LDA
DFN	Several consecutive terms with membership degrees	Compute with membership degrees	DFN
PLTS	A probabilistic distribution of several terms	Compute with terms and probabilities	PLTS or EHFLTS
2DLT	Two terms	Compute with terms	2DLT

EHFLTSs [29]. The basic aggregation operation of LTWHs is implemented by two steps. The first step is similar to the operation in the virtual linguistic model, and the second step makes the results more coarse but interpretable.

2.5.3 Compared with Other Techniques

There are some other linguistic representational and computational models, such as the proportional linguistic terms (PpLTs), linguistic distribution assessments (LDAs), discrete fuzzy numbers (DFNs), probabilistic linguistic term sets (PLTSs), 2-dimensional linguistic terms (2DLTs). Their main characteristics are shown in Table 2.2.

As can be seen in Table 2.2, most of these linguistic representation models include at least two linguistic terms for the purpose of modeling uncertainties. Some techniques need more information, such as complete or incomplete probabilistic distribution and membership degrees. However, EHFLTSs and LTWHs focus on the expressions which frequently emerged in natural languages. EHFLTSs list all the possible terms, and LTWHs begin with only one linguistic term which is modified by a weakened hedge. The uncertainty of using the linguistic term is represented by the hedge.

2.6 Concluding Remarks

This chapter has focused on the theoretical foundations of uncertain linguistic expressions, such as the theory of virtual linguistic terms, two models of uncertain linguistic expressions (EHFLTSs and LTWHs). The syntactical and semantic rules, order relations, negations and basic operations of the models have been introduced.

The virtual linguistic model serves as the basis of the other two models. This chapter has presented the rule of generating virtual terms based on an atomic term and a real number, introduced the semantics of virtual terms by using specific types of linguistic hedges, and then reconstructed the computational model of virtual terms.

EHFLTSs are not a simple extension of HFLTSs. They not only possess better mathematical properties than HFLTSs, but also serve as a computational model of HFLTSs. This chapter has analyzed the derivation of EHFLTSs and their focused linguistic expressions, introduced the corresponding computational model, especially the order relations on the set of EHFLTSs.

The model of LTWHs has also been introduced to model another type of natural linguistic expressions, which enable the application of LTWHs in GDM problems. In fact, if an expert is not confident enough to use a single term, then the weakened linguistic hedges could be employed to describe the degree of uncertainty in a qualitative manner. This chapter has introduced the representational and computational models of LTWHs. The models are easy to use, and possess very good interpretability.

References

1. Brouwer, L.E.J.: Über abbildung von mannigfaltigkeiten. Math. Ann. **71**(1), 97–115 (1911)
2. Bustince, H., Fernández, J., Kolesárová, A., Mesiar, R.: Generation of linear orders for intervals by means of aggregation functions. Fuzzy Sets Syst. **220**, 69–77 (2013)
3. Casillas, J., Cordón, O., Del Jesus, M.J., Herrera, F.: Genetic tuning of fuzzy rule deep structures preserving interpretability and its interaction with fuzzy rule set reduction. IEEE Trans. Fuzzy Syst. **13**(1), 13–29 (2005)
4. Cordón, O., del Jesus, M.J., Herrera, F.: Genetic learning of fuzzy rule-based classification systems cooperating with fuzzy reasoning methods. Int. J. Intell. Syst. **13**(10–11), 1025–1053 (1998)
5. De Cock, M., Kerre, E.E.: Fuzzy modifiers based on fuzzy relations. Inf. Sci. **160**(1), 173–199 (2004)
6. De Miguel, L., Bustince, H., Fernández, J., Induráin, E., Kolesárová, A., Mesiar, R.: Construction of admissible linear orders for interval-valued atanassov intuitionistic fuzzy sets with an application to decision making. Inf. Fusion **27**, 189–197 (2016)
7. De Cock, M., Radzikowska, A.M., Kerre, E.E.: A fuzzy-rough approach to the representation of linguistic hedges. In: Technologies for Constructing Intelligent Systems 1, pp. 33–42. Springer (2002)
8. Degani, R., Bortolan, G.: The problem of linguistic approximation in clinical decision making. Int. J. Approx. Reason. **2**(2), 143–162 (1988)
9. Dong, Y.C., Xu, Y.F., Yu, S.: Linguistic multiperson decision making based on the use of multiple preference relations. Fuzzy Sets Syst. **160**(5), 603–623 (2009)
10. Dubois, D., Prade, H.: Rough fuzzy sets and fuzzy rough sets. Int. J. Gen. Syst. **17**(2–3), 191–209 (1990)

11. Falcó, E., García-Lapresta, J.L., Roselló, L.: Allowing agents to be imprecise: a proposal using multiple linguistic terms. Inf. Sci. **258**, 249–265 (2014)
12. Herrera, F., Herrera-Viedma, E.: Linguistic decision analysis: Steps for solving decision problems under linguistic information. Fuzzy Sets Syst. **115**(1), 67–82 (2000)
13. Herrera, F., Martínez, L.: A 2-tuple fuzzy linguistic representation model for computing with words. IEEE Trans. Fuzzy Syst. **8**(6), 746–752 (2000)
14. Komorníková, M., Mesiar, R.: Aggregation functions on bounded partially ordered sets and their classification. Fuzzy Sets Syst. **175**(1), 48–56 (2011)
15. Kyselová, D., Dubois, D., Komorníková, M., Mesiar, R.: Refining aggregation operator-based orderings in multifactorial evaluation-Part I: continuous scales. IEEE Trans. Fuzzy Syst. **15**(6), 1100–1106 (2007)
16. Lakoff, G.: Hedges: a study in meaning criteria and the logic of fuzzy concepts. In: Contemporary Research in Philosophical Logic and Linguistic Semantics, pp. 221–271. Springer (1975)
17. Lewis, M., Lawry, J.: A label semantics approach to linguistic hedges. Int. J. Approx. Reason. **55**(5), 1147–1163 (2014)
18. Liang, Q.L., Mendel, J.M.: Interval type-2 fuzzy logic systems: theory and design. IEEE Trans. Fuzzy Syst. **8**(5), 535–550 (2000)
19. Liao, H.C., Xu, Z.S., Zeng, X.J.: Distance and similarity measures for hesitant fuzzy linguistic term sets and their application in multi-criteria decision making. Inf. Sci. **271**, 125–142 (2014)
20. Liao, H.C., Xu, Z.S., Zeng, X.J.: Hesitant fuzzy linguistic VIKOR method and its application in qualitative multiple criteria decision making. IEEE Trans. Fuzzy Syst. **23**(5), 1343–1355 (2015)
21. Merigó, J.M., Palacios-Marqués, D., Zeng, S.Z.: Subjective and objective information in linguistic multi-criteria group decision making. Eur. J. Oper. Res. **248**(2), 522–531 (2016)
22. Rodríguez, R.M., Martínez, L.: An analysis of symbolic linguistic computing models in decision making. Int. J. Gen. Syst. **42**(1), 121–136 (2013)
23. Rodríguez, R.M., Martínez, L., Herrera, F.: Hesitant fuzzy linguistic term sets for decision making. IEEE Trans. Fuzzy Syst. **20**(1), 109–119 (2012)
24. Torra, V.: Negation functions based semantics for ordered linguistic labels. Int. J. Intell. Syst. **11**(11), 975–988 (1996)
25. Türkşen, I.B.: Type 2 representation and reasoning for CWW. Fuzzy Sets Syst. **127**(1), 17–36 (2002)
26. Wang, H.: Extended hesitant fuzzy linguistic term sets and their aggregation in group decision making. Int. J. Comput. Intell. Syst. **8**(1), 14–33 (2015)
27. Wang, H., Xu, Z.S.: Total orders of extended hesitant fuzzy linguistic term sets: definitions, generations and applications. Knowl. Based Syst. **107**, 142–154 (2016)
28. Wang, H., Xu, Z.S., Zeng, X.J.: Linguistic terms with weakened hedges: a model for qualitative decision making under uncertainty. Inf. Sci. **433–434**(3), 37–54 (2018a)
29. Wang, H., Xu, Z.S., Zeng, X.J.: Hesitant fuzzy linguistic term sets for linguistic decision making: current developments, issues and challenges. Inf. Fusion **43**, 1–12 (2018b)
30. Xu, Z.S.: Uncertain linguistic aggregation operators based approach to multiple attribute group decision making under uncertain linguistic environment. Inf. Sci. **168**(1), 171–184 (2004a)
31. Xu, Z.S.: A method based on linguistic aggregation operators for group decision making with linguistic preference relations. Inf. Sci. **166**(1), 19–30 (2004b)
32. Xu, Z.S.: Deviation measures of linguistic preference relations in group decision making. Omega **33**(3), 249–254 (2005)
33. Xu, Z.S.: On generalized induced linguistic aggregation operators. Int. J. General Syst. **35**(1), 17–28 (2006)
34. Xu, Z.S.: Linguistic aggregation operators: an overview. In: Fuzzy Sets and Their Extensions: Representation, Aggregation and Models, pp. 163–181. Springer (2008a)
35. Xu, Z.S.: Group decision making based on multiple types of linguistic preference relations. Inf. Sci. **178**(2), 452–467 (2008b)

36. Xu, Z.S.: An interactive approach to multiple attribute group decision making with multigranular uncertain linguistic information. Group Decis. Negot. **18**(2), 119–145 (2009)
37. Xu, Z.S., Wang, H.: On the syntax and semantics of virtual linguistic terms for information fusion in decision making. Inf. Fusion **34**, 43–48 (2017)
38. Yager, R.R.: A new methodology for ordinal multiobjective decisions based on fuzzy sets. Decis. Sci. **12**(4), 589–600 (1981)
39. Yang, J.B., Xu, D.L.: On the evidential reasoning algorithm for multiple attribute decision analysis under uncertainty. IEEE Trans. Syst. Man Cybern. Part A Syst. Hum. **32**(3), 289–304 (2002)
40. Yu, X.H., Xu, Z.S., Chen, Q.: A method based on preference degrees for handling hybrid multiple attribute decision making problems. Expert Syst. Appl. **38**(4), 3147–3154 (2011)
41. Zadeh, L.A.: The concept of a linguistic variable and its application to approximate reasoning-II. Inf. Sci. **8**(4), 301–357 (1975)
42. Zadeh, L.A.: Fuzzy logic = computing with words. IEEE Trans. Fuzzy Syst. **4**(2), 103–111 (1996)

Part III
Group Decision-Making Based on a Single Type of Uncertain Linguistic Expressions

Chapter 3
Group Decision-Making Based on EHFLTSs Under the Framework of Decision Matrix

Under the framework of decision matrix, this chapter focuses on GDM problems whose decision information takes the form of EHFLTSs. A general framework of multiple groups decision-making (MGDM) will be introduced at first for the problems with complex structure of groups. Then some specific MGDM approaches will be introduced based on information fusion of EHFLTSs. Espccially, an admissible order-based GDM approach will be presented based on the admissible order defined in Sect. 2.3.

3.1 A Framework of Multiple Groups Decision-Making

In complex GDM problems, the scale of a group would be big or huge, and the structure of a group would be very complex. The existing contributions mainly focus on the sizes of groups, but pay little attention on the structures of groups. This section treats a group as several sub-groups based on its inner structure where members of each sub-groups own similar or the same knowledge and expertise. The GDM problems are thus called MGDM problems [19, 21]. The necessity of considering structures of groups could be summarized as follows:

In real applications, GDM is usually taken into account instead of individual decision-making although the derived decisions might be not always better than those derived by individual decision-making. This is caused by several reasons. Firstly, one expert can not afford the whole task of assessments due to the complexities of the problems. Then a group is necessary, in which each expert only needs to complete partial work. Secondly, groups own some notable advantages. It can be expected that a group takes advantage of the diverse strengths and expertise of its members, and reaches the superior solutions than the individuals. Michaelsen et al. [13]

H. Wang and Z. Xu, *Theory and Approaches of Group Decision-Making with Uncertain Linguistic Expressions*, Uncertainty and Operations Research,
https://doi.org/10.1007/978-981-13-3735-2_3

demonstrated that groups outperform their most proficient group members 97% of the time. Daily and Steiner [3] also showed that groups can achieve a higher number of brainstormed ideas.

However, there are also some disadvantages involved with GDM. It is apparent that groups are generally slower to arrive at decisions than individuals. Groupthink, sometimes, occurs when the members in the group feel pressure to confront what seems to be the dominant view of the group. Group polarization is another potential disadvantage of GDM. In addition, the members may perform the tasks quite differently. For example, individuals tend to take more risks [7] and act more selfishly [8] when they make decisions in a group.

In order to overcome the limitations of GDM, Wang and Xu [21] presented a novel decision-making framework, i.e., MGDM, to serve as a generation of traditional GDM. MGDM refers to as making decisions over available alternatives by a decision organization that is characterized by several groups. There are generally two categories of groups: heterogeneous groups and homogeneous groups. The experts in a heterogeneous group are adept at distinct fields of disciplines, and have diverse cultural backgrounds. Each expert is good at evaluating alternatives with respect to a subset of criteria. Heterogeneous group is adapted for the problems whose evaluations are interdisciplinary. The experts in a homogeneous group are from adjacent (or the same) disciplines. They have the same or similar cultural backgrounds. Each expert can conduct the same evaluation task in isolation. This kind of group is used to overcome the potential disadvantages of individuals. In the novel framework of [21], as can be seen in Part 1 of Fig. 3.3, the experts in each group are homogeneous while the experts in different groups are heterogeneous. Each group deals with partial evaluations according to its disciplines and backgrounds. The individuals of a group work in isolation if possible. The organization acts collectively to complete the whole work. Obviously, if there is only one group, the organization is reduced to a homogeneous group; while if there is only one member in each homogeneous group, the organization is reduced to a heterogeneous group.

3.1.1 Mathematical Description of MGDM

In the MGDM problems, several groups of experts act collectively to select the most relevant alternative(s) among the available ones. Formally, this problem can be described as follows [21]:

A decision organization is formed by r groups (denoted by $\{G_l | l = 1, 2, \ldots, r\}$) of experts. The t homogeneous experts in G_l are denoted by $E = \{e_{lk} | k = 1, 2, \ldots, t, l = 1, 2, \ldots, r\}$. The experts of different groups are heterogeneous. The relative weights of experts within a group are indifferent. The organization is authorized to evaluate a set of m alternatives $A = \{a_1, a_2, \ldots, a_m\}$ in terms of n criteria $C = \{c_1, c_2, \ldots, c_n\}$. The weight vector of criteria is $\mathbf{w} = (w_1, w_2, \ldots, w_n)$, where $\sum_{j=1}^{n} w_j = 1, w_j \in [0, 1] (j = 1, 2, \ldots, n)$. The group G_l evaluates a subset of C in isolation, denoted by SC_l, such that $SC_l \neq \emptyset (l = 1, 2, \ldots, r), \cup_{l=1}^{r} SC_l = C$.

The performance of a_i, provided by e_{lk}, with respect to the criterion c_j, is represented by a function $V : A \times E \times C \rightarrow S$, where S represents the range of performance values in specific problems and could be [0, 1], the LTS $S^{(\tau)}$ or $2^{S^{(\tau)}}$. Thus, the performance is denoted by $V(a_i, c_j, e_{lk})$. The aim of the MGDM problem is to synthesize the evaluation values of each alternative and then reach a final decision.

3.1.2 *Process of MGDM*

In this section, we mainly focus on the solutions of three specific MGDM problems based on different scenarios. Let's begin with a simple example. Suppose that a company is going to select and import the most valuable product from some alternatives. Three main criteria are the production cost, marketing cost and after-sales service cost. The manager authorizes three relative departments, i.e., the producing department, the marketing department and after-sales service department, to evaluate the product. If one criterion is only evaluated by a single department (for instance, the production costs of alternatives are only focused by the producing department), we call this case the 1-to-n scenario (because more than one criterion may be assessed by the same department). Moreover, distinct departments may pay their attention on the same criterion. For example, the production cost influences the work of all departments. Thus, they will all express their opinions about the costs of alternatives. We call this case the m-to-n scenarios. We focus on the solution of these scenarios in this section.

(1) *The process for the 1-to-n scenario*

As shown in Fig. 3.1, we have $SC_{l_1} \cap SC_{l_2} = \emptyset (\forall l_1, l_2 = 1, 2, \ldots, r)$ in this scenario. This is close to the case of traditional GDM problems. The process of this scenario is as follows [21]:

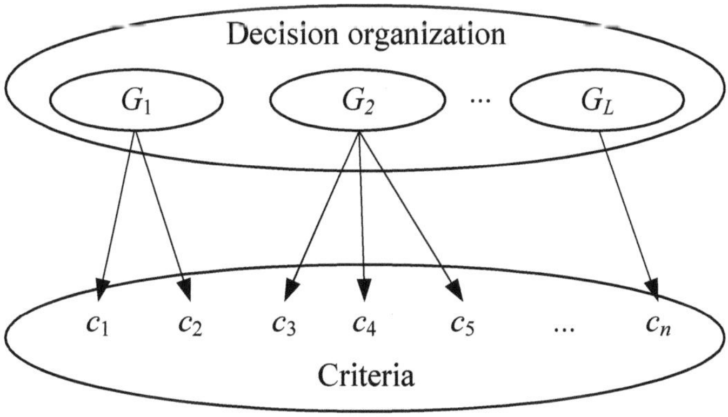

Fig. 3.1 The structure of the 1-to-n scenario

Step 1: Forming the decision matrix $D = (V(a_i, c_j))_{m\times n}$. The performance of a_i with respect to c_j, denoted by $V(a_i, c_j)$, is synthesized by the opinions of all experts who contribute the corresponding piece of opinion, i.e.,

$$V(a_i, c_j) = \cup_{k=1,2,\dots,t} V(a_i, c_j, e_{lk})$$

where $\cup$ means the consideration of all the opinions.

Step 2: The choice of the aggregation operator Agg. Associated with $\mathbf{w}$, we obtain the overall performance of each alternative $V(a_i)$ by one aggregation operator:

$$V(a_i) = Agg_{\mathbf{w}}(V(a_i, c_1), V(a_i, c_2), \dots, V(a_i, c_n))$$

Step 3: The choice of the best alternative(s).

(2) *The processes for the m-to-n scenario*

Generally, as shown in Fig. 3.2, a criterion may be evaluated by more than one group. Formally, there may exist $l_1, l_2 \in \{1, 2, \dots, r\}$ such that $SC_{l_1} \cap SC_{l_2} \neq \emptyset$. Given c_j, the groups which participate in evaluating c_j are denoted by $G^{(j)}$. Apparently, $G^{(j)} \subseteq G$ and $\cup_{j=1,2,\dots,n} G^{(j)} = G$. The experts in $G^{(j)}$ are denoted by $e_k^{(j)}(m = 1, 2, \dots, \#G^{(j)})$, where $\#G^{(j)}$ is the number of experts in $G^{(j)}$. In the following, we discuss two distinct cases of this scenario and present the corresponding processes.

Firstly, we assume that the weights of groups in $G^{(j)}$ are equal. In other words, they have the same confidence level when evaluating c_j. The corresponding decision-making process is [21]:

Step 1: Forming the decision matrix $D = (V(a_i, c_j))_{m\times n}$. For c_j, $V(a_i, c_j)$ is derived by

$$V(a_i, c_j) = \cup_{k=1,2,\dots,t} V(a_i, c_j, e_k^{(j)})$$

where $\cup$ means the consideration of all the opinions.

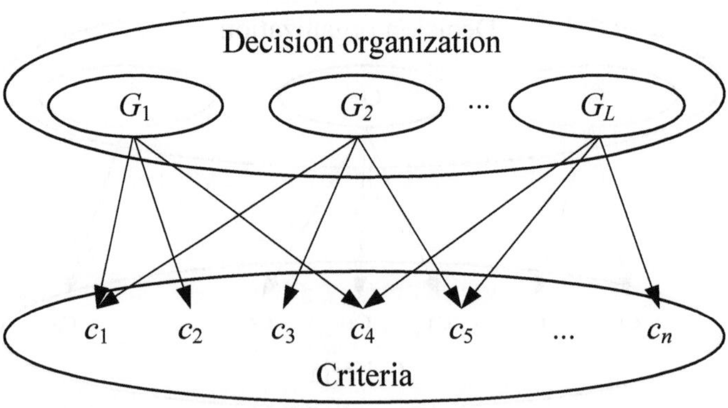

Fig. 3.2 The structure of the m-to-n scenario

Step 2: See Step 2 of the process for the 1-to-n scenario.

Step 3: See Step 3 of the process for the 1-to-n scenario.

Secondly, we assume that the weights of groups in $G^{(j)}$ cannot be ignored. Generally, because of the distinguished professional area, the groups in $G^{(j)}$ may have different confidence levels when evaluating c_j. The $L^{(j)}$ groups in $G^{(j)}$ are denoted by $G_l^{(j)}$, $l = 1, 2, \ldots, L^{(j)}$. For simplicity, the group $G_l^{(j)}$ is advised to provide a confidence level associated with the evaluation of $G_l^{(j)}$, denoted by $cl_l^{(j)} (\in [0, 1])$. The decision-making process is [21]:

Step 1: Synthesizing evaluations within each group. Similar to the above cases, we consider all the opinions in each group by the operator $\cup$, and then the performance of a_i with respect to c_j provided by G_l, denoted by $V(a_i, c_j, G_l)$, can be derived.

Step 2: Forming the decision matrix $D = (V(a_i, c_j))_{m \times n}$. The weights of groups in $G^{(j)}$ can be derived by $\lambda = (\lambda_1, \lambda_2, \ldots, \lambda_{L^{(j)}})$, where $\lambda_l = cl_l^{(j)} / \sum_{l=1}^{L^{(j)}} cl_l^{(j)}$. Utilize the aggregation operator $Agg1$ to synthesize the opinions of the $L^{(j)}$ groups:

$$V(a_i, c_j) = Agg1_{\lambda}(V(a_i, c_j, G_1^{(j)}), V(a_i, c_j, G_2^{(j)}), \ldots, V(a_i, c_j, G_{L^{(j)}}^{(j)}))$$

Step 3: The choice of the aggregation operator $Agg2$. See Step 2 of the process for the 1-to-n scenario.

Step 4: See Step 3 of the process for the 1-to-n scenario.

Obviously, we only present the general framework of the decision-making processes. In application, the operator $\cup$ and the aggregation operators should be specified based on the forms of performance values and the preferences of decision makers. If the performance values take the form of EHFLTSs, the implementation of these processes will be developed in the next section.

3.2 A MGDM Approach Based on Information Fusion

3.2.1 Some Aggregation Operators of EHFLTSs

Information fusion is a key technique for GDM. Similar to Torra [17], we have the following extension principle:

Definition 3.1 ([19]) Let Θ be a mapping $\Theta : (\bar{S}^{(g)})^n \rightarrow \bar{S}^{(g)}$, where $\bar{S}^{(g)} = \{s_\alpha | \alpha \in [-g, g]\}$, $H = \{h_S^1, h_S^2, \ldots, h_S^n\}$ is a set of n EHFLTSs defined on the reference set X based on $\bar{S}^{(g)}$. The extension of Θ on H is defined for each $x \in X$ by:

$$\Theta_H(x) = \cup_{(s_{\alpha_1}, s_{\alpha_2}, \ldots, s_{\alpha_n}) \in \{h_S^1 \times h_S^2 \times \cdots \times h_S^n\}} \{\Theta(s_{\alpha_1}, s_{\alpha_2}, \ldots, s_{\alpha_n})\} \tag{3.1}$$

According to Definition 3.1, the existing aggregation operators of VLTs can be extended to the setting of EHFLTSs. In the rest of this section, two sets of EHFLTSs are denoted by $H = \{h_S^j\}$ and $\dot{H} = \{\dot{h}_S^j\}$, $j = 1, 2, \ldots, n$. The number of linguistic terms in h_S^j and $\dot{h}_S^j$ are denoted by $\#h_S^j$ and $\#\dot{h}_S^j$. Linguistic terms in h_S^j and $\dot{h}_S^j$ are denoted by s_{α_j} and $s_{\dot{\alpha}_j}$, respectively. Furthermore, the i_j linguistic terms in h_S^j and $\dot{h}_S^j$ are specified by $s_{\alpha_{ji_j}}$ and $s_{\dot{\alpha}_{ji_j}}$ if necessary. We will introduce two classes of aggregation operators according to the form of weighting vector in the sequel.

3.2.1.1 Aggregation Operators with Linguistic Weights

Given a set of n EHFLTs are denoted by $\{h_S^j\}(j = 1, 2, \ldots, n)$, their corresponding weights take the form of linguistic terms from $\bar{S}^{(g)}$. Herrera and Herrera-Viedma [5] provided the linguistic weighted disjunction (LWD) operators in the setting values and the weights of objects are represented by simple linguistic terms. As the extension of the LWD operator, we have the following operator:

Definition 3.2 ([19]) Let $\{h_S^j\}(j = 1, 2, \ldots, n)$ be n EHFLTSs, $\omega = (\omega_1, \omega_2, \ldots, \omega_n)$ be the weighting vector such that $\omega_j \in \bar{S}^{(g)}(j = 1, 2, \ldots, n)$. A mapping $EHFLWD : (\bar{S}^{(g)})^n \to \bar{S}^{(g)}$ is called an extended hesitant fuzzy linguistic weighted disjunction (EHFLWD) operator of dimension n if

$$EHFLWD(h_S^1, h_S^2, \ldots, h_S^n) = \mathop{\vee}_{j=1}^{n} (\omega_j \wedge h_S^j)$$
$$= \cup_{s_{\alpha_1} \in h_S^1, \ldots, s_{\alpha_n} \in h_S^n} \{\max_j \{\min\{\omega_j, s_{\alpha_j}\}\}\} \tag{3.2}$$

If $\omega = (s_g, \ldots, s_g)$, where s_g is the largest term in $\bar{S}^{(g)}$, then $\omega_j \wedge h_S^j = h_S^j$, we have

$$EHFLWD(h_S^1, h_S^2, \ldots, h_S^n) = \mathop{\vee}_{j=1}^{n} h_S^j$$

However, $\mathop{\vee}_{j=1}^{n} h_S^j \neq \max_j\{h_S^j\}$.

The OWA operator [25] provides an aggregation strategy to lie between the max and min operators because of its re-ordering step. In linguistic setting, Yager [26] presented an ordinal form of the OWA operator. Motivated by which, we introduce the OWA operator in the extended hesitant fuzzy linguistic setting.

Definition 3.3 ([19]) Let $\{h_S^j\}(j = 1, 2, \ldots, n)$ be n EHFLTSs. An extended hesitant fuzzy ordinal OWA (EHFOOWA) operator of dimension n is a mapping $EHFOOWA : (\bar{S}^{(g)})^n \to \bar{S}^{(g)}$ such that

$$EHFOOWA(h_S^1, h_S^2, \ldots, h_S^n) = \mathop{\vee}_{j=1}^{n} (w_j \wedge h_S^{\sigma(j)})$$
$$= \cup_{s_{\alpha_{\sigma(1)}} \in h_S^{\sigma(1)}, \ldots, s_{\alpha_{\sigma(n)}} \in h_S^{\sigma(n)}} \{\max_j \{\min\{w_j, s_{\alpha_{\sigma(j)}}\}\}\} \tag{3.3}$$

where $\mathbf{w} = (w_1, w_2, \ldots, w_n)$ is the associated weighting vector, $w_j \in \bar{S}^{(g)}(j = 1, 2, \ldots, n)$, $h_S^{\sigma(j)}$is the j-th largest element of $\{h_S^j\}$.

If $\mathbf{w} = (s_g, s_{-g}, \ldots, s_{-g})$, then $w_1 \wedge h_S^{\sigma(1)} = h_S^{\sigma(1)}$, $w_j \wedge h_S^{\sigma(j)} = w_j (\forall j = 2, 3, \ldots, n)$, we have

$$EHFOOWA(h_S^1, h_S^2, \ldots, h_S^n) = h_S^{\sigma(1)} \vee s_{-g} \vee \cdots \vee s_{-g} = h_S^{\sigma(1)} = \max_j \{h_S^j\}$$

The EHFOOWA operator is reduced to the extended hesitant fuzzy linguistic max (EHFLM1) operator. Similarly, if $\mathbf{w} = (s_{-g}, \ldots, s_{-g}, s_g)$, $EHFOOWA(h_S^1, h_S^2, \ldots, h_S^n) = \min_j \{h_S^j\}$, The EHFOOWA operator is reduced to the extended hesitant fuzzy linguistic min (EHFLM2) operator in this case.

Consider that the LWD operator weights only the values themselves, while the ordinal OWA operator weights the re-ordered positions of the values only, Xu [23] proposed an ordinal hybrid aggregation (OHA) operator to reflect the importance degrees of both the linguistic arguments and their ordered positions. Based on the same idea, the follow aggregation operator can be defined:

Definition 3.4 ([19]) Let $\{h_S^j\} (j = 1, 2, \ldots, n)$ be n EHFLTSs. An extended hesitant fuzzy ordinal hybrid aggregation (EHFOHA) operator of dimension n is a mapping $EHFOHA : (\bar{S}^{(g)})^n \rightarrow \bar{S}^{(g)}$ such that

$$\begin{aligned} EHFOHA(h_S^1, h_S^2, \ldots, h_S^n) &= \bigvee_{j=1}^{n} (w_j \wedge h_S^{\dot{\sigma}(j)}) \\ &= \bigcup_{s_{\alpha_{\dot{\sigma}(1)}} \in h_S^{\dot{\sigma}(1)}, \ldots, s_{\alpha_{\dot{\sigma}(n)}} \in h_S^{\dot{\sigma}(n)}} \{\max_j \{\min\{w_j, s_{\alpha_{\dot{\sigma}(j)}}\}\}\} \end{aligned} \quad (3.4)$$

where $\mathbf{w} = (w_1, w_2, \ldots, w_n)$ is the associated weighting vector, $w_j \in \bar{S}^{(g)}$ $(j = 1, 2, \ldots, n)$, $h_S^{\dot{\sigma}(j)}$ is the j-th largest element in $\{\bar{h}_S^j = \omega_j \wedge h_S^j\}$, $\omega = (\omega_1, \omega_2, \ldots, \omega_n)$ is the weighting vector of $\{h_S^j\}$, $\omega_j \in \bar{S}^{(g)} (j = 1, 2, \ldots, n)$.

Especially, if $\mathbf{w} = (s_g, s_g, \ldots, s_g)$, then $\forall h_S^{\dot{\sigma}(j)}$, $w_j \wedge h_S^{\dot{\sigma}(j)} = h_S^{\dot{\sigma}(j)}$,

$$EHFOHA(h_S^1, h_S^2, \ldots, h_S^n) = \bigvee_{j=1}^{n} (w_j \wedge h_S^{\dot{\sigma}(j)}) = \bigvee_{j=1}^{n} h_S^{\dot{\sigma}(j)} = \bigvee_{j=1}^{n} (\omega \wedge h_S^j)$$

thus the EHFOHA operator is reduced to the EHFLWD operator. If $\omega = (s_g, s_g, \ldots, s_g)$, then $\omega_j \wedge h_S^j = h_S^j (\forall h_S^j)$, thus the EHFOHA operator is reduced to the EHFOOWA operator.

3.2.1.2 Aggregation Operators with Numerical Weights

Except for linguistic weights, numerical weights are often used in application as well. In this case, several aggregation operators are developed in linguistic setting, such as the linguistic weighted averaging (LWA) operator [24], the linguistic OWA operator [24], the linguistic hybrid aggregation (LHA) operator [23], the induced linguistic

OWA operator [24] and so on. Based on the extension principle and some existing linguistic aggregation operator, some new aggregation operators can be developed as follows:

Definition 3.5 ([19]) Let $\{h_S^j\}(j = 1, 2, \ldots, n)$ be n EHFLTSs, their weighting vector is $\omega = (\omega_1, \omega_2, \ldots, \omega_n)$, where $\omega_j \in [0, 1](j = 1, 2, \ldots, n)$ and $\sum_{j=1}^n \omega_j = 1$. A mapping $EHFLWA : (\bar{S}^{(g)})^n \to \bar{S}^{(g)}$ is called an extended hesitant fuzzy linguistic weighted averaging (EHFLWA) operator of dimension n if

$$EHFLWA(h_S^1, h_S^2, \ldots, h_S^n) = \overset{n}{\underset{j=1}{\oplus}} (\omega_j h_S^j)$$

$$= \cup_{s_{\alpha_1} \in h_S^1, \ldots, s_{\alpha_n} \in h_S^n} \{\overset{n}{\underset{j=1}{\oplus}} (\omega_j s_{\alpha_j})\} = \cup_{s_{\alpha_1} \in h_S^1, \ldots, s_{\alpha_n} \in h_S^n} \{s_{\dot{\bar{\alpha}}}\} \tag{3.5}$$

where $\dot{\bar{\alpha}} = \sum_{j=1}^n \omega s_{\alpha_j}$.

The EHFLWA operator extends both the weighted averaging (WA) operator and the LWA operator. In fact, if $\omega = (1/n, 1/n, \ldots, 1/n)$, then the EHFLWA operator is reduced to the extended hesitant fuzzy linguistic averaging (EHFLA) operator:

$$EHFLWA(h_S^1, h_S^2, \ldots, h_S^n) = \cup_{s_{\alpha_1} \in h_S^1, \ldots, s_{\alpha_n} \in h_S^n} \{(\sum\nolimits_{j=1}^n s_{\alpha_j})/n\}$$

Definition 3.6 ([19]) Let $\{h_S^j\}(j = 1, 2, \ldots, n)$ be n EHFLTSs. An EHFLOWA operator of dimension n is a mapping $EHFLOWA : (\bar{S}^{(g)})^n \to \bar{S}^{(g)}$such that

$$EHFLOWA(h_S^1, h_S^2, \ldots, h_S^n) = \overset{n}{\underset{j=1}{\oplus}} (w_j h_S^{\sigma(j)})$$

$$= \cup_{s_{\beta_1} \in h_S^{\sigma(1)}, \ldots, s_{\beta_n} \in h_S^{\sigma(n)}} \{\overset{n}{\underset{j=1}{\oplus}} (w_j s_{\beta_j})\} = \cup_{s_{\beta_1} \in h_S^{\sigma(1)}, \ldots, s_{\beta_n} \in h_S^{\sigma(n)}} \{s_{\bar{\beta}}\} \tag{3.6}$$

where $\bar{\beta} = \sum_{j=1}^n w_j \beta_j$, $h_S^{\sigma(j)}$ is the j-th biggest element of $\{h_S^j\}$, $\mathbf{w} = (w_1, w_2, \ldots, w_n)$ is the associated weighting vector such that $w_j \in [0, 1](j = 1, 2, \ldots, n)$ and $\sum_{j=1}^n w_j = 1$.

If $\mathbf{w} = (1, 0, \ldots, 0)$, then $w_1 h_S^{\sigma(1)} = h_S^{\sigma(1)}$ and $w_j h_S^{\sigma(j)} = s_0$ $(\forall j = 2, 3, \ldots, n)$, thus

$$EHFLOWA(h_S^1, h_S^2, \ldots, h_S^n) = h_S^{\sigma(1)} \oplus s_0 \oplus \cdots \oplus s_0 = \max_j \{h_S^j\}$$

The EHFLOWA operator is reduced to the EHFLM1 operator. Similarly, if $\mathbf{w} = (0, \ldots, 0, 1)$, then the EHFLOWA operator is reduced to the EHFLM2 operator.

According to Definitions 3.5 and 3.6, it is clear that the EHFLWA operator weights the input EHFLTs, while the EHFLOWA operator weights the ordered position instead. The weights represent distinct aspects of inputs in these two operators. The following operator could overcome this drawback:

Definition 3.7 ([19]) Let $\{h_S^j\}(j = 1, 2, \ldots, n)$ be n EHFLTSs, An extended hesitant fuzzy linguistic hybrid aggregation (EHFLHA) operator of dimension n is a mapping $EHFLHA : (\bar{S}^{(g)})^n \rightarrow \bar{S}^{(g)}$ such that

$$EHFLHA(h_S^1, h_S^2, \ldots, h_S^n) = \bigoplus_{j=1}^{n} (w_j h_S^{\dot{\sigma}(j)})$$

$$= \cup_{s_{\dot{\beta}_1} \in h_S^{\sigma(1)}, \ldots, s_{\dot{\beta}_n} \in h_S^{\sigma(n)}} \{ \bigoplus_{j=1}^{n} (w_j s_{\dot{\beta}_j}) \} = \cup_{s_{\dot{\beta}_1} \in h_S^{\sigma(1)}, \ldots, s_{\dot{\beta}_n} \in h_S^{\sigma(n)}} \{ s_{\dot{\bar{\beta}}} \} \quad (3.7)$$

where $\dot{\bar{\beta}} = \sum_{j=1}^{n} w_j \dot{\beta}_j$, $h_S^{\dot{\sigma}(j)}$ is the j-th biggest element of $\{\bar{h}_S^j = n\omega_j h_S^j\}$, $\omega = (\omega_1, \omega_1, \ldots, \omega_n)$ is the weighting vector of $\{h_S^j\}$ such that $\omega_j \in [0, 1] (j = 1, 2, \ldots, n)$ and $\sum_{j=1}^{n} \omega_j = 1$, n is the balancing coefficient, $\mathbf{w} = (w_1, w_2, \ldots, w_n)$ is the associated weighting vector such that $w_j \in [0, 1] (j = 1, 2, \ldots, n)$ and $\sum_{j=1}^{n} w_j = 1$.

If $\mathbf{w} = (1/n, 1/n, \ldots, 1/n)$, according to Theorems 2.15 and 2.16,

$$EHFLHA(h_S^1, h_S^2, \ldots, h_S^n) = \bigoplus_{j=1}^{n} (\frac{1}{n} h_S^{\dot{\sigma}(j)}) = \bigoplus_{j=1}^{n} (\frac{1}{n} n\omega_j h_S^j) = \bigoplus_{j=1}^{n} (\omega_j h_S^j)$$

then the EHFLHA operator is reduced to the EHFLWA operator. Similarly, if $\omega = (1/n, 1/n, \ldots, 1/n)$, then $\bar{h}_S^j = h_S^j$, the EHFLHA operator is reduced to the EHFLOWA operator.

3.2.2 Properties of the Aggregation Operators

We will discuss some properties of the presented aggregation operators in this subsection. Because of the operation $\cup$, most of the operators do not possess excellent mathematical properties, such as monotonicity, idempotency, commutativity and boundary. But, luckily, we will see some operators own properties like these four.

Theorem 3.8 ([19]) *Let* $\{h_S^j\}$ *and* $\{\dot{h}_S^j\}$ $(j = 1, 2, \ldots, n)$ *be two sets of EHFLTSs. If* $\exists i \in \{1, 2, \ldots, n\}$ *such that* $\#h_S^i = \#\dot{h}_S^i = N_i$ *and* $\forall s_{\alpha_{ij_i}} \in h_S^1, s_{\dot{\alpha}_{ij_i}} \in \dot{h}_S^i, s_{\alpha_{ij_i}} \leq s_{\dot{\alpha}_{ij_i}}$, *and* $\forall j \neq i$, $h_S^i = \dot{h}_S^i$, *then we have*

$$EHFLWD(h_S^1, h_S^2, \ldots, h_S^n) \leq EHFLWD(\dot{h}_S^1, \dot{h}_S^2, \ldots, \dot{h}_S^n)$$

Proof Since $s_{\alpha_{ij_i}} \leq s_{\dot{\alpha}_{ij_i}}$, we have $\forall \omega_i \in S^{(g)}, \omega_i \wedge s_{\alpha_{ij_i}} \leq \omega_i \wedge s_{\dot{\alpha}_{ij_i}}$, then

$$\cup_{s_{\alpha_{ij_i}} \in h_S^i} \{\omega_i \wedge s_{\alpha_{ij_i}}\} \leq \cup_{s_{\dot{\alpha}_{ij_i}} \in \dot{h}_S^i} \{\omega_i \wedge s_{\dot{\alpha}_{ij_i}}\}$$

which means $\omega_i \wedge h_S^i \leq \omega_i \wedge \dot{h}_S^i$, thus $EHFLWD(h_S^1, h_S^2, \ldots, h_S^n) = (\omega_1 \wedge h_S^1) \vee \cdots \vee (\omega_i \wedge h_S^i) \vee \cdots \vee (\omega_n \wedge h_S^n) \leq (\omega_1 \wedge h_S^1) \vee \cdots \vee (\omega_i \wedge \dot{h}_S^i) \vee \cdots \vee (\omega_n \wedge h_S^n) = (\omega_1 \wedge \dot{h}_S^1) \vee \cdots \vee (\omega_i \wedge \dot{h}_S^i) \vee \cdots \vee (\omega_n \wedge \dot{h}_S^n) = EHFLWD(\dot{h}_S^1, \dot{h}_S^2, \ldots, \dot{h}_S^n)$. □

Theorem 3.9 ([19] Quasi-Boundary) *Let* $\{h_S^j\}(j = 1, 2, \ldots, n)$ *be* n *EHFLTSs. Then*

$$s_{-L} \leq EHFLWD(h_S^1, h_S^2, \ldots, h_S^n) \leq s_L$$

where $s_{-L} = \min_j\{\min\{\omega_j, \min_{s_{\alpha_j} \in h_S^j}\{s_{\alpha_j}\}\}\}$, $s_L = \max_j\{\max\{\omega_j, \max_{s_{\alpha_j} \in h_S^j}\{s_{\alpha_j}\}\}\}$.

Proof $\forall s_{\alpha_1} \in h_S^1, s_{\alpha_2} \in h_S^2, \ldots, s_{\alpha_n} \in h_S^n$,

$$\begin{aligned}\min_j\{\min\{\omega_j, \min_{s_{\alpha_j} \in h_S^j}\{s_{\alpha_j}\}\}\} &\leq \max_j\{\min\{\omega_j, s_{\alpha_j}\}\}\\ &\leq \max_j\{\max\{\omega_j, \max_{s_{\alpha_j} \in h_S^j}\{s_{\alpha_j}\}\}\}\end{aligned}$$

Thus $s_{-L} \leq E(\cup_{s_{\alpha_1} \in h_S^1, \ldots, s_{\alpha_n} \in h_S^n}\{\max_j\{\min\{\omega_j, s_{\alpha_j}\}\}\}) \leq s_L$, where $E()$ is the expected term defined in Definition 2.18. According to Definition 2.20, $s_{-L} \leq EHFLWD(h_S^1, h_S^2, \ldots, h_S^n) \leq s_L$. □

Similarly, using the same approach, we can easily prove the following theorem:

Theorem 3.10 ([19] Quasi-Boundary) *Let* $\{h_S^j\}(j = 1, 2, \ldots, n)$ *be* n *EHFLTSs. Then*

$$s_{-L} \leq EHFOOWA(h_S^1, h_S^2, \ldots, h_S^n) \leq s_L$$

where $s_{-L} = \min_j\{\min\{w_j, \min_{s_{\alpha_j} \in h_S^j}\{s_{\alpha_j}\}\}\}$, $s_L = \max_j\{\max\{w_j, \max_{s_{\alpha_j} \in h_S^j}\{s_{\alpha_j}\}\}\}$.

Theorem 3.11 ([19] Commutativity) *Let* $\{h_S^j\}(j = 1, 2, \ldots, n)$ *be* n *EHFLTSs. Then we have*

(1) $EHFOOWA(h_S^1, h_S^2, \ldots, h_S^n) = EHFOOWA(\dot{h}_S^1, \dot{h}_S^2, \ldots, \dot{h}_S^n)$;

(2) $EHFLOWA(h_S^1, h_S^2, \ldots, h_S^n) = EHFLOWA(\dot{h}_S^1, \dot{h}_S^2, \ldots, \dot{h}_S^n)$;

where $\dot{h}_S^1, \dot{h}_S^2, \ldots, \dot{h}_S^n$ *is any permutation of* $h_S^1, h_S^2, \ldots, h_S^n$.

Proof (1) Since $\dot{h}_S^1, \dot{h}_S^2, \ldots, \dot{h}_S^n$ is any permutation of $h_S^1, h_S^2, \ldots, h_S^n$, then $h_S^{\sigma(j)} = \dot{h}_S^{\sigma(j)}(\forall j = 1, 2, \ldots, n)$, and thus $EHFOOWA(h_S^1, h_S^2, \ldots, h_S^n) = \overset{n}{\underset{j=1}{\vee}}(w_j \wedge h_S^{\sigma(j)})$ $= \overset{n}{\underset{j=1}{\vee}}(w_j \wedge \dot{h}_S^{\sigma(j)}) = EHFOOWA(\dot{h}_S^1, \dot{h}_S^2, \ldots, \dot{h}_S^n)$.

(2) The proof is similar to (1). □

Theorem 3.12 ([19] Quasi-Idempotency) *Let* h_S *be an EHFLTS,* $\cong$ *be the equivalent relation defined in Definition 2.20, then*

$$EHFLWA(h_S, h_S, \ldots, h_S) \cong h_S$$

Proof Assume $\#h_S = N$, $h_S = \{s_{\beta_1}, s_{\beta_2}, \ldots, s_{\alpha_N}\}$, then

$$E(h_S) = \frac{1}{N} \overset{N}{\underset{j=1}{\oplus}} s_{\beta_j} = s_{\frac{1}{N}\sum_{j=1}^{N}\beta_j}$$

Firstly, we prove $E(EHFLWA(h_S, h_S, \ldots, h_S)) = E(h_S)$. We only prove the case of $n = 2$, other cases ($n \geq 2$) could be proven by mathematical induction. Since $n = 2$,

$$EHFLWA(h_S, h_S) = \omega_1 h_S \oplus \omega_2 h_S = \cup_{s_{\alpha_1} \in h_S, s_{\alpha_2} \in h_S}\{s_{\omega_1\alpha_1+\omega_2\alpha_2}\} \tag{3.8}$$

When α_1 and α_2 traverse $\beta_1, \beta_2, \ldots, \beta_N$, Eq. (3.8) includes N^2 possible values whose sum is $N\omega_1\sum_{j=1}^{N}\beta_j + N\omega_2\sum_{j=1}^{N}\beta_j = N\sum_{j=1}^{N}\beta_j$. Therefore,

$$E(EHFLWA(h_S, h_S)) = s_{\frac{1}{N^2}N\sum_{j=1}^{N}\beta_j} = s_{\frac{1}{N}\sum_{j=1}^{N}\beta_j} = E(h_S)$$

Secondly, we prove $D(EHFLWA(h_S, h_S, \ldots, h_S)) = D(h_S)$, where the function D is the hesitation degree defined in Definition 2.19. The max and min linguistic terms of h_S are denoted by s_{α^+} and s_{α^-}, thus $D(h_S) = (\alpha^+ - \alpha^-)/(2g+1)$. According to the basic operations of EHFLTSs and the definition of the EHFLWA operator, the max virtual linguistic term in $EHFLWA(h_S, h_S, \ldots, h_S)$ is derived if $s_{\alpha_1} = \cdots = s_{\alpha_N} = s_{\alpha^+}$, thus $\overset{N}{\underset{j=1}{\oplus}} \omega_j s_{\alpha_j} = s_{\alpha^+}$. Similarly, the min virtual linguistic term in $EHFLWA(h_S, h_S, \ldots, h_S)$ is s_{α^-}, thus $D(EHFLWA(h_S, h_S, \ldots, h_S)) = D(h_S)$.

According to Definition 2.20, $EHFLWA(h_S, h_S, \ldots, h_S) \cong h_S$. □

Theorem 3.13 ([19] Quasi-Boundary) *Let $\{h_S^j\}(j = 1, 2, \ldots, n)$ be n EHFLTSs. Then*

$$s_{-L} \leq EHFLWA(h_S^1, h_S^2, \ldots, h_S^n) \leq s_L$$

where $s_{-L} = \min_j\{\min_{s_{\alpha_j} \in h_S^j}\{s_{\alpha_j}\}\}$, $s_L = \max_j\{\max_{s_{\alpha_j} \in h_S^j}\{s_{\alpha_j}\}\}$.

Proof Since $\forall i = 1, 2, \ldots, n$,

$$s_{-L} = \min_j\{\min_{s_{\alpha_j} \in h_S^j}\{s_{\alpha_j}\}\} \leq s_{\alpha_i} \leq \max_j\{\max_{s_{\alpha_j} \in h_S^j}\{s_{\alpha_j}\}\} = s_L$$

Then $s_{-L} \leq \overset{n}{\underset{i=1}{\oplus}} \omega_i s_{\alpha_i} \leq s_L$, which leads to

$$s_{-L} \leq E(EHFLWA(h_S^1, h_S^2, \ldots, h_S^n)) \leq s_L$$

Thus $s_{-L} \leq EHFLWA(h_S^1, h_S^2, \ldots, h_S^n) \leq s_L$. □

3.2.3 Implementation of the MGDM Processes

This section will implement the MGDM processes presented in Sect. 3.1 in the setting of EHFLTSs. The problem description can be found in Sect. 3.1.1. Figure 3.3 illustrates the three parts of the proposed approach [19].

Part 1. Structure of groups in the organization. Experts in each group are homogeneous while experts in different groups are heterogeneous. Each group deals with a part of evaluations according to its knowledge and speciality. Individuals of a group work in isolation if possible. The whole organization works collectively to complete the entire evaluations.

Part 2. Evaluation and transformation. Given a linguistic term set $S^{(g)}$, HFLTSs can be directly used by the experts to elicit several linguistic values for a linguistic variable when they hesitate among several values. However, such elements are not similar to human beings' way of thinking and reasoning. Therefore, Rogríguez et al. [16] defined a context-free grammar to generate linguistic expressions that are more similar to human beings' expressions. Then the linguistic expressions provided by experts are transformed into HFLTSs by using a transformation function. According to the way of individual thinking in fuzzy uncertain circumstance and the proposed construction axiom, in this model, individual evaluations are represented by linguistic expressions similar to human beings' way of thinking and reasoning and then transformed to HFLTSs.

Part 3. Synthesis for decision-making. In this phase, two tools are used for synthesis. The union operation is used to transform HFLTSs to a generalized case, EHFLTSs. Aggregation operators are used to synthesize opinions represented by EHFLTSs. The most difference between union and aggregation operator is that all the original information are kept when the former is used while averaging value is obtained by some means when an aggregation operator is used. Thus this model can reduce the use of aggregation operators and eliminate loss of information.

Suppose that the decision organization G is divided into r groups $G = \{G_l | l = 1, 2, \ldots, r\}$ whose weights are denoted by $\omega^{(G)} = (\omega_1^{(G)}, \omega_2^{(G)}, \ldots, \omega_r^{(G)})$. The weights of criteria $C = \{c_j | j = 1, 2, \ldots, n\}$ are denoted by $\omega^{(C)} = (\omega_1^{(C)}, \omega_2^{(C)}, \ldots, \omega_n^{(C)})$. Group G_l is authorized to evaluate the set of alternatives $A = \{a_1, a_2, \ldots, a_m\}$ with respect to a subset of criteria SC_l. In this section, we implement the MGDM processes in Sect. 3.1.2 by two different scenarios with different types of weights [19]. For simplicity, we suppose that every group is authorized to evaluate alternatives with respect to the whole set of criteria.

(1) *Weights take the form of linguistic terms*. Suppose $\omega_l^{(G)} \in S^{(g)}$, $\omega_j^{(C)} \in S^{(g)}$, $l = 1, 2, \ldots, r$, $j = 1, 2, \ldots, n$. The process of the second scenario in Sect. 3.1.2 can be specified by the following Approach 1.

Step 1: Union within each group. The evaluation information of a_i, with respect to the criterion c_j, provided by the group G_l, denoted by $h_S(a_i, c_j, G_l)$, is derived by:

$$h_S(a_i, c_j, G_l) = \cup_{k=1}^{\#G_l} h_S(a_i, c_j, e_{lk})$$

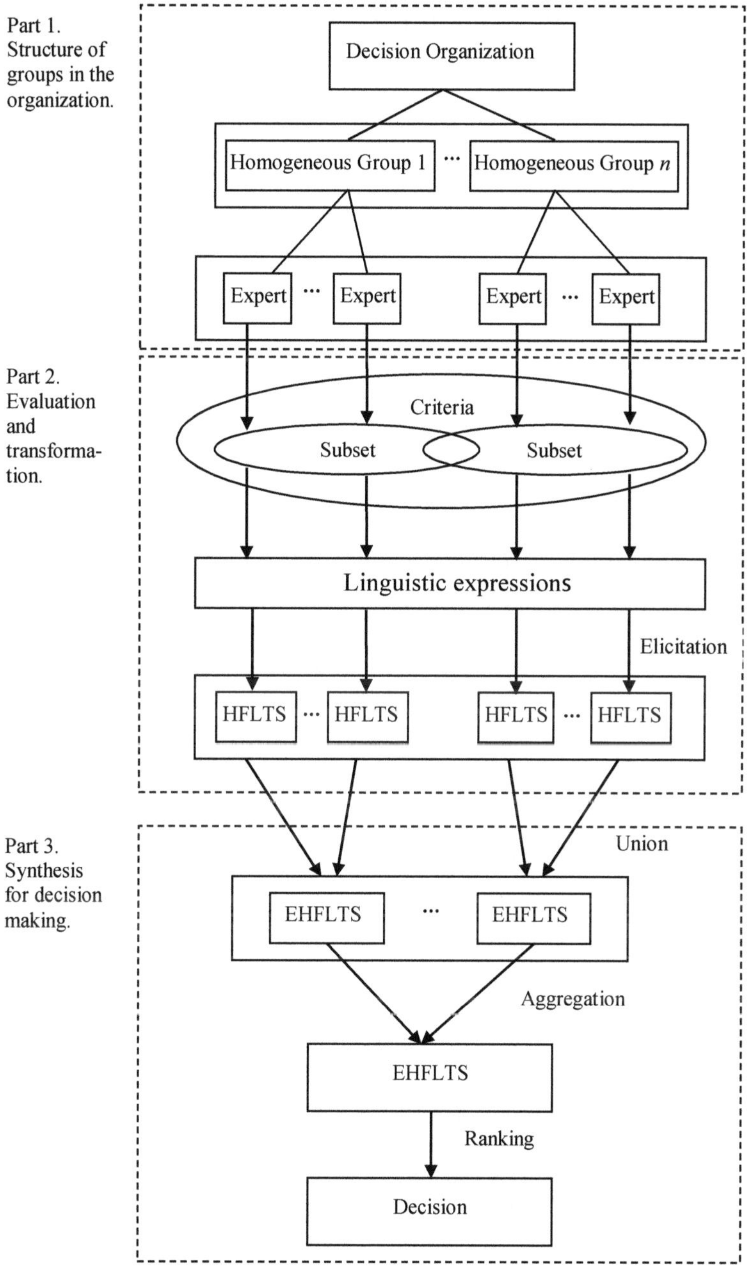

Fig. 3.3 Implementation of MGDM processes in the setting of EHFLTSs

where $\#G_l$ is the number of experts in G_l, $l = 1, 2, \ldots, r$, $i = 1, 2, \ldots, m$, $j = 1, 2, \ldots, n$.

Step 2: The collective overall preference values of a_i with respect to the criterion c_j, denoted by $h_S(a_i, c_j)$, are obtained by the EHFOHA operator:

$$h_S(a_i, c_j) = EHFOHA(h_S(a_i, c_j, G_1), h_S(a_i, c_j, G_2), \ldots, h_S(a_i, c_j, G_r))$$

where $i = 1, 2, \ldots, m$, $j = 1, 2, \ldots, n$, $\mathbf{w} = (w_1, w_2, \ldots, w_r)$ is the associated weighting vector of the EHFOHA operator, $w_l \in S^{(g)}$, $l = 1, 2, \ldots, r$.

Step 3: The overall preference values of a_i, denoted by $h_S(a_i)$, are obtained by utilizing the EHFLWD operator:

$$h_S(a_i) = EHFLWD(h_S(a_i, c_1), h_S(a_i, c_2), \ldots, h_S(a_i, c_n))$$

where $i = 1, 2, \ldots, m$.

Step 4: Utilize the overall preference values $h_S(a_i)$ to rank the alternatives.

(2) *Weights take the form of real numbers*. Let $\omega_l^{(G)} \in [0, 1]$, $l = 1, 2, \ldots, r$, $\sum_{l=1}^{r} \omega_l^{(G)} = 1$, $\omega_j^{(C)} \in [0, 1]$, $j = 1, 2, \ldots, n$, $\sum_{j=1}^{n} \omega_l^{(C)} = 1$. Then the process of the second scenario in Sect. 3.1.2 can be specified by the following Approach 2.

Step 1: See Step 1 of Approach 1.

Step 2: The collective overall preference values of a_i with respect to the criterion c_j, denoted by $h_S(a_i, c_j)$, are obtained by the EHFLHA operator:

$$h_S(a_i, c_j) = EHFLHA(h_S(a_i, c_j, G_1), h_S(a_i, c_j, G_2), \ldots, h_S(a_i, c_j, G_r))$$

where $i = 1, 2, \ldots, m$, $j = 1, 2, \ldots, n$, $\mathbf{w} = (w_1, w_2, \ldots, w_r)$ is the associated weighting vector of the EHFLHA operator such that $w_l \in [0, 1]$, $l = 1, 2, \ldots, r$, $\sum_{l=1}^{n} w_l = 1$.

Step 3: The overall preference values of a_i, denoted by $h_S(a_i)$, are obtained utilizing the EHFLWA operator:

$$h_S(a_i) = EHFLWA(h_S(a_i, c_1), h_S(a_i, c_2), \ldots, h_S(a_i, c_n))$$

where $i = 1, 2, \ldots, m$.

Step 4: See Step 4 of Approach 1.

We assumed that the weighting vectors are completely known in the above scenarios. In fact, if the weighting vector of criteria is absolutely unknown, then we can use the corresponding OWA operator instead of the weighted averaging operator. That is, in Step 3 of the two scenarios, we can replace the EHFLWD operator and the EHFLWA operator with the EHFOOWA operator and the EHFLOWA operator respectively. Further, the associated weighting vector of the EHFLOWA operator can be determined by the normal distribution based method or others [22].

3.2.4 Applications

In this section, we apply the proposed linguistic MGDM approaches in a practical example of evaluating university faculty for tenure and promotion [1, 23]. The criteria used in some universities are c_1: teaching, c_2: research, and c_3: service (whose weighting vector is $\omega^{(C)} = (0.14, 0.26, 0.6)$). Five alternatives (faculty candidates), $\{a_i | i = 1, 2, 3, 4, 5\}$, are to be evaluated using the LTS $S^{(3)} = \{s_{-3}, \ldots, s_0, \ldots, s_3\}$ by two groups of experts (whose weighting vector is $\omega^{(G)} = (0.6, 0.4)$). After elicitation, the experts' evaluation information is listed in Table 3.1. As the weighting vectors take the form of real numbers, we utilize Approach 2 to meet a decision [19].

Step 1: The evaluation information of the two groups is derived by the union of HFLTSs provided by the experts of each group. The results are listed in Table 3.2.

Table 3.1 Decision information provided by the two groups of experts

Group	Expert	Criterion	a_1	a_2	a_3	a_4	a_5
G_1	e_{11}	c_1	$\{s_{-1}, s_0\}$	$\{s_{-2}\}$	$\{s_{-1}, s_0\}$	$\{s_2\}$	$\{s_1, s_2\}$
		c_2	$\{s_0\}$	$\{s_1, s_2\}$	$\{s_{-2}\}$	$\{s_1, s_2\}$	$\{s_1\}$
		c_3	$\{s_2\}$	$\{s_2, s_3\}$	$\{s_2\}$	$\{s_{-1}\}$	$\{s_{-1}, s_0\}$
	e_{12}	c_1	$\{s_{-1}\}$	$\{s_{-2}\}$	$\{s_{-1}\}$	$\{s_2\}$	$\{s_{-1}\}$
		c_2	$\{s_2, s_3\}$	$\{s_1\}$	$\{s_{-2}\}$	$\{s_1\}$	$\{s_1, s_2\}$
		c_3	$\{s_2\}$	$\{s_1, s_2\}$	$\{s_2\}$	$\{s_1\}$	$\{s_2\}$
	e_{13}	c_1	$\{s_{-1}, s_0\}$	$\{s_0\}$	$\{s_0, s_1\}$	$\{s_2, s_3\}$	$\{s_{-1}\}$
		c_2	$\{s_0\}$	$\{s_1, s_2\}$	$\{s_{-2}\}$	$\{s_2\}$	$\{s_1\}$
		c_3	$\{s_0\}$	$\{s_1, s_2\}$	$\{s_2\}$	$\{s_{-1}\}$	$\{s_{-1}, s_0\}$
G_2	e_{21}	c_1	$\{s_0\}$	$\{s_1, s_2\}$	$\{s_1\}$	$\{s_2\}$	$\{s_{-1}\}$
		c_2	$\{s_1, s_2\}$	$\{s_1\}$	$\{s_0, s_1\}$	$\{s_1, s_2\}$	$\{s_2\}$
		c_3	$\{s_0\}$	$\{s_3\}$	$\{s_2\}$	$\{s_2\}$	$\{s_2\}$
	e_{22}	c_1	$\{s_2\}$	$\{s_2\}$	$\{s_0, s_1\}$	$\{s_2\}$	$\{s_2\}$
		c_2	$\{s_2, s_3\}$	$\{s_1\}$	$\{s_{-2}\}$	$\{s_1\}$	$\{s_2\}$
		c_3	$\{s_1\}$	$\{s_0\}$	$\{s_1\}$	$\{s_{-1}, s_0\}$	$\{s_{-1}, s_0\}$

Table 3.2 The collective decision information represented by EHFLTSs

Group	Criterion	a_1	a_2	a_3	a_4	a_5
G_1	c_1	$\{s_{-1}, s_0\}$	$\{s_{-2}, s_0\}$	$\{s_{-1}, s_0, s_1\}$	$\{s_2, s_3\}$	$\{s_{-1}, s_1, s_2\}$
	c_2	$\{s_0, s_2, s_3\}$	$\{s_1, s_2\}$	$\{s_{-2}\}$	$\{s_1, s_2\}$	$\{s_1, s_2\}$
	c_3	$\{s_0, s_2\}$	$\{s_1, s_2, s_3\}$	$\{s_2\}$	$\{s_{-1}, s_1\}$	$\{s_{-1}, s_0, s_2\}$
G_2	c_1	$\{s_{-2}, s_0\}$	$\{s_1, s_2\}$	$\{s_0, s_1\}$	$\{s_2\}$	$\{s_{-1}, s_2\}$
	c_2	$\{s_1, s_2, s_3\}$	$\{s_1\}$	$\{s_{-2}, s_0, s_1\}$	$\{s_1, s_2\}$	$\{s_2\}$
	c_3	$\{s_0, s_1\}$	$\{s_0, s_3\}$	$\{s_1, s_2\}$	$\{s_{-1}, s_0, s_2\}$	$\{s_{-1}, s_1, s_3\}$

Table 3.3 Group decision matrix represented by EHFLTSs

	c_1	c_2	c_3
a_1	$\{s_{0.6}, s_0, s_{0.2}, s_{0.8}\}$	$\{s_{0.4}, s_{0.8}, s_{1.2}, s_{1.6}, s_2, s_{2.2}, s_{2.4}, s_{2.6}, s_3\}$	$\{s_0, s_{0.4}, s_{1.2}, s_{1.6}\}$
a_2	$\{s_{0.4}, s_{0.8}, s_{1.6}, s_2\}$	$\{s_1, s_{1.6}\}$	$\{s_{0.6}, s_{1.2}, s_{1.8}, s_{2.4}, s_3\}$
a_3	$\{s_{-1}, s_{-0.6}, s_{-0.4}, s_0, s_{0.2}, s_{0.6}\}$	$\{s_{-2}, s_{-1.2}, s_{0.8}\}$	$\{s_{-1.6}, s_2\}$
a_4	$\{s_2, s_{2.6}\}$	$\{s_1, s_{1.4}, s_{1.6}, s_2\}$	$\{s_{-1}, s_{-0.6}, s_{0.2}, s_{0.6}, s_{1.4}\}$
a_5	$\{s_{-1}, s_{0.2}, s_{0.8}, s_{1.4}, s_2\}$	$\{s_{1.4}, s_2\}$	$\{s_{-1}, s_{-0.4}, s_{-0.2}, s_{0.4}, s_{0.6}, s_{0.8}, s_{1.2}, s_{1.6}, s_{2.4}\}$

Step 2: The performances of alternatives with respect to the set of criteria can be derived by using the EHFLHA operator with $\mathbf{w} = (0.5, 0.5)$, which are shown in Table 3.3.

Step 3: The overall performances of alternatives are derived by the EHFLWA operator. The resultant expected terms are:

$$E(h_S(a_1)) = s_{0.797},\ E(h_S(a_2)) = s_{1.586},\ E(h_S(a_3)) = s_{0.7053},$$
$$E(h_S(a_4)) = s_{0.792},\ E(h_S(a_5)) = s_{0.886}$$

Step 4: Based on Definition 2.20, the ranking of 5 alternatives is:

$$a_3 \prec a_4 \prec a_1 \prec a_5 \prec a_2$$

Thus a_2 is the best alternative.

3.2.5 *Comparative Analysis*

As an alternative solution of the above problem, the LA operator, the LWA operator and LHA operator are used for comparison. Without the idea of hesitation, we cannot deal with several possible values at the same time. Thus if experts have hesitancy among several possible linguistic terms, a pre-aggregation step has to be done, and then an averaging value is computed by some means. Following the advice of Xu [23], the problem can be processed by some steps.

Step 1: If an expert has hesitancy among several possible linguistic terms, the LA operator is used to obtain the corresponding averaging values. For example, the resultant decision matrix provided by e_{11} is transformed into Table 3.4.

Step 2: The evaluations within each group are synthesized by the LA operator as well as the relative weights of experts within a group are indifferent. For example, the resultant decision matrix of G_1 is shown in Table 3.5.

Table 3.4 Decision matrix derived by e_{11} after pre-aggregation

Criterion	a_1	a_2	a_3	a_4	a_5
c_1	$s_{-0.5}$	s_{-2}	$s_{-0.5}$	s_2	$s_{1.5}$
c_2	s_0	$s_{1.5}$	s_{-2}	$s_{1.5}$	s_1
c_3	s_2	$s_{2.5}$	s_2	s_{-1}	$s_{-0.5}$

Table 3.5 Decision matrix of G_1 after second aggregation

Criteria	a_1	a_2	a_3	a_4	a_5
c_1	$s_{-0.6667}$	s_{-1}	$s_{-0.3333}$	$s_{2.1667}$	$s_{0.1667}$
c_2	$s_{0.8333}$	$s_{1.3333}$	s_{-2}	$s_{1.5}$	$s_{1.1667}$
c_3	$s_{1.3333}$	$s_{1.8333}$	s_2	$s_{0.3333}$	$s_{0.3333}$

Table 3.6 The final decision matrix after third aggregation

Criterion	a_1	a_2	a_3	a_4	a_5
c_1	s_0	$s_{0.1}$	$s_{0.1}$	$s_{2.1}$	$s_{0.3}$
c_2	$s_{1.3}$	$s_{0.6}$	$s_{-0.5}$	$s_{1.4}$	$s_{1.5}$
c_3	s_1	$s_{1.7}$	$s_{1.8}$	$s_{-0.5}$	$s_{0.5}$

Step 3: We aggregate the results of Step 2 by the LHA operator to obtain the final decision matrix. The weighting vector and the associated weighting vector are the same as those of Sect. 3.2.4. The result is presented in Table 3.6.

Step 4: The overall performances of alternatives are:

$$z_1 = s_{0.938}, z_2 = s_{1.19}, z_3 = s_{0.704}, z_4 = s_{0.958}, z_5 = s_{0.732}$$

Step 5: The alternatives can be ranked as: $a_3 \prec a_5 \prec a_1 \prec a_4 \prec a_2$.

Based on the procedures of the comparable processes, we discuss their differences by the following aspects:

(1) Number of times of using aggregation operators. As the idea of HFS is used, the introduced model and process need less aggregation. Compared to the existing process, the pre-aggregation step in expert level is eliminated. Further, aggregation within each group is conducted by the operation $\cup$ rather than an aggregation operator.

(2) Possible values versus averaging values. Because of less aggregation operator is used, all possible values, rather than only averaging values, are maintained for consideration. As in Tables 3.1 and 3.4, the introduced process uses HFLTSs to represent experts' opinions, while the existing process has to synthesize all possible linguistic terms to an averaging value. The same phenomenon happens in each level of aggregation. Therefore, the introduced process handles all possible values along with the procedure of aggregation, it is more meaningful than considering just averaging values as there is no loss of information.

(3) Final decisions. The two methods are different but agree on the first choice a_2, which validates that the introduced process is reasonable and it is useful to consider all possible values. We can also see that the priorities of five alternatives are distinct. There is a rank reversal between a_4 and a_5. The introduced process uses all possible values for synthesis and needs less aggregation, as analyzed above, thus the final decision would be more rational.

3.3 A Two-Phase GDM Approach Based on Admissible Orders

We shall focus on the use of admissible orders developed in Sect. 2.3 in GDM in this section. In order that, the extended hesitant fuzzy linguistic OWA (EHFLOWA) operator based on admissible orders is introduced at first.

3.3.1 Defining the EHFLOWA Operator Based on Admissible Orders

Zhang and Wu [27] proposed the EHFLOWA operator by defining the order of EHFLTSs with the expected term. Moreover, Wang [19] defined an improved version according to the partial order $\preceq_W$ defined in Eq. (2.25). However, it is not sufficient if some input elements are not comparable with respect to these partial orders. This section introduces a new definition of the EHFLOWA operator. The linguistic OWA operator for CWW is as follows:

Definition 3.14 ([24]) Let $\{s_{\alpha_1}, s_{\alpha_2}, \ldots, s_{\alpha_m}\}$ be m linguistic terms, $\mathbf{w} = (w_1, w_2, \ldots, w_m) \in [0, 1]^m$ be the associated vector such that $\sum_{i=1}^m w_i = 1$. A linguistic OWA operator of dimension m associated with $\mathbf{w}$ is a mapping $LOWA_{\mathbf{w}} : (S^{(g)})^m \to S^{(g)}$ such that

$$LOWA_{\mathbf{w}}(s_{\alpha_1}, s_{\alpha_2}, \ldots, s_{\alpha_m}) = \bigoplus_{i=1}^{m} (w_i s_{\alpha_{\sigma(i)}}) \tag{3.9}$$

where $s_{\alpha_{\sigma(i)}}$ is the i-th largest of $\{s_{\alpha_1}, s_{\alpha_2}, \ldots, s_{\alpha_m}\}$.

For convenience, a set of m EHFLTSs, normalized by the technique of Sect. 2.3, is denoted by $H = \{h_S^i | i = 1, 2, \ldots, m\}$, where $h_S^i = \{s_{\alpha_j}^i | j = 1, 2, \ldots, n\} \in \mathcal{E}^n(S)$. Given the admissible order $\preceq$ defined in Definition 2.24, the EHFLOWA operator can be generalized as follows [20]:

Definition 3.15 ([24]) Let $H = \{h_S^i | i = 1, 2, \ldots, m\}$ be m EHFLTSs, $\mathbf{w} = (w_1, w_2, \ldots, w_m) \in [0, 1]^m$ be the associated vector such that $\sum_{i=1}^m w_i = 1$, and $\preceq$ be an admissible order on $\mathcal{E}^n(S)$. An EHFLOWA operator of dimension m associated with $\preceq$ and $\mathbf{w}$ is a mapping $EHFLOWA_{\mathbf{w}}^{\preceq} : (\mathcal{E}^n(S))^m \to \mathcal{E}^n(S)$ such that

$$EHFLOWA_{\mathbf{w}}^{\preceq}(h_S^1, h_S^2, \ldots, h_S^m) = \bigoplus_{i=1}^{m} (w_i h_S^{\sigma(i)}) \tag{3.10}$$

where $h_S^{\sigma(i)}$ is the i-th largest of H with respect to the order $\preceq$.

Based on Definition 2.22, Eq. (3.10) can be rewritten as [20]:

$$EHFLOWA_{\mathbf{w}}^{\preceq}(h_S^1, h_S^2, \ldots, h_S^m) = \cup_{j=1}^{n}\{\bigoplus_{i=1}^{m} (w_i s_{\alpha_j}^{\sigma(i)})\} \tag{3.11}$$

where $s_{\alpha_j}^{\sigma(i)}$ is the j-th linguistic term in $h_S^{\sigma(i)}$, $i = 1, 2, \ldots, m$, $j = 1, 2, \ldots, n$.

Example 3.16 Given the LTS $S^{(3)} = \{s_{-3}, \ldots, s_0, \ldots, s_3\}$, let $h_S^1 = \{s_1, s_3\}$ and $h_S^2 = \{s_{-1}, s_0, s_2, s_3\}$, $\mathbf{w} = (0.4, 0.6)$. If we let $\xi = 0.5$, then h_S^1 is normalized to $h_S^1 = \{s_1, s_2, s_2, s_3\}$. Using the order $\preceq_{D_n}$ defined in Eq. (2.37), we have $h_S^2 \preceq_{D_n} h_S^1$, and $EHFLOWA_{\mathbf{w}}^{\preceq}(h_S^1, h_S^2) = \{0.4s_1 \oplus 0.6s_{-1}, 0.4s_2 \oplus 0.6s_0, 0.4s_2 \oplus s_2, 0, 4s_3 \oplus 0.6s_3\} = \{s_{-0.2}, s_{0.8}, s_2, s_3\}$. Furthermore, let $h_S^3 = \{s_0, s_2, s_2, s_4\}$, then $h_S^2 \preceq_{D_n} h_S^3$, $EHFLOWA_{\mathbf{w}}^{\preceq}(h_S^3, h_S^2) = \{s_{-0.6}, s_{0.8}, s_2, s_{3.4}\}$. Thus we have

$$EHFLOWA_{\mathbf{w}}^{\preceq}(h_S^1, h_S^2) \preceq_{D_n} EHFLOWA_{\mathbf{w}}^{\preceq}(h_S^3, h_S^2)$$

but $h_S^3 \preceq_{D_n} h_S^1$.

Example 3.16 demonstrates that the EHFLOWA operator may be not increasingly monotonic with respect to the admissible order $\preceq$. According to Sect. 3.2.2, the EHFLOWA operator based on the partial order $\preceq_W$ is not monotonic as well. Fortunately, if the admissible order is generated by the mapping K_λ defined in Eq. (2.41), we have the following theorem [20]:

Theorem 3.17 ([24]) *Let $\preceq$ be an admissible order on $\mathcal{E}^n(S)$ generated by the n-tuple $(K_\lambda, f_2, \ldots, f_n)$, $EHFLOWA_{\mathbf{w}}^{\preceq}$ be the EHFLOWA operator defined by Eq. (3.11). Then*

$$\begin{aligned} &K_\lambda(EHFLOWA_{\mathbf{w}}^{\preceq}(h_S^1, h_S^2, \ldots, h_S^m)) \\ &= LOWA_{\mathbf{w}}(K_\lambda(h_S^1), K_\lambda(h_S^2), \ldots, K_\lambda(h_S^m)) \end{aligned} \tag{3.12}$$

Proof According to the definition of K_λ, it is obvious that $h_S^{\sigma(1)} \preceq h_S^{\sigma(2)} \preceq \cdots \preceq h_S^{\sigma(m)}$ if $K_\lambda(h_S^{\sigma(1)}) \leq K_\lambda(h_S^{\sigma(2)}) \leq \cdots \leq K_\lambda(h_S^{\sigma(m)})$. Thus,

$$\begin{aligned} K_\lambda(EHFLOWA_{\mathbf{w}}^{\preceq}(h_S^1, h_S^2, \ldots, h_S^m)) &= K_\lambda(\cup_{j=1}^{n}\{\bigoplus_{i=1}^{m} (w_i s_{\alpha_j}^{\sigma(i)})\}) \\ = \bigoplus_{i=1}^{m} w_i K_\lambda(\cup_{j=1}^{n}\{s_{\alpha_j}^{\sigma(i)}\}) &= \bigoplus_{i=1}^{m} w_i K_\lambda(h_S^{\sigma(i)}) \\ = LOWA_{\mathbf{w}}(K_\lambda(h_S^1), K_\lambda(h_S^2), \ldots, K_\lambda(h_S^m)) & \end{aligned}$$

□

We can see that Eq. (3.12) is irrelevant to $(f_2, \ldots, f_n)$. Then the increasing monotonicity of the EHFLOWA operator can be clarified [20]:

Theorem 3.18 ([24]) *Let $\preceq$ be an admissible order on $\mathcal{E}^n(S)$ generated by $(K_{\lambda_1}, K_{\lambda_2}, \ldots, K_{\lambda_n})$. Then the EHFLOWA operator $EHFLOWA_{\mathbf{w}}^{\preceq}$ is an aggregation function on $\mathcal{E}^n(S)$ with respect to $\preceq$.*

Proof Suppose that the inputs of the EHFLOWA operator are $H = \{h_S^i | i = 1, 2, \ldots, m\}$, where $S^{(g)} = \{s_{-g}, \ldots, s_0, \ldots, s_g\}$.

(1) Since the top and the bottom of $(\mathcal{E}^n(S), \preceq)$ are $\{s_g\}$ and $\{s_{-g}\}$, it is obvious that $EHFLOWA_{\mathbf{w}}^{\preceq}(\{s_g\}, \{s_g\}, \ldots, \{s_g\}) = \{s_g\}$, $EHFLOWA_{\mathbf{w}}^{\preceq}(\{s_{-g}\}, \{s_{-g}\}, \ldots, \{s_{-g}\}) = \{s_{-g}\}$.

(2) To show the increasing monotonicity of $EHFLOWA_{\mathbf{w}}^{\preceq}$, we increase any EHFLTS h_S^i to $\dot{h}_S^i$. Because $h_S^i \preceq \dot{h}_S^i$, $K_{\lambda_j}(h_S^i) \leq K_{\lambda_j}(\dot{h}_S^i) (\forall j = 1, 2, \ldots, n)$. According to Theorem 3.17,

$$\begin{aligned}
&K_{\lambda_1}(EHFLOWA_{\mathbf{w}}^{\preceq}(h_S^1, \ldots, h_S^i, \ldots, h_S^m)) \\
&= LOWA_{\mathbf{w}}(K_{\lambda_1}(h_S^1), \ldots, K_{\lambda_1}(h_S^i), \ldots, K_{\lambda_1}(h_S^m)) \\
&\leq LOWA_{\mathbf{w}}(K_{\lambda_1}(h_S^1), \ldots, K_{\lambda_1}(\dot{h}_S^i), \ldots, K_{\lambda_1}(h_S^m)) \\
&= K_{\lambda_1}(EHFLOWA_{\mathbf{w}}^{\preceq}(h_S^1, \ldots, \dot{h}_S^i, \ldots, h_S^m))
\end{aligned}$$

If this inequality is strict, then the result follows. If it reduces to equality, it must be caused by $K_{\lambda_1}(h_S^i) = K_{\lambda_1}(\dot{h}_S^i)$. Then there exists $j \in \{2, 3, \ldots, n\}$ such that $K_{\lambda_1}(h_S^i) < K_{\lambda_1}(\dot{h}_S^i)$. We discuss the problem in two situations:

(i) If the increase from h_S^i to $\dot{h}_S^i$ does not change the ordinal relation of the m inputs, then

$$\begin{aligned}
&K_{\lambda_j}(EHFLOWA_{\mathbf{w}}^{\preceq}(h_S^1, \ldots, h_S^i, \ldots, h_S^m)) \\
&= w_1 K_{\lambda_j}(h_S^{\sigma(1)}) + \cdots + w_i K_{\lambda_j}(h_S^{\sigma(i)}) + \cdots + w_m K_{\lambda_j}(h_S^{\sigma(m)}) \\
&\leq w_1 K_{\lambda_j}(h_S^{\sigma(1)}) + \cdots + w_i K_{\lambda_j}(\dot{h}_S^{\sigma(i)}) + \cdots + w_m K_{\lambda_j}(h_S^{\sigma(m)}) \\
&= K_{\lambda_j}(EHFLOWA_{\mathbf{w}}^{\preceq}(h_S^1, \ldots, \dot{h}_S^i, \ldots, h_S^m))
\end{aligned}$$

(ii) Otherwise, there exists an EHFLTS h_S^k such that

$$K_{\lambda_1}(h_S^i) = K_{\lambda_1}(h_S^k), \ldots, K_{\lambda_{j-1}}(h_S^i) = K_{\lambda_{j-1}}(h_S^k)$$

and $K_{\lambda_j}(h_S^i) < K_{\lambda_j}(h_S^k)$. Moreover,

$$\begin{aligned}
\delta = &K_{\lambda_j}(EHFLOWA_{\mathbf{w}}^{\preceq}(h_S^1, \ldots, h_S^i, \ldots, h_S^m)) \\
&- K_{\lambda_j}(EHFLOWA_{\mathbf{w}}^{\preceq}(h_S^1, \ldots, \dot{h}_S^i, \ldots, h_S^m))
\end{aligned}$$

only depends on h_S^i, $\dot{h}_S^i$ and h_S^k. Simply speaking, if there is only one h_S^k, then the ordered positions of h_S^i and h_S^k in $EHFLOWA_{\mathbf{w}}^{\preceq}(h_S^1, \ldots, h_S^i, \ldots, h_S^m)$ are replaced by h_S^k and $\dot{h}_S^i$, respectively, in $EHFLOWA_{\mathbf{w}}^{\preceq}(h_S^1, \ldots, \dot{h}_S^i, \ldots, h_S^m)$. Due to the linearity of K_{λ_j}, we have $\delta < 0$.

According to (i) and (ii), the increasing monotonicity of the EHFLOWA operator is demonstrated. Then, the result follows immediately. □

Based on Theorem 3.18, it is clear that the EHFLOWA operators $EHFLOWA_{\mathbf{w}}^{\preceq_{Lex1}}$ and $EHFLOWA_{\mathbf{w}}^{\preceq_{Lex2}}$ are aggregation functions.

In practice, the associated weights may take the form of linguistic terms as well, like the case of Definition 3.3. Apparently, it is easy to extend Definition 3.15 to this kind of weighting vectors. We omit the discussion in this section.

3.3.2 The Two-Phase GDM Approach

The mathematical description of the focused GDM problem is: t experts in the set $E = \{e_1, e_2, \ldots, e_t\}$ are authorized to evaluate the set of alternatives $A = \{a_1, a_2, \ldots, a_m\}$ with respect to the set of criteria $C = \{c_1, c_2, \ldots, c_n\}$. Our aim is to figure out the most desirable alternative from A according to the experts' opinions. It is common that the experts prefer to express their evaluations by linguistic terms in qualitative setting. Moreover, the experts may have hesitancy on several terms. Thus, we assume that, generally, the experts express their opinions by the form of EHFLTSs based on the predefined LTS $S^{(g)} = \{s_{-g}, \ldots, s_0, \ldots, s_g\}$. The performance of a_i with respect to c_j, provided by e_k, is an EHFLTS denoted by $h_S(a_i, c_j, e_k)$, $i = 1, 2, \ldots, m$, $j = 1, 2, \ldots, n$, $k = 1, 2, \ldots, t$. Then the linguistic information of e_k can be represented by a matrix $MH_k = (h_S(a_i, c_j, e_k))_{m \times n}$, $k = 1, 2, \ldots, t$.

The two-phase GDM approach is divided into two phases [20]: the aggregation phase and the exploitation phase. The former obtains the overall evaluation of each alternative by the EHFLOWA operator and ranks alternatives according to the selected parameters. If different rankings are derived by distinct parameters, then the latter synthesizes all possible rankings by the social choice theory to obtain a final ranking.

Phase 1. Aggregating through the EHFLOWA operator

In the aggregation phase, the following aggregation process is presented [20].

Step 1: Determine the risk preference and choose an admissible order $\preceq$. The risk preference has to be determined at first so that original linguistic information can be normalized and an admissible order can be selected. It should be noted that obtaining the risk preference is very complicated because both the decision maker's preferences and the practical problem should be considered simultaneously. For example, if the decision maker is optimistic, then ξ can be close to 1 and the order $\preceq_{Lex2}$ can be used; if he/she is pessimistic, then ξ should be close to 0 and the order $\preceq_{Lex1}$ is more logical; if he/she is more or less risk-neutral, then ξ should be close to 0.5 and the order $\preceq_{D_n}$ is more suitable.

Step 2: Determine the weighting vector $\mathbf{w}$. Suppose that the weights of experts and criteria are unknown or indifferent, or the decision maker prefers to conduct aggregations only according to the provided information, then the EHFLOWA operator is very suitable. In this case, some existing methods for determining OWA weights can be used, such as the quantifiers proposed in [25] and the method based on normal distribution [22].

Step 3: Aggregation. Firstly, the set of experts' opinions are aggregated to form the group's decision matrix by the EHFLOWA operator. The resultant matrix is denoted by $MH = (h_S(a_i, c_j))_{m\times n}$, where $h_S(a_i, c_j)$ is the averaging performance of a_i with respect to c_j, $i = 1, 2, \ldots, m$, $j = 1, 2, \ldots, n$. Secondly, the overall performance of a_i, denoted by $h_S(a_i)$, is obtained by aggregating the i-th row of MH using the EHFLOWA operator, $i = 1, 2, \ldots, m$.

Step 4: Ranking. The solution is the alternative which is superior to others with respect to the order $\preceq$.

Comparing with the methods proposed by Rodríguez et al. [16], we use the EHFLOWA operator to fuse information provided by the experts based on the admissible order $\preceq$. The order used here is a total order rather than partial order. Moreover, according to Theorem 3.18, the operator we used is an aggregation function which is of increasing monotonicity. While the advantage of Rodríguez et al. [16] is that it uses all possible terms directly in the aggregation of the criteria level.

Phase 2. Exploiting by the social choice theory

The result of the aggregation algorithm is highly restricted to ξ, $\mathbf{w}$ and $\preceq$. If this information is completely known in the application, we use the above process straightly and the final decision can be reached. However, some of them, such as the order which reflects the risk preferences of the decision makers, are very complex to determine. If we hesitate about some weighting strategies or some appropriate orders, we can run the aggregation process with each combination. Also, if all combinations return the same result, then we can choose the best alternative easily. Generally, if we obtain different rankings of alternatives, an exploiting algorithm based on the social choice theory is introduced as follows [20]: Suppose that a collection of rankings are derived by running the aggregation process.

Step 1: Construct the defeat relation $DR = (dr_{ij})_{m\times m}$, in which dr_{ij} represents the percentage of defeat of a_i by a_j, $i, j = 1, 2, \ldots, m$.

Step 2: Run the MinLexMax Algorithm 1, with DR.

Step 3: Select the winning alternative according to the output of Step 2.

Algorithm 1 The MinLexMax algorithm. Input: DR; Output: Ranking of alternatives

1: Let $k = 1$, $DR^{(k)} = DR$;
2: Find out the maximum value dr_i^{max} of each row of $DR^{(k)}$; Let $Ind_i^{(k)} = \{i|argmin\{dr_i^{max}\}\}$;
3: If $k \geq m$, then output $\{a_i | i \in Ind_i^{(k)}\}$; else go to Step 4;
4: If $\#Ind_i^{(k)} = 1$, then a_i has the minimum largest defeat and is the winning alternative, output a_i; else go to Step 5;
5: Select the rows whose indices are in $Ind_i^{(k)}$ and remove $\min\{dr_i^{max}\}$ from each row, the resultant matrix is denoted by $DR^{(k+1)}$; $k = k + 1$; go to Step 2.

The MinLexMax algorithm outputs a sole winning alternative if a tiny condition is satisfied.

Theorem 3.19 ([20]) *The MinLexMax algorithm returns a sole winning alternative if and only if there does not exist two equal row vectors (after rearrangements in ascending order) in $DR^{(2)}$.*

Proof According to the MinLexMax algorithm, the largest value of each column is removed from the matrix in each loop. If the algorithm stops with $k \geq m$, then there exist at least two rows in $DR^{(2)}$ such that:

(1) In each loop the same value is removed;

(2) The only entries of each of the two rows in the $(m - 1)$-th loop are equal.

Thus, after rearrangements in ascending order, the two row vectors are equal. □

Using the social choice theory, the alternative defeated by the smallest percentages of other alternatives can be figured out. The algorithm enables each possible ranking serves as a voter. All information of the rankings is used to form the defeat relation. The algorithm is very easy to use in real application. We will apply this algorithm in a real GDM problem to clarify its reasonableness.

3.3.3 Application in Evaluations of Energy Technologies

Nowadays, a sustainable energy system is crucial for any countries. The implementation of new and innovative energy technologies is very important for governments [4]. The function of governments is to appraise and select energy technologies and then support the outstanding ones with funding and other incentives for private sector efforts. However, the process of evaluations is really complex because a series of uncertainties and implications might be encountered, such as: (1) the analysis has to face several uncertainties such as fossil fuel price, environmental regulations, market structure, technological, and demand and supply uncertainty [18]; (2) sustainability is inherently vague and complex, and the implications of sustainable developments as a policy objective is difficult to be defined or measured [14]; (3) the necessary information for the evaluations of technologies with respect to their sustainability may be unquantifiable due to its nature or even unavailable since the cost of its computation is too high [4].

The government formed a working organization with 4 experts from the relevant energy "actors". To assess the technologies' impact on the environmental, social, economical and technological dimension of sustainable development, a number of criteria have been selected and shown in Table 3.7. Furthermore, the organization looked systematically into the longer-term future, sought for the technologies which have not been used in any energy sector or have been applied at the initial stage, but are likely to uphold the sustainable development by the four dimensions in Table 3.7. At last, the technologies listed in Table 3.8 have been pre-selected as alternatives. We solve the problem by the approach proposed in the above subsection.

It is natural that most of the criteria are qualitative and cannot be quantified. When expressing the evaluation results, it is more convenient for the experts to use

Table 3.7 Selected criteria of appraising energy technologies

Dimension	Criterion
Economic	c_1: Investment cost, c_2: Economic viability using payback period
Environmental	c_3: Contribution to confrontation of the climate change phenomenon, c_4: Effects on natural environment
Technological	c_5: Efficiency rate, c_6: Knowledge of the innovative technology
Social	c_7: Contribution to employment opportunities' creation, c_8: Contribution to regional development

Table 3.8 Pre-selected technologies

Category	Technology
The natural fossil fuels technologies	a_1: Pressurized fluidized bed combustion
	a_2: Pressurized pulverized coal combustion
	a_3: Natural gas combined cycle
The hydrogen technologies	a_4: Molten carbonate fuel cell
	a_5: Fuel cell/turbine hybrids
Renewable energy technologies	a_6: Biomass co-firing
	a_7: Biomass gasification
	a_8: Off-shore wind farms
	a_9: Large-scale wind farms
	a_{10}: Building integrated photovoltaics

linguistic expressions instead of crisp numbers. Moreover, because of the high level of uncertainties mentioned above, the experts may feel not very confident to use a certain term to represent their opinions. Assume that the experts agree with evaluating alternatives with the LTS $S^{(4)} = \{s_{-4}, \ldots, s_0, \ldots, s_4\}$ in Fig. 2.1. Whenever they can not express their opinions by a certain term, EHFLTSs or HFLTSs can be used. Tables 3.9, 3.10, 3.11 and 3.12 show the linguistic information provided by 4 experts.

Phase 1. Suppose that the decision maker hesitates about choosing the values of parameters of the aggregation process, we run it by the combination of several reasonable values. Specifically, $\xi = 0, 0.5, 1$, $\preceq = \preceq_{Lex1}, \preceq_{Lex2}, \preceq_{D_n}$, $\mathbf{w}$ is implemented by the fuzzy quantifiers: "at least half", "as many as possible" and "most" [6]. Then all the possible rankings of alternatives are summarized in Table 3.13. Note that the values of parameters used here is only for the purpose of illustration.

As can be seen in Table 3.13, there are 12 distinct rankings among 27 combinations of values of parameters. The only thing we are sure is that a_5 is the one with the worst performance. The alternatives a_1, a_3 and a_6 win the first place for 9, 15 and 3 times, respectively. Thus, it is necessary to derive a more admissible ranking by the proposed exploitation algorithm.

Phase 2. The defeat relation of 10 alternatives is derived as follows:

Table 3.9 Performances of technologies per criterion provided by the 1st expert

	c_1	c_2	c_3	c_4	c_5	c_6	c_7	c_8
a_1	$\{s_3\}$	$\{s_2\}$	$\{s_3\}$	$\{s_2, s_3\}$	$\{s_2\}$	$\{s_2\}$	$\{s_2\}$	$\{s_1, s_2\}$
a_2	$\{s_2\}$	$\{s_2\}$	$\{s_2\}$	$\{s_3, s_4\}$	$\{s_0\}$	$\{s_1\}$	$\{s_2\}$	$\{s_2\}$
a_3	$\{s_3\}$	$\{s_1, s_2\}$	$\{s_3\}$	$\{s_1, s_2\}$	$\{s_3\}$	$\{s_3\}$	$\{s_3\}$	$\{s_1, s_2\}$
a_4	$\{s_{-1}\}$	$\{s_2\}$	$\{s_2\}$	$\{s_3\}$	$\{s_2\}$	$\{s_0, s_1\}$	$\{s_2\}$	$\{s_1\}$
a_5	$\{s_{-2}, s_{-1}\}$	$\{s_1\}$	$\{s_2\}$	$\{s_3\}$	$\{s_1\}$	$\{s_{-1}\}$	$\{s_0, s_1\}$	$\{s_0\}$
a_6	$\{s_2\}$	$\{s_4\}$	$\{s_0, s_1\}$	$\{s_2\}$	$\{s_2\}$	$\{s_2\}$	$\{s_3\}$	$\{s_2\}$
a_7	$\{s_1\}$	$\{s_2\}$	$\{s_0\}$	$\{s_2\}$	$\{s_2, s_3\}$	$\{s_2\}$	$\{s_4\}$	$\{s_3\}$
a_8	$\{s_2\}$	$\{s_1\}$	$\{s_0\}$	$\{s_0\}$	$\{s_1\}$	$\{s_2\}$	$\{s_2, s_3\}$	$\{s_3\}$
a_9	$\{s_2\}$	$\{s_2\}$	$\{s_0\}$	$\{s_0\}$	$\{s_1\}$	$\{s_3\}$	$\{s_3\}$	$\{s_2, s_3, s_4\}$
a_{10}	$\{s_{-1}\}$	$\{s_{-1}, s_0\}$	$\{s_2\}$	$\{s_2, s_3\}$	$\{s_3\}$	$\{s_3\}$	$\{s_2\}$	$\{s_1\}$

Table 3.10 Performances of technologies per criterion provided by the 2nd expert

	c_1	c_2	c_3	c_4	c_5	c_6	c_7	c_8
a_1	$\{s_2, s_3\}$	$\{s_2\}$	$\{s_2, s_3\}$	$\{s_2\}$	$\{s_2\}$	$\{s_2, s_3\}$	$\{s_2\}$	$\{s_2, s_3\}$
a_2	$\{s_2\}$	$\{s_1\}$	$\{s_2\}$	$\{s_2, s_3\}$	$\{s_0\}$	$\{s_1\}$	$\{s_1, s_2\}$	$\{s_2\}$
a_3	$\{s_2, s_3\}$	$\{s_2\}$	$\{s_3\}$	$\{s_1, s_2\}$	$\{s_3\}$	$\{s_1, s_2\}$	$\{s_3\}$	$\{s_2, s_3\}$
a_4	$\{s_1\}$	$\{s_1, s_2\}$	$\{s_1, s_2\}$	$\{s_3\}$	$\{s_2, s_3\}$	$\{s_0\}$	$\{s_2\}$	$\{s_1, s_2\}$
a_5	$\{s_{-1}, s_0\}$	$\{s_1, s_2\}$	$\{s_2\}$	$\{s_0, s_1\}$	$\{s_1\}$	$\{s_0\}$	$\{s_0\}$	$\{s_0, s_1\}$
a_6	$\{s_2\}$	$\{s_2, s_3, s_4\}$	$\{s_1\}$	$\{s_2\}$	$\{s_2, s_3\}$	$\{s_2\}$	$\{s_2, s_3\}$	$\{s_2\}$
a_7	$\{s_1, s_2\}$	$\{s_2\}$	$\{s_1, s_2\}$	$\{s_2\}$	$\{s_2, s_3\}$	$\{s_1, s_2, s_3\}$	$\{s_4\}$	$\{s_2, s_3\}$
a_8	$\{s_2\}$	$\{s_1, s_2\}$	$\{s_0\}$	$\{s_0\}$	$\{s_1\}$	$\{s_2\}$	$\{s_2, s_3\}$	$\{s_3\}$
a_9	$\{s_1, s_2\}$	$\{s_2\}$	$\{s_{-1}\}$	$\{s_0\}$	$\{s_0, s_1\}$	$\{s_3\}$	$\{s_3\}$	$\{s_2, s_3\}$
a_{10}	$\{s_1\}$	$\{s_1, s_2\}$	$\{s_2\}$	$\{s_2, s_3\}$	$\{s_3\}$	$\{s_3\}$	$\{s_1\}$	$\{s_1, s_2\}$

Table 3.11 Performances of technologies per criterion provided by the 3rd expert

	c_1	c_2	c_3	c_4	c_5	c_6	c_7	c_8
a_1	$\{s_2\}$	$\{s_2, s_3\}$	$\{s_2, s_3\}$	$\{s_2, s_3\}$	$\{s_2\}$	$\{s_2\}$	$\{s_2, s_3\}$	$\{s_3\}$
a_2	$\{s_1, s_2, s_3\}$	$\{s_1\}$	$\{s_2\}$	$\{s_2\}$	$\{s_0, s_1\}$	$\{s_1, s_2\}$	$\{s_2\}$	$\{s_2, s_3\}$
a_3	$\{s_3\}$	$\{s_1, s_2\}$	$\{s_2, s_3, s_4\}$	$\{s_1\}$	$\{s_2, s_3\}$	$\{s_3\}$	$\{s_1, s_2\}$	$\{s_2, s_3\}$
a_4	$\{s_1\}$	$\{s_1, s_2\}$	$\{s_1, s_2\}$	$\{s_3, s_4\}$	$\{s_2, s_3\}$	$\{s_0, s_1\}$	$\{s_2, s_3\}$	$\{s_1\}$
a_5	$\{s_{-2}, s_{-1}\}$	$\{s_2\}$	$\{s_2\}$	$\{s_0, s_1\}$	$\{s_1\}$	$\{s_0\}$	$\{s_0\}$	$\{s_0, s_1\}$
a_6	$\{s_2, s_3\}$	$\{s_2, s_3\}$	$\{s_1, s_2, s_3\}$	$\{s_1, s_2\}$	$\{s_3\}$	$\{s_2, s_3\}$	$\{s_1\}$	$\{s_2\}$
a_7	$\{s_1, s_2\}$	$\{s_2\}$	$\{s_1, s_2\}$	$\{s_2\}$	$\{s_2, s_3\}$	$\{s_0, s_1\}$	$\{s_2\}$	$\{s_2, s_3\}$
a_8	$\{s_2\}$	$\{s_1, s_2\}$	$\{s_0\}$	$\{s_0\}$	$\{s_1\}$	$\{s_2, s_3\}$	$\{s_2, s_3\}$	$\{s_1\}$
a_9	$\{s_2\}$	$\{s_1\}$	$\{s_0\}$	$\{s_0, s_1\}$	$\{s_0\}$	$\{s_2, s_3\}$	$\{s_1, s_2\}$	$\{s_3\}$
a_{10}	$\{s_1, s_2\}$	$\{s_{-1}\}$	$\{s_1, s_2\}$	$\{s_2\}$	$\{s_3\}$	$\{s_0, s_1\}$	$\{s_1\}$	$\{s_2\}$

Table 3.12 Performances of technologies per criterion provided by the 4th expert

	c_1	c_2	c_3	c_4	c_5	c_6	c_7	c_8
a_1	$\{s_1\}$	$\{s_2, s_3\}$	$\{s_3\}$	$\{s_2\}$	$\{s_1, s_2\}$	$\{s_2\}$	$\{s_3\}$	$\{s_2\}$
a_2	$\{s_3\}$	$\{s_1\}$	$\{s_1, s_2\}$	$\{s_1, s_2\}$	$\{s_1\}$	$\{s_1, s_2\}$	$\{s_2, s_3\}$	$\{s_2, s_3\}$
a_3	$\{s_2, s_3\}$	$\{s_1\}$	$\{s_3\}$	$\{s_1, s_2\}$	$\{s_2\}$	$\{s_2, s_3\}$	$\{s_2\}$	$\{s_1\}$
a_4	$\{s_1, s_2, s_3\}$	$\{s_1, s_2\}$	$\{s_1\}$	$\{s_2, s_3\}$	$\{s_3\}$	$\{s_0\}$	$\{s_2, s_3\}$	$\{s_2, s_3\}$
a_5	$\{s_{-2}, s_{-1}\}$	$\{s_3, s_4\}$	$\{s_1, s_2\}$	$\{s_0\}$	$\{s_0, s_1\}$	$\{s_1\}$	$\{s_0, s_1\}$	$\{s_0, s_1\}$
a_6	$\{s_2\}$	$\{s_2, s_3\}$	$\{s_2, s_3\}$	$\{s_2\}$	$\{s_3\}$	$\{s_2, s_3\}$	$\{s_{-1}, s_0\}$	$\{s_2\}$
a_7	$\{s_1\}$	$\{s_2, s_3\}$	$\{s_0, s_1\}$	$\{s_2, s_3\}$	$\{s_1, s_2, s_3\}$	$\{s_0, s_1\}$	$\{s_2\}$	$\{s_2, s_3\}$
a_8	$\{s_2\}$	$\{s_1, s_2\}$	$\{s_0\}$	$\{s_0\}$	$\{s_1\}$	$\{s_2, s_3\}$	$\{s_2, s_3\}$	$\{s_1\}$
a_9	$\{s_1, s_2\}$	$\{s_0\}$	$\{s_0, s_1\}$	$\{s_1, s_2\}$	$\{s_0, s_1, s_2\}$	$\{s_1, s_2\}$	$\{s_0, s_1\}$	$\{s_3\}$
a_{10}	$\{s_{-1}, s_0\}$	$\{s_0, s_1\}$	$\{s_1, s_2\}$	$\{s_2, s_3\}$	$\{s_1, s_2, s_3\}$	$\{s_1\}$	$\{s_1, s_2\}$	$\{s_2, s_3\}$

$$DR = \begin{pmatrix} - & 0 & 0.67 & 0.11 & 0 & 0.33 & 0.33 & 0 & 0.19 & 0 \\ 1 & - & 1 & 0.33 & 0 & 1 & 0.89 & 0.33 & 0.33 & 0.33 \\ 0.33 & 0 & - & 0 & 0 & 0.11 & 0.11 & 0 & 0 & 0 \\ 0.89 & 0.67 & 1 & - & 0 & 1 & 1 & 0.11 & 0.22 & 0.11 \\ 1 & 1 & 1 & 1 & - & 1 & 1 & 1 & 1 & 1 \\ 0.67 & 0 & 0.89 & 0 & 0 & - & 0.22 & 0 & 0.11 & 0 \\ 0.67 & 0.11 & 0.89 & 0 & 0 & 0.78 & - & 0 & 0.11 & 0 \\ 1 & 0.67 & 1 & 0.89 & 0 & 1 & 1 & - & 0.44 & 0.44 \\ 0.82 & 0.67 & 1 & 0.78 & 0 & 0.89 & 0.89 & 0.56 & - & 0.44 \\ 1 & 0.67 & 1 & 0.89 & 0 & 1 & 1 & 0.56 & 0.56 & - \end{pmatrix}$$

The maximum defeats of alternatives are

$$\left(0.67\ 1\ 0.33\ 1\ 1\ 0.89\ 0.89\ 1\ 0.89\ 1\right)$$

Then the minimum of maximum defeats is 0.33, which corresponds to the alternative a_3. Therefore, it reaches the conclusion that a_3 (Natural Gas Combined Cycle) is the wining technology.

3.3.4 Comparisons and Further Discussions

In the approach proposed by Zhang and Wu [27], the EHFLTSs are aggregated at the group level and the criteria level, respectively. Then, the alternatives are ranked by comparing the scores of overall performances. Besides, the approach in Sect. 3.2 aggregated EHFLTSs at the group level using the union operation rather than any other aggregation operators so that all possible linguistic terms provided by the

Table 3.13 The overall rankings of 10 technologies with respect to different values of parameters

ξ	Order	Quantifier	Ranking
0	$\preceq_{Lex1}$	"Most"	$a_5 \preceq a_9 \preceq a_{10} \preceq a_4 \preceq a_8 \preceq a_2 \preceq a_7 \preceq a_6 \preceq a_1 \preceq a_3$
		"At least half"	$a_5 \preceq a_2 \preceq a_8 \preceq a_4 \preceq a_{10} \preceq a_1 \preceq a_7 \preceq a_6 \preceq a_9 \preceq a_3$
		"As many as possible"	$a_5 \preceq a_{10} \preceq a_9 \preceq a_8 \preceq a_4 \preceq a_7 \preceq a_2 \preceq a_6 \preceq a_3 \preceq a_1$
	$\preceq_{Lex2}$	"Most"	$a_5 \preceq a_8 \preceq a_{10} \preceq a_9 \preceq a_4 \preceq a_2 \preceq a_6 \preceq a_7 \preceq a_1 \preceq a_3$
		"At least half"	$a_5 \preceq a_2 \preceq a_8 \preceq a_{10} \preceq a_9 \preceq a_1 \preceq a_4 \preceq a_3 \preceq a_7 \preceq a_6$
		"As many as possible"	$a_5 \preceq a_9 \preceq a_{10} \preceq a_8 \preceq a_4 \preceq a_2 \preceq a_6 \preceq a_7 \preceq a_3 \preceq a_1$
	$\preceq_{D_n}$	"Most"	$a_5 \preceq a_9 \preceq a_{10} \preceq a_8 \preceq a_4 \preceq a_2 \preceq a_7 \preceq a_6 \preceq a_1 \preceq a_3$
		"At least half"	$a_5 \preceq a_2 \preceq a_8 \preceq a_{10} \preceq a_4 \preceq a_1 \preceq a_9 \preceq a_7 \preceq a_6 \preceq a_3$
		"As many as possible"	$a_5 \preceq a_9 \preceq a_{10} \preceq a_8 \preceq a_4 \preceq a_2 \preceq a_7 \preceq a_6 \preceq a_3 \preceq a_1$
0.5	$\preceq_{Lex1}$	"Most"	$a_5 \preceq a_9 \preceq a_{10} \preceq a_4 \preceq a_8 \preceq a_2 \preceq a_7 \preceq a_6 \preceq a_1 \preceq a_3$
		"At least half"	$a_5 \preceq a_2 \preceq a_8 \preceq a_4 \preceq a_{10} \preceq a_1 \preceq a_7 \preceq a_6 \preceq a_9 \preceq a_3$
		"As many as possible"	$a_5 \preceq a_{10} \preceq a_9 \preceq a_8 \preceq a_4 \preceq a_7 \preceq a_2 \preceq a_6 \preceq a_3 \preceq a_1$
	$\preceq_{Lex2}$	"Most"	$a_5 \preceq a_8 \preceq a_{10} \preceq a_9 \preceq a_4 \preceq a_2 \preceq a_6 \preceq a_7 \preceq a_1 \preceq a_3$
		"At least half"	$a_5 \preceq a_2 \preceq a_8 \preceq a_{10} \preceq a_9 \preceq a_1 \preceq a_4 \preceq a_3 \preceq a_7 \preceq a_6$
		"As many as possible"	$a_5 \preceq a_9 \preceq a_{10} \preceq a_8 \preceq a_4 \preceq a_2 \preceq a_6 \preceq a_7 \preceq a_3 \preceq a_1$
	$\preceq_{D_n}$	"Most"	$a_5 \preceq a_9 \preceq a_{10} \preceq a_8 \preceq a_4 \preceq a_2 \preceq a_6 \preceq a_7 \preceq a_1 \preceq a_3$
		"At least half"	$a_5 \preceq a_2 \preceq a_8 \preceq a_{10} \preceq a_4 \preceq a_1 \preceq a_9 \preceq a_7 \preceq a_6 \preceq a_3$
		"As many as possible"	$a_5 \preceq a_9 \preceq a_{10} \preceq a_8 \preceq a_4 \preceq a_2 \preceq a_7 \preceq a_6 \preceq a_3 \preceq a_1$
1	$\preceq_{Lex1}$	"Most"	$a_5 \preceq a_9 \preceq a_{10} \preceq a_4 \preceq a_8 \preceq a_2 \preceq a_7 \preceq a_6 \preceq a_1 \preceq a_2$
		"At least half"	$a_5 \preceq a_2 \preceq a_8 \preceq a_4 \preceq a_{10} \preceq a_1 \preceq a_7 \preceq a_6 \preceq a_9 \preceq a_3$
		"As many as possible"	$a_5 \preceq a_{10} \preceq a_9 \preceq a_8 \preceq a_4 \preceq a_7 \preceq a_2 \preceq a_6 \preceq a_3 \preceq a_1$
	$\preceq_{Lex2}$	"Most"	$a_5 \preceq a_8 \preceq a_{10} \preceq a_9 \preceq a_4 \preceq a_2 \preceq a_6 \preceq a_7 \preceq a_1 \preceq a_3$
		"At least half"	$a_5 \preceq a_2 \preceq a_8 \preceq a_{10} \preceq a_9 \preceq a_1 \preceq a_4 \preceq a_3 \preceq a_7 \preceq a_6$
		"As many as possible"	$a_5 \preceq a_9 \preceq a_{10} \preceq a_8 \preceq a_4 \preceq a_2 \preceq a_6 \preceq a_7 \preceq a_3 \preceq a_1$
	$\preceq_{D_n}$	"Most"	$a_5 \preceq a_9 \preceq a_{10} \preceq a_8 \preceq a_4 \preceq a_2 \preceq a_7 \preceq a_6 \preceq a_1 \preceq a_3$
		"At least half"	$a_5 \preceq a_2 \preceq a_8 \preceq a_{10} \preceq a_4 \preceq a_9 \preceq a_1 \preceq a_7 \preceq a_6 \preceq a_3$
		"As many as possible"	$a_5 \preceq a_9 \preceq a_{10} \preceq a_8 \preceq a_4 \preceq a_2 \preceq a_7 \preceq a_6 \preceq a_3 \preceq a_1$

experts can be considered directly in the second aggregation. The selected order is $\preceq_W$.

Furthermore, as can be seen in Tables 3.9, 3.10, 3.11 and 3.12, all provided linguistic information is HFLTSs. Thus, the proposed approach can be compared with the existing methods proposed for this special setting. Liu and Rodríguez [11] developed a MCDM method based on the fuzzy envelopes of HFLTSs and the classical TOPSIS method. The fuzzy envelope of a HFLTS is represented by a trapezoidal fuzzy numbers. A kind of Minkowski distance is utilized to measure the distance of an alternative to the fuzzy positive and negative ideal solutions. To enable their method in GDM, we use the trapezoidal fuzzy OWA operator proposed in [10] to aggregate 4 matrices of the above example. In this sense, the approach proposed by Riera et al. [15] based on DNFs is also interesting for comparison. As the degree of

Table 3.14 Some features of the comparable approaches

Approach	Setting	Normalization	Order	Monotonicity
Zhang and Wu [27]	EHFLTS	Not needed	Partial order	Not monotonic
Liu and Rodríguez [11]	HFLTS	N/A	N/A	N/A
Chen and Hong [2]	HFLTS	N/A	Partial order	Monotonic
Riera et al. [15]	DFNs	N/A	Partial order	Monotonic
The approach of Sect. 3.2	EHFLTS	Not needed	Partial order	Not monotonic
The approach of this section	EHFLTS	Needed	Admissible order	Monotonic

one alternative satisfying each criterion is unknown, each evaluation is transformed into a DFN by fixing the degree to 1. For instance, the chain corresponding to the used LTS is $L_n = \{0, 1, \ldots, 8\}$ and the subjective evaluation $\{s_1, s_2, s_3\}$ is transformed into $\{1/5, 1/6, 1/7\}$. In addition, Tables 3.9, 3.10, 3.11 and 3.12 should be aggregated to form the final decision table because DFNs can only used for expressing individual opinions (the support of a DFN is consecutive natural numbers). Then, the aggregation among criteria can reach the overall performances of the alternative. In this comparison, the extension of the kernel aggregation function [12] is used and the parameter is fixed to 4.

Another similar approach based on membership functions can be found in [2], in which, a HFLTS is transformed into a trapezoidal fuzzy number and then reduces to an interval associated with the risk preferences of the decision maker. The order of intervals is defined by a likelihood-based method. The operators they used are based on the min and max operators.

Some features of the proposed approach and five existing approaches are summarized in Table 3.14. Notice that the approach of Liu and Rodríguez [11] orders the alternatives by distances to ideal solutions rather than comparing HFLTSs. Chen and Hong's approach [2] takes use of a partial order of intervals. Riera et al. [15] compared DFNs by constructing a dominance relation which does not define a total order either. Due to the basic operation of EHFLTSs used in Zhang and Wu's approach [27] and the approach in Sect. 3.2, the increasing monotonicity of their selected operators is not satisfied. However, the EHFLOWA operator used in the proposed approach is increasingly monotonic if the total order satisfies Theorem 3.18. Although the total order of DFNs has not been developed, the aggregation function on DFNs can be monotonic with respect to the predefined partial orders [9].

The rankings of six approaches are listed in Table 3.15. Notice that in the computational process, we use the OWA strategy associated with the quantifier "most" whenever an operator is needed (except for Chen and Hong's approach [2] and Riera's approach [15]). We set $\xi = 0.5$ and $\preceq = \preceq_{Lex1}$ in the proposed approach and consider the optimistic risk preference in Chen and Hong's approach [2].

We discuss the comparable approaches in the following aspects:

Table 3.15 Rankings derived by the comparable approaches

Approach	Ranking
Zhang and Wu [27]	$a_5 \preceq a_9 \preceq a_{10} = a_4 \preceq a_8 = a_2 \preceq a_6 \preceq a_7 \preceq a_1 \preceq a_3$
Liu and Rodríguez [11]	$a_5 \preceq a_9 \preceq a_{10} \preceq a_4 \preceq a_8 \preceq a_2 \preceq a_6 \preceq a_7 \preceq a_1 \preceq a_3$
Chen and Hong [2]	$a_5 \preceq a_{10} \preceq a_9 \preceq a_4 \preceq a_8 \preceq a_2 \preceq a_6 \preceq a_7 \preceq a_1 \preceq a_3$
Riera and [15]	$a_5 \preceq a_9 \preceq a_{10} \preceq a_4 \preceq a_8 \preceq a_2 \preceq a_7 \preceq a_6 \preceq a_1 \preceq a_3$
The approach of Sect. 3.2	$a_5 \preceq a_9 \preceq a_{10} \preceq a_4 \preceq a_8 \preceq a_2 \preceq a_6 \preceq a_7 \preceq a_1 \preceq a_3$
The approach of this section	$a_5 \preceq a_9 \preceq a_{10} \preceq a_4 \preceq a_8 \preceq a_2 \preceq a_7 \preceq a_6 \preceq a_1 \preceq a_3$

(1) *Concerning the orders.* Total orders are essential to rank a set of values. If partial orders are considered, two values, which are not equal, may be unable to distinguish. As shown in Table 3.15, $a_{10} = a_4$ is derived by $E(a_{10}) = E(a_4)$. In fact, a_{10} and a_4 do not coincide but are equivalent with respect to the partial order defined by expected terms. If the degree of hesitancy is further considered, we have $a_{10} \preceq_W a_4$ according to the partial order $\preceq_W$. However, this would not happen if total orders, such as total orders introduced in this book, are taken into account.

(2) *Concerning risk preferences of the experts.* Generally, modeling risk preferences are indispensable and inevitable for decision-making. In Zhang and Wu's approach [27] and the approach of Sect. 3.2, this is reflected by the weighting strategies of aggregation operators. In Chen and Hong's approach [2], the trapezoidal membership functions are converted into numerical intervals with the help of risk preferences. In Riera's approach [15], the risk preference is represented by the parameter of the aggregation function. While in the approach of this section, risk preferences are reflected by the parameter ξ and the total orders. It is common that risk preferences can affect the final decision-making but are very complex to be determined accurately. Thus this approach is a solution to consider all possible situations to reach a sounder decision.

(3) *Concerning the EHFLOWA operators.* The EHFLOWA operator was used in Zhang and Wu's approach [27], the approach of Sect. 3.2 and the approach of this section. However, there are some differences: (i) The operator in the two existing approaches is based on partial orders rather than total orders in the approach of this section. (ii) They utilize the basic operation defined in Definition 2.13. But the resultant operator is not increasingly monotonic. We use a special form of the operator as shown in Eq. (2.22). According to the main idea of hesitant fuzzy sets, we may ignore some possible values. But the monotonicity of the EHFLOWA operator can be satisfied by appropriate definition of admissible orders.

(4) *EHFLTSs (HFLTSs) vs. DFNs.* All the six approaches can solve the problems whose decision information takes the form of HFLTSs. Whereas Liu and Rodríguez's approach [11], Chen and Hong's approach [2] and Riera's approach [15] can not deal with linguistic information with the form of EHFLTSs. But this fact is not an evidence to show that EHFLTSs are more advanced than HFLTSs and DFNs. We can only draw the following conclusions: (i) HFLTSs and DFNs are more rational

to express individual evaluations than EHFLTSs; (ii) EHFLTSs and DFNs are more convenient for computation. EHFLTSs enable us to conduct computation by each possible term involved in them. If the computation is not conducted according to each involved term, then HFLTSs would be reduced to the uncertain linguistic terms. (iii) DFNs are more general and flexible linguistic representational model because they can include more information than EHFLTSs. However, it leads to additional work for the experts to provide this kind of information. If the membership degrees are available, then DFNs are the best choice; otherwise, EHFLTSs (or HFLTSs) can be used instead.

3.4 Conclusions

This chapter has studied GDM problems in the setting of EHFLTSs, based on the framework of decision matrices. Different from traditional GDM approaches, we have started with the analysis of inner structures of groups, and introduced the processes of MGDM. The processes have been implemented in the setting of EHFLTSs. The involved aggregation operators possess very good properties. Besides, a new OWA operator has been introduced based on the admissible order on the set of EHFLTSs. The operator has been applied in a GDM approach. We have discussed how subjective preferences of decision makers affect final decisions. The presented approach based on social choice theory could provide admissible decisions if different rankings are derived by using different values of parameters.

References

1. Bryson, N., Mobolurin, A.: An action learning evaluation procedure for multiple criteria decision making problems. Eur. J. Oper. Res. **96**(2), 379–386 (1997)
2. Chen, S.M., Hong, J.A.: Multicriteria linguistic decision making based on hesitant fuzzy linguistic term sets and the aggregation of fuzzy sets. Inf. Sci. **286**, 63–74 (2014)
3. Daily, B.F., Steiner, R.L.: The influence of group decision support systems on contribution and commitment levels in multicultural and culturally homogeneous decision-making groups. Comput. Hum. Behav. **14**(1), 147–162 (1998)
4. Doukas, H.C., Andreas, B.M., Psarras, J.E.: Multi-criteria decision aid for the formulation of sustainable technological energy priorities using linguistic variables. Eur. J. Oper. Res. **182**(2), 844–855 (2007)
5. Herrera, F., Herrera-Viedma, E.: Aggregation operators for linguistic weighted information. IEEE Trans. Syst., Man Cybern.-Part A: Syst. Hum. **27**(5), 646–656 (1997)
6. Herrera, F., Herrera-Viedma, E.: Linguistic decision analysis: steps for solving decision problems under linguistic information. Fuzzy Sets Syst. **115**(1), 67–82 (2000)
7. Hong, L.K.: Risky shift and cautious shift: some direct evidence on the culture-value theory. Soc. Psychol. **41**(4), 342–346 (1978)
8. Insko, C.A., Schopler, J., Hoyle, R.H., Dardis, G.J., Graetz, K.A.: Individual-group discontinuity as a function of fear and greed. J. Pers. Soc. Psychol. **58**(1), 68–79 (1990)
9. Komorníková, M., Mesiar, R.: Aggregation functions on bounded partially ordered sets and their classification. Fuzzy Sets Syst. **175**(1), 48–56 (2011)

10. Liu, P.D.: A weighted aggregation operators multi-attribute group decision-making method based on interval-valued trapezoidal fuzzy numbers. Expert. Syst. Appl. **38**(1), 1053–1060 (2011)
11. Liu, H.B., Rodríguez, R.M.: A fuzzy envelope for hesitant fuzzy linguistic term set and its application to multicriteria decision making. Inf. Sci. **258**, 220–238 (2014)
12. Mas, M., Monserrat, M., Torrens, J.: Kernel aggregation functions on finite scales. Constructions from their marginals. Fuzzy Sets Syst. **241**, 27–40 (2014)
13. Michaelsen, L.K., Watson, W.E., Black, R.H.: A realistic test of individual versus group consensus decision making. J. Appl. Psychol. **74**(5), 834–839 (1989)
14. Phillis, Y.A., Andriantiatsaholiniaina, L.A.: Sustainability: an ill-defined concept and its assessment using fuzzy logic. Ecol. Econ. **37**(3), 435–456 (2001)
15. Riera, J.V., Massanet, S., Herrera-Viedma, E., Torrens, J.: Some interesting properties of the fuzzy linguistic model based on discrete fuzzy numbers to manage hesitant fuzzy linguistic information. Appl. Soft Comput. **36**, 383–391 (2015)
16. Rodríguez, R.M., Martínez, L., Herrera, F.: Hesitant fuzzy linguistic term sets for decision making. IEEE Trans. Fuzzy Syst. **20**(1), 109–119 (2012)
17. Torra, V.: Hesitant fuzzy sets. Int. J. Intell. Syst. **25**(6), 529–539 (2010)
18. Venetsanos, K., Angelopoulou, P., Tsoutsos, T.: Renewable energy sources project appraisal under uncertainty: the case of wind energy exploitation within a changing energy market environment. Energy Policy **30**(4), 293–307 (2002)
19. Wang, H.: Extended hesitant fuzzy linguistic term sets and their aggregation in group decision making. Int. J. Comput. Intell. Syst. **8**(1), 14–33 (2015)
20. Wang, H., Xu, Z.S.: Total orders of extended hesitant fuzzy linguistic term sets: definitions, generations and applications. Knowl.-Based Syst. **107**, 142–154 (2016)
21. Wang, H., Xu, Z.S.: Multi-groups decision making using intuitionistic-valued hesitant fuzzy information. Int. J. Comput. Intell. Syst. **9**(3), 468–482 (2016)
22. Xu, Z.S.: An overview of methods for determining OWA weights. Int. J. Intell. Syst. **20**(8), 843–865 (2005)
23. Xu, Z.S.: A note on linguistic hybrid arithmetic averaging operator in multiple attribute group decision making with linguistic information. Group Decis. Negot. **15**(6), 593–604 (2006)
24. Xu, Z.S.: On generalized induced linguistic aggregation operators. Int. J. Gen. Syst. **35**(1), 17–28 (2006)
25. Yager, R.R.: On ordered weighted averaging aggregation operators in multicriteria decision making. IEEE Trans. Syst., Man Cybern. **18**(1), 183–190 (1988)
26. Yager, R.R.: Applications and extensions of OWA aggregations. Int. J. Man-Mach. Stud. **37**(1), 103–122 (1992)
27. Zhang, Z.M., Wu, C.: Hesitant fuzzy linguistic aggregation operators and their applications to multiple attribute group decision making. J. Intell. Fuzzy Syst. **26**(5), 2185–2202 (2014)

Chapter 4
Preference Analysis and Applications Based on EHFLTSs

LPRs enable decision makers to express preferences by pair-wise comparisons in qualitative setting. The fundamental aspect of LPRs is to measure the degrees of consistency when applying them in decision-making. The model of EHFLTSs introduced in Chap. 2 is an effective technique to represent uncertainty in QDM problems. Based on EHFLTSs, this chapter focuses on the following two aspects:

(1) Consistency measures of extended hesitant fuzzy linguistic preference relations (EHFLPRs). Many contributions mainly focus on LPRs, uncertain LPRs and hesitant fuzzy LPRs in qualitative setting. Due to the employment of virtual terms, some of the involved HFLPRs are, actually, EHFLPRs [19]. However, there are some limitations in these contributions, such as the necessity of normalization, the requirement of strict consistency, and the lack of obtaining priorities from EHFLPRs. This chapter will specify the concept of EHFLPRs, introduce the additive and weak consistencies, discuss consistencies based on preference graphs visually, and then introduce two algorithms to reduce EHFLPRs to LPRs.

(2) Application of EHFLPRs in the improvement of incomplete LPRs. Based on specific consistency measures, this chapter will focus on the estimation of missing entries. Due to the fact that incomplete LPRs do not usually reach the strict additive consistency, different estimated values could be derived by different known entries. We introduce an approach to collect all the possible values by EHFLTSs and support experts to complete missing entries interactively. Compared with other contributions, the algorithms in this chapter could help experts figure out the reasonable values of missing entries and realize the deviations between known entries and their real opinions.

H. Wang and Z. Xu, *Theory and Approaches of Group Decision-Making with Uncertain Linguistic Expressions*, Uncertainty and Operations Research,
https://doi.org/10.1007/978-981-13-3735-2_4

4.1 Some Consistency Measures of EHFLPRs

The LTS defined in Eq. (2.20) is more suitable to represent preference information. Thus, in this chapter, all the LTSs take the form of $S^{(g)} = \{s_{-g}, \ldots, s_0, \ldots, s_g\}$. When virtual terms are involved, $S^{(g)}$ is extended to $\bar{S}^{(g)} = \{s_\alpha | \alpha \in [-q, q]\} (q \geq g)$. For convenience, an equivalent relation based on the expected terms is defined as follows:

Definition 4.1 ([11]) Given two EHFLTSs h_S^1 and h_S^2, if $E(h_S^1) = E(h_S^2)$, then h_S^1 and h_S^2 are said to be approximately equivalent, denoted by $h_S^1 \cong h_S^2$.

4.1.1 The Concept of EHFLPRs

Let $V = \{v_1, v_2, \ldots, v_n\}$ be a set of n alternatives. Comparisons between each pair of alternatives are provided by the experts using the LTS $S^{(g)}$ (or $\bar{S}^{(g)}$), and then a LPR is constructed. In the situations where the experts provide pair-wise comparisons of alternatives by using linguistic expressions, Zhu and Xu [19] presented the following concept of HFLPRs:

Definition 4.2 ([19]) A HFLPR is presented by a matrix $\tilde{H} = (\tilde{h}_{ij})_{n \times n} \subset V \times V$, where $\tilde{h}_{ij} = \{s_{\alpha_{ij}^l} | l = 1, 2, \ldots, \#\tilde{h}_{ij}\}$ is a HFLTS indicating that hesitant degrees to which v_i is preferred to v_j, $\#\tilde{h}_{ij}$ is the number of linguistic terms in $\tilde{h}_{ij}$, $s_{\alpha_{ij}^l}$ is the l-th linguistic term of $\tilde{h}_{ij}$, and $\forall l = 1, 2, \ldots, \#\tilde{h}_{ij}, i, j = 1, 2, \ldots, n, i < j$:

$$s_{\alpha_{ij}^l} \oplus s_{\alpha_{ji}^l} = s_0, \ \tilde{h}_{ii} = \{s_0\}, \ \#\tilde{h}_{ij} = \#\tilde{h}_{ji} \tag{4.1}$$

We can see that, in Definition 4.2, the linguistic terms in the upper triangular elements of $\tilde{H}$ are arranged in ascending order, and the linguistic terms in the lower triangular elements are arranged in descending order. In the rest of this chapter, we organize the elements in each preference matrix in the same way.

EHFLTSs have already been considered by Zhu and Xu [19] because of the use of Eq. (2.30), although they presented this definition based on HFLTSs. However, the operation of Eq. (2.30) does not consider all the possible values. This chapter specifies the concept of EHFLPRs based on the operation of Eq. (2.13).

Definition 4.3 ([11]) An EHFLPR is presented by a matrix $HP = (h_{ij})_{n \times n} \subset V \times V$, where $h_{ij} = \{s_{\alpha_{ij}^l} | l = 1, 2, \ldots, \#h_{ij}\}$ is an EHFLTS indicating that the hesitant degrees to which v_i is preferred to v_j, such that $\forall l = 1, 2, \ldots, \#h_{ij}, i, j = 1, 2, \ldots, n, i < j$:

$$s_{\alpha_{ij}^l} \oplus s_{\alpha_{ji}^l} = s_0, \ h_{ii} = \{s_0\}, \ \#h_{ij} = \#h_{ji} \tag{4.2}$$

Because of the distinct operators, Definition 4.3 can be regarded as a generalization of Definition 4.2. Specifically, according to Eq. (2.30), Definition 4.2 satisfies:

$$\tilde{h}_{ij} \oplus \tilde{h}_{ji} = \{s_0\} \tag{4.3}$$

But EHFLPRs defined hereinabove is based on Definition 2.13, which means:

$$h_{ij} \oplus h_{ji} \cong \{s_0\} \tag{4.4}$$

In fact, if Eq. (4.2) holds, then $\alpha_{ij}^{l} + \alpha_{ji}^{l} = 0(\forall i, j, l)$, we have

$$h_{ij} \oplus h_{ji} = \cup_{s_{\alpha_{ij}^{l_1}} \in h_{ij}, s_{\alpha_{ji}^{l_2}} \in h_{ji}} \{s_{\alpha_{ij}^{l_1}} \oplus s_{\alpha_{ji}^{l_2}}\} = \cup_{s_{\alpha_{ij}^{l_1}} \in h_{ij}, s_{\alpha_{ji}^{l_2}} \in h_{ji}} \{s_{\alpha_{ij}^{l_1} + \alpha_{ji}^{l_2}}\} \tag{4.5}$$

Therefore,

$$\begin{aligned} I(E(h_{ij} \oplus h_{ji})) &= \frac{1}{(\#h_{ij})(\#h_{ji})} \sum_{l_1=1}^{\#h_{ij}} \sum_{l_2=1}^{\#h_{ji}} (\alpha_{ij}^{l_1} + \alpha_{ji}^{l_2}) \\ &= \frac{1}{(\#h_{ij})^2} \sum_{l_1=1}^{\#h_{ij}} \left((\#h_{ij})\alpha_{ij}^{l_1} + \sum_{l_2=1}^{\#h_{ij}} \alpha_{ji}^{l_2} \right) \\ &= \frac{1}{(\#h_{ij})^2} \left((\#h_{ij}) \sum_{l_1=1}^{\#h_{ij}} \alpha_{ij}^{l_1} + (\#h_{ij}) \sum_{l_2=1}^{\#h_{ij}} \alpha_{ji}^{l_2} \right) \\ &= \frac{1}{(\#h_{ij})} \sum_{l_1=1}^{\#h_{ij}} \left(\alpha_{ij}^{l_1} + \alpha_{ji}^{l_1} \right) = 0 \end{aligned}$$

which means $h_{ij} \oplus h_{ji} \cong \{s_0\}$.

4.1.2 *Preference Relation Graphs*

In what follows, we begin with some basic concepts related to graphical representation of preference relations:

Definition 4.4 ([11]) Let $R = (r_{ij})_{n \times n}$ be a LPR. the preference relation graph (P-graph) associated with R is a weighted digraph $G_P = (V, A)$, where $V = \{v_1, v_2, \ldots, v_n\}$ is the set of vertices and $A = \{(v_i, v_j)\}$ is the set of arcs, arc (v_i, v_j) joins the vertex v_i to v_j if $r_{ij} \geq s_0$, with its weight being $w(v_i, v_j) = Ind(r_{ij})$, $i \neq j, i, j = 1, 2, \ldots, n$, Ind is the index function defined in Eq. (2.12).

In a P-graph, V represents the set of alternatives considered in the LPR, an arc (v_i, v_j) indicates that v_i is superior to v_j with the degree $s_{w(v_i, v_j)} = r_{ij}$. P-graphs have some interesting properties, for example, if the comparison "indifference" is not taken into account, then there are $n(n-1)/2$ arcs in G_P, the underlying graph of G_P is a simple and complete graph. The P-graph only displays the information that v_i is superior to v_j. We further present the following definition to show all preference information in a digraph:

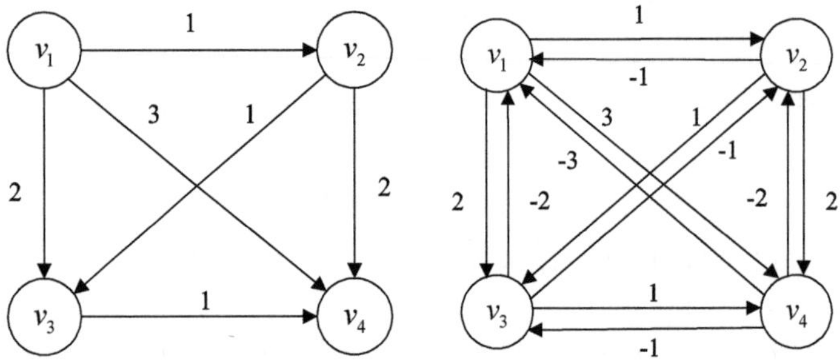

Fig. 4.1 The P-graph and the S-P-graph of LPR in Example 4.6

Definition 4.5 ([11]) Let $R = (r_{ij})_{n\times n}$ be a LPR, the symmetric preference relation graph (S-P-graph) associated with R is a symmetric weighted digraph $G_{S-P} = (V, A)$, where $V = \{v_1, v_2, \ldots, v_n\}$ is the set of vertices and $A = \{(v_i, v_j)|i \neq j, i, j = 1, 2, \ldots, n\}$ is the set of arcs, and arc (v_i, v_j) joins the vertex v_i to the vertex v_j, with its weight being $w(v_i, v_j) = Ind(r_{ij}), i \neq j, i, j = 1, 2, \ldots, n$.

Obviously, the S-P-graph keeps all preference information as the weights of arcs. There are $n(n-1)$ arcs in G_{S-P}. The indegree and the outdegree of each vertex v_i are equal to $n-1$. Note that the weights in G_{S-P} might be any values in $[-g, g]$.

Example 4.6 Given a LPR (based on the LTS in Example 2.3):

$$R_1 = \begin{pmatrix} s_0 & s_1 & s_2 & s_3 \\ s_{-1} & s_0 & s_1 & s_2 \\ s_{-2} & s_{-1} & s_0 & s_1 \\ s_{-3} & s_{-2} & s_{-1} & s_0 \end{pmatrix}$$

Its associated P-graph and S-P-graph are shown in Fig. 4.1.

Some concepts corresponding to EHFLPRs are introduced as follows:

Definition 4.7 ([11]) Let $HP = (h_{ij})_{n\times n}$ be an EHFLPR, then the hesitant preference relation graph (HP-graph) associated with HP is a weighted digraph $G_{HP} = (V, A)$ where $V = \{v_1, v_2, \ldots, v_n\}$ is the set of vertices and $A = \{(v_i^l, v_j^l)\}$ is the set of arcs, and arc (v_i^l, v_j^l) joins the vertex v_i to the vertex v_j if $s_{\alpha_{ij}^l} \geq s_0$, with its weight being $w(v_i^l, v_j^l) = \alpha_{ij}^l, l = 1, 2, \ldots, \#h_{ij}, i \neq j, i, j = 1, 2, \ldots, n$.

Generally, there may be multiple arcs which come out of the vertex v_i and enter into the vertex v_j if $\#h_{ij} \geq 2$. It should be noted that the arcs (v_i^l, v_j^l) are numbered according to the order of the corresponding hesitant elements emerged in h_{ij}. Similar to Definition 4.5, we further give the following definition:

Definition 4.8 ([11]) Let $HP = (h_{ij})_{n\times n}$ be an EHFLPR, then the symmetric hesitant preference relation graph (S-HP-graph) associated with HP is a symmetric

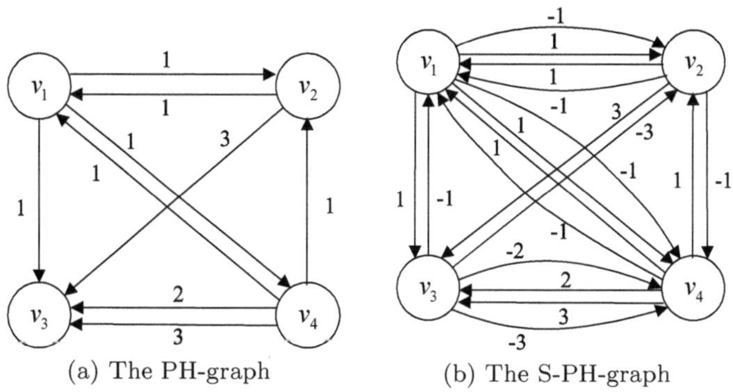

Fig. 4.2 The PH-graph and the S-PH-graph of HP_1 in Example 4.9

weighted digraph $G_{S-HP} = (V, A)$, with $V = \{v_1, v_2, \ldots, v_n\}$ being the set of vertices, and $A = \{(v_i^l, v_j^l) | l = 1, 2, \ldots, \#h_{ij}, i \neq j, i, j = 1, 2, \ldots, n\}$ being the set of arcs, where arc (v_i^l, v_j^l) is the l-th arc that joins the vertex v_i to the vertex v_j, with its weight being $w(v_i^l, v_j^l) = \alpha_{ij}^l$, $l = 1, 2, \ldots, \#h_{ij}, i \neq j, i, j = 1, 2, \ldots, n$.

Example 4.9 Given an EHFLPR (based on the LTS in Example 2.3):

$$HP_1 = \begin{pmatrix} \{s_0\} & \{s_{-1}, s_1\} & \{s_1\} & \{s_{-1}, s_1\} \\ \{s_1, s_{-1}\} & \{s_0\} & \{s_3\} & \{s_{-1}\} \\ \{s_{-1}\} & \{s_{-3}\} & \{s_0\} & \{s_{-3}, s_{-2}\} \\ \{s_1, s_{-1}\} & \{s_1\} & \{s_3, s_2\} & \{s_0\} \end{pmatrix}$$

Its associated PH-graph and S-PH-graph are shown in Fig. 4.2.

Some other denotations used in the rest of the book are list below: Given a digraph $G = (V, A)$, a walk is a sequence of the form:

$$(v_{i_1}, (v_{i_1}, v_{i_2}), v_{i_2}, \ldots, (v_{i_{k-1}}, v_{i_k}), v_{i_k}) \tag{4.6}$$

where k is an integer, $v_{i_1}, v_{i_2}, \cdots, v_{i_k} \in V$, and $(v_{i_1}, v_{i_2}), \ldots, (v_{i_{k-1}}, v_{i_k}) \in A$. A walk is a path if its vertices, and $v_{i_1}, v_{i_2}, \ldots, v_{i_k}$ are pair-wise distinct. Given a weighted digraph, the length of a path, denoted by $len(v_{i_1}, (v_{i_1}, v_{i_2}), v_{i_2}, \ldots, (v_{i_{k-1}}, v_{i_k}), v_{i_k})$, is defined by the sum of the weights of its arcs. The distance from v_i to v_j, denoted by $d(v_i, v_j)$, is the shortest length of the paths from v_i to v_j in the weighted digraph.

In general, given an EHFLPR, the corresponding PH-graph and S-PH-graph are multiple graphs. In the rest of the chapter, the multiplicity of an arc is the number of multiple edges (obtained by removing the directed information from arcs) sharing the same end vertices. The aim of introducing four preference graphs is to make a visible view of preference relations. Although there are several studies which use graphs as tools, most of them use graphs to discuss the weak consistency only, and very few of them use the weight information of arcs, and therefore, few of them deal with the additive consistency by graphs.

4.1.3 Additive Consistency for EHFLPRs

Xu [13] introduced the concept of additive consistency of LPRs as follows:

Definition 4.10 ([13]) Let $R = (r_{ij})_{n\times n}$ be a LPR, R is called an additively consistent LPR if

$$r_{ij} = r_{ik} \oplus r_{kj},\ i, j, k = 1, 2, \ldots, n \tag{4.7}$$

Example 4.11 Given a LPR R_1 shown in Example 4.6, according to Definition 4.10, R_1 is additively consistent.

Take the vertices v_1 and v_2 for example, as clearly shown in Fig. 4.1, the distance from v_1 to v_2 is that $d(v_1, v_2) = 1$. Moreover, $len(v_1, (v_1, v_2), v_2) = len(v_1, (v_1, v_3), v_3, (v_3, v_2), v_2) = len(v_1, (v_1, v_4), v_4, (v_4, v_2), v_2) = 1$, from which we can know that the length of path from v_i to v_j directly is equal to the length of path from v_i to v_j through any other intermediary vertex v_k if a LPR is additively consistent. Hence one could redefine the additive consistency as follows:

Definition 4.12 ([11]) Let $R = (r_{ij})_{n\times n}$ be a LPR, and $G_{S-P} = (V, A)$ be the associated S-P-graph, then R is called an additively consistent LPR if for any $\forall i \neq j, i, j = 1, 2, \ldots, n$,

$$len(v_i, (v_i, v_j), v_j) = len(v_i, (v_i, v_k), v_k, (v_k, v_j), v_j) \tag{4.8}$$

holds for any $k = 1, 2, \ldots, n$.

The equivalence of Definitions 4.10 and 4.12 is apparent. Motivated by Definition 4.12, the consistency degree of a judgement can be determined by the similarity of $len(v_i, (v_i, v_j), v_j)$ and $len(v_i, (v_i, v_k), v_k, (v_k, v_j), v_j)(k = 1, 2, \ldots, n, k \neq i, k \neq j)$. More generally, we can utilize the arithmetical mean $\sum_{k\neq i,k\neq j} len(v_i, (v_i, v_k), v_k, (v_k, v_j), v_j)/(n-2)$ to estimate $len(v_i, (v_i, v_j), v_j)$. Thus s_α is the approximate value of the judgement r_{ij}, where

$$\alpha = \frac{1}{n-2} \sum_{k\neq i,k\neq j} len(v_i, (v_i, v_k), v_k, (v_k, v_j), v_j) \tag{4.9}$$

Based on the idea of Definition 4.10, the additive consistency of EHFLPRs can be defined as follows:

Definition 4.13 ([11]) Let $HP = (h_{ij})_{n\times n}$ be an EHFLPR, HP is called an additively consistent EHFLPR if

$$h_{ij} \cong h_{ik} \oplus h_{kj},\ i, j, k = 1, 2, \ldots, n \tag{4.10}$$

Equation (4.10) can be interpreted as follows: For an additively consistent EHFLPR, the averaging preference degree of v_i preferred to v_j is equal to the averaging preference degree of v_i preferred to v_k plus that of v_k preferred to v_j when hesitations emerge in judgements. Associated with the S-HP-graph, the length of paths $(v_i, (v_i^l, v_j^l), v_j)$ should be equal to the averaging length of the paths $(v_i, (v_i^{l_1}, v_k^{l_1}), v_k, (v_k^{l_1}, v_j^{l_1}), v_j)$. Based on the above analysis, we can construct an additively consistent EHFLPR by a given EHFLPR, which can be shown in the following theorem:

Theorem 4.14 ([11]) *Given the EHFLPR $HP = (h_{ij})_{n\times n}$, $HP' = (\bar{h}_{ij})_{n\times n}$ is an additively consistent EHFLPR if*

$$\bar{h}_{ij} = \begin{cases} \frac{1}{n}(\bigoplus_{k=1}^{n}(h_{ik} \oplus h_{kj})), \ i, j = 1, 2, \cdots, n, i \neq j \\ \{s_0\}, \qquad\qquad otherwise \end{cases} \tag{4.11}$$

Proof For any $i, j = 1, 2, \cdots, n, i \neq j$,

$$E(\bar{h}_{ij}) = E(\frac{1}{n}(\bigoplus_{k=1}^{n}(h_{ik} \oplus h_{kj}))) = \frac{1}{n}E(\bigoplus_{k=1}^{n}(h_{ik} \oplus h_{kj}))$$

Moreover,

$$\begin{aligned} E(\bar{h}_{ik} \oplus \bar{h}_{kj}) &= E(\frac{1}{n}(\bigoplus_{e=1}^{n}(h_{ie} \oplus h_{ek})) \oplus \frac{1}{n}(\bigoplus_{e=1}^{n}(h_{ke} \oplus h_{ej}))) \\ &= \frac{1}{n}E(\bigoplus_{e=1}^{n}(h_{ie} \oplus h_{ek} \oplus h_{ke} \oplus h_{ej})) \\ &= \frac{1}{n}E((\bigoplus_{e=1}^{n}(h_{ke} \oplus h_{ek})) \oplus (\bigoplus_{e=1}^{n}(h_{ie} \oplus h_{ej}))) \\ &= \frac{1}{n}(E(\bigoplus_{e=1}^{n}(h_{ke} \oplus h_{ek})) \oplus E(\bigoplus_{e=1}^{n}(h_{ie} \oplus h_{ej}))) \\ &= s_0 \oplus \frac{1}{n}E(\bigoplus_{e=1}^{n}(h_{ie} \oplus h_{ej})) = E(\bar{h}_{ij}) \end{aligned}$$

Thus $\bar{h}_{ij} \cong \bar{h}_{ik} \oplus \bar{h}_{kj}$. According to Definition 4.13, HP' is additively consistent. □

4.1.4 Selective Algorithm for Reducing EHFLPRs to LPRs Based on Additive Consistency

Based on the associated S-HP-graph, in this section we introduce a selective approach to obtain the reduced LPR with the highest additive consistency level from the given EHFLPR [11]. Motivated by Definition 4.13, the additive consistency level of the judgement h_{ij} can be estimated by the averaging length of paths from v_i to v_j through v_k, where $k \neq i, k \neq j$. For brevity, we let $K = \{1, 2, \ldots, n\} \setminus \{i, j\}$, then for any $k \in K$,

$$len(v_i, (v_i^{l_1}, v_k^{l_1}), v_k, (v_k^{l_2}, v_j^{l_2}), v_j) = w(v_i^{l_1}, v_k^{l_1}) + w(v_k^{l_2}, v_j^{l_2}) \tag{4.12}$$

Thus, the averaging length of paths from v_i to v_j through v_k is:

$$\frac{1}{(\#h_{ik})(\#h_{kj})} \sum_{l_1=1}^{\#h_{ik}} \sum_{l_2=1}^{\#h_{kj}} \left(w(v_i^{l_1}, v_k^{l_1}) + w(v_k^{l_2}, v_j^{l_2}) \right) \tag{4.13}$$

If k goes through all the values in K, then the estimated value of weight of arcs from v_i to v_j, denoted by $\hat{w}(v_i, v_j)$, is:

$$\hat{w}(v_i, v_j) = \frac{1}{n-2} \sum_{k \in K} \frac{1}{(\#h_{ik})(\#h_{kj})} \sum_{l_1=1}^{\#h_{ik}} \sum_{l_2=1}^{\#h_{kj}} \left(w(v_i^{l_1}, v_k^{l_1}) + w(v_k^{l_2}, v_j^{l_2}) \right) \tag{4.14}$$

and the estimated value of the judgement h_{ij}, denoted by $\hat{h}_{ij}$, is:

$$\hat{h}_{ij} = \{s_{\hat{\alpha}}\}, \text{ where } \hat{\alpha} = \hat{w}(v_i, v_j) \tag{4.15}$$

If the arc (v_i^l, v_j^l) is the judgement with the highest additive consistency level, then its weight $w(v_i^l, v_j^l)$ should be the closest to $\hat{w}(v_i, v_j)$, then the optimal weight of the arc from v_i to v_j, denoted by $w^*(v_i, v_j)$, is

$$w^*(v_i, v_j) = w(v_i^{l^*}, v_j^{l^*}), \text{ where } l^* = \underset{l}{argmin}\{|w(v_i^l, v_j^l) - \hat{w}(v_i, v_j)|\} \tag{4.16}$$

Meanwhile the additive consistency level of the judgement h_{ij}, denoted by CI_{ij}, can be defined by

$$CI_{ij} = 1 - |w^*(v_i, v_j) - \hat{w}(v_i, v_j)|/2g \tag{4.17}$$

where $2g$ is the length of the interval $[-g, g]$, which depends on the original LTS $S^{(g)}$.

According to the above analysis, a selective algorithm (Algorithm 2) can be developed to obtain the reduced LPR from the given EHFLPR with the highest additive consistency level [11].

Algorithm 2 The selective algorithm. Input: EHFLPR $HP = (h_{ij})_{n \times n}$; Ouput: the reduced LPR $R = (r_{ij})_{n \times n}$, the consistency level of R (CI)

1: Construct the S-HP-graph by utilizing HP; Initialize R by $r_{ij} = s_0$, $i, j = 1, 2, \ldots, n$;
2: Calculate $\hat{w}(v_i, v_j)$ by using Eq. (4.14), $i, j = 1, 2, \ldots, n$, $i \neq j$;
3: Calculate $w^*(v_i, v_j)$ by using Eq. (4.16); Let $r_{ij} = s_{w^*(v_i, v_j)}$; Calculate CI_{ij} by using Eq. (4.17), $i, j = 1, 2, \ldots, n$, $i \neq j$;
4: The consistency level of R is derived from $CI = \frac{1}{n^2-n} \sum_{i=1}^{n} \sum_{j=1, j \neq i}^{n} CI_{ij}$.

Example 4.15 Given an EHFLPR (based on the LTS in Example 2.3):

$$HP_2 = \begin{pmatrix} \{s_0\} & \{s_{-1}, s_1\} & \{s_1\} & \{s_{-1}\} \\ \{s_1, s_{-1}\} & \{s_0\} & \{s_3\} & \{s_{-1}\} \\ \{s_{-1}\} & \{s_{-3}\} & \{s_0\} & \{s_{-3}, s_{-2}\} \\ \{s_1\} & \{s_1\} & \{s_3, s_2\} & \{s_0\} \end{pmatrix}$$

Then we can obtain a reduced LPR by Algorithm 2, as shown below:

1: The S-HP-graph of HP_2 is given in Fig. 4.3. Initialize R by $R = (s_0)_{4\times 4}$;

2: Calculate the length of the paths from v_1 to v_2 through v_3 and the length of the path from v_1 to v_2 through v_4:

$$len(v_1, (v_1^1, v_3^1), v_3, (v_3^1, v_2^1), v_2) = 1 + (-3) = -2,$$
$$len(v_1, (v_1^1, v_4^1), v_4, (v_4^1, v_2^1), v_2) = \frac{1}{2}(-1 + 1) = 0$$

Thus $\hat{w}(v_1, v_2) = \frac{1}{2}(-2 + 0) = -1$. Similarly, the resultant estimated weights are shown in the following matrix:

$$\hat{W} = \left(\hat{w}(v_i, v_j)\right)_{4\times 4} = \begin{pmatrix} - & -1 & 2.25 & -1.25 \\ 1 & - & 1.25 & -0.25 \\ -2.25 & -1.25 & - & -3 \\ 1.25 & 0.25 & 3 & - \end{pmatrix}$$

3: According to Eq. (4.16), the optimal estimated weights of arcs form the following matrix:

$$W^* = \left(w^*(v_i, v_j)\right)_{4\times 4} = \begin{pmatrix} - & -1 & 1 & -1 \\ 1 & - & 3 & -1 \\ -1 & -3 & - & -3 \\ 1 & 1 & 3 & - \end{pmatrix}$$

and the reduced LPR is:

$$R = \begin{pmatrix} s_0 & s_{-1} & s_1 & s_{-1} \\ s_1 & s_0 & s_3 & s_{-1} \\ s_{-1} & s_{-3} & s_0 & s_{-3} \\ s_1 & s_1 & s_3 & s_0 \end{pmatrix}$$

By using Eq. (4.17), we can calculate $CI_{ij}(i, j = 1, 2, 3, 4, i \neq j)$ as:

$$\left(CI_{ij}\right)_{n\times n} = \begin{pmatrix} - & 1 & 0.7917 & 0.9583 \\ 1 & - & 0.7083 & 0.875 \\ 0.7917 & 0.7083 & - & 1 \\ 0.9583 & 0.875 & 1 & - \end{pmatrix}$$

4: The consistency level of R is $CI = 0.8889$.

In addition, the selected arcs from the original S-HP-graph are shown in Fig. 4.3.

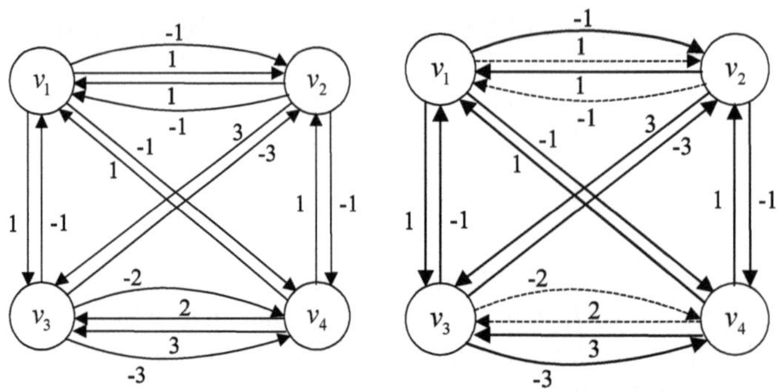

Fig. 4.3 The original S-PH-graph and the reduced S-PH-graph of the EHFLPR in Example 4.15

4.1.5 *Weak Consistency for EHFLPRs*

The strictly additive consistency is a strong condition to evaluate the consistency of the experts' judgements, and thus, it is sometimes unnecessary due to the complex environment and the experts' cognitive diversity. But the weak consistency can avoid logically contradictory judgements in preference relations. In this section, we present the concept of weak consistency for EHFLPRs, and also give a graph theory-based interpretation of weak consistency. After that, an algorithm is introduced to search the reduced LPRs with weak consistency from the original EHFLPR.

Tanino [8] introduced the following concept of weak consistency for fuzzy preference relations:

Definition 4.16 ([8]) Let $R = (r_{ij})_{n\times n}$ be a fuzzy preference relation, for all $i, j, k \in \{1, 2, \ldots, n\}, i \neq j \neq k$, if $r_{ik} \geq 0.5$, $r_{kj} \geq 0.5$, we have $r_{ij} \geq 0.5$, then R is said to have weak transitivity (weak consistency).

Based on this idea, the weak consistency for LPRs can be defined as follows:

Definition 4.17 ([11]) Let $R = (r_{ij})_{n\times n}$ be a LPR, for all $i, j, k \in \{1, 2, \ldots, n\}, i \neq j \neq k$, if $r_{ik} \geq s_0$, and $r_{kj} \geq s_0$, we have $r_{ij} \geq s_0$, then R is said to have weak consistency.

Associated with the P-graph of R, if $r_{ik} \geq s_0$, then there is an arc (v_i, v_k) in G_P; if $r_{kj} \geq s_0$, then there is an arc (v_k, v_j); while if $r_{ij} < s_0$, then there is an arc (v_j, v_i), which leads to a circular triad. Therefore, the weak consistency of R can be checked by its P-graph. As shown in Fig. 4.1, the LPR R_1 in Example 4.6 is weakly consistent. Below we introduce the concept of the weak consistency of EHFLPRs:

Definition 4.18 ([11]) Let $HP = (h_{ij})_{n\times n}$ be an EHFLPR, then HP is said to be of weak consistency if there exists no circular triad in its PH-graph.

However, since all the possible values of the judgements in EHFLPRs are considered, then the possibility of the appearance of circular triad in PH-graphs is usually high. A rational way is to remove illogical arcs from the original EHFLPRs for the derivation of weak consistent HFLPRs, and then to search for LPRs from the weak consistent EHFLPRs.

4.1.6 Broken Circle Algorithm for Reducing EHFLPRs to LPRs Based on Weak Consistency

Xu et al. [15] presented a method to detect circular triads from a digraph of fuzzy preference relations. Zhu and Xu [18] introduced a similar approach to search circular triads from a digraph of hesitant fuzzy preference relation. The approaches can be used in this section directly. Our purpose is to seek for weak consistent LPRs from a given EHFLPR. However, there may be more than one possible LPR with weak consistency. As additive consistency is a more wonderful property of a LPR, we aim at searching the possible LPR with higher additive consistency level. In other words, when we have some different choices to break contradictory judgements by removing arcs from circular triads, the criterion is to remove the arc(s) with the lowest additive consistency level.

Given an EHFLPR $HP = (h_{ij})_{n\times n}$ and its PH-graph $G_{HP} = (V, A)$, all circular triads are found out at first (according to the methods presented in [15, 18]), then one arc is removed at a time. Specifically, each circular triads is denoted by

$$(v_i, (v_i^{l_1}, v_k^{l_1}), v_k, (v_k^{l_2}, v_j^{l_2}), v_j, (v_j^{l_3}, v_i^{l_3}), v_i) \tag{4.18}$$

and the set of arcs included in at least one circular triad is denoted by

$$A_{TRI} = \{(v_i^{l_m}, v_j^{l_m}) | m \text{ is the number of arcs in } A_{TRI}\} \tag{4.19}$$

Then the additive consistency level of each arc can be computed by using Eq. (4.17), for example,

$$CI_{ij}^{l_m} = 1 - |w(v_i^{l_m}, v_j^{l_m}) - \hat{w}(v_i, v_j)|/2g \tag{4.20}$$

The arc with the lowest $CI_{ij}^{l_m}$ implies that it possesses the highest contradictory degree and should be removed from G_{HP} (if the multiplicity of the arc is bigger than 1). Based on the discussion above, we introduce the broken circle algorithm (Algorithm 3).

Algorithm 3 The broken circle algorithm. Input: $HP = (h_{ij})_{n\times n}$; Output: the possible reduced LPRs with weak consistency $R = (r_{ij})_{n\times n}$.

1: Let $p = 0$, $HP^{(p)} = HP$;
2: Construct the HP-graph G_{HP} by utilizing $HP^{(p)}$;
3: If $HP^{(p)}$ is of weak consistency, then go to Step 6; else, go to Step 4;
4: Find out all circular triads and form A_{TRI}; Calculate $CI_{ij}^{l_k}$ $(k = 1, 2, \ldots, m)$; Select the arc with the lowest additive consistency level whose multiplicity is bigger than 1, if there is no such arc, go to Step 7, else, remove the arc from G_{HP} and delete the corresponding linguistic term from $HP^{(p)}$;
5: $HP^{(p+1)} = HP^{(p)}$, $p = p + 1$, go to Step 3;
6: Divide $HP^{(p)}$ into all possible reduced LPRs;
7: End.

Furthermore, if Step 6 of Algorithm 3 is replaced by the selective algorithm, then at most one LPR with both weak consistency and the highest additive consistency level can be output. If the output is null, there exists no possible LPR with weak consistency, and thus, the original EHFLPR does not satisfy weak consistency.

Example 4.19 Let HP_1 be the EHFLPR as in Example 4.9. We can obtain the reduced LPRs with weak consistency from HP_1 by using Algorithm 3, as shown below:

1: Let $p = 0$, $HP^{(0)} = HP_1$;

2: The HP-graph G_{HP} of $HP^{(0)}$ is given in Fig. 4.2;

3: There is a circular triad $(v_1, (v_1^2, v_4^2), v_4, (v_4^1, v_2^1), v_2, (v_2^1, v_1^1), v_1)$ in $HP^{(0)}$, go to Step 4;

4: $A_{TRI} = \{(v_1^2, v_4^2), (v_4^1, v_2^1), (v_2^1, v_1^1)\}$, the estimated weights are $\hat{w}(v_1, v_4) = -1.75$, $\hat{w}(v_4, v_2) = -0.25$, $\hat{w}(v_2, v_1) = 0.5$. Their consistency levels are 0.5417, 0.7917, 0.9167, respectively. The arc (v_1^2, v_4^2) possesses the lowest additive consistency level and its multiplicity is 2. Therefore, we remove (v_1^2, v_4^2) from $HP^{(0)}$, s_1 from h_{14} and s_{-1} from h_{41};

5: Let $HP^{(1)} = HP^{(0)}$, then

$$HP^{(1)} = \begin{pmatrix} \{s_0\} & \{s_{-1}, s_1\} & \{s_1\} & \{s_{-1}\} \\ \{s_1, s_{-1}\} & \{s_0\} & \{s_3\} & \{s_{-1}\} \\ \{s_{-1}\} & \{s_{-3}\} & \{s_0\} & \{s_{-3}, s_{-2}\} \\ \{s_1\} & \{s_1\} & \{s_3, s_2\} & \{s_0\} \end{pmatrix}$$

The HP-graph of $HP^{(1)}$ is shown in Fig. 4.4; $p = 1$; go to Step 3;

3: There is no circular triad in $HP^{(1)}$, thus go to Step 6;

6: Divide $HP^{(1)}$ into four possible reduced LPRs with weak consistency:

$$R_1^{H_1} = \begin{pmatrix} s_0 & s_{-1} & s_1 & s_{-1} \\ s_1 & s_0 & s_3 & s_{-1} \\ s_{-1} & s_{-3} & s_0 & s_{-3} \\ s_1 & s_1 & s_3 & s_0 \end{pmatrix}, \quad R_2^{H_1} = \begin{pmatrix} s_0 & s_{-1} & s_1 & s_{-1} \\ s_1 & s_0 & s_3 & s_{-1} \\ s_{-1} & s_{-3} & s_0 & s_{-2} \\ s_1 & s_1 & s_2 & s_0 \end{pmatrix}$$

$$R_3^{H_1} = \begin{pmatrix} s_0 & s_1 & s_1 & s_{-1} \\ s_{-1} & s_0 & s_3 & s_{-1} \\ s_{-1} & s_{-3} & s_0 & s_{-3} \\ s_1 & s_1 & s_3 & s_0 \end{pmatrix}, \quad R_4^{H_1} = \begin{pmatrix} s_0 & s_1 & s_1 & s_{-1} \\ s_{-1} & s_0 & s_3 & s_{-1} \\ s_{-1} & s_{-3} & s_0 & s_{-2} \\ s_1 & s_1 & s_2 & s_0 \end{pmatrix}$$

4.1.7 Comparative Analyses

(1) *Rationality of the two algorithms*

In the selective algorithm, the arcs with the highest additive consistency degree are selected for each pair of vertices by estimating the averaging weights. The ratio-

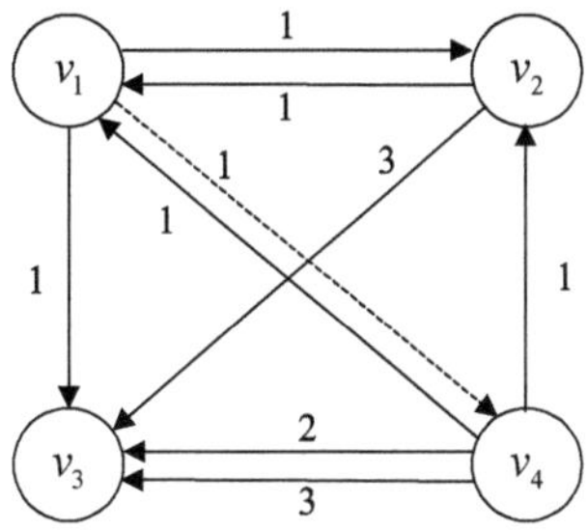

Fig. 4.4 The resultant S-HP-graph of Example 4.19 after completing the broken circle algorithm. The dotted arc is the one removed from the original S-HP-graph

nality of the reduced LPR can be easily clarified as follows: The given EHFLPR HP_2 in Example 4.15 is first divided into four possible LPRs which are just listed in Step 6 of Example 4.19. Then we can employ the approach for additive consistency checking [4] to calculate the consistency levels of four LPRs, denoted by $(CI(R_i^{H_1})(i = 1, 2, 3, 4)$, the results are (Note that the consistency level defined by [4] is the smaller the better):

$$CI(R_1^{H_1}) = 0.0962, CI(R_2^{H_1}) = 0.1179, CI(R_3^{H_1}) = 0.1667, CI(R_4^{H_1}) = 0.1800$$

Therefore, $R_1^{H_1}$ is the LPR with the highest additive consistency level, which is the LPR derived by the selective algorithm.

The rationality of the broken circle algorithm is apparent according to the definition of weak consistency.

(2) *Compared with similar techniques*

Zhu and Xu [19] presented the additive consistency of HFLPRs as well. We compare our method with the technique of [19] by using the HFLPR (based on the LTS $S^{(4)}$):

$$HP_3 = \begin{pmatrix} \{s_0\} & \{s_1\} & \{s_2, s_3\} & \{s_1\} \\ \{s_{-1}\} & \{s_0\} & \{s_{-4}, s_{-3}\} & \{s_2\} \\ \{s_{-2}, s_{-3}\} & \{s_4, s_3\} & \{s_0\} & \{s_{-3}, s_{-2}\} \\ \{s_{-1}\} & \{s_{-2}\} & \{s_3, s_2\} & \{s_0\} \end{pmatrix}$$

Firstly, we need to analyze the constructive additively consistent EHFLPRs: According to [19], the normalized EHFLPR can be obtained by $\beta-$normalization at first:

$$HP_3^N = \begin{pmatrix} \{s_0\} & \{s_1, s_1\} & \{s_2, s_3\} & \{s_1, s_1\} \\ \{s_{-1}, s_{-1}\} & \{s_0\} & \{s_{-4}, s_{-3}\} & \{s_2, s_2\} \\ \{s_{-2}, s_{-3}\} & \{s_4, s_3\} & \{s_0\} & \{s_{-3}, s_{-2}\} \\ \{s_{-1}, s_{-1}\} & \{s_{-2}, s_{-2}\} & \{s_3, s_2\} & \{s_0\} \end{pmatrix}$$

Then the additively consistent EHFLPR can be constructed as:

$$HP_3' = \begin{pmatrix} \{s_0\} & \{s_{1.75}, s_{1.75}\} & \{s_{1.25}, s_{1.75}\} & \{s_1, s_{1.5}\} \\ \{s_{-1.75}, s_{-1.75}\} & \{s_0\} & \{s_{-0.5}, s_0\} & \{s_{-0.75}, s_{-0.25}\} \\ \{s_{-1.25}, s_{-1.75}\} & \{s_{0.5}, s_0\} & \{s_0\} & \{s_{-0.25}, s_{-0.25}\} \\ \{s_{-1}, s_{-1.5}\} & \{s_{0.75}, s_{0.25}\} & \{s_{0.25}, s_{0.25}\} & \{s_0\} \end{pmatrix}$$

Whereas if we use Definition 2.13 and Theorem 4.14, then the additive consistent EHFLPR can be constructed as:

$$HP_3'' = \begin{pmatrix} \{s_0\} & \{s_{1.25}, s_{1.75}, s_2\} & \{s_1, s_{1.25}, s_{1.5}, s_{1.75}, s_2\} & \{s_1, s_{1.25}, s_{1.5}\} \\ \{s_{-1.25}, s_{-1.75}, s_{-2}\} & \{s_0\} & \{s_{-0.75}, s_{-0.5}, s_{-0.25}, s_0, s_{0.25}\}\} & \{s_{-0.75}, s_{-0.5}, s_{-0.25}\} \\ \{s_{-1}, s_{-1.25}, s_{-1.5}, s_{-1.75}, s_{-2}\} & \{s_{0.75}, s_{0.5}, s_{0.25}, s_0, s_{-0.25}\}\} & \{s_0\} & \{s_{-0.75}, s_{-0.5}, s_{-0.25}, s_0, s_{0.25}\} \\ \{s_{-1}, s_{-1.25}, s_{-1.5}\} & \{s_{0.75}, s_{0.5}, s_{0.25}\} & \{s_{0.75}, s_{0.5}, s_{0.25}, s_0, s_{-0.25}\} & \{s_0\} \end{pmatrix}$$

The advantages of the selective algorithm are obvious: It considers all possible values during the process of computation. Furthermore, we do not need a normalization procedure which may bring the values that are not included in the original EHFLPRs.

In addition, the additive consistency levels are also discussed in [19]. However, it is meaningless to compare the numerical results of consistency levels because Zhu and Xu [19] investigated the consistency level of the given HFLPR, while this chapter focuses on the consistency level of the reduced LPR. Therefore, we can conclude that the focuses of these two are different. Zhu and Xu [19] further gave the approaches to improve the HFLPR if its consistency level is unacceptable, while in this chapter, the additive consistency and the consistency level are defined by a general form. The defined concepts are used as measures to reduce an EHFLPR to a LPR with the highest consistency level so that the existing techniques of LPRs can be used directly. Then the decision-making problems with preference relations can be solved completely. We note that the two are not aiming at the same topic but complementary with each other. The introduced results of this chapter can be seen as a sequential study of [19]. In practice, if an EHFLPR is derived, then it can be improved to an acceptable one by the approaches in [19] (more properly, designing the approaches by the idea and framework in [19] while using the algorithms in this chapter), and then can be reduced to a LPR with highest consistency level, and the ranking or priorities can be obtained by the existing techniques for LPRs, such as the approaches proposed in [13].

Another consistency measure, i.e., the weak consistency measure, has been introduced for EHFLPRs. There are some other similar techniques in the existing literature, for example, Zhu and Xu [18] gave the algorithms for the regression of hesitant fuzzy preference relations, and thus, the uncertain setting is different from that in this chapter. Besides, it is more visible to use graph theory to deal with two mentioned consistency measures. However, the graphs are only used for weak consistency in [18]. Ma et al. [7] and Xu et al. [15] investigated weak consistency by graph theory as well, but they all focused on fuzzy preference relations.

(3) *Additive consistency versus weak consistency*

Generally speaking, weak consistency helps to avoid logic contradictions in preference relations, and additive consistency indicates the complete consistency. Therefore, it is natural to consider weak consistency at first, and then to reach a high level of additive consistency. It is obvious that the EHFLPR HP_2 provided in Example 4.15 is $HP^{(1)}$ derived by Step 5 of Example 4.19. Thus it can be known that for a given EHFLPR, the broken circle algorithm should be used at first to ensure its weak consistency and then the selective algorithm can be employed to reach a high additive consistency level.

(4) *Regarding to "indifference" (s_0)*

In pair-wise judgements, "indifference" may emerge, i.e., there exists $w(v_i^l, v_j^l) = 0$ and thus $w(v_j^l, v_i^l) = 0$, which is corresponding to two arcs between v_i and v_j with the opposite direction in PH-graphs. In such a case, circular triads may not indicate the dissatisfaction of weak consistency. Xu et al. [15] investigated the problem in detail. It is not an issue when the additive consistency is considered in this chapter because symmetric graphs are used in the selective algorithm. When it comes to weak consistency, the EHFLPRs including "indifference" can also be reduced to weak consistent EHFLPRs by the broken circle algorithm. We can clarify this issue by the following additional example:

Example 4.20 Given an EHFLPR (based on the LTS in Example 2.3):

$$HP_4 = \begin{pmatrix} \{s_0\} & \{s_{-1}, s_0\} & \{s_1, s_2\} & \{s_1\} \\ \{s_1, s_0\} & \{s_0\} & \{s_3\} & \{s_{-1}\} \\ \{s_{-1}, s_{-2}\} & \{s_{-3}\} & \{s_0\} & \{s_{-4}, s_{-3}\} \\ \{s_{-1}\} & \{s_1\} & \{s_4, s_3\} & \{s_0\} \end{pmatrix}$$

Using Algorithm 3, the PH-graph of $HP^{(0)}$ is shown in Fig. 4.5. There are two circles among v_1, v_4, and v_2. As $\hat{w}(v_2, v_1) = -0.25$, the second arc from v_2 to v_1 should be removed at first. Then the other arc from v_2 to v_1 will also be deleted as long as the algorithm goes on (see Fig. 4.5). Actually, the second operation makes no sense for the EHFLPR. The resultant weak consistent EHFLPR is:

$$HP_4^{(2)} = \begin{pmatrix} \{s_0\} & \{s_0\} & \{s_1, s_2\} & \{s_1\} \\ \{s_0\} & \{s_0\} & \{s_3\} & \{s_{-1}\} \\ \{s_{-1}, s_{-2}\} & \{s_{-3}\} & \{s_0\} & \{s_{-4}, s_{-3}\} \\ \{s_{-1}\} & \{s_1\} & \{s_4, s_3\} & \{s_0\} \end{pmatrix}$$

Therefore, this algorithm can effectively deal with "indifference" although some redundant operations might be done.

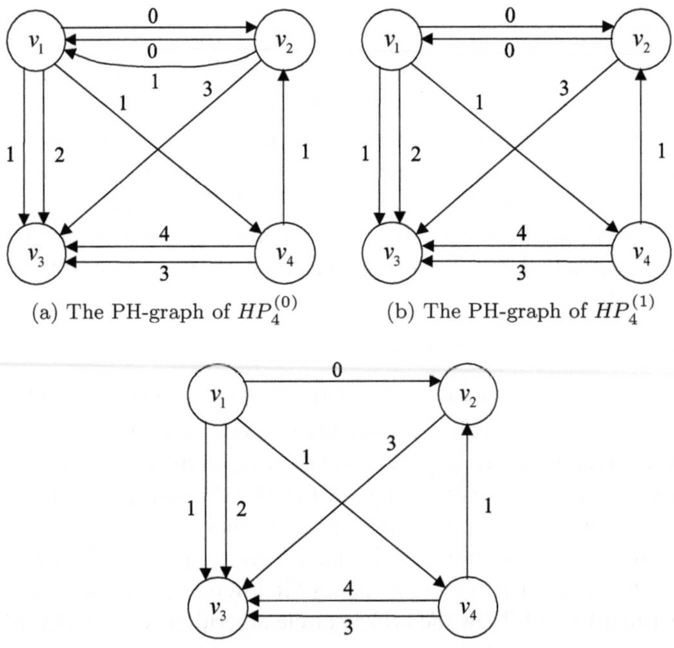

(a) The PH-graph of $HP_4^{(0)}$ (b) The PH-graph of $HP_4^{(1)}$

(c) The PH-graph of $HP_4^{(2)}$

Fig. 4.5 The PH-graphs of HP_4 during the procedure of Algorithm 3 in Example 4.20

4.2 Improving Incomplete LPRs Based on Consistency Measures of EHFLPRs

As discussed in Sect. 1.3.3, most of the existing contributions regarding incomplete LPRs focus on automatic approaches to complete missing entries and to obtain priorities. However, when expressing preferences, there might be deviations between experts' provided information and their real opinions. More accurate preferences could be obtained if interactive processes are employed. It should be noted that completing missing entries is not the only aim of interactive processes. These processes improve incomplete LPRs and obtain more accurate decision information. Thus, it is rational and meaningful to interact with experts. For one thing, if the provided information coincides with their real opinion, then the estimated values of missing entries could be reviewed, selected and revised by experts. For another, if the deviations exist, then they could be delivered to the estimated values and the deviations of missing entries between the estimated values and the potential opinions of experts could become greater and greater. When receiving the estimated values, experts might realize the deviations. Both the original known entries and the missing entries could be improved.

Based on this idea, in this section, we focus on the interactive algorithms for improving the incomplete LPRs. We begin the discussion with an acceptable incomplete LPRs given by the experts. As the weak consistency is the basic condition that LPRs should satisfy, we introduce the corresponding definition of incomplete LPRs and then present an algorithm to ensure that a given incomplete LPRs is of weak consistency. Then two algorithms for the completion of weak consistent incomplete LPRs are introduced [12]. Similar to the above section, we assume that a LPR is a binary relation defined on $V \times V$, where $V = (v_1, v_2, \ldots, v_n)$.

4.2.1 Incomplete LPRs and Their Consistency Measures

In order to model LPRs with missing entries, Xu [14] presented the following definition:

Definition 4.21 ([14]) Let $R = (r_{ij})_{n\times n}$ be a LPR, then R is called an incomplete LPR if some of its elements cannot be given by the experts, which we denote by the unknown variable "x", and the others can be provided by the experts, which satisfy:

$$r_{ij} \in S^{(g)},\ r_{ij} \oplus r_{ji} = s_0, r_{ii} = s_0, \forall i, j \tag{4.21}$$

Similar to Definition 4.21, we introduce the concept of incomplete EHFLPRs in the next definition, based on the concept of EHFLPRs defined in Sect. 4.1:

Definition 4.22 ([12]) Let $HP = (h_{ij})_{n\times n}$ be an EHFLPR, where $h_{ij} = \{s_{\alpha^l_{ij}} | l = 1, 2, \ldots, \#h_{ij}\}$ is an EHFLTS. If some elements in HP are unknown, and all the existing entries satisfy: $\forall l = 1, 2, \ldots, \#h_{ij}, i, j = 1, 2, \ldots, n, i < j$,

$$s_{\alpha^l_{ij}} \oplus s_{\alpha^l_{ji}},\ h_{ii} = \{s_0\},\ \#h_{ij} = \#h_{ji} \tag{4.22}$$

then HP is called an incomplete EHFLPR. The unknown entries are denoted as "x".

In this section, a LPR $R = (r_{ij})_{n\times n}$ is considered as the special case of an EHFLPR $HP = (h_{ij})_{n\times n}$, where $h_{ij} = \{r_{ij}\}$. Considering a LPR, Xu [14] defined the acceptable incomplete LPR by checking if every alternative is compared at least once.

Definition 4.23 ([14]) Let $R = (r_{ij})_{n\times n}$ be an incomplete LPR, R is acceptable if there exists at least one known entry (except diagonal elements) in each line or each column of R, i.e., there exist at least $n - 1$ judgements provided by the experts.

We only discuss the acceptable incomplete LPRs in this book. Some studies related to the unacceptable cases can be found in [2, 16]. The concept of acceptable incomplete EHFLPRs can be defined similarly. Xu [13] defined the additive consistency of incomplete LPRs by letting Eq. (4.7) hold for any known entries. A better idea to define the additive consistency is to take the completeness of the incomplete LPRs into account (see [6] for detail).

This section employs preference graphs defined in Sect. 4.1.2 as a tool. Different from complete LPRs, the weak consistency of an incomplete LPR can not be checked by the presence of circular triads. Generally, a cycle $(v_{i_1}, (v_{i_1}, v_{i_2}), v_{i_2}, \ldots, (v_{i_{k-1}}, v_{i_k}), v_{i_k}, (v_{i_k}, v_{i_1}), v_{i_1})$ with k vertices is denoted as a k-cycle, $3 \leq k \leq n$. A k-cycle may lead to weak inconsistency of a given LPRs. We refer it to as illogical k-cycle in the following definition:

Definition 4.24 ([12]) A k-cycle $(v_{i_1}, (v_{i_1}, v_{i_2}), v_{i_2}, \ldots, (v_{i_{k-1}}, v_{i_k}), v_{i_k}, (v_{i_k}, v_{i_1}), v_{i_1})$ of P-graph (or PH-graph) is an illogical k-cycle if there exists at least an arc (v_i, v_j) such that $w(v_i, v_j) > 0$.

Based on Definition 4.24, the weak consistency of incomplete LPRs and incomplete EHFLPRs can be redefined by the absence of illogical k-cycles.

Definition 4.25 ([12]) Let $R = (r_{ij})_{n \times n}$ be an incomplete LPR, R is said to be of weak consistency if there exists no illogical k-cycle ($3 \leq k \leq n$) in its P-graph.

Definition 4.26 ([12]) Let $HP = (h_{ij})_{n \times n}$ be an incomplete EHFLPR, HP is said to be of weak consistency if there exists no illogical k-cycle ($3 \leq k \leq n$) in its PH-graph.

4.2.2 An Interactive Algorithm to Reach Weak Consistency of Incomplete LPRs

The first task of decision support is to ensure the incomplete LPRs provided by experts are logically rational, i.e., weakly consistent. Thus, we introduce an interactive algorithm to detect and repair inconsistencies of given incomplete LPRs [12].

The most significant procedure of weak consistency detection is to find out k-cycles in the P-graph of an incomplete LPRs. Xu et al. [17] developed an algorithm to search for k-cycles based on the numerical matrix of incomplete fuzzy preference relations. In this section, weak consistency is tested based on the P-graph. The elementary cycle (EC) algorithm proposed by Tiernan [9] can be employed to list all k-cycles because it can be implemented by programming languages directly.

When the k-cycles of a P-graph are figured out, some advices should be given to the exerts to repair weak inconsistencies. Two classes of arcs which appear in k-cycles might be illogical judgements with high possibilities. The first class includes those who appear most frequently in the list of k-cycles. If this class of arcs is repaired, k-cycles would be removed rapidly. Another class is those who possess smaller weights. It is clear that only the directions of arcs can influence the weak consistency. Considering the provided r_{ij} and the actual value in the experts' mind r_{ij}^*, it is rational to hypothesize that the deviation between them are random. Thus if r_{ij}^* is close to s_0, then r_{ij}^* falls into a range nearby s_0, which results to the direction of arc defined by r_{ij} may be opposite to that defined by r_{ij}^*. In the following interactive algorithm, the experts are suggested to consider revising the two classes of arcs in the P-graph. The criterion of deriving the recommended values is to revise the direction of the corresponding arc. Specifically, if an illogical entry $r_{ij} > s_0$ needs revision, then

r_{ij} should be revised to any term of $\{s_{-g}, s_{-g+1}, \ldots, s_0\}$, and r_{ji} should be revised to the corresponding term of $\{s_0, s_1, \ldots, s_g\}$. The interactive weak consistency reaching (WCR) algorithm is described in Algorithm 4 [12].

Algorithm 4 The WCR algorithm. Input: an incomplete LPR $R = (r_{ij})_{n\times n}$; Output: an incomplete LPR with weak consistency.

1: Initiation. Construct the P-graph of R, denoted as $G_P = (V, A)$; let $m = 0$, $R^{(m)} = r$, $G_P^{(m)} = G_P$;
2: Find all k-cycles ($3 \le k \le n$) in $G_P^{(m)}$ by the EC algorithm. Remove the logical cycles whose weights of arcs are equal to 0. The resultant set of cycles is denoted by C;
3: If $C = \emptyset$, then $R^{(m)}$ is weak consistent, go to Step 7; else go to Step 4;
4: Find the arc(s) (v_i, v_j) which is the most frequent in C. The set of position indices of entries need to be revised is denoted by $E_1 = \{(i, j)|(v_i, v_j)\text{is the most frequent arc in } C\}$. Find the arc(s)whose weight is the closest (not equal) to 0 and let $E = E_1 \cup \{(i, j)|w(x_i, x_j) \text{ is the closest to 0 in } C\}$;
5: For each $(i, j) \in E$, recommend $h_{ji} = \{s_0, s_1, \ldots, s_g\}$ to the experts. The experts should choose the entry with the highest confident level to revise, using one of the recommended linguistic terms. If the experts choose $r^*_{ji} \in h_{ji}$ as the revised value of s_{ji}, then let $r_{ji} = r^*_{ji}$ (correspondingly, $r_{ij} = neg(r_{ji})$), the new incomplete LPR is denoted by $R^{(m+1)}$ and its G-graph is denoted by $G_P^{(m+1)}$;
6: $m = m + 1$, go to Step 2;
7: End.

The following theorem can be easily obtained from the procedure of the WCR algorithm:

Theorem 4.27 ([12]) *Algorithm 4 is finite and returns the weakly consistent incomplete LPR of a given incomplete LPR.*

Proof (1) The finiteness of the WCR algorithm is proven at first by clarifying that the number of k-cycles would be decreased once the direction of an arc is revised. Suppose that the algorithm revises the direction of the arc (v_i, v_j), and consider that there is a path from v_l to v_m, then there can be three possible relations between the arc (v_i, v_j) and the path from v_l to v_m, which is illustrated in Fig. 4.6. In Case 1 and Case 2, the original cycles, which include (v_i, v_j), are removed from the P-graph, and no new cycle emerges. Whereas in Case 3, it seems a new cycle raises up when (v_i, v_j) is revised to (v_j, v_i). In fact, if the original cycle includes (v_i, v_j), there must be another cycle including the path $(v_i, (v_i, v_l), v_l, \ldots, v_m, (v_m, v_j), v_j)$. Thus the arc (v_i, v_j) is suggested to be revised only because its weight is close to 0. After revision, a new cycle $(v_i, (v_i, v_l), v_l, \ldots, v_m, (v_m, v_j), v_j, (v_j, v_i), v_i)$ is constructed and (v_j, v_i) would not be recommended any more. The relation between a recommended arc and another path can be transformed to Cases 1 and 2, which completes the proof of the finiteness of the WCR algorithm.

(2) The weak consistency can be obtained immediately by the procedure of the algorithm. □

We further present an example to illustrate the validity of Algorithm 4.

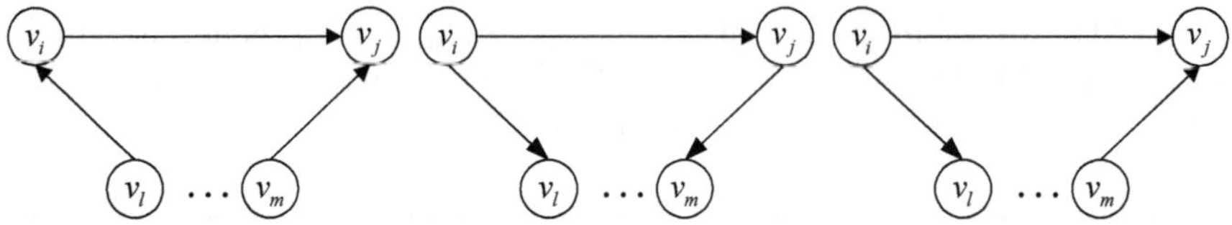

(a) Case 1 (b) Case 2 (c) Case 3

Fig. 4.6 The possible relations between the arc (v_i, v_j) and the path from v_l to v_m

Example 4.28 Suppose that an incomplete LPR is provided by an expert as follows (based on the LTS in Example 2.3):

$$R_1 = \begin{pmatrix} s_0 & s_{-2} & x & x & s_3 & s_{-3} \\ s_2 & s_0 & s_1 & s_{-1} & x & s_{-3} \\ x & s_{-1} & s_0 & x & x & s_4 \\ x & s_1 & x & s_0 & s_{-3} & x \\ s_{-3} & x & x & s_3 & s_0 & x \\ s_3 & s_3 & s_{-4} & x & x & s_0 \end{pmatrix}$$

1: Let $m = 0$; $R^{(0)} = R_1$; $G_P^{(0)}$ is shown in Fig. 4.7;

2: There are a 3-cycles $(v_2, (v_2, v_3), v_3, (v_3, v_6), v_6, (v_6, v_2), v_2)$, a 4-cycle $(x_1, (v_1, v_5), v_5, (v_5, v_4), v_4, (v_4, v_2), v_2, (v_2, v_1), v_1)$ and a 6-cycle $(v_1, (v_1, v_5), v_5, (v_5, v_4), v_4, (v_4, v_2), v_2, (v_2, v_3), v_3, (v_3, v_6), v_6, (v_6, v_1), v_1)$ in $G_P^{(0)}$;

3: C is not empty, go to Step 4;

4: The arcs $(v_1, v_5), (v_5, v_4), (v_4, v_2), (v_2, v_3), (v_3, v_6)$ appear twice. The arcs $(v_2, v_3), (v_4, v_2)$ possess the smallest weights (1). Thus $E = \{(1, 5), (5, 4), (4, 2), (2, 3), (3, 6)\}$;

5: For each $(i, j) \in E$, recommend $h_{ji} = \{s_0, s_1, \ldots, s_4\}$ to the experts. Suppose that the experts realize that $r_{32} = s_1$ ($r_{23} = s_{-1}$), then new incomplete LPR is denoted by $R^{(1)}$; $G_P^{(1)}$ is shown in Fig. 4.7;

6: $m = 1$, go to Step 2;

2: There is only one 4-cycle in $G_P^{(1)}$: $(v_1, (v_1, v_5), v_5, (v_5, v_4), v_4, (v_4, v_2), v_2, (v_2, v_1), v_1)$;

3: C is not empty, go to Step 4;

4: The 4 arcs appear once; and the weight of (x_4, x_2) is the smallest, then $E = \{(1, 5), (5, 4), (4, 2), (2, 1)\}$;

5: For each $(i, j) \in E$, recommend $h_{ji} = \{s_0, s_1, \ldots, s_4\}$ to the experts. Suppose that the experts realize that r_{24} should be s_1 (correspondingly, $r_{42} = s_{-1}$), the new incomplete LPR is denoted by $R^{(2)}$ and its G-graph, which is shown in (c) of Fig. 4.7, is denoted by $G_P^{(2)}$;

6: $m = 2$, go to Step 2;

2: There is no cycle in $G_P^{(2)}$;

3: C is empty. Thus $R^{(2)}$ is weakly consistent, go to Step 7;

7: End.

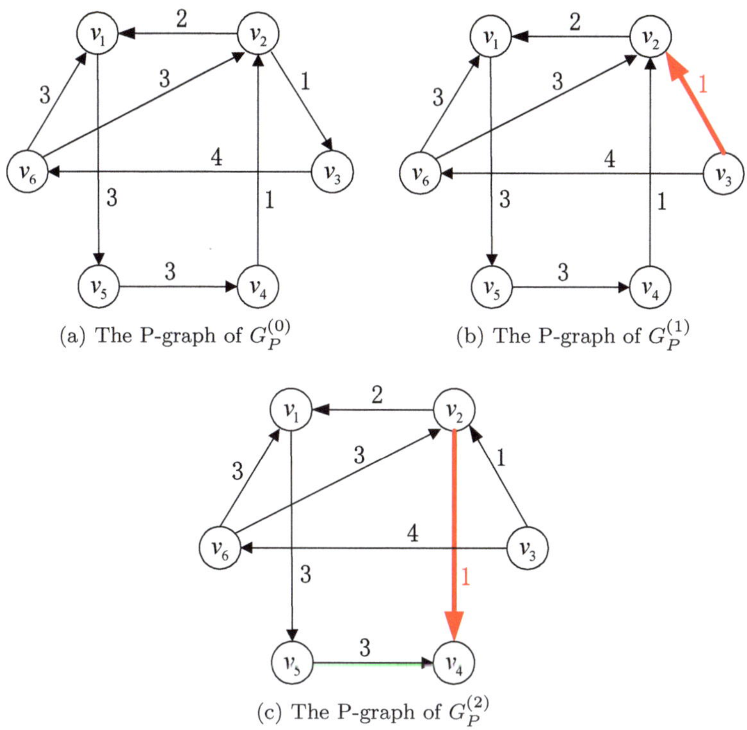

Fig. 4.7 The P-graphs of the incomplete LPRs in Example 4.28

Note that the weak inconsistency of incomplete HFLPRs can be detected and repaired by a completely similar way to the above algorithm. Further, if the experts are enabled to have hesitancy on the recommended linguistic terms, then the incomplete LPR becomes an incomplete HFLPR during the interaction. A similar algorithm can be developed for this situation.

4.2.3 A Consistency-Based Interactive Algorithm to Complete Incomplete LPRs

Given a weak consistent incomplete LPR, in this section, we introduce an interactive algorithms to complete it for supporting decision-making. For a given incomplete LPR $R = (r_{ij})_{n\times n}$ associated with its P-graph $G_P = (V, A_P)$ and SP-graph $G_{S-P} = (V, A_{S-P})$, the set of all possible arcs is denoted by:

$$A = \{(v_i, v_j)|i, j = 1, 2, \ldots, n, i \neq j\} \tag{4.23}$$

The set of known arcs of G_P is:

$$EA_P = \{(v_i, v_j) \in A | (v_i, v_j) \in A_P\} \tag{4.24}$$

The set of known arcs of G_{S-P} is:

$$EA_{S-P} = \{(v_i, v_j) \in A | (v_i, v_j) \in A_{S-P}\} \tag{4.25}$$

The set of missing arcs of G_{S-P} is:

$$MA_{S-P} = A \backslash EA_{S-P} \tag{4.26}$$

Two useful sets of lower indices are:

$$J_{ik}^{(WC)} = \{j | (v_i, v_j), (v_j, v_k) \in EA_P\} \tag{4.27}$$

$$J_{ik}^{(AC)} = \{j | (v_i, v_j), (v_j, v_k) \in EA_{S-P}\} \tag{4.28}$$

Below we consider the estimating all the possible values of missing entries of a incomplete LPR based on additive consistency and weak consistency, represent the values by EHFLTSs, and recommend experts to select from EFHLTSs. Specifically, for a missing entry r_{ik}, if there exists j such that r_{ij} and r_{jk} are known then r_{ik} can be estimated by $r_{ij} \oplus r_{jk}$ according to the definition of additive consistency. This is the very approach presented in [14]. However, the incomplete LPR may be not strictly additive consistent. Thus if there exist j_1 and j_2 such that $r_{ij_1}, r_{j_1k}, r_{ij_2}, r_{j_2k}$ are known, but $r_{ij_1} \oplus r_{j_1k} \neq r_{ij_2} \oplus r_{j_2k}$, the existing methods calculate the averaging value of the two results by some means. Moreover, when presenting a LPR by pairwise comparisons, the experts may have deviations between the provided values and their actual opinions. In this case, it is rational to elicit them to seek out the deviations by a third-party object (alternative). Thus the introduce algorithm first calculates all the possible linguistic terms for the missing elements of an incomplete LPR, and recommends these values to the experts [12]. The experts can select the most possible term(s) to complete the incomplete LPR. The introduce algorithm use EHFLTSs as they can represent all possible linguistic terms simultaneously. Thus the output of this algorithm is generally an EHFLPR.

The main advantage of this idea is the consideration of all possible linguistic terms and the recommendation to the experts for completing incomplete LPRs by interaction. However, an incomplete LPR may be not weakly consistent any more if the missing entries are completed only by the additive consistency because some of the possible linguistic terms may be illogical. These illogical terms should be removed from the estimated sets of linguistic terms. Therefore, when estimating a missing entry, the proposed algorithm calculates the possible linguistic terms according to weak consistency and then computes the possible terms based on additive consistency. The intersection of these two classes of possible terms serves as the set of recommended values of a missing entry. The procedures are specified in Algorithm 5 [12].

Algorithm 5 The additive consistency and weak consistency-based inter-active algorithm (ACWC algorithm). Input: a weakly consistent incomplete LPR $R = (r_{ij})_{n\times n}$; Output: a weakly consistent EHFLPR.

1: Initiate $HP = (h_{ij})_{n\times n}$: if r_{ij} is known, then $h_{ij} = \{r_{ij}\}$, else $h_{ij} = \{\}$;
2: If HP is complete, go to Step 7; else go to Step 3;
3: For any $(v_i, v_k) \in MA_{S-P}$, if $\#J_{ik}^{(WC)} > 0$, then there should be an arc from v_i to v_k, thus the weakly consistent estimated value is $\hat{h}_{ik}^{(WC)} = \{s_0, s_1, \ldots, s_g\}$ ($\hat{h}_{ki}^{(WC)} = \{s_{-g}, s_{-g+1}, \ldots, s_0\}$), $EA_P = EA_P \cup \{(v_i, v_k)\}$; else if $\#J_{ki}^{(WC)} > 0$, let $\hat{h}_{ki}^{(WC)} = \{s_0, s_1, \ldots, s_g\}$ ($\hat{h}_{ik}^{(WC)} = \{s_{-g}, s_{-g+1}, \ldots, s_0\}$), $EA_P = EA_P \cup \{(v_k, v_i)\}$. Repeat the procedures till no new arc is added into EA_P; let $\hat{h}_{ik}^{(WC)} = \hat{h}_{ki}^{(WC)} = \{s_{-g}, \ldots, s_0, \ldots, s_g\}$, where $(v_i, v_k) \notin EA_P$ and $(v_k, v_i) \notin EA_P, i \neq k$;
4: For any $(v_i, v_k) \in MA_{S-P}$, if $\#J_{ik}^{(AC)} > 0$, let $\hat{h}_{ik}^j = h_{ij} \oplus h_{jk} (\forall j \in J_{ik}^{(AC)})$, then the additive consistent estimated value is $\hat{h}_{ik}^{(AC)} = \cup_{j\in J_{ik}^{(AC)}} \hat{h}_{ik}^j$;
5: The estimated value of h_{ik} is $\hat{h}_{ik} = \hat{h}_{ik}^{(WC)} \bigcap \hat{h}_{ik}^{(AC)}$, where $(v_i, v_k) \in MA_{S-P}$;
6: Recommend all the estimated values to the experts and suggest acknowledging the entry with the highest confident level. If a subset of $\hat{h}_{ik}$, denoted by h_{ik}, is selected by the experts, then h_{ik} is the confirmed value of v_i over v_k and h_{ki} can be obtained by Definition 4.3. Let $EA_{S-P} = EA_{S-P} \cup \{(v_i, v_k), (v_k, v_i)\}$, $MA_{S-P} = MA_{S-P} \setminus \{(v_i, v_k), (v_k, v_i)\}$. If $h_{ik} \geq s_0$, $EA_P = EA_P \cup \{(v_i, v_k)\}$; if $h_{ki} \geq s_0$, $EA_P = EA_P \cup \{(v_k, v_i)\}$; go to Step 2. If the experts fail to determine which one(s) should be selected, go to Step 7;
7: Output HP.

It is apparent that Algorithm 5 is finite and its output is weakly consistent. The algorithm enables the experts to complete only one missing entry at each interaction to keep the weak consistency of the given incomplete LPR. Note that some estimated possible linguistic terms may lie outside the interval $[s_{-g}, s_g]$. Thus the following transformative function is introduced to normalize the extreme values:

$$f(s_\alpha) = \begin{cases} s_{-g}, & s_\alpha < s_{-g} \\ s_g, & s_\alpha > s_g \\ s_\alpha, & otherwise \end{cases} \tag{4.29}$$

Example 4.29 Given the following weak consistent incomplete LPR resulted from Example 4.28:

$$R_1 = \begin{pmatrix} s_0 & s_{-2} & x & x & s_3 & s_{-3} \\ s_2 & s_0 & s_{-1} & s_1 & x & s_{-3} \\ x & s_1 & s_0 & x & x & s_4 \\ x & s_{-1} & x & s_0 & s_{-3} & x \\ s_{-3} & x & x & s_3 & s_0 & x \\ s_3 & s_3 & s_{-4} & x & x & s_0 \end{pmatrix}$$

1: Initiate HP:

$$HP = \begin{pmatrix} \{s_0\} & \{s_{-2}\} & \{\} & \{\} & \{s_3\} & \{s_{-3}\} \\ \{s_2\} & \{s_0\} & \{s_{-1}\} & \{s_1\} & \{\} & \{s_{-3}\} \\ \{\} & \{s_1\} & \{s_0\} & \{\} & \{\} & \{s_4\} \\ \{\} & \{s_{-1}\} & \{\} & \{s_0\} & \{s_{-3}\} & \{\} \\ \{s_{-3}\} & \{\} & \{\} & \{s_3\} & \{s_0\} & \{\} \\ \{s_3\} & \{s_3\} & \{s_{-4}\} & \{\} & \{\} & \{s_0\} \end{pmatrix}$$

2: HP is not complete, go to Step 3;

3–5: Take $(v_1, v_3) \in MA_{S-P}$ for instance. As $\#J_{13}^{(WC)} = 0, \#J_{31}^{(WC)} = 2, J_{13}^{(AC)} = \{2, 6\}$, we have $\hat{h}_{31}^{(WC)} = \{s_0, s_1, \ldots, s_4\}$ ($\hat{h}_{13}^{(WC)} = \{s_{-4}, s_{-3}, \ldots, s_0\}$), $\hat{h}_{13}^{(AC)} = (h_{12} \oplus h_{23}) \cup (h_{16} \oplus h_{63}) = \{s_{-7}, s_{-3}\}$. According to Eq. (4.29), $\hat{h}_{13}^{(AC)} = \{s_{-4}, s_{-3}\}$. Thus, the estimated value of h_{13} is $\hat{h}_{13} = \hat{h}_{13}^{(AC)} \bigcap \hat{h}_{13}^{(AC)} = \{s_{-4}, s_{-3}\}$. Similarly, other missing arcs (in the upper triangular) are calculated and shown in Table 4.1;

6: Suppose that the experts select $h_{34} = \{s_2\}$ with the highest confident level, go to Step 2;

2: HP is not complete, go to Step 3;

3–5: The estimating procedure and recommended values are shown in Table 4.2;

Table 4.1 The estimating procedure and the recommended values of Example 4.29: the first interaction

Arc	$\hat{h}_{ik}^{(WC)}$	$\hat{h}_{ik}^{(AC)}$	$\hat{h}_{ik}$
(v_1, v_3)	$\{s_{-4}, s_{-3}, \ldots, s_0\}$	$\{s_{-4}, s_{-3}\}$	$\{s_{-4}, s_{-3}\}$
(v_1, v_4)	$\{s_0, s_1, \ldots, s_4\}$	$\{s_{-1}, s_4\}$	$\{s_4\}$
(v_2, v_5)	$\{s_0, s_1, \ldots, s_4\}$	$\{s_{-2}, s_4\}$	$\{s_4\}$
(v_3, v_4)	$\{s_0, s_1, \ldots, s_4\}$	$\{s_2\}$	$\{s_2\}$
(v_3, v_5)	$\{s_0, s_1, \ldots, s_4\}$	$\{\}$	$\{\}$
(v_4, v_6)	$\{s_{-4}, s_{-3}, \ldots, s_0\}$	$\{s_{-4}\}$	$\{s_{-4}\}$
(v_5, v_6)	$\{s_{-4}, s_{-3}, \ldots, s_0\}$	$\{s_{-4}\}$	$\{s_{-4}\}$

Table 4.2 The estimating procedure and the recommended values of Example 4.29: the second interaction

Arc	$\hat{h}_{ik}^{(WC)}$	$\hat{h}_{ik}^{(AC)}$	$\hat{h}_{ik}$
(v_1, v_3)	$\{s_{-4}, s_{-3}, \ldots, s_0\}$	$\{s_{-4}, s_{-3}\}$	$\{s_{-4}, s_{-3}\}$
(v_1, v_4)	$\{s_0, s_1, \ldots, s_4\}$	$\{s_{-1}, s_4\}$	$\{s_4\}$
(v_2, v_5)	$\{s_0, s_1, \ldots, s_4\}$	$\{s_{-2}, s_4\}$	$\{s_4\}$
(v_3, v_5)	$\{s_0, s_1, \ldots, s_4\}$	$\{s_{-1}\}$	$\{\}$
(v_4, v_6)	$\{s_{-4}, s_{-3}, \ldots, s_0\}$	$\{s_{-4}, s_2\}$	$\{s_{-4}\}$
(v_5, v_6)	$\{s_{-4}, s_{-3}, \ldots, s_0\}$	$\{s_{-4}\}$	$\{s_{-4}\}$

6: Suppose that the experts select $h_{13} = \{s_{-4}, s_{-3}\}, h_{14} = \{s_4\}, h_{25} = \{s_1\}, h_{35} = \{s_4\}, h_{46} = \{s_{-4}\}, h_{56} = \{s_{-4}\}$ in the next interactions, then HP is completed to the following form:

$$HP = \begin{pmatrix} \{s_0\} & \{s_{-2}\} & \{s_{-4}, s_{-3}\} & \{s_4\} & \{s_3\} & \{s_{-3}\} \\ \{s_2\} & \{s_0\} & \{s_{-1}\} & \{s_1\} & \{s_1\} & \{s_{-3}\} \\ \{s_4, s_3\} & \{s_1\} & \{s_0\} & \{s_2\} & \{s_4\} & \{s_4\} \\ \{s_{-4}\} & \{s_{-1}\} & \{s_{-2}\} & \{s_0\} & \{s_{-3}\} & \{s_{-4}\} \\ \{s_{-3}\} & \{s_{-1}\} & \{s_{-4}\} & \{s_3\} & \{s_0\} & \{s_{-4}\} \\ \{s_3\} & \{s_3\} & \{s_{-4}\} & \{s_4\} & \{s_4\} & \{s_0\} \end{pmatrix}$$

We can see that the outcome is generally an EHFLPR with weak consistency. The proposed algorithm recommends all possible values, which are calculated by additive consistency and subjected to weak consistency, to the experts to improve the incomplete LPR.

4.2.4 The Interactive Algorithm with Self-adaptive Evolution to Complete Incomplete LPRs

Algorithm 5 improves an incomplete LPR based on not only additive consistency but also weak consistency. By which we enable the experts to take part in the interactions. An incomplete LPR is completed by both objective computing based on certain criteria and the experts' subjective information elicited by interactions. However, there are some drawbacks in the algorithm. It aims to mine the actual values of the experts' preferences, but the experts' can only select terms from some possible values provided by algorithms. When completing the incomplete LPR by interaction, the experts may realize the appearance of deviations between existing entries and their minds. Then the experts' preferred values may be not included in the recommended set. Thus the first drawback of Algorithm 5 is that the experts cannot provide preference values not included in the recommended set. Furthermore, when a subset of recommended values is selected by the experts, it means that other values are not appropriate to express the preferences. Therefore, some existing entries should be revised based on this new opinion to increase the consistency level of the preference relation. In this section, we introduce an interactive algorithm to construct a complete LPR with additive consistency [12].

Without loss of generality, we assume that the experts begin comparisons from the first row (column) of the LPR. As the minimum condition of an acceptable incomplete LPR is $n - 1$ pair-wise comparisons should be given (and each object should be compared at least once), we begin the following discussion based on the assumption that the first row and column of the LPR is completely provided by the experts. For the convenience of description, we introduce a new operation of linguistic terms as follows:

Definition 4.30 ([12]) Given three linguistic terms $s_\alpha, s_\beta, s_\gamma \in S^{(g)}$, if $s_\gamma \oplus s_\beta = s_\alpha$, then we denote $s_\gamma = s_\alpha \ominus s_\beta$.

In fact, the subtraction can be done by the lower indices, that is $s_\alpha \ominus s_\beta = s_{\alpha-\beta}$. Moreover, we have $r_{ij} \oplus r_{ji} = s_0$ in a LPR. It means $r_{ij} = s_0 \ominus r_{ji}$, thus $r_{ij} \oplus r_{kl} = r_{kl} \oplus (s_0 \ominus r_{ji}) = r_{kl} \ominus r_{ji}$ holds for any $r_{kl} \in R$. Consequently, this new operation enables us to focus on the upper triangle of R because of the relationship between the upper triangle and the lower triangle. In the rest of this section, only the elements in the upper triangle are focused on.

Given a weakly consistent incomplete LPR:

$$R = (r_{ij})_{n\times n} = \begin{pmatrix} r_{11} & r_{12} & \cdots & r_{1n} \\ r_{21} & x & \cdots & x \\ \vdots & \vdots & \ddots & \vdots \\ r_{n1} & x & \cdots & x \end{pmatrix} \tag{4.30}$$

for any missing entry $(v_2, v_k) \in MA_{S-P}, k \geq 3$, there exists $j = 1 \in J_{2k}^{(AC)}$ such that $(v_2, v_1), (v_1, v_k) \in EA_{S-P}$. Thus r_{2k} can be estimated by $\hat{r}_{2k} = r_{21} \oplus r_{ik}$, or equivalently $\hat{r}_{2k} = r_{ik} \ominus r_{12}$. If the estimated values of the second row are returned to the experts, there might be the following cases:

(1) The experts believe that $\hat{r}_{2k}$ is the actual value of r_{2k}, then the entry is completed by $r_{2k} = \hat{r}_{2k}$.

(2) The experts argue that $\hat{r}_{2k}$ is not the actual value of r_{2k}, and insist that another linguistic term $\dot{h}_{2k}$ is more suitable, then the entry is completed by $r_{2k} = \dot{r}_{2k}$. Furthermore, the provided term $\dot{r}_{2k}$ indicates that there are deviations when evaluating r_{12} and/or r_{1k}. Thus, the experts should revise them according to their knowledge and experiences. If the experts think that r_{12} should be r'_{12}, then $r_{12} = r'_{12}$ and r_{1k} should be automatically revised to $r'_{1k} = r'_{12} \oplus \dot{r}_{2k}$ so as to satisfy the additive consistency. Similarly, if the experts revise r_{1k} to r'_{1k}, then r_{12} should be automatically changed to $r'_{12} = \dot{r}_{2k} \ominus r'_{1k}$. In addition, the entry r_{12} was used to estimate the values of the second row. We have to estimate the second row again by r'_{12}.

Based on the above idea, we develop the interactive algorithm with self-adaptive evolution (SAE algorithm) to complete an incomplete LPR row by row, as shown in Algorithm 6 [12].

Algorithm 6 The SAE algorithm. Input: a weakly consistent incomplete LPR $R = (r_{ij})_{n\times n}$ in Eq. (4.30); Output: an additively consistent LPR.

1: Let $i = 1$;
2: Estimate the $(i+1)$-th row of R by $\hat{r}_{i+1,j} = r_{ij} \ominus r_{i,i+1}$, $j = i+2, i+3, \ldots, n$;
3: Recommend $\hat{r}_{i+1,j}(j = i+2, i+3, \ldots, n)$ to the experts;
4: Let $j = i+2$;
5: If the experts agree with $\hat{r}_{i+1,j}$, then $r_{i+1,j} = \hat{r}_{i+1,j}$, go to Step 7; else, go to Step 6;
6: Assume that the experts insist that the actual value of $r_{i+1,j}$ is $\dot{r}_{i+1,j}$, then $r_{i+1,j} = \dot{r}_{i+1,j}$, wait for the experts to adjust r_{ij} and/or $r_{i,i+1}$. If the experts input $\dot{r}_{ij}$ as the adjusted value of r_{ij}, then $r_{ij} = \dot{r}_{ij}$, $r_{i,i+1} = \dot{r}_{ij} \ominus \dot{r}_{i+1,j}$; if the experts input $\dot{r}_{i,i+1}$ as the adjusted value of $r_{i,i+1}$, then $r_{i,i+1} = \dot{r}_{i,i+1}$, $r_{ij} = \dot{r}_{i,i+1} \oplus \dot{r}_{i+1,j}$. Adjust the $(i+1)$-th column by $r_{l,i+1} = r_{li} \oplus r_{i,i+1}$ and the j-th column by $r_{lj} = r_{l,i+1} \oplus r_{i+1,j}$, where $l \in \{1, 2, \ldots, i-1\}$. Re-estimate the $(i+1)$-th row by $\hat{r}_{i+1,l} = r_{il} \ominus r_{i,i+1}$, where $l \in \{i+2, i+3, \ldots, n\} \setminus \{j\}$;
7: If $j < n$, then $j = j+1$, go to Step 5; else, go to Step 8;
8: Let $i = i+1$. If $i \geq n-1$, go to Step 9; else, go to Step 2;
9: For any $j > i$, $r_{ji} = neg(r_{ij})$; $r_{ii} = s_0$; Output R.

In Algorithm 6, the additive consistency of the output R can be clarified by the following theorem [12]:

Theorem 4.31 ([12]) *Algorithm 6 outputs an additively consistent LPR.*

Proof Assume that R is not additively consistent, then there exists k such that $K_{ij} = \{k | r_{ij} \neq r_{ik} \oplus r_{kj}\}$ is not empty. Without loss of generality, let $i < j$.

(1) If r_{ij} is determined by the recommended value, then we have $r_{ij} = r_{ik} \oplus r_{kj}$ according to Step 2 and Step 5.

(2) If r_{ij} is determined by the experts, then according to Step 6, $r_{ij} = r_{ik} \oplus r_{kj}$ holds after the procedure of adjustments and self-adaptive evolution is finished.

Thus we have $K_{ij} = \emptyset$, which is contradictory to the assumption. Thus, R is additively consistent. □

Example 4.32 Given the following weakly consistent incomplete LPR (based on the LTS in Example 2.3):

$$R_3 = \begin{pmatrix} s_0 & s_1 & s_{-1} & s_2 & s_3 \\ s_{-1} & s_0 & x & x & x \\ s_1 & x & s_0 & x & x \\ s_{-2} & x & x & s_0 & x \\ s_{-3} & x & x & x & s_0 \end{pmatrix}$$

1: Let $i = 1$;

2: Estimate the second row of R_3, for example, $\hat{r}_{23} = r_{13} \ominus r_{12} = s_{-1} \ominus s_1 = s_{-2}$. The first two rows of R_3 is:

$$\begin{pmatrix} s_0 & s_1 & s_{-1} & s_2 & s_3 \\ & s_0 & s_{-2} & s_1 & s_2 \end{pmatrix}$$

3: Recommend $\hat{r}_{2j}(j = 3, 4, 5)$ to the experts;

4: Let $j = 3$;

5: Suppose that the experts do not agree with $\hat{r}_{23} = s_{-2}$. They insist that s_{-1} is more suitable. Go to Step 6;

6: $r_{23} = s_{-1}$, wait for the experts to adjust r_{13} and/or r_{12}. If the experts consider that r_{13} is not necessary to revise, then r_{12} should be revised to $r_{12} = r_{13} \ominus r_{23} = s_{-1} \ominus s_{-1} = s_0$. Thus, the second row is re-estimated as:

$$\begin{pmatrix} s_0 & s_0 & s_{-1} & s_2 & s_3 \\ & s_0 & s_{-1} & s_2 & s_3 \end{pmatrix}$$

7: $j < n$, let $j = 4$, go to Step 5;
5: Suppose that the experts agree with $\hat{r}_{24} = s_2$, then $r_{24} = s_2$. Go to Step 7;
7: $j < n$, let $j = 5$, go to Step 5;
5: Suppose that the experts agree with $\hat{r}_{25} = s_3$, then $r_{2s} = s_3$. Go to Step 7;
7: $j \geq n$; go to Step 8;
8: $i = 2$; go to Step 2 to estimate the third row of R_3;
Run the algorithm till $i = 4$, and then go to Step 9.
9: R_3 might be completed as:

$$P_3 = \begin{pmatrix} s_0 & s_0 & s_{-0.5} & s_1 & s_{3.5} \\ s_0 & s_0 & s_{-0.5} & s_1 & s_{3.5} \\ s_{0.5} & s_{0.5} & s_0 & s_{1.5} & s_4 \\ s_{-1} & s_{-1} & s_{-1.5} & s_0 & s_{2.5} \\ s_{-3.5} & s_{-3.5} & s_{-4} & s_{-2.5} & s_0 \end{pmatrix}$$

4.2.5 An Example Regarding the Evaluation of Energy Channels

Energy channels, which are used to transport oil, natural gas, electricity and other resources, play an important role in the economic and social development of any country. However, the safety of energy channels is threatened by various terrorist forces, such as piracy, in recent years. More than 80% of Chinese international trades rely on South Sea, Strait of Malacca, Gulf of Aden, etc. An institute including 100 military experts is authorized to evaluate the level of risk of energy channels related to Chinese international trades in order to provide the support for the military deployment and emergency response. By means of data collection and case study, a network analysis model is formed for the problem. The model includes five clusters of elements, which are Piracy, Sea control capability, Island chain blockade capability, Risk elements and Energy channels. Specifically, the elements in Sea control capability (C) are Military bases (C_1), Number of garrison (C_2), Reconnaissance capabilities (C_3), Military support capabilities (C_4) and Logistical capacity (C_5); the elements in Energy channels (E) are South Sea (E_1), Strait of Malacca (E_2), Indian Ocean (E_3), Gulf of Aden (E_4), East Africa (E_5), Cape of Good Hope (E_6), Arafura Sea (E_7) and Okhotsk (E_8). When conducting pair-wise judgements, some preference relations can be derived by the existing objective data, while most of preference relations can only be obtained by subjective opinions of the experts because of the absence of necessary data and various kinds of uncertainties. To obtain decision information with high confident level, the military experts are given enough time to provide their opinions.

Because what we concern in this section is to obtain LPRs as accurate as possible based on incomplete LPRs, we do not plan to solve the whole problem here. Only two specific cases are presented to illustrate the introduced algorithms as well as to compare them with the existing techniques.

Case 1. Compare five elements of the cluster C with respect to E_1.

Suppose that an expert uses the following LTS for pair-wise judgements: $S^{(2)} = \{s_{-2} = very\ \ poor, s_{-1} = poor, s_0 = fair, s_1 = good, s_2 = very\ \ good\}$, and the initial incomplete LPR is:

$$R_{C\_E1} = \begin{pmatrix} s_0 & x & s_{-2} & s_{-1} & x \\ x & s_0 & s_2 & x & s_2 \\ s_2 & s_{-2} & s_0 & s_1 & x \\ s_1 & x & s_{-1} & s_0 & s_2 \\ x & s_{-2} & x & s_{-2} & s_0 \end{pmatrix}$$

Obviously, it is a weakly consistent incomplete LPR. Using Algorithm 5, the estimated values of the missing entries are:

$$\hat{h}_{12} = \{s_{-2}\},\ \hat{h}_{15} = \{s_1\},\ \hat{h}_{24} = \{s_0, s_2\},\ \hat{h}_{35} = \{s_0, s_2\}$$

If the expert chooses $h_{24} = \{s_0\}$ in this interaction, then the estimated values of the second round are:

$$\hat{h}_{12} = \{s_{-2}, s_{-1}\},\ \hat{h}_{15} = \{s_1\},\ \hat{h}_{35} = \{s_0, s_2\}$$

When the algorithm ends, the output LPR might be:

$$R^{(1)}_{C\_E1} = \begin{pmatrix} s_0 & s_{-2} & s_{-2} & s_{-1} & s_1 \\ s_2 & s_0 & s_2 & \mathbf{s_0} & s_2 \\ s_2 & s_{-2} & s_0 & s_1 & s_1 \\ s_1 & \mathbf{s_0} & s_{-1} & s_0 & s_2 \\ s_{-1} & s_{-2} & s_{-1} & s_{-2} & s_0 \end{pmatrix}$$

Moreover, there are several studies focusing on managing missing preference values of incomplete preference relations, which can be divided into two different strategies: the iterative approaches and the optimization approaches. There are not any studies using optimization approaches in linguistic setting because of the difficulty of forming optimal models using linguistic terms directly. Herrera-Viedmaet al. [6] proposed an additive consistency based iterative procedure to estimate the missing preference values of incomplete fuzzy preference relations. Motivated by which,

Alonso et al. [1] proposed a method for incomplete 2-tuple LPRs which converts a 2-tuple LPR into a fuzzy preference relation and estimates the missing values using the additive transitivity property, Alonso et al. [3] designed an iterative procedure similar to [6] to estimate the missing entries of an incomplete 2-tuple LPR, Xu et al. [16] further introduced a revised version of the iterative procedure proposed in [3].

If Alonso et al. [1]'s algorithm is used, then it is completed as:

$$R^{(2)}_{C\_E1} = \begin{pmatrix} s_0 & s_{-2} & s_{-2} & s_{-1} & s_1 \\ s_2 & s_0 & s_2 & \mathbf{s_{1.5}} & s_2 \\ s_2 & s_{-2} & s_0 & s_1 & s_1 \\ s_1 & \mathbf{s_{-1.5}} & s_{-1} & s_0 & s_2 \\ s_{-1} & s_{-2} & s_{-1} & s_{-2} & s_0 \end{pmatrix}$$

In this case, the same result can be derived by the Alonso et al. [3]'s algorithm and the Xu et al. [16]'s algorithm. Note that all these three algorithms stop at the first round of iteration.

Case 2. Compare 8 elements of the cluster E with respect to C_3.

Suppose that an expert considers the LTS in Example 2.3 for pair-wise judgements. The initial incomplete LPR is:

$$R_{E\_C3} = \begin{pmatrix} s_0 & s_2 & s_1 & s_{-1} & s_0 & s_3 & s_2 & s_3 \\ s_{-2} & s_0 & x & x & x & x & x & x \\ s_{-1} & x & s_0 & x & x & x & x & x \\ s_1 & x & x & s_0 & x & x & x & x \\ s_0 & x & x & x & s_0 & x & x & x \\ s_{-3} & x & x & x & x & s_0 & x & x \\ s_{-2} & x & x & x & x & x & s_0 & x \\ s_{-3} & x & x & x & x & x & x & s_0 \end{pmatrix}$$

It is a weakly consistent incomplete LPR as well. Using the SAE algorithm, the first two rows (after estimating) are:

$$\begin{pmatrix} s_0 & s_2 & s_1 & s_{-1} & s_0 & s_3 & s_2 & s_3 \\ & s_0 & s_{-1} & s_{-3} & s_{-2} & s_1 & s_0 & s_1 \end{pmatrix}$$

If the expert does not agree with the estimated values and realizes the entry of row 1 and column 2, i.e., s_2, should be s_1, then the first two rows (after re-estimating) are:

$$\begin{pmatrix} s_0 & s_1 & s_1 & s_{-1} & s_0 & s_3 & s_2 & s_3 \\ & s_0 & s_0 & s_{-2} & s_{-1} & s_2 & s_1 & s_2 \end{pmatrix}$$

When the algorithm is over, the output LPR might be:

$$R_{E\_C3}^{(1)} = \begin{pmatrix} s_0 & \mathbf{s_1} & s_1 & s_{-1} & s_0 & s_3 & s_2 & s_3 \\ \mathbf{s_{-1}} & s_0 & \mathbf{s_0} & \mathbf{s_{-2}} & \mathbf{s_{-1}} & \mathbf{s_2} & \mathbf{s_1} & \mathbf{s_2} \\ s_{-1} & \mathbf{s_0} & s_0 & s_{-2} & s_{-1} & s_2 & s_1 & s_2 \\ s_1 & \mathbf{s_2} & s_2 & s_0 & s_1 & s_4 & s_3 & s_4 \\ s_0 & \mathbf{s_1} & s_1 & s_{-1} & s_0 & s_3 & s_2 & s_3 \\ s_{-3} & \mathbf{s_{-2}} & s_{-2} & s_{-4} & s_{-3} & s_0 & s_{-1} & s_0 \\ s_{-2} & \mathbf{s_{-1}} & s_{-1} & s_{-3} & s_{-2} & s_1 & s_0 & s_1 \\ s_{-3} & \mathbf{s_{-2}} & s_{-2} & s_{-4} & s_{-3} & s_0 & s_{-1} & s_0 \end{pmatrix}$$

Moreover, Xu [14] is the first paper that presented an iterative algorithm to complete incomplete LPRs based on additive consistency. If the algorithm in [14] is used, then the output LPR is:

$$R_{E\_C3}^{(2)} = \begin{pmatrix} s_0 & \mathbf{s_2} & s_1 & s_{-1} & s_0 & s_3 & s_2 & s_3 \\ \mathbf{s_{-2}} & s_0 & \mathbf{s_1} & \mathbf{s_{-3}} & \mathbf{s_{-2}} & \mathbf{s_1} & \mathbf{s_0} & \mathbf{s_1} \\ s_{-1} & \mathbf{s_{-1}} & s_0 & s_{-2} & s_{-1} & s_2 & s_1 & s_2 \\ s_1 & \mathbf{s_3} & s_2 & s_0 & s_1 & s_4 & s_3 & s_4 \\ s_0 & \mathbf{s_2} & s_1 & s_{-1} & s_0 & s_3 & s_2 & s_3 \\ s_{-3} & \mathbf{s_{-1}} & s_{-2} & s_{-4} & s_{-3} & s_0 & s_{-1} & s_0 \\ s_{-2} & \mathbf{s_0} & s_{-1} & s_{-3} & s_{-2} & s_1 & s_0 & s_1 \\ s_{-3} & \mathbf{s_{-1}} & s_{-2} & s_{-4} & s_{-3} & s_0 & s_{-1} & s_0 \end{pmatrix}$$

4.2.6 Comparisions and Discussions

(1) *Regarding the computational results*

We can see that the computational results derived by the algorithms of this section and the existing algorithms are generally different in both cases. The existing algorithms only use the information of the initial incomplete LPRs and estimate missing entries iteratively. No extra information is needed. While the ACWC algorithm and the SAE algorithm estimate the missing entries and improve the incomplete LPRs by interacting with the experts. Thus, if new opinion is provided by the experts, the computational results would be different. Because all missing entries are determined by the experts, it is rational to conclude that the outputs of the two algorithms are more accurate and closer to the real opinion of the experts.

Nevertheless, it is meaningless to compare the consistency level of the resultant LPRs derived by the ACWA algorithm and the existing algorithms. Because what we are doing is to let the improved version of the incomplete LPRs be close to the actual values rather than to reach a high level of consistency. In fact, whenever the ACWA algorithm is over, another system like the one proposed in [5] can be designed to find out the most inconsistent entries and then to give advice for revision. By which we can reach a satisfactory consistency level.

Table 4.3 A summary of different techniques dealing with incomplete LPRs

Algorithm	Linguistic representation model	Consistency measures	Completing strategy	Output
Xu [14]	Virtual term set	Additive consistency	Iterative method	LPR
Alonso et al. [1]	2-tuple term set	Additive consistency	Iterative method	LPR
Alonso et al. [3]	2-tuple term set	Additive consistency	Iterative method	LPR
Xu et al. [16]	2-tuple term set	Additive consistency	Iterative method	LPR
Wang and Chen [10]	Cardinal representation	Additive consistency	Iterative method	LPR
Algorithm 5	Virtual term set	Additive consistency & Weak consistency	Interactive method	EHFLPR
Algorithm 6	Virtual term set	Additive consistency	Interactive method	LPR

(2) *Regarding the algorithms of weak consistency*

Xu et al. [17] presented the definition of weak consistency of incomplete fuzzy preference relations, developed an algorithm to check the weak consistency as well as a method to repair weak inconsistency. There are some common aspects between the algorithm in [17] and the WCR algorithm. Weak inconsistencies of both algorithms are judged by detecting k-cycles ($3 \leq k \leq n$) the digraphs of preference relations. The strategies for selecting illogical arcs of both algorithms are based on the frequency and the distance to "indifference". But the differences are apparent as well. Firstly, the fuzzy settings are different. The algorithm in [17] focuses on fuzzy setting whereas this section concentrates on LPRs. In addition, the algorithms for detecting k-cycles are distinct. Finally, the approaches to repair inconsistencies are disparate. The algorithm in [17] designs a set of fixed rules to repair the incomplete LPRs by the predefined way. Yet the WCR algorithm selects the most possible incorrect entries for the experts to elicit their actual values of preferences. Only if no new opinion is mined out, then the WCR algorithm may reduce to the one similar to [17].

(3) *Regarding the algorithms of completing incomplete LPRs*

Except for the algorithms mentioned in this section, Wang and Chen [10] presented an approach denoted based on the cardinal linguistic computational approach and the additive consistency. The algorithm in [10] utilizes the membership functions of linguistic terms (taking the form of TriFNs) for computation, and thus relies on the pre-defined semantics of terms. The differences between the algorithms in this section and the above-mentioned studies in linguistic setting are summarized in Table 4.3.

Furthermore, we illustrate the advantages and the disadvantages of the algorithms in this section as follows: (1) The algorithm in [14] outputs an additive consistent LPR if all the known entries satisfy the additive transitivity. The same result can be obtained in the SAE algorithms. But, as seen in Step 3 of Example 4.29, if there are two possible linguistic terms obtained by the additive transitivity, the algorithm in [14] cannot solve this case. (2) The algorithms in [1, 3, 16] are based on the idea proposed in [6]. The local estimated value of a missing entry is derived by an intermediate vertex and the additive consistency. Then the overall estimated value is obtained by the averaging of those local estimated values. As in Step 3 of Example 4.29, according to v_2, a local estimated value of (v_1, v_3) is s_{-4}, and another local estimated value, s_{-3} is derived by v_6. Then the overall estimated value of (v_1, v_3) is the averaging value of s_{-3} and s_{-4}. Therefore, these three algorithms consider only the averaging value as the estimated value of a missing entry. But the ACWC algorithm takes all possible linguistic terms into account by EHFLTSs and the final decision of the missing entries is determined by the interaction with the experts. It is useful if some new opinions could be expressed by the experts because the outputs of the proposed algorithms can represent the experts' actual preferences more accurately. Whereas the iterative methods have to assume that the original preference values coincide with the experts' opinions and cannot be revised during the steps of completing. The main disadvantage of the ACWC and SAE algorithms is the necessity of participation during the completing procedure. The speed of reaching a decision might be slower, and if no new opinion can be provided by the experts, then the proposed algorithms reduce to iterative algorithms.

4.3 Conclusions

This chapter has focused on the concept of EHFLPRs, their consistency measures and corresponding applications. Firstly, Sect. 4.1 has introduced the additive consistency and weak consistency of EHFLPRs, represented them by graphs visually. Based on specific consistency measures, two algorithms have been introduced to reduce EHFLPRs to LPRs. In addition, Sect. 4.2 has represented the set of possible values of a missing entry of an incomplete LPR, improved incomplete LPRs based on consistency measures. The major advantages of the techniques of this chapter are:

(1) EHFLPRs are introduced and some consistency measures are developed to ensure their rationality. Based on the presented algorithms, the existing techniques of LPRs can be employed directly to obtain the priorities of an EHFLPR.

(2) The introduced concepts and algorithms are based on the defined preference graphs. This makes the algorithms visible and thus are easy to be acknowledged by experts. The idea of preference graphs could be used in the study of other types of preference relations.

(3) The improving algorithms of incomplete LPRs could mine experts' real opinions more accurately by interactions. When estimating missing entries, the introduced algorithms consider not only weak consistency but also additive consistency.

(4) The interactive algorithms sit on the basis of EHFLTSs. EHFLTSs could collect all the possible values of missing entries, enable experts to represent uncertain preferences. Thus the interactive algorithms could deal with uncertainties more flexibly.

References

1. Alonso, S., Chiclana, F., Herrera, F., Herrera-Viedma, E., Alcalá-Fdez, J., Porcel, C.: A consistency-based procedure to estimate missing pairwise preference values. Int. J. Intell. Syst. **23**(2), 155–175 (2008)
2. Alonso, S., Herrera-Viedma, E., Chiclana, F., Herrera, F.: Individual and social strategies to deal with ignorance situations in multi-person decision making. Int. J. Inf. Technol. Decis. Mak. **8**(02), 313–333 (2009)
3. Alonso, S., Cabrerizo, F.J., Chiclana, F., Herrera, F., Herrera-Viedma, E.: Group decision making with incomplete fuzzy linguistic preference relations. Int. J. Intell. Syst. **24**(2), 201–222 (2009)
4. Dong, Y.C., Xu, Y.F., Li, H.Y.: On consistency measures of linguistic preference relations. Eur. J. Oper. Res. **189**(2), 430–444 (2008)
5. Herrera-Viedma, E., Martínez, L., Mata, F., Chiclana, F.: A consensus support system model for group decision-making problems with multigranular linguistic preference relations. IEEE Trans. Fuzzy Syst. **13**(5), 644–658 (2005)
6. Herrera-Viedma, E., Chiclana, F., Herrera, F., Alonso, S.: Group decision-making model with incomplete fuzzy preference relations based on additive consistency. IEEE Trans. Syst. Man Cybern. Part B: Cybern. **37**(1), 176–189 (2007)
7. Ma, J., Fan, Z.P., Jiang, Y.P., Mao, J.Y., Ma, L.: A method for repairing the inconsistency of fuzzy preference relations. Fuzzy Sets Syst. **157**(1), 20–33 (2006)
8. Tanino, T.: Fuzzy preference orderings in group decision making. Fuzzy Sets Syst. **12**(2), 117–131 (1984)
9. Tiernan, J.C.: An efficient search algorithm to find the elementary circuits of a graph. Commun. ACM **13**(12), 722–726 (1970)
10. Wang, T.C., Chen, Y.H.: Incomplete fuzzy linguistic preference relations under uncertain environments. Inf. Fus. **11**(2), 201–207 (2010)
11. Wang, H., Xu, Z.S.: Some consistency measures of extended hesitant fuzzy linguistic preference relations. Inf. Sci. **297**, 316–331 (2015)
12. Wang, H., Xu, Z.S.: Interactive algorithms for improving incomplete linguistic preference relations based on consistency measures. Appl. Soft Comput. **42**, 66–79 (2016)
13. Xu, Z.S.: EOWA and EOWG operators for aggregating linguistic labels based on linguistic preference relations. Int. J. Uncertain. Fuzziness Knowl. Based Syst. **12**(6), 791–810 (2004)
14. Xu, Z.S.: Incomplete linguistic preference relations and their fusion. Inf. Fus. **7**(3), 331–337 (2006)
15. Xu, Y.J., Patnayakuni, R., Wang, H.M.: The ordinal consistency of a fuzzy preference relation. Inf. Sci. **224**, 152–164 (2013)
16. Xu, Y.J., Ma, F., Tao, F.F., Wang, H.M.: Some methods to deal with unacceptable incomplete 2-tuple fuzzy linguistic preference relations in group decision making. Knowl. Based Syst. **56**, 179–190 (2014)
17. Xu, Y.J., Gupta, J.N., Wang, H.M.: The ordinal consistency of an incomplete reciprocal preference relation. Fuzzy Sets Syst. **246**, 62–77 (2014)
18. Zhu, B., Xu, Z.S.: Regression methods for hesitant fuzzy preference relations. Technol. Econ. Dev. Econ. **19**(sup1), S214–S227 (2013)
19. Zhu, B., Xu, Z.S.: Consistency measures for hesitant fuzzy linguistic preference relations. IEEE Trans. Fuzzy Syst. **22**(1), 35–45 (2014)

Chapter 5
Preference Analysis and Group Decision-Making Based on LTWHs

This chapter focuses on GDM problems whose information takes the form of LTWHs defined in Sect. 2.4. We introduce a multi-granular linguistic decision-making (MGLDM) approach and discuss the consistency measures of LPRs based on LTWHs.

As a tool of representing granularities, linguistic hedges depict the uncertainty of using single terms qualitatively. A LTWH can be considered as a term in a relatively coarser granularity, and thus is a natural technique to model multi-granular linguistic information. As a typical application of LTWHs, this chapter introduces a new technique for multi-granularity transformation and then applies it to MGLDM problems.

LTWHs will be introduced to the framework of decision-making with preference relations in order that the forms of preference representation could be extended. Similar to Sect. 4.1, this chapter deals with this type of preference relations based on graphs.

5.1 Multi-granular Linguistic Decision-Making with LTWHs

5.1.1 *The Framework of MGLDM Problems*

Formally, a MGLDM problem refers to a set of alternatives $A = \{a_1, a_2, \ldots, a_m\}$ which are evaluated with respect to a collection of criteria $C = \{c_1, c_2, \ldots, c_n\}$ using several LTSs with different granularities and/or semantics, associated with the weights of criteria $\mathbf{w} = (w_1, w_2, \ldots, w_n)$, where $\sum_{j=1}^{n} w_n = 1$ and $w_j \in [0, 1] (j = 1, 2, \ldots, n)$. These LTSs can be denoted by $S^{(MG)} = \{S^{(\tau_q)} | q = 1, 2, \ldots, Q\}$, where

H. Wang and Z. Xu, *Theory and Approaches of Group Decision-Making with Uncertain Linguistic Expressions*, Uncertainty and Operations Research,
https://doi.org/10.1007/978-981-13-3735-2_5

the q-th LTS is $S^{(\tau_q)} = \{s_\alpha^{(q)} | \alpha = 0, 1, \ldots, \tau_q\}$. LTSs with different granularities are necessary because the granules of knowledge of experts are different and then uncertainty exists when expressing opinions by a certain linguistic term. Moreover, certain hierarchical relationship often exists in the set of LTSs and thus hierarchical representational models are easy and effective for applications. A general version of hierarchical representational models, namely hierarchical tree [7], represents the set of LTSs by

$$HT = \cup_{q=1}^{Q} \{S^{(\tau_q)}\} \tag{5.1}$$

where $S^{(\tau_q)}$ is the LTS of level q with a granularity of $\tau_q + 1$. The hierarchical tree can be constructed by a top-down strategy. Given a LTS $S^{(\tau_q)}$ in the q-th level, the new LTS in the $(q+1)$-th level should satisfy: (1) $\tau_q < \tau_{q+1}$; and (2) there exists only one mapping which implements the semantics derivation of $S^{(\tau_{q+1})}$ from the previous level of $S^{(\tau_q)}$. Especially, a frequently considered version, which is called linguistic hierarchy [2, 4], can be formed by preserving all modal points of the membership functions of linguistic terms from the q-th level to the $(q+1)$-th level and then adding a new linguistic term between each pair of terms of the q-th level. Therefore, we have $\tau_{q+1} = 2\tau_q$ in this case, as the example shown in Fig. 5.1. In this section, we focus on the hierarchical representational model to represent of multi-granular linguistic information. For more representational models as well as the recent advance in MGLDM, please refer to [10, 17].

It is frequently assumed that a criterion is evaluated based on a single LTS in MGLDM. The aim of a MGLDM problem is to select the most desirable one(s) from the set A. Generally, the problem can be solved by the following three phases [5]:

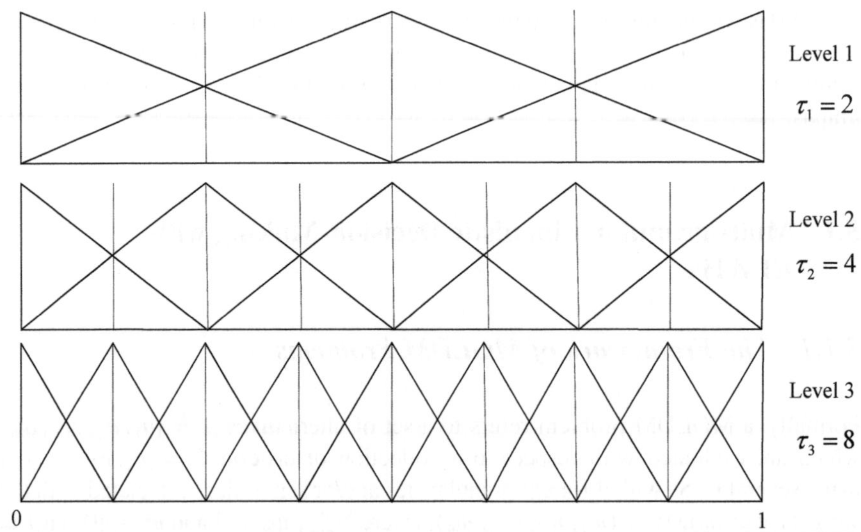

Fig. 5.1 An example of linguistic hierarchy of three, five, and nine terms

(1) *Unifying the linguistic information.* The provided decision information, expressed by multi-granularity linguistic terms, is transferred into linguistic information in one specific domain.

(2) *Computing the collective performances.* The unified information is fused and the collective linguistic performance of each alternative is therefore obtained. This phase is usually implemented by aggregation operators.

(3) *Exploiting the ranking of alternatives.* Based on the collective performances, a ranking method is adopted so that the priority of alternatives can be exploited. For example, this can be achieved by constructing fuzzy preference relations.

5.1.2 Constructing Multi-granular Linguistic Model Based on Hedges

The existing models generate a hierarchical model to represent the values of a linguistic variable by a top-down strategy. The underlying reason of this strategy is that a LTS with the refined granularity is necessary if the previous LTS is too coarse to express the values accurately. Different from such a strategy, we construct a hierarchical model by the opposite strategy. This bottom-up strategy assumes that a LTS with coarse granularity is considered if the previous LTS is so refined that experts are not sure which term can be used. Simultaneously, if uncertainty exists, experts can express it by means of linguistic hedges. This idea results in the recursive algorithm (Algorithm 7) to construct a hierarchical tree with Q levels based on a predefined and refined enough LTS [14].

Algorithm 7 The recursive algorithm to construct a hierarchical tree. Input: The number of levels Q, the LTS of the Q-th level $S^{(\tau_Q)} = \{s_\alpha^{(Q)} | \alpha = 0, 1, \ldots, \tau_Q\}$, where $\tau_Q = 2^{Q_0}$ and $Q_0 (\geq Q)$ is an integer, a WHS $H^{(\varsigma)} = \{h_t | t = 1, 2, \ldots, \varsigma\}$; Output: a hierarchical tree HT

1: Let $q = Q$, $\tau_q = \tau_Q$, $S^{(\tau_q)} = S^{(\tau_Q)}$;
2: If $q > 1$, go to Step 3; else, go to Step 4;
3: Fix t; $S^{(\tau_{q-1})} = \{l_\beta^{(q-1)} = \langle h_t, s_\alpha^{(q)} \rangle | h_t \in H^{(\varsigma)}, s_\alpha^{(q)} \in S^{(\tau_q)}, \alpha = 0, 2^t, 2 \cdot 2^t, \ldots, \tau_q\}$;
$q = q - 1$; go to Step 2;
4: $HT = \cup_{q=1}^{Q} \{S^{(\tau_q)}\}$;

In the third step of Algorithm 7, the value of hedge h_t is assigned according to the degree of uncertainty. Moreover, t is fixed in each loop. Because $t \geq 1$, we have $\tau_q \geq 2\tau_{q-1}$. Especially, if $t = 1$, then $\tau_q = 2\tau_{q-1}$, the derived hierarchical tree reduces to a linguistic hierarchy. Formally, the step of constructing LTS $S^{(\tau_{q-1})}$ can be rewritten as [14]:

$$S^{(\tau_{q-1})} = \{l_\beta^{(q-1)} = \langle h_1, s_\alpha^{(q)} \rangle | s_\alpha^{(q)} \in S^{(\tau_q)}, \alpha = 0, 2, 4, \ldots, \tau_q\} \tag{5.2}$$

in this case. Note that the condition $Q_0 \geq Q$ is given to make sure that a hierarchy with Q levels can be constructed. If $t = 1$ holds throughout the algorithm, then it is sufficient to set $\tau_Q = 2^Q$, i.e., $Q_0 = Q$. Algorithm 7 can be further illustrated by the next example:

Example 5.1 Given the LTS shown at the 3rd level in Fig. 5.1, denoted by $S^{(8)}$, we show how to generate the linguistic hierarchy. Initially, let $q = 3, \tau_3 = 8, S^{(\tau_3)} = S^{(8)}$. If $t = 1$, then $\alpha = 0, 2, 4, 6, 8$ and

$$\begin{aligned} S^{(\tau_2)} &= \{l_\beta^{(2)} = \langle h_1, s_\alpha^{(3)} \rangle | s_\alpha^{(3)} \in S^{(8)}, \alpha = 0, 2, 4, 6, 8\} \\ &= \{\langle h_1, s_0^{(3)} \rangle, \langle h_1, s_2^{(3)} \rangle, \langle h_1, s_4^{(3)} \rangle, \langle h_1, s_6^{(3)} \rangle, \langle h_1, s_8^{(3)} \rangle\} \end{aligned}$$

There are 5 LTWHs in $S^{(\tau_2)}$, and $\tau_2 = 4$. According to Theorem 2.41, $S^{(\tau_2)}$ is the one shown at the 2nd level in Fig. 5.1. If $q = 2$, similarly, we can obtain the 1st level in Fig. 5.1. Moreover, in the case $q = 3$, if we let $t = 2$, then $\alpha = 0, 4, 8$, thus $S^{(\tau_2)} = \{l_\beta^{(2)} = \langle h_2, s_\alpha^{(3)} \rangle | s_\alpha^{(3)} \in S^{(8)}, \alpha = 0, 4, 8\} = \{\langle h_2, s_0^{(3)} \rangle, \langle h_2, s_4^{(3)} \rangle, \langle h_2, s_8^{(3)} \rangle\}$. Then we generate the LTS shown in the 1st level of Fig. 5.1.

Compared with the existing hierarchical tree model, Algorithm 7 creates the set of LTSs through the natural way of human thinking. In fact, it is always indispensable and valuable to describe information as accurate as possible. If one object cannot be evaluated by numerical values because of the limitation of knowledge and/or expertise, then fuzzy techniques, including linguistic terms, could be considered as an alternative; In the even worse situation where the opinions cannot be expressed with sufficient confidence by a linguistic term, then we shall seek for another LTS with a coarser knowledge granule. The proposed LTWHs can act as a natural way to make the granule coarser.

However, it should be clarified that the proposed Algorithm 7 does not aim at constructing linguistic hierarchy for MGLDM. On the contrast, given a linguistic hierarchy which can be constructed by the algorithm, we have drawn the inherent connection between the linguistic terms of different levels. This fact could lead to a simple and effective information unification process, which will be introduced in the coming subsection.

5.1.3 An Approach for MGLDM with LTWHs

Suppose that the experts evaluate the set of alternative based on the hierarchical tree $HT = \cup_{q=1}^{Q}\{S^{(\tau_q)}\}$ which can be constructed by Algorithm 7, and the decision information forms a matrix $M^{(MG)} = (s_{ij})_{m\times n}$ where s_{ij} is the linguistic value of the alternative a_i with respect to the criterion c_j, $i = 1, 2, \ldots, m$, $j = 1, 2, \ldots, n$. We present a solution for MGLDM problems based on LTWHs, following the traditional three phases [14].

Step 1. Unification. The decision information is unified and represented by the linguistic terms in the Q-th level and the linguistic hedges $h_t \in H^{(\varsigma)}$. Especially, the value of t can be determined according to how a linguistic term is generated by Algorithm 7. Given a linguistic term $s_\alpha^{(q)}$ in the q-th level, the unification process can be depicted by Algorithm 8.

Algorithm 8 The transformation algorithm of multi-granular linguistic information. Input: A hierarchical tree $HT = \cup_{q=1}^{Q}\{S^{(\tau_q)}\}$, the linguistic term $s_\alpha^{(q)} \in S^{(\tau_q)}$; Output: The unified value l.

1: Find the linguistic term $s_\beta^{(Q)}$, in $S^{(\tau_Q)}$, whose core coincides with the core of $s_\alpha^{(q)}$;
2: $i = 0$, $h_{t_i} = h_0$;
3: If $i < Q - q$, go to Step 4; else, go to Step 5;
4: Find h_{t_i} which is used to construct the LTS $S^{(\tau_{q+i})}$ in Algorithm 7; $i = i + 1$, go to Step 3;
5: $l = \langle h_{t_{Q-q-1}}, \langle h_{t_{Q-q-2}}, \ldots, \langle h_{t_1}, \langle h_{t_0}, s_\beta^{(Q)}\rangle\rangle\rangle\rangle$;

According to Theorem 2.42, the outcome of Algorithm 8 can be rewritten as $l = \langle h_{t_0+t_1+\cdots+t_{Q-q-1}}, s_\beta^{(Q)}\rangle$. In application, the number of levels Q is usually not big, thus Algorithm 8 can be finished in a few loops. The unified decision matrix is denoted by $M^{(LTWH)} = (l_{mn})_{M\times N}$, where $l_{mn} = \langle h_{mn}, \dot{s}_{mn}\rangle$ is the LTWH transformed from $s_{mn}, i = 1, 2, \ldots, m, j = 1, 2, \ldots, n$.

Step 2. Aggregation. The overall performance of each alternative a_i, denoted by $l_m = \langle h_{t_m}, \dot{s}_{\alpha_m}\rangle$, can be calculated by a specific aggregation operator, associated with the weights of criteria **w**.

Step 3. Exploitation. The ranking of alternatives can be exploited directly by the total order defined in Definition 2.46.

5.1.4 An Application of Evaluating the Non-financial Performance of Banks

Banks, which mediate between the ones who possess capital surplus and the ones who need capital, play a critical role in an economic system. Many sectors of the economy, especially real economy, could be deeply affected by the development in the banking sector. All stakeholders (including the State and individuals) can be influenced directly if any problems occur in the current system of banks. To ensure and maintain the efficient and healthy status of banks, financial performance evaluations are necessary. However, their non-financial performance should be evaluated as well, in terms of careful monitoring and solid auditing. The reasons for evaluating non-financial performance includes the competition pressure from other competitors, the necessity of specific socio-economic and political situation, the inevitable technological and economic developments and so on (See [6] for more details about this issue). As suggested by [1, 12], five main non-financial criteria, which are Pricing,

Table 5.1 Selected criteria of evaluating the non-financial performance of banks

Criterion	Weight	Involved sub-criteria
Pricing (c_1)	0.364	Deposit rate, transaction fee and loan interest rates
Differentiation (c_2)	0.131	Professional banking services, international linkages, international image and reputation, continuing development, company privilege, penetration rate to a market, working hours
Marketing (c_3)	0.190	Type and quality of the product, service quality (including concrete characteristics, quality of employees, responding to customer needs), market dimension (including market share, newly added customer)
Service delivery (c_4)	0.062	Location branch, transaction duration, internet banking
Productivity (c_5)	0.254	Productivity

Differentiation, Marketing, Service delivery and Productivity, are considered in this section. Table 5.1 explains the meaning and the scopes of the criteria.

Considering three private banks anonymized by a_1, a_2, a_3, a government auditor is going to evaluate their non-financial performances with respect to the five criteria. The weighting vector of the criteria is shown in Table 5.1. Obviously, it is hard to obtain accurate and real values to measure these criteria. Some criteria, such as service quality, can only be evaluated by customers' experience. Thus all the evaluations are expressed by linguistic terms. Moreover, due to the lack of information (or the asymmetric information), different degrees of uncertainties could exist when evaluating based on the set of criteria. In this section, we use the linguistic hierarchy shown in Fig. 5.1, denoted by $S^{MG} = \{S^{(2)}, S^{(4)}, S^{(8)}\}$, for evaluation. Specifically, Pricing is evaluated by $S^{(8)}$ because it is very important and most of the needed information could be found by some means; Marketing is evaluated by $S^{(2)}$ because there are many factors to be considered and most of them are subjective experiences of customers; others are evaluated by $S^{(4)}$. After collecting all the evidences, the auditor presents the linguistic information as the following matrix:

$$M^{(MG)} = \begin{pmatrix} s_4^{(3)} & s_3^{(2)} & s_2^{(1)} & s_1^{(2)} & s_2^{(2)} \\ s_7^{(3)} & s_2^{(2)} & s_1^{(1)} & s_2^{(2)} & s_3^{(2)} \\ s_6^{(3)} & s_4^{(2)} & s_0^{(1)} & s_3^{(2)} & s_3^{(2)} \end{pmatrix} \quad (5.3)$$

Based on the MGLDM approach in Sect. 5.1.3, we solve the problem as follows:

Step 1. Unification. Each entry of the matrix is unified by Algorithm 8. For instance,

$$s_3^{(2)} \to \langle h_1, s_6^{(3)} \rangle (more\ or\ less\ s_6^{(3)})$$
$$s_1^{(1)} \to \langle h_1, s_2^{(2)} \rangle \to \langle h_1, \langle h_1, s_4^{(3)} \rangle \rangle = \langle h_2, s_4^{(3)} \rangle (roughly\ s_6^{(3)})$$

Then the matrix is transformed into:

$$M^{(LTWH)} = \begin{pmatrix} s_4^{(3)} & \langle h_1, s_6^{(3)} \rangle & \langle h_2, s_8^{(3)} \rangle & \langle h_1, s_2^{(3)} \rangle & \langle h_1, s_4^{(3)} \rangle \\ s_7^{(3)} & \langle h_1, s_4^{(3)} \rangle & \langle h_2, s_4^{(3)} \rangle & \langle h_1, s_4^{(3)} \rangle & \langle h_1, s_6^{(3)} \rangle \\ s_6^{(3)} & \langle h_1, s_8^{(3)} \rangle & \langle h_2, s_0^{(3)} \rangle & \langle h_1, s_6^{(3)} \rangle & \langle h_1, s_6^{(3)} \rangle \end{pmatrix} \tag{5.4}$$

Step 2. Aggregation. Associated with the weights shown in Table 5.1, each row of matrix $M^{(LTWH)}$ can be aggregated so that the overall performance of each alternative can be derived. Based on the LTWHWA operator defined by Eq. (2.64), the overall performance of a_1 is:

$$\begin{aligned}\langle h_{t_1}, \dot{s}_{\alpha_1} \rangle &= 0.364\langle h_0, s_4^{(3)} \rangle \oplus 0.131\langle h_1, s_6^{(3)} \rangle \oplus 0.19\langle h_2, s_8^{(3)} \rangle \\ &\oplus 0.062\langle h_1, s_2^{(3)} \rangle \oplus 0.254\langle h_1, s_4^{(3)} \rangle\end{aligned}$$

where $t_1 = round(0.364 \cdot 0 + 0.131 \cdot 1 + 0.19 \cdot 2 + 0.062 \cdot 1 + 0.254 \cdot 1) = round$ $(0.827) = 1$, $\alpha_1 = round(0.364 \cdot 4 + 0.131 \cdot 6 + 0.19 \cdot 8 + 0.062 \cdot 2 + 0.254 \cdot 4)$ $= round(4.902) = 5$, thus $l_1 = \langle h_1, s_5^{(3)} \rangle (more\ or\ less\ s_5^{(3)})$. Similarly, the overall performances of a_2 and a_3 are, respectively, $l_2 = \langle h_1, s_6^{(3)} \rangle$ and $l_3 = \langle h_1, s_5^{(3)} \rangle$. Note that, for l_3, we have $t_3 = round(0.827) = 1$ and $\alpha_3 = round(5.128) = 5$.

Step 3. Exploitation. According to the total order defined in Eq. (2.61), we have $l_1 \preceq_{Lex} l_2$ and $l_3 \preceq_{Lex} l_2$. Thus the bank a_2 is the best one among the three.

As has been mentioned in Sect. 2.4.2, the approximation step used in the linear operation of LTWHs may lead to a rough solution. In the above case, the overall performances of a_1 and a_3 are equal because of the approximation. If the decision maker persists in obtaining a priority of the two alternatives, then the results in the aggregation step can be used. Thus we can denote them by $l_1 = \langle h_{0.827}, s_{4.902}^{(3)} \rangle$ and $l_3 = \langle h_{0.827}, s_{5.128}^{(3)} \rangle$. The order $\preceq_{Lex}$ works well in this case. Based on $\preceq_{Lex}$, we have $l_1 \preceq_{Lex} l_3$. Note that the intermediate results can only be used for ranking because they are not interpretable at all.

5.1.5 Compared with Similar MGLDM Approaches

To analyze the strengths and drawbacks of the introduced MGLDM approach, we solve the problem in the above subsection by three similar approaches proposed by Herrera et al. [5], Herrera and Martínez [4] and Espinilla et al. [2], which are named by the fuzzy set-based approach, the linguistic 2-tuple-based approach and the extended hierarchical approach respectively.

The fuzzy set-based approach [5] does not bring any restriction on the LTSs in the set S^{MG}. To deal with the arbitrariness of semantic distributions of the LTSs, a so-called basic LTS which is uniformly distributed in the domain is employed to unify multi-granular linguistic information. Once the basic LTS $S^{(\tau_T)} = \{s_\alpha^{(T)} | \alpha =$

$0, 1, \ldots, \tau_T\}$ is chosen, a linguistic term $s_\alpha^{(q)} \in S^{MG}$ can be expressed by a fuzzy set defined in $S^{(\tau_T)}$ according to the following function:

$$\begin{aligned} &TF_{q,T} : S^{(\tau_q)} \rightarrow \mathcal{F}(S^{(\tau_T)}), \\ &TF_{q,T}(s_\alpha^{(q)}) = \{(s_\beta^{(T)}, \gamma_\beta^\alpha) | \beta = 0, 1, \ldots, \tau_T\}, \forall s_\alpha^{(q)} \in S^{(\tau_q)}, \\ &\gamma_\beta^\alpha = \max_y \min(\mu_{s_\alpha^{(q)}}(y), \mu_{s_\beta^{(T)}}(y)) \end{aligned} \tag{5.5}$$

where $\mathcal{F}(S^{(\tau_T)})$ is the set of fuzzy sets defined in $S^{(\tau_T)}$. For the problem of Sect. 5.1.4, it is natural to let LTS $S^{(8)}$ in the third level act as the basic LTS. Then each entry of the matrix $M^{(MG)}$ can be unified and represented by a fuzzy set defined in $S^{(8)}$. For instance, the unified result of $s_3^{(2)}$ is shown in Table 5.2. After unification, the fuzzy sets corresponding to the entries of $M^{(MG)}$ in the same row are fused by means of aggregation operators and the overall performance of each alternative is derived. Using the weighted averaging operator and the weighting vector $\mathbf{w}$, the overall performance of a_1 is derived and shown in Table 5.2. Then based on a fuzzy preference relation-based method, we get a_2 as the maximal non-dominated alternative.

The linguistic 2-tuple-based approach [4] aims at introducing a symbolic and precise approach for MGLDM based on the linguistic 2-tuple model. This approach begins with constructing a linguistic hierarchy, like the one shown in Fig. 5.1. In the unification phase, the following transformation function is defined to transform the linguistic 2-tuple $s_\alpha^{(q)} = (s_i^{(q)}, t^{(q)})$ in the q-th level to another linguistic 2-tuple $s_\alpha^{(q')} = (s_i^{(q')}, t^{(q')})$ in the q'-th level:

$$TF'_{q,q'}(s_i^{(q)}, t^{(q)}) = \Delta\left(\frac{\Delta^{-1}(s_i^{(q)}, t^{(q)}) \cdot (\tau_{q'})}{\tau_q}\right) \tag{5.6}$$

where Δ and Δ^{-1} are a pair of functions which are used to transform information between a real number and a linguistic 2-tuple [3]. For the purpose of comparison,

Table 5.2 Some computational results of the 4 comparable MGLDM approaches

Approach	Unified result of $s_3^{(2)}$	Overall performance of a_1
Fuzzy set-based approach [5]	$\{(s_0^{(3)}, 0), (s_1^{(3)}, 0), (s_2^{(3)}, 0),$ $(s_3^{(3)}, 0), (s_4^{(3)}, 1/3), (s_5^{(3)}, 2/3),$ $(s_6^{(3)}, 1), (s_7^{(3)}, 2/3), (s_8^{(3)}, 1/3)\}$	$\{(s_0^{(3)}, 0.02), (s_1^{(3)}, 0.04), (s_2^{(3)}, 0.15),$ $(s_3^{(3)}, 0.39), (s_4^{(3)}, 0.72), (s_5^{(3)}, 0.52),$ $(s_6^{(3)}, 0.33), (s_7^{(3)}, 0.24), (s_8^{(3)}, 0.23)\}$
Linguistic 2-tuple based approach [4]	$(s_6^{(3)}, 0)$	$(s_5^{(3)}, -0.098)$
Extended hierarchical approach [2]	$(s_6^{(3)}, 0)$	$(s_5^{(3)}, -0.098)$
LTWH-based approach	more or less $s_6^{(3)}$	more or less $s_5^{(3)}$

the unified information is represented based on $S^{(8)}$. For instance, the linguistic term $s_3^{(2)}$ is transformed and shown in Table 5.2. Associating with the weighting vector $\mathbf{w}$, we can obtain the overall performance of each alternative by the 2-tuple weighted averaging operator. The overall performance of a_1 is $(s_5^{(3)}, -0.098)$. After aggregation and based on the total order defined in the set of linguistic 2-tuple, we obtain the ranking: $a_1 \prec a_3 \prec a_2$.

The extended hierarchical approach [2] is based on the extended hierarchical model which generalizes the linguistic hierarchy [4] by using $\tau_{q+1} > \tau_q$ instead of $\tau_{q+1} = 2\tau_q$. An additional LTS, serving as the position of basic LTS, is employed so that the transformation between linguistic terms in any two levels can be conducted using the manner of Eq. (5.6). Specifically, the given linguistic term is transformed into a linguistic term of the basic LTS at first, and then the resultant term can be transformed into the target level. Thus, linguistic information could be unified after using Eq. (5.6) twice. The computational phase of this model is the same as that of [4]. Because of the special linguistic hierarchy used in our case, the computational results coincide with the one of the linguistic 2-tuple-based approach.

Based on the above computational procedures, we can summarize some features regarding these approaches, as listed in Table 5.3. The fuzzy set-based approach brings no limitation to multi-granular LTSs because it introduces an additional basic LTS for unification. The others are based on a linguistic hierarchy and thus the LTS in the bottom level can serve as the role of basic LTS. In the unification phase, the LTWH-based approach uses linguistic hedges to transform linguistic terms based on semantics. The semantics of the unified results coincide with the semantics of the original terms. Thus, the LTWH-based approach is accurate in its unification phase in the sense of semantics. In this sense, the linguistic 2-tuple-based approach and the extended hierarchical approach are not so accurate. As shown in Table 5.2, the 2-tuple $(s_3^{(2)}, 0)$ is transformed to $(s_6^{(3)}, 0)$. The semantics of these two are different. However, it should be noted that the change of semantics does not mean that these two approaches lose information in the unification phase. In fact, Eq. (5.6) is a one-to-one mapping. The unified results can be transformed into original information by means of the inverse function of Eq. (5.6). In the aggregation phase, the linguistic 2-tuple-

Table 5.3 Features of four comparable MGLDM approaches

Approach	Basic LTS	Unification results	Semantics of unified terms	Multi-granular LTSs	Interpretability
Fuzzy set based approach [5]	Needed	Fuzzy sets	Changed	Any	Hard
Linguistic 2-tuple based approach [4]	No	Linguistic 2-tuples	Changed	Linguistic hierarchy	Easy
Extended hierarchical approach [2]	Needed	Linguistic 2-tuples	Changed	Any	Easy
LTWH based approach	No	LTWH	Unchanged	Linguistic hierarchy	Very easy

based approach is accurate because of the employed linguistic 2-tuple model. The LTWH-based model includes an approximation step which leads to an interpretable yet not accurate result.

Based on the above analysis, we can draw some conclusions with regard to the strengths and weaknesses of using LTWHs in MGLDM problems. The strengths are:

(1) The use of linguistic hedges enables to unify linguistic information while maintaining its semantics. The uncertainty included in a linguistic term with a coarser granularity can be modelled by means of a certain hedge.

(2) The LTWH-based approach possesses the best interpretability, comparing with other approaches. The result in each phase can be interpreted by a linguistic expression which is close to human thinking. In addition, the aggregation results fall into the same domain of the unified information. To avoid the loss of information caused by high interpretability, an alternative way to obtain accurate and fine aggregation results, by ignoring the approximation step, is also available if the alternatives cannot be ranked by interpretable results.

(3) In real application, the original information may not take the form of Eq. (5.3) but Eq. (5.4). In this case, the experts present their evaluations by means of natural linguistic expressions taking the form of LTWHs. Therefore, the LTWH-based MGLDM approach can be considered as a MCDM approach in the setting of LTWHs.

However, the weakness is the limitation of multi-granularity LTSs. Given two adjacent LTSs $S^{(\tau_q)}$ and $S^{(\tau_{q+1})}$, Algorithm 7 requires that τ_{q+1}/τ_q must be a multiple of 2. When constructing the set of multi-granularity LTSs, we have to start with a fine enough LTS which serves as the bottom level of the linguistic hierarchy. This is caused by the definition of the semantics of LTWHs.

5.2 Consistency Measures of Linguistic Preference Relations with Hedges

Similar to Chap. 4, the LTS of Eq. (2.20) is considered in this section for representing preferences. Given WHS $\bar{H}^{(\varsigma)} = \{h_t | t = 0, 1, \ldots, \varsigma\}$, the set of all LTWHs based on $S^{(g)}$ and $\bar{H}^{(\varsigma)}$ is denoted as $\mathcal{L}$. In the virtual linguistic model, $S^{(g)}$ is usually extended as $\bar{S}^{(g)} = \{s_\alpha | \alpha = [-q, q], q \geq g\}$. For convenience, 2-tuple $\langle h_t, s_\alpha \rangle$, where $s_\alpha \in \bar{S}^{(g)}$ is also called a LTWH. The set of LTWHs generated by $\bar{S}^{(g)}$ and $\bar{H}^{(\varsigma)}$ is denoted as $\bar{\mathcal{L}}$. Let $\langle h_t, s_\alpha \rangle \in \bar{\mathcal{L}}$, if $\langle h_t, s_\alpha \rangle \notin \mathcal{L}$, then we refer to it as a virtual LTWH which could only emerge in the process of computation.

5.2.1 Some Basic Operations and Order Relations of LTWHs

According to the semantics of LTWHs, the term s_α in $\langle h_t, s_\alpha\rangle$ somewhat acts as the expectation. This motivates us to define the following strictly partial order $\prec$:

Definition 5.2 ([13]) Given two LTWHs $l_1 = \langle h_{t_1}, s_{\alpha_1}\rangle, l_2 = \langle h_{t_2}, s_{\alpha_2}\rangle \in \bar{\mathcal{L}}$, then

$$l_1 \prec l_2 \Leftrightarrow s_{\alpha_1} < s_{\alpha_2} \tag{5.7}$$

If $s_{\alpha_1} = s_{\alpha_2}$, then l_1 and l_2 are incomparable according to Definition 5.2. In fact, this can be depicted by the following equivalent relation:

Definition 5.3 ([13]) Given two LTWHs $l_1 = \langle h_{t_1}, s_{\alpha_1}\rangle, l_2 = \langle h_{t_2}, s_{\alpha_2}\rangle \in \bar{\mathcal{L}}$, then

$$l_1 \simeq l_2 \Leftrightarrow s_{\alpha_1} = s_{\alpha_2} \tag{5.8}$$

Moreover, given two matrices P_1 and P_2, the notation $P_1 \simeq P_2$ means that their corresponding entries are equivalent in the sense of Definition 5.3. Notice that two binary relations, i.e., $=$ and $\simeq$, will be used in the sequel. $\langle h_{t_1}, s_{\alpha_1}\rangle = \langle h_{t_2}, s_{\alpha_2}\rangle$ always means $t_1 = t_2$ and $\alpha_1 = \alpha_2$. Therefore, $l_1 = l_2$ always implies $l_1 \simeq l_2$. Eqs. (5.7) and (5.8) implies a poset $(\bar{\mathcal{L}}, \preceq)$, where $\preceq$ is defined by $(\forall l_1, l_2 \in \bar{\mathcal{L}})$

$$l_1 \preceq l_2 \Leftrightarrow (l_1 \prec l_2) \vee (l_1 \simeq l_2) \tag{5.9}$$

For convenience, if $l_1 \preceq l_2$ (or $l_1 \prec l_2$), then we also write $l_2 \succeq l_1$ (or $l_2 \succ l_1$). To ease the development in this section, the following basic operations are necessary:

Definition 5.4 ([13]) Given three LTWHs $l = \langle h_t, s_\alpha\rangle, l_1 = \langle h_{t_1}, s_{\alpha_1}\rangle, l_2 = \langle h_{t_2}, s_{\alpha_2}\rangle \in \bar{\mathcal{L}}, \lambda > 0$, we define
(1) $l_1 \oplus l_2 = \langle h_{max\{t_1,t_2\}}, s_{\alpha_1+\alpha_2}\rangle$;
(2) $\lambda l = \langle h_t, s_{\lambda\alpha}\rangle$.

Apparently, if $h_t = h_{t_1} = h_{t_2} = h_0$ in Definition 5.4, then the operations are reduced to the version defined in Xu [15]. For the convenience of representation in some cases, the subtraction of two LTWHs can be defined [13]. Given $l_1, l_2, l_3 \in \bar{\mathcal{L}}$, if $l_2 \oplus l_3 = l_1$, then we denote $l_3 = l_1 \ominus l_2$. Associated with the operation $\oplus$, we obtain:

$$l_1 \ominus l_2 = \langle h_{max\{t_1,t_2\}}, s_{\alpha_1-\alpha_2}\rangle \tag{5.10}$$

The following properties are required in the sequel:

Theorem 5.5 ([13]) *For any* $l, l_1, l_2, l_3 \in \bar{\mathcal{L}}, \lambda_1, \lambda_2 > 0$, *we have*
(1) $Neg(Neg(l)) = l$, $Neg(l) = s_0 \ominus l$;
(2) $l \oplus s_0 = l$, $l \ominus s_0 = l$;
(3) Associative: $l_1 \oplus l_2 \oplus l_3 = l_1 \oplus (l_2 \oplus l_3)$, $l_1 \ominus l_2 \ominus l_3 = l_1 \ominus (l_2 \oplus l_3)$;

(4) Distributive: $\lambda(l_1 \oplus l_2) = (\lambda l_1) \oplus (\lambda l_2)$, $(\lambda_1 + \lambda_2)l = (\lambda_1 l) \oplus (\lambda_2 l)$;
(5) $Neg(l_1) \oplus Neg(l_2) = Neg(l_1 \oplus l_2)$;
where $s_0 = \langle h_0, s_0 \rangle$ *is the middle element in* $\bar{S}^{(g)}$.

The proof of this properties is straightforward according to the above definitions. Moreover, different from the idea of [16] which uses a number in [0, 1] to represent the deviation between two linguistic terms in $\bar{S}^{(g)}$, we measure the deviation between two LTWHs in $\bar{\mathcal{L}}$ by means of a LTWH as follows:

Definition 5.6 ([13]) Given $l_1 = \langle h_{t_1}, s_{\alpha_1} \rangle, l_2 = \langle h_{t_2}, s_{\alpha_2} \rangle \in \bar{\mathcal{L}}$, the deviation between l_1 and l_2 is defined by:

$$d(l_1, l_2) = \begin{cases} l_1 \ominus l_2, \ l_1 \succeq l_2 \\ l_2 \ominus l_1, \ otherwise \end{cases} \tag{5.11}$$

The linguistic form of deviations make use of LTWHs in $\{\langle h_t, s_\alpha \rangle | h_t \in \bar{H}, s_\alpha \in \bar{S}, s_\alpha \succeq s_0\}$ to represent the gap between two LTWHs. The uncertainty implied by the hedges of the two LTWHs is remained in the deviation measure. For instance, let $l_1 = s_1$ and $l_2 = \langle h_1, s_1 \rangle$ be two LTWHs based on $S^{(4)}$ and $\bar{H}^{(2)}$ specified in Eq. (2.47), then $d(l_1, l_2) = \langle h_1, s_0 \rangle$, which means that the deviation between *slightly good* and *more or less slightly good* is *more or less indifferent*. The deviation measure possesses some interesting properties.

Theorem 5.7 ([13]) *Let* $l_1 = \langle h_{t_1}, s_{\alpha_1} \rangle, l_2 = \langle h_{t_2}, s_{\alpha_2} \rangle \in \bar{\mathcal{L}}$, *then we have*
(1) $d(l_1, l_2) = \langle h_{max\{t_1,t_2\}}, s_{|\alpha_1-\alpha_2|} \rangle$;
(2) If $l_1 \simeq l_2$, *then* $d(l_1, l_2) \simeq s_0$;
(3) If $l_1 \simeq l_2$, *then* $d(l, l_1) \simeq d(l, l_2)$ *for any* $l \in \bar{\mathcal{L}}$;
(4) $d(l_1, l) \oplus d(l, l_1) \succeq d(l_1, l_2)$ *for any* $l \in \bar{\mathcal{L}}$.

Proof Let $l = \langle h_t, s_\alpha \rangle \in \bar{\mathcal{L}}$,

(1) If $l_1 \succeq l_2$, $d(l_1, l_2) = l_1 \ominus l_2 = \langle h_{max\{t_1,t_2\}}, s_{\alpha_1-\alpha_2} \rangle$; If $l_2 \succeq l_1$, then $d(l_1, l_2) = l_2 \ominus l_1 = \langle h_{max\{t_1,t_2\}}, s_{\alpha_2-\alpha_1} \rangle$. Thus $d(l_1, l_2) = \langle h_{max\{t_1,t_2\}}, s_{|\alpha_1-\alpha_2|} \rangle$.

(2)–(3) If $l_1 \simeq l_2$, then $s_{\alpha_1} = s_{\alpha_2}$. $d(l_1, l_2) = \langle h_{max\{t_1,t_2\}}, s_0 \rangle \simeq s_0$; $d(l, l_1) = \langle h_{max\{t,t_1\}}, s_{|\alpha-\alpha_1|} \rangle = \langle h_{max\{t,t_1\}}, s_{|\alpha-\alpha_2|} \rangle \simeq \langle h_{max\{t,t_2\}}, s_{|\alpha-\alpha_2|} \rangle = d(l, l_2)$.

(4) $d(l_1, l) \oplus d(l, l_2) = \langle h_{max\{t,t_1\}}, s_{|\alpha-\alpha_1|} \rangle \oplus \langle h_{max\{t,t_2\}}, s_{|\alpha-\alpha_2|} \rangle = \langle h_{max\{t,t_1,t_2\}}, s_{|\alpha-\alpha_1|+|\alpha-\alpha_2|} \rangle \succeq \langle h_{max\{t,t_1,t_2\}}, s_{|\alpha_1-\alpha_2|} \rangle \simeq d(l_1, l_2)$. □

5.2.2 *Linguistic Preference Relations with Weakened Hedges*

When expressing preference degrees over a set of objects, weakened hedges would be quite natural to be considered if the expert is not confident enough to use a certain term. This leads to the appearance of LTWHs in preference relations. Thus, we introduce the following definition:

Definition 5.8 ([13]) Given $\bar{S}^{(g)}$, $\bar{H}^{(\varsigma)}$ and a set of objects $V = \{v_1, v_2, \ldots, v_n\}$, a binary relation P defined on the set V is called a linguistic preference relation with hedges (LHPR) if, for any $i, j = 1, 2, \ldots, n$, $P(v_i, v_j) = l_{ij} \in \bar{\mathcal{L}}$ represents the degree of v_i being preferred to v_j. Formally, a LHPR is denoted by $P = (l_{ij})_{n\times n} = (\langle h_{t_{ij}}, s_{\alpha_{ij}}\rangle)_{n\times n}$, where $h_{t_{ij}} \in \bar{H}$, $s_{\alpha_{ij}} \in \bar{S}$. P is said to be reciprocal if $l_{ij} = Neg(l_{ji})$ for any $i, j = 1, 2, \ldots, n$.

Two conclusions are transparent: (1) If $t_{ij} = 0$, i.e., $h_{t_{ij}} = h_0$, for any $i, j = 1, 2, \ldots, n$, then the LHPR is reduced to a traditional LPR; (2) For any $i = 1, 2, \ldots, n$, $l_{ii} \simeq \langle h_0, s_0\rangle$. In fact, $l_{ii} = Neg(l_{ii})$ means $\langle h_{t_{ii}}, s_{\alpha_{ii}}\rangle = \langle h_{t_{ii}}, s_{-\alpha_{ii}}\rangle$. Thus $\alpha_{ii} = -\alpha_{ii}$, which results in $\alpha_{ii} = 0$. Notice that we use $l_{ii} \simeq s_0$ instead of the traditional form $l_{ii} = s_0$. This is just a theoretical generalization for the convenience of inducing some necessary properties. The generalization does not mean that there exists any uncertainty in self comparisons.

Similar to Chap. 4, the graph theory is considered to handle consistency measures of LHPRs in a visible manner. In a fuzzy weighted graph [8], the vertices and arcs (or edges) are crisp, but the weights of arcs (or edges) are fuzzy. In this section, we specify the weights of arcs by LTWHs which come from the entries of a LHPR. The LHPR is visualized by its associated fuzzy weighted digraph:

Definition 5.9 ([13]) Let $P = (l_{ij})_{n\times n}$ be a LHPR defined on $V = \{v_1, v_2, \ldots, v_n\}$. A preference relation graph (P-graph) associated with P is a fuzzy weighted digraph $G_P = (V, A)$, where the set of vertices is V, the set of arcs is denoted by $A = \{(v_i, v_j)\}$, and the arc (v_i, v_j) which joins v_i to v_j exists if $l_{ij} \succeq s_0 (i \neq j)$. If (v_i, v_j) exists, then its fuzzy weight is defined by $w(v_i, v_j) = l_{ij}$.

In a P-graph, the arc (v_i, v_j) indicates that v_i is preferred to v_j. Preference values which are equivalent to s_0 are considered as a special case of preferences. Given a LHPR $P = (l_{ij})_{n\times n}$, the number of arcs is $n(n-1)/2 + c_0$, where c_0 is the number of upper diagonal entries which are equivalent to s_0. The following digraph is specified to highlight each entry of P:

Definition 5.10 ([13]) Let $P = (l_{ij})_{n\times n}$ be a LHPR defined on $V = \{v_1, v_2, \ldots, v_n\}$. A symmetric preference relation graph (SP-graph) associated with P is fuzzy weighted digraph $G_{S-P} = (V, A)$, where the set of vertices is V, the set of edges is denoted by $A = \{(v_i, v_j)\}$, and the arc (v_i, v_j) joins v_i to v_j with its fuzzy weight $w(v_i, v_j) = l_{ij}, i \neq j$.

Different from P-graphs, there are $n(n-1)$ arcs in a SP-graph associated with $P = (l_{ij})_{n\times n}$. In the P-graph (or SP-graph) $G = (V, A)$ associated with the LHPR P, a sequence $(v_{i_1}, (v_{i_1}, v_{i_2}), v_{i_2}, \ldots, v_{i_{k-1}}, (v_{i_{k-1}}, v_{i_k}), v_{i_k})$ is a walk from v_{i_1} to v_{i_k}, where $v_{i_1}, v_{i_2}, \ldots, v_{i_k} \in V$ and $(v_{i_1}, v_{i_2}), \ldots, (v_{i_{k-1}}, v_{i_k}) \in A$. A walk is called a path if $v_{i_1}, v_{i_2}, \ldots, v_{i_k}$ are distinct. The fuzzy length of the path is defined by the sum of weights of its arcs, i.e.,

$$len(v_{i_1}, (v_{i_1}, v_{i_2}), v_{i_2}, \ldots, v_{i_{k-1}}, (v_{i_{k-1}}, v_{i_k}), v_{i_k}) = l_{i_1 i_2} \oplus \cdots \oplus l_{i_{k-1} i_k}$$

The fuzzy distance from v_{i_1} to v_{i_k} is the shortest fuzzy length of the paths from v_{i_1} to v_{i_k}. If $v_{i_1} = v_{i_k}$ and $v_{i_1}, v_{i_2}, \ldots, v_{i_{k-1}}$ are distinct, then a walk is a cycle.

Traditionally, the arcs in a digraph G with n vertices are represented by an adjacent matrix $M = (M_{ij})_{n\times n}$, having $M_{ij} = 1$ if and only if there is an arc (v_i, v_j). Given a LHPR $P = (l_{ij})_{n\times n}$, the arcs of its associated P-graph G_P can be represented by the adjacent matrix $M_P = (M_{ij})_{n\times n}$, where

$$M_{ij} = \begin{cases} 1, & w(v_i, v_j) \succeq s_0 \\ 0, & w(v_i, v_j) \prec s_0 \end{cases} \tag{5.12}$$

According to Definition 5.9, $M_{ii} = 0 (\forall i = 1, 2, \ldots, n)$. Moreover, if $l_{ij} \simeq s_0, i \neq j$, then $M_{ij} = M_{ji} = 1$. In this sense, the adjacent matrix of the SP-graph of a LHPR P is not so interesting because all its off-diagonal elements are equal to 1.

Example 5.11 Given $S^{(4)}$ in Example 2.3 and $\bar{H}^{(2)}$ in Eq. (2.47), a LHPR could be:

$$P = \begin{pmatrix} s_0 & \langle h_1, s_{-2}\rangle & \langle h_1, s_{-3}\rangle & s_{-1} & \langle h_2, s_2\rangle \\ \langle h_1, s_2\rangle & s_0 & s_2 & \langle h_1, s_1\rangle & s_2 \\ \langle h_1, s_3\rangle & s_{-2} & s_0 & s_3 & s_1 \\ s_1 & \langle h_1, s_{-1}\rangle & s_{-3} & s_0 & \langle h_1, s_2\rangle \\ \langle h_2, s_{-2}\rangle & s_{-2} & s_{-1} & \langle h_1, s_{-2}\rangle & s_0 \end{pmatrix}$$

For example, the entry $\langle h_1, s_2\rangle$ means that v_2 is *more or less good* when compared with v_1. Its P-graph and SP-graph are shown in Figs. 5.2 and 5.3, respectively.

5.2.3 Consistency Measures of LHPRs

Based on the concept and the associated P-graph of LHPRs, several kinds of consistency measures can be defined to implement the idea of transitivity.

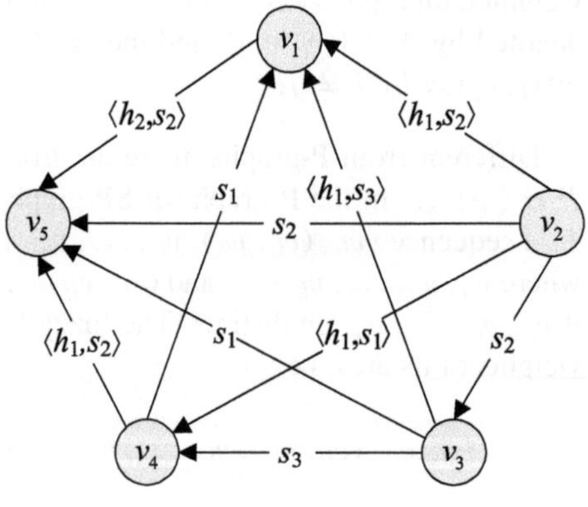

Fig. 5.2 The P-graph associated with the LHPR in Example 5.11

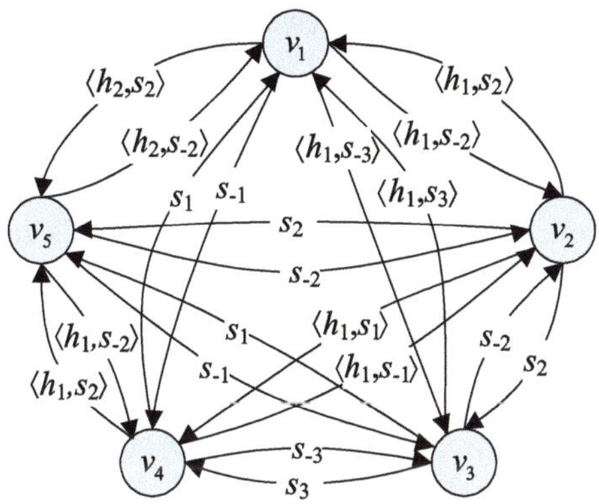

Fig. 5.3 The SP-graph associated with the LHPR in Example 5.11

Definition 5.12 ([13]) Given a reciprocal LHPR $P = (l_{ij})_{n\times n}$, where $l_{ij} = \langle h_{t_{ij}}, s_{\alpha_{ij}}\rangle \in \bar{\mathcal{L}}i, j = 1, 2, \ldots, n$, then
(1) P satisfies the triangle condition if

$$l_{ik} \oplus l_{kj} \succeq l_{ij}, \forall i, j, k = 1, 2, \ldots, n$$

(2) P satisfies the weak transitivity if

$$l_{ik} \succeq s_0, l_{kj} \succeq s_0 \Rightarrow l_{ij} \succeq s_0, \forall i, j, k = 1, 2, \ldots, n$$

(3) P satisfies the restricted max-max transitivity if

$$l_{ik} \succeq s_0, l_{kj} \succeq s_0 \Rightarrow l_{ij} \succeq max\{l_{ik}, l_{kj}\}, \forall i, j, k = 1, 2, \ldots, n$$

(4) P satisfies the restricted max-min transitivity if

$$l_{ik} \succeq s_0, l_{kj} \succeq s_0 \Rightarrow l_{ij} \succeq min\{l_{ik}, l_{kj}\}, \forall i, j, k = 1, 2, \ldots, n$$

(5) P satisfies the additive transitivity if

$$l_{ik} \oplus l_{kj} \simeq l_{ij}, \forall i, j, k = 1, 2, \ldots, n$$

Especially, P is said to be of weakly consistent if it satisfies the weak transitivity; P is said to be of additively consistent if it satisfies the additive transitivity.

It is very simple to interpret the transitivity visually by using P-graphs and SP-graphs. For any $i, j, k = 1, 2, \ldots, n$, if v_i is preferred to v_k and v_k is preferred to v_j, then the triangle condition and the weak transitivity stipulate the upper and lower bounds of $w(v_i, v_j)$, respectively. Specifically, in a P-graph, if there is an arc directed from v_i to v_k and another arc directed from v_k to v_j, then the weak transitivity requires that there should be an arc directed from v_i to v_j. Simultaneously, the triangle condition calls for that the fuzzy weight of (v_i, v_j) should not exceed the fuzzy length of $(v_i, (v_i, v_k), v_k, (v_k, v_j), v_j)$. As seen in Fig. 5.2, because there are two arcs (v_2, v_3) and (v_3, v_1), then there should be an arc (v_2, v_1) according to the weak transitivity and $w(v_2, v_1)$ should not exceed $w(v_2, v_3) \oplus w(v_3, v_1)$ according to the triangle condition. From the angle of lower bounds, the restricted max-min transitivity requires that $w(v_i, v_j)$ should be no less than $min\{w(v_i, v_k), w(v_k, v_j)\}$; the restricted max-max transitivity demands that $w(v_i, v_j)$ should be at least $max\{w(v_i, v_k), w(v_k, v_j)\}$. The additive transitivity defines $w(v_i, v_j)$ by a precise angle, i.e., $w(v_i, v_j)$ should be equivalent to $w(v_i, v_k) \oplus w(v_k, v_j)$. Associated with its SP-graph, a LHPR satisfies the additive transitivity if the fuzzy lengths of all paths which start from v_i and end by v_j are equivalent. As seen in Fig. 5.2, $len(v_2, (v_2, v_1), v_1) = l_{21} = \langle h_1, s_2 \rangle$ and $len(v_2, (v_2, v_3), v_3, (v_3, v_1), v_1) = l_{21} \oplus l_{31} = s_2 \oplus \langle h_1, s_3 \rangle = \langle h_1, s_5 \rangle$. Then we have $\langle h_1, s_2 \rangle \prec \langle h_1, s_5 \rangle$ and thus P in Example 5.11 is not additively consistent. The relationship among the transitivity can be summarized directly based on the definition and the above analyses.

Theorem 5.13 ([13]) *Given a LHPR P and five propositions: (i) P satisfies the triangle condition; (ii) P satisfies the weak consistency; (iii) P satisfies the restricted max-max transitivity; (iv) P satisfies the restricted max-min transitivity; (v) P satisfies the additive transitivity, then:*
(1) (v) ⇒ (i);
(2) (v) ⇒ (iii) ⇒ (iv) ⇒ (ii).

Similar to many studies regarding preference relations, the additive consistency is an ideal property for a LHPR if satisfied. The weak consistency, which ensures that a LHPR is logically correct, is the property that the LHPR should at least satisfy. We mainly focus on these two types of transitivity and start with identifying whether a LHPR is of weak consistency.

5.2.4 Weak Consistency of LHPRs

According to Definition 5.12, weak transitivity can be checked directly by the P-graph. Similar to Sect. 4.2, a cycle with k vertices and k arcs is referred to as a k-cycle. Weak transitivity requires that there is no k-cycle in the P-graph, $3 \leq k \leq n$. Fortunately, it does not have to check all $k \in \{3, 4, \ldots, n\}$.

Theorem 5.14 ([13]) *For any P-graph associated with a reciprocal LHPR, if there is a k-cycle, $k \in \{3, 4, \ldots, n\}$, then there is a 3-cycle.*

Proof For any P-garph, according to Definition 5.9, there is at least one arc located between any two vertices. Given a k-cycle denoted by $(v_{i_1}, (v_{i_1}, v_{i_2}), v_{i_2}, \ldots, v_{i_k}, (v_{i_k}, v_{i_1}), v_{i_1})$, where $k \in \{3, 4, \ldots, n\}$,

(1) If $w(v_{i_2}, v_{i_k}) \succeq s_0$, as shown in Fig. 5.4(a), there is a 3-cycle $(v_{i_1}, (v_{i_1}, v_{i_2}), v_{i_2}, (v_{i_2}, v_{i_k}), v_{i_k}, (v_{i_k}, v_{i_1}), v_{i_1})$;

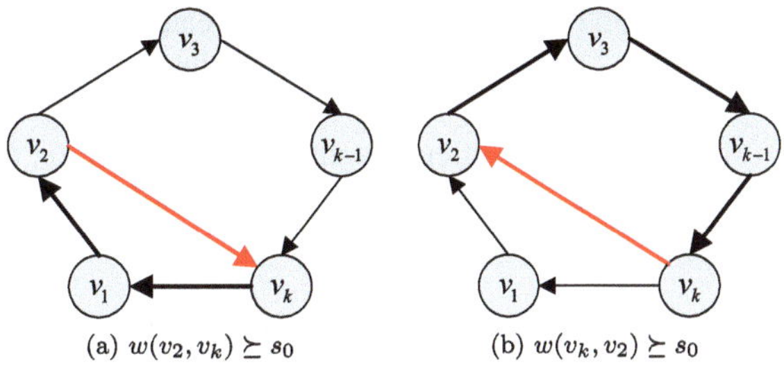

Fig. 5.4 Illustration of finding a 3-cycle from a k-cycle. **a** a 3-cycle is found; **b** the k-cycle is reduced to a $(k-1)$-cycle

(2) If $w(v_{i_2}, v_{i_k}) \prec s_0$, according to the reciprocal property, there is an arc (v_{i_k}, v_{i_2}). Ignoring v_1, we obtain a new $(k-1)$-cycle $(v_{i_2}, (v_{i_2}, v_{i_3}), v_{i_3}, \ldots, v_{i_k}, (v_{i_k}, v_{i_2}), v_{i_2})$, as shown in Fig 5.4(b).

Similarly, when considering $w(v_{i_3}, v_{i_k})$, we could get either a 3-cycle or a new $(k-2)$-cycle. Repeating this process, it is apparent that a 3-cycle can be found. □

Therefore, it is enough to check all the 3-cycles in a P-graph for weak consistency judgement. However, not all the 3-cycles means illogical judgements in a preference relation because the weights of arcs in a 3-cycle might be equivalent to s_0. Similar to Sect. 4.1.5, the following definition could be considered to identify real cycles.

Definition 5.15 ([13]) A k-cycle in a P-graph is said to be a strict k-cycle if there exists at least one arc (v_i, v_j) whose weight is greater than s_0, i.e., $w(v_i, v_j) \succ s_0$.

The definition is straightforward. In fact, if the weight of each arc in a cycle is equivalent to s_0, then the cycle is meaningless for weak consistency judgement. Formally, we have the following theorem:

Theorem 5.16 ([13]) *A LHPR is weakly consistent if and only if there is no strict 3-cycle in its associated P-graph.*

Proof The theorem can be rephrased as: A LHPR is not weakly consistent if and only of there exists at least one strict 3-cycle in its P-graph. Let $P = (l_{ij})_{n\times n}$ be a LHPR defined on the set V, associated with the P-graph G_P.

($\Rightarrow$) If P is not weakly consistent, then there exist $i, j, k \in \{1, 2, \ldots, n\}$ such that $l_{ij} \succeq s_0$, $l_{jk} \succeq s_0$ and $l_{ik} \prec s_0$. Then the 3-cycle $(v_i, (v_i, v_j), v_j, (v_j, v_k), v_k, (v_k, v_i), v_i)$ always exists.

(1) If $l_{ij} \succ s_0$ and $l_{jk} \succ s_0$, then the weights of three arcs of the 3-cycle are greater than s_0. Thus, it is a strict 3-cycle.

(2) If $l_{ij} \succ s_0$ and $l_{jk} \simeq s_0$, then we have $w(v_i, v_j) \succ s_0$ and $w(v_k, v_i) \succ s_0$. It is also a strict 3-cycle.

(3) If $l_{ij} \simeq s_0$ and $l_{jk} \simeq s_0$, then the 3-cycle is strict because $w(v_k, v_i) \succ s_0$.

($\Leftarrow$) Suppose that there exist $i, j, k \in \{1, 2, \ldots, n\}$ which form a strict 3-cycle $(v_i, (v_i, v_j), v_j, (v_j, v_k), v_k, (v_k, v_i), v_i)$. The cycle is strict, and thus, there is at least one arc whose weight is greater than s_0.

(1) If all the three weights are greater than s_0, then it is obvious that P is not weakly consistent.

(2) If two of the three weights are greater than s_0, then we denote $w(v_i, v_j) \succ s_0$, $w(v_j, v_k) \succ s_0$, and $w(v_k, v_i) \simeq s_0$. We have $l_{jk} \succ s_0$ (i.e., $l_{jk} \succeq s_0$) and $l_{ki} \simeq s_0$ (i.e., $l_{ki} \succeq s_0$), but $l_{ji} \prec s_0$. Thus, P is not weakly consistent.

(3) If one of the three weights is greater than s_0, then we denote $w(v_i, v_j) \succ s_0$, $w(v_j, v_k) \simeq s_0$, and $w(v_k, v_i) \simeq s_0$. Accordingly, $l_{jk} \succeq s_0$ and $l_{ki} \succeq s_0$. However, $l_{ji} \prec s_0$. Thus, P is not weakly consistent. □

Theorem 5.16 ensures that the weak consistency can be identified by checking the existence of strict 3-cycle. In order to identify whether a 3-cycle is strict or not, we need to find out the walk of a cycle at first. This could be achieved by Algorithm 9 [13].

Algorithm 9 The identification algorithm of weak consistency of a LHPR. Input: a LHPR $P = (l_{ij})_{n\times n}$; Output: P is weakly consistent or not.

1: Construct the adjacent matrix M of P according to Eq. (5.12); let $c = 1$;
2: For any $i, j, k = 1, 2, \ldots, n$, if $M_{ij}M_{jk}M_{ki} = 1$, then let $l_{max} = max\{l_{ij}, l_{jk}, l_{ki}\}$; if $l_{max} \succ s_0$, then $c = 0$, break; else, continue;
3: If $c = 1$, then P is weakly consistent; else P is not.

Note that, different from the similar weak consistency identification algorithms [9, 18], Algorithm 9 checks the P-graph of P based on two levels. First, $M_{ij}M_{jk}M_{ki} = 1$ is to identify the existence of a 3-cycle. In addition, if $l_{max} \succ s_0$, then the found 3-cycle is a strict 3-cycle. The algorithm is terminated if a strict 3-cycle is found or i, j, k have gone through $\{1, 2, \ldots, n\}$. Moreover, for a preference relation, n is usually suggested to be less than 9 [11]. Thus, the complexity of Algorithm 9 is acceptable.

Example 5.17 Consider the LHPR P in Example 5.11, according to Algorithm 9, there is no 3-cycle in the P-graph, then P is weakly consistent.

5.2.5 Additive Consistency of LHPRs

Below we consider how to identify whether a LHPR is additively consistent or not.

Theorem 5.18 ([13]) *If a LHPR $P = (l_{ij})_{n\times n}$ is reciprocal, then the following statements are equivalent:*

(1) $l_{ij} \oplus l_{jk} \simeq l_{ik}, \forall i, j, k;$
(2) $l_{ij} \oplus l_{jk} \simeq l_{ik}, \forall i < j < k;$
(3) $l_{i,i+1} \oplus l_{i+1,i+2} \oplus \cdots \oplus l_{j-1,j} \oplus l_{j,i} \simeq s_0, \forall i < j.$

Proof (1)⇒(2): It is obvious.

(2)⇒(1): Let us consider the order of i, j, k. If $i = j = k$, $l_{ij} \oplus l_{jk} = s_0 = l_{ik}$; if two of the three are equal, say, if $i = j \neq k$, $l_{ij} \oplus l_{jk} = s_0 \oplus l_{ik} = l_{ik}$. Then we consider the case $i \neq j \neq k$:

(i) If $i < j < k$, then apparently $l_{ij} \oplus l_{jk} \simeq l_{ik}$ according to (2);

(ii) If $i < k < j$, then $l_{ik} \oplus l_{kj} \simeq l_{ij}$. Thus $l_{ij} \oplus l_{jk} = (l_{ik} \oplus l_{kj}) \oplus l_{jk} = l_{ik} \oplus (l_{kj} \oplus l_{jk}) \simeq l_{ik} \oplus s_0 = l_{ik}$;

(iii) Similar to (ii), it is obvious if $j < i < k, j < k < i, k < i < j$ and $k < j < i$, then $l_{ij} \oplus l_{jk} \simeq l_{ik}$.

Thus for any $i, j, k = 1, 2, \ldots, n$, $l_{ij} \oplus l_{jk} \simeq l_{ik}$.

(2)⇒(3): Let $j = i + 1$ and $k = i + 2$ in (2), we get $l_{i,i+1} \oplus l_{i+1,i+2} \simeq l_{i,i+2}$. Similarly, we can get a collection of equations: $l_{i,i+2} \oplus l_{i+2,i+3} \simeq l_{i,i+3}, \ldots, l_{i,j-1} \oplus l_{j-1,j} \simeq l_{ij}$. Moreover, $l_{ij} \oplus l_{j,i} \simeq s_0$. The accumulation of these equations leads to $l_{i,i+1} \oplus l_{i+1,i+2} \oplus \cdots \oplus l_{j-1,j} \oplus l_{j,i} \simeq s_0$.

(3)⇒(2): Let $i < j < k$, we get $l_{i,i+1} \oplus l_{i+1,i+2} \oplus \cdots \oplus l_{j-1,j} \oplus l_{ji} \simeq s_0, l_{j,j+1} \oplus l_{j+1,j+2} \oplus \cdots \oplus l_{k-1,k} \oplus l_{kj} \simeq s_0$ and $l_{i,i+1} \oplus l_{i+1,i+2} \oplus \cdots \oplus l_{k-1,k} \oplus l_{ki} \simeq s_0$ from (3). Accumulating the first two, we get $l_{i,i+1} \oplus l_{i+1,i+2} \oplus \cdots \oplus l_{k-1,k} \oplus l_{ji} \oplus l_{kj} \simeq s_0$. Comparing it with the third equation, it is obvious that $l_{ji} \oplus l_{kj} \simeq l_{ki}$, which means $(s_0 \ominus l_{ij}) \oplus (s_0 \ominus l_{jk}) \simeq (s_0 \ominus l_{ik})$. According to Theorem 5.5, $l_{ji} \oplus l_{kj} \simeq l_{ki}$. □

In Theorem 5.18, (2) presents a simple way to check the additive consistency of a LHPR. In fact, it is enough to check the values of l_{ij}, l_{jk}, and l_{ik} having $i \leq j \leq k$ for a given reciprocal LHPR. Besides, (3) enables to generate an additively consistent LHPR by means of $n - 1$ entries: $l_{12}, l_{23}, \ldots, l_{n-1,n}$. Below we consider the construction of an additively consistent LHPR.

5.2.5.1 Constructing an Additively Consistent LHPR from $n - 1$ Entries

As discussed in Sect. 4.2, incomplete preference relations are frequently considered to facilitate experts providing their preference information. Ideally, if each object is compared by only one time, then we have $n - 1$ known entries of the preference relation. An additively consistent preference relation can always be generated in this case, as shown in Algorithm 10 [13]. The algorithm can be depicted by two phases: computation and normalization. The first phase (Steps 1–2) computes all the missing entries, and then the second phase (Steps 3–4) normalizes the results so that they could be interpretable in the original domain.

Theorem 5.19 ([13]) *Algorithm 10 outputs an additively consistent LHPR.*

Proof Given $l_{12}, l_{23}, \ldots, l_{n-1,n} \in \bar{\mathcal{L}}$, it is apparent that the computational results of Step 2 satisfy $l_{ij} \oplus l_{jk} \simeq l_{ik}, \forall i, j, k$, according to Theorem 5.18. Thus, if $s_{\alpha_{i_0 \cdot j_0}} \leq s_g$, then the resultant P is additively consistent; else we have to clarify that f maps P to an additively consistent LHPR whose entries are in $\bar{\mathcal{L}}$.

Algorithm 10 The algorithm of constructing an additively consistent LHPR from $n-1$ entries. Input: An incomplete LHPR $P=(l_{ij})_{n\times n}$ with $n-1$ known entries $l_{12}, l_{23}, \ldots, l_{n-1,n} \in \bar{\mathcal{L}}$; Output: A completed additively consistent LHPR P.

1: For any $i<j$, if $l_{ij} \notin \{l_{12}, l_{23}, \ldots, l_{n-1,n}\}$, do $l_{ij}=l_{i,i+1} \oplus l_{i+1,i+2} \oplus \cdots \oplus l_{j-1,j}$;
2: For any $i=j$, let $l_{ii}=s_0$; for any $i>j$, let $l_{ij}=Neg(l_{ji})$;
3: Find an entry satisfying $l_{i_0,j_0} \succeq l_{ij} (\forall i,j=1,2,\ldots,n)$, denoted as $l_{i_0,j_0}=\langle h_{t_{i_0,j_0}}, s_{\alpha_{i_0,j_0}}\rangle$; if $s_{\alpha_{i_0,j_0}} \leq s_g$, then go to Step 5; else, go to Step 4.
4: A new LHPR $P'=f(P)$, where the function $f:[s_{-\alpha_{i_0,j_0}}, s_{\alpha_{i_0,j_0}}] \to [s_g, s_g]$ normalizes the second component of each LTWH in P, such that $f(s_\alpha)=s_\beta$ with $\beta=g\alpha/\alpha_{i_0,j_0}$. Let $P=P'$.
5: End.

Let $P=(l_{ij})_{n\times n}=(\langle h_{t_{ij}}, s_{\alpha_{ij}}\rangle)_{n\times n}$, $P'=(l'_{ij})_{n\times n}=(\langle h_{t_{ij}}, s'_{\alpha_{ij}}\rangle)_{n\times n}$.

(1) Obviously, $f(s_{-\alpha_{i_0,j_0}})=s_{-g}$, $f(s_{\alpha_{i_0,j_0}})=s_g$. Thus, the entries are normalized into the range $\bar{\mathcal{L}}$.

(2) For any $i,j=1,2,\ldots,n$, we have $\langle h_{t_{ij}}, s'_{\alpha_{ij}}\rangle \oplus \langle h_{t_{ji}}, s'_{\alpha_{ji}}\rangle = \langle h_{t_{ij}}, f(s_{\alpha_{ij}})\rangle \oplus \langle h_{t_{ji}}, f(s_{\alpha_{ji}})\rangle$, where $f(s_{\alpha_{ij}}) \oplus f(s_{\alpha_{ji}}) = (g/\alpha_{i_0,j_0})s_{\alpha_{ij}} \oplus s_{\alpha_{ji}} = (g/\alpha_{i_0,j_0})s_0$ according to Step 2. Thus, $\langle h_{t_{ij}}, s'_{\alpha_{ij}}\rangle \oplus \langle h_{t_{ji}}, s'_{\alpha_{ji}}\rangle \simeq s_0$, which means that P' is reciprocal.

(3) For any $i,j,k=1,2,\ldots,n$, according to Step 1 and Theorem 5.18, we have $l'_{ij} \oplus l'_{jk} = \langle h_{t_{ij}}, s'_{\alpha_{ij}}\rangle \oplus \langle h_{t_{jk}}, s'_{\alpha_{jk}}\rangle = \langle h_{max\{t_{ij},t_{jk}\}}, f(s_{\alpha_{ij}}) \oplus f(s_{\alpha_{jk}})\rangle$, where $f(s_{\alpha_{ij}}) \oplus f(s_{\alpha_{jk}}) = (g/\alpha_{i_0,j_0})s_{\alpha_{ij}} \oplus s_{\alpha_{jk}} = (g/\alpha_{i_0,j_0})s_{\alpha_{ik}} = f(s_{\alpha_{ik}})$. Thus $l'_{ij} \oplus l'_{jk} = \langle h_{max\{t_{ij},t_{jk}\}}, s'_{\alpha_{ik}}\rangle \simeq l'_{ik}$. The additive consistency is proven. □

Note that, due to the basic operations in Definition 5.4, the uncertainties of the known entries which are expressed by weakened hedges, will be transferred to the missing entries during the generating process.

Example 5.20 Given an incomplete LHPR $P=(l_{ij})_{4\times 4}$ with three known entries: $l_{12}=s_1$, $l_{23}=\langle h_1, s_2\rangle$, $l_{34}=\langle h_2, s_{-1}\rangle$ based on the LTS $S^{(4)}$ in Example 2.3 and the WHS $\bar{H}^{(2)}$ in Eq. (2.47). According to Steps 1–2 of Algorithm 10, P can be completed as:

$$P=\begin{pmatrix} s_0 & s_1 & \langle h_1, s_3\rangle & \langle h_2, s_2\rangle \\ s_{-1} & s_0 & \langle h_1, s_2\rangle & \langle h_2, s_1\rangle \\ \langle h_1, s_{-3}\rangle & \langle h_1, s_{-2}\rangle & s_0 & \langle h_2, s_{-1}\rangle \\ \langle h_2, s_{-2}\rangle & \langle h_2, s_{-1}\rangle & \langle h_2, s_1\rangle & s_0 \end{pmatrix}$$

where, for example, $l_{14}=l_{12} \oplus l_{23} \oplus l_{34} = s_1 \oplus \langle h_1, s_2\rangle \oplus \langle h_2, s_{-1}\rangle = \langle h_2, s_2\rangle$, $l_{41}=Neg(l_{14})=\langle h_2, s_{-2}\rangle$. We can see that the greatest element is $l_{13}=\langle h_1, s_3\rangle$. Because $s_3 \prec s_\tau = s_4$, the algorithm is terminated.

5.2.5.2 Constructing an Additively Consistent LHPR by a Reciprocal LHPR

Besides, an additively consistent LHPR can be generated based on a given LHPR. Consider the SP-graph of a LHPR P, if P is additively consistent, then given $i, j = 1, 2, \ldots, n$, $w(v_i, v_j)$ should be equivalent to the fuzzy length of path $(v_i, (v_i, v_k), v_k, (k_i, v_j), v_j)$, for any $k = 1, 2, \ldots, n$. This fact motivates us to estimate l_{ij} the set of paths which are from v_i to v_j through any intermediate vertices. Formally, we have:

Theorem 5.21 ([13]) *Given a reciprocal LHPR $P = (l_{ij})_{n\times n}$, let $\bar{P} = (\bar{l}_{ij})_{n\times n}$ and $\forall i, j = 1, 2, \ldots, n$,*

$$\bar{l}_{ij} = \frac{1}{n} \bigoplus_{k=1}^{n} (l_{ik} \oplus l_{kj}) \tag{5.13}$$

then $\bar{P}$ is additively consistent.

Proof (1) For any $i, j = 1, 2, \ldots, n$,

$$\begin{aligned}\bar{l}_{ji} &= \tfrac{1}{n} \bigoplus_{k=1}^{n} (l_{jk} \oplus l_{ki}) = \tfrac{1}{n} \bigoplus_{k=1}^{n} (Neg(l_{kj}) \oplus Neg(l_{ik})) \\ &= \tfrac{1}{n} Neg(\bigoplus_{k=1}^{n} (l_{ik} \oplus l_{kj})) = Neg(\bar{l}_{ij})\end{aligned}$$

thus $\bar{P}$ is reciprocal.

(2) For any $i, j = 1, 2, \ldots, n$,

$$\begin{aligned}\bar{l}_{ik} \oplus \bar{l}_{kj} &= \tfrac{1}{n} \bigoplus_{k_1=1}^{n} (l_{i,k_1} \oplus l_{k_1,k}) \oplus \tfrac{1}{n} \bigoplus_{k_2=1}^{n} (l_{k,k_2} \oplus l_{k_2,j}) \\ &= \tfrac{1}{n} \bigoplus_{k_1=1}^{n} (l_{i,k_1} \oplus l_{k_1,k} \oplus l_{k,k_1} \oplus l_{k_1,j}) = \tfrac{1}{n} \bigoplus_{k_1=1}^{n} (l_{i,k_1} \oplus l_{k_1,j}) = \bar{l}_{ij}\end{aligned}$$

thus, $\bar{P}$ is additively consistent. □

In practice, it is not very interesting to generate such a LHPR based on arbitrary reciprocal LHPR. However, the generation process implies another way to check if a LHPR is additively consistent.

Theorem 5.22 ([13]) *Let $P = (l_{ij})_{n\times n}$ be a reciprocal LHPR and $\bar{P} = (\bar{l}_{ij})_{n\times n}$ be the LHPR generated by Eq. (5.13) based on P. P is additively consistent if and only if $P \simeq \bar{P}$.*

Proof ($\Leftarrow$): If $P \simeq \bar{P}$, according to Theorem 5.21, $\bar{P}$ is additively consistent. For any $i, j, k = 1, 2, \ldots, n$, $l_{ik} \oplus l_{kj} \simeq \bar{l}_{ik} \oplus \bar{l}_{kj} \simeq \bar{l}_{ij} \simeq l_{ij}$, then P is also additively consistent.

($\Rightarrow$): If P is additively consistent, then $l_{ik} \oplus l_{kj} \simeq l_{ij} (\forall i, j, k = 1, 2, \ldots, n)$. Accordingly, $\forall i, j, k = 1, 2, \ldots, n, \bar{l}_{ij} = \frac{1}{n} \bigoplus_{k=1}^{n} (l_{ik} \oplus l_{kj}) \simeq \frac{1}{n} \bigoplus_{k=1}^{n} l_{ij} = l_{ij}$. Thus $P \simeq \bar{P}$. □

According to Theorem 5.22, an additively consistent LHPR should be equivalent to the LHPR generated by Eq. (5.13).

Example 5.23 We have proven that the LHPR in Example 5.11 is weakly consistent. According to Eq. (5.13), a new LHPR $\bar{P} = (\bar{l}_{ij})_{5\times 5}$ can be generated. For instance, $\bar{l}_{12} = \frac{1}{5} \overset{5}{\underset{k=1}{\oplus}} (l_{1k} \oplus l_{k2}) = \frac{1}{5}(s_0 \oplus \langle h_1, s_{-2}\rangle) \oplus (\langle h_1, s_{-2}\rangle \oplus s_0) \oplus (\langle h_1, s_{-3}\rangle \oplus s_{-2}) \oplus (s_{-1} \oplus \langle h_1, s_{-1}\rangle) \oplus (\langle h_2, s_2\rangle \oplus s_{-2}) = \langle h_2, s_{-2.2}\rangle$. Moreover, we have:

$$\bar{P} = \begin{pmatrix} \langle h_2, s_0\rangle & \langle h_2, s_{-2.2}\rangle & \langle h_2, s_{-1.8}\rangle & \langle h_2, s_{-0.6}\rangle & \langle h_2, s_{0.6}\rangle \\ \langle h_2, s_{2.2}\rangle & \langle h_1, s_0\rangle & \langle h_1, s_{0.4}\rangle & \langle h_1, s_{1.6}\rangle & \langle h_2, s_{2.8}\rangle \\ \langle h_2, s_{1.8}\rangle & \langle h_1, s_{-0.4}\rangle & \langle h_1, s_0\rangle & \langle h_1, s_{1.2}\rangle & \langle h_2, s_{2.4}\rangle \\ \langle h_2, s_{0.6}\rangle & \langle h_1, s_{-1.6}\rangle & \langle h_1, s_{-1.2}\rangle & \langle h_1, s_0\rangle & \langle h_2, s_{1.2}\rangle \\ \langle h_2, s_{-0.6}\rangle & \langle h_2, s_{-2.8}\rangle & \langle h_2, s_{-2.4}\rangle & \langle h_2, s_{-1.2}\rangle & \langle h_2, s_0\rangle \end{pmatrix}$$

Obviously, $P \simeq \bar{P}$ is not true, thus P is not additively consistent.

If a LHPR is not additively consistent, then the degree of additive consistency could be measured by the similarity or deviation between P and $\bar{P}$. This will be presented in detail in the next subsection.

5.2.6 Consistency Improving of LHPRs

The deviation between two LHPRs, which is vital to quantify the degree of consistency, could be defined based on the deviation between each pair of upper diagonal elements in the LTWHs:

Definition 5.24 ([13]) Given two reciprocal LHPRs $P = (l_{ij})_{n\times n}$ and $P' = (l'_{ij})_{n\times n}$, their deviation is defined as:

$$d(P, P') = \frac{2}{n(n-1)} \underset{i<j}{\oplus} d(l_{ij}, l'_{ij}) \tag{5.14}$$

Definition 5.27 can be regarded as a tool of consistency improving. Firstly, we will employ it to improve a LHPR to satisfy the weak transitivity.

5.2.6.1 Improving a LHPR to Satisfy Weak Consistency

It is generally required that a LHPR is weakly consistent. If not, an approach should be developed to improve the consistency of the LHPR. Interactive approaches, such as the idea in Sect. 4.2, detect the illogical arcs in the graph and receive feedbacks from experts. Automatic approaches improves the preference relation based on the original information and some specific revision rules. In the sequel, we introduce an automatic approach (Algorithm 11) to improve a LHPR which is not weakly consistent [13].

Algorithm 11 The weak consistency improving algorithm of LHPR. Input: a reciprocal LHPR $P = (l_{ij})_{n\times n}$, $\lambda \in (0, 1)$; Output: a weakly consistent LHPR $P^{(m)}$.

1: Let $P^{(0)} = P, m = 0$;
2: According to Algorithm 9, if $P^{(m)}$ is weakly consistent, go to Step 4; else, generate $\bar{P}^{(m)}$ by using Eq. (5.13), go to Step 3;
3: Let $P^{(m+1)} = (1-\lambda)P^{(m)} \oplus \lambda \bar{P}^{(m)}, m = m + 1$; go to Step 2;
4: Output $P^{(m)}$.

Algorithm 11 revises the entries of a given LHPR automatically and maintains the original opinions as much as possible. To this end, λ plays an important role. In fact, λ implies to what extent the original information should be maintained. If $\lambda = 0$, then only the original information in P is considered; if $\lambda = 1$, then the original information is completely ignored. In Algorithm 11, the additively consistent LHPR $\bar{P}^{(m)}$ is generated in each iteration. This is rational but results in the complexity of the algorithm. To improve Algorithm 11, the following theorem is required:

Theorem 5.25 ([13]) *For any $m \geq 0$, $\lambda \in (0, 1)$, $\bar{P}^{(m)}$ and $\bar{P}^{(m+1)}$ derived in Algorithm 11 satisfy: $\bar{P}^{(m)} \simeq \bar{P}^{(m+1)}$.*

Proof Let $P^{(m)} = (l_{ij}^{(m)})_{n\times n} = (\langle h_{t_{ij}^{(m)}}, s_{\alpha_{ij}^{(m)}}\rangle)_{n\times n}$, $\bar{P}^{(m)} = (\bar{l}^{(m)})_{n\times n}$,

(1) Firstly, we have to prove that $P^{(m+1)}$ is a reciprocal LHPR. In fact,

$$\begin{aligned} l_{ij}^{(m+1)} &= (1-\lambda)l_{ij}^{(m)} \oplus \lambda \frac{1}{n} \bigoplus_{k=1}^{n} (l_{ik}^{(m)} \oplus l_{kj}^{(m)}) \\ &= \langle h_{t_{ij}^{(m)}}, s_{(1-\lambda)\alpha_{ij}^{(m)}}\rangle \oplus \lambda \frac{1}{n} \bigoplus_{k=1}^{n} \langle h_{max\{t_{ik}^{(m)}, t_{kj}^{(m)}\}}, s_{\alpha_{ik}^{(m)}+\alpha_{kj}^{(m)}}\rangle \\ &= \langle h_{t_{ij}^{(m)}}, s_{(1-\lambda)\alpha_{ij}^{(m)}}\rangle \oplus \langle h_{t_0^{(ij)}}, s_{\lambda\alpha_0^{(ij)}}\rangle \end{aligned}$$

where $t_0^{(ij)} = \max_k\{\max\{t_{ik}^{(m)}, t_{kj}^{(m)}\}\}$, $\alpha_0^{(ij)} = \frac{1}{n}\sum_{k=1}^{n}(\alpha_{ik}^{(m)} + \alpha_{kj}^{(m)})$. Then we have $l_{ij}^{(m+1)} = \langle h_{max\{t_{ij}^{(m)}, t_0^{(ij)}\}}, s_{(1-\lambda)\alpha_{ij}^{(m)}+\lambda\alpha_0^{(ij)}}\rangle$. Obviously, $h_{max\{t_{ij}^{(m)}, t_0^{(ij)}\}} \in \bar{H}, s_{(1-\lambda)\alpha_{ij}^{(m)}+\lambda\alpha_0^{(ij)}} \in \bar{S}$, thus $l_{ij}^{(m+1)} \in \bar{\mathcal{L}}$ and $P^{(m+1)}$ is a LHPR. Furthermore, if $m = 0$, P is reciprocal. Assume that $P^{(m)}$ is reciprocal, which means $l_{ij}^{(m)} = Neg(l_{ji}^{(m)})(\forall i, j = 1, 2, \ldots, n)$. Then

$$\begin{aligned} l_{ji}^{(m+1)} &= \langle h_{max\{t_{ji}^{(m)}, t_0^{(ji)}\}}, s_{(1-\lambda)\alpha_{ji}^{(m)}+\lambda\alpha_0^{(ji)}}\rangle \\ &= \langle h_{max\{t_{ij}^{(m)}, t_0^{(ij)}\}}, s_{-((1-\lambda)\alpha_{ij}^{(m)}+\lambda\alpha_0^{(ij)})}\rangle = Neg(l_{ij}^{(m+1)}) \end{aligned}$$

Thus $P^{(m+1)}$ is reciprocal.

(2) We prove $\bar{P}^{(m)} \simeq \bar{P}^{(m+1)}$. According to $l_{ij}^{(m+1)}$ derived in (1), we have:

$$\begin{aligned}\bar{l}_{ij}^{(m+1)} &= \frac{1}{n} \bigoplus_{k=1}^{n} (\langle h_{t_0^{(ik)}}, s_{\alpha_0^{(ik)}} \rangle \oplus \langle h_{t_0^{(kj)}}, s_{\alpha_0^{(kj)}} \rangle) \\ &= \frac{1}{n} \bigoplus_{k=1}^{n} \langle h_{max\{t_0^{(ik)}, t_0^{(kj)}\}}, s_{\alpha_0^{(ik)}+\alpha_0^{(kj)}} \rangle = \langle h_{t_1^{(ij)}}, s_{\alpha_1^{(ij)}} \rangle\end{aligned}$$

where $t_1^{(ij)} = \max_k \{\max\{t_0^{(ik)}, t_0^{(kj)}\}\}$, $\alpha_1^{(ij)} = \frac{1}{n} \sum_{k=1}^{n} (\alpha_0^{(ik)} + \alpha_0^{(kj)})$. Especially,

$$\begin{aligned}\alpha_1^{(ij)} &= \frac{1}{n} \sum_{k=1}^{n} (\frac{1}{n} \sum_{k_1=1}^{n} (\alpha_{ik_1}^{(m)} + \alpha_{k_1 k}^{(m)}) + \frac{1}{n} \sum_{k_2=1}^{n} (\alpha_{kk_2}^{(m)} + \alpha_{k_2 j}^{(m)})) \\ &= \frac{1}{n^2} \sum_{k=1}^{n} \sum_{k_1=1}^{n} (\alpha_{ik_1}^{(m)} + \alpha_{k_1 k}^{(m)} + \alpha_{kk_1}^{(m)} + \alpha_{k_1 j}^{(m)}) \\ &= \frac{1}{n^2} \sum_{k=1}^{n} \sum_{k_1=1}^{n} (\alpha_{ik_1}^{(m)} + \alpha_{k_1 j}^{(m)}) = \frac{1}{n} \sum_{k_1=1}^{n} (\alpha_{ik_1}^{(m)} + \alpha_{k_1 j}^{(m)}) = \alpha_0^{(ij)}\end{aligned}$$

this means $\bar{l}_{ij}^{(m+1)} \simeq \bar{l}_{ij}^{(m)}$. Thus $\bar{P}^{(m)} \simeq \bar{P}^{(m+1)}$. □

Thus, according to (3) of Theorems 5.7 and 5.25, it is not necessary to generate $\bar{P}^{(m)}$ in each loop of Algorithm 11. The algorithm can be improved to the new version of Algorithm 12 [13].

Algorithm 12 The improved version of weak consistency improving algorithm of LHPR. Input: a reciprocal LHPR $P = (l_{ij})_{n \times n}$, $\lambda \in (0, 1)$; Output: a weakly consistent LHPR $P^{(m)}$.

1: Let $P^{(0)} = P$, $m = 0$, generate $\bar{P}$ by using Eq. (5.13);
2: According to Algorithm 9, if $P^{(m)}$ is weakly consistent, then go to Step 4; else, go to Step 3;
3: Let $P^{(m+1)} = (1 - \lambda) P^{(m)} \oplus \lambda \bar{P}$, $m = m + 1$; go to Step 2;
4: Output $P^{(m)}$.

The convergence of Algorithm 12 can be identified as follows:

Theorem 5.26 ([13]) *Algorithm 12 outputs a weakly consistent LHPR within finite loops.*

Proof Let $P^{(m)} = (l_{ij}^{(m)})_{n \times n}$ and $\bar{P} = (\bar{l}_{ij})_{n \times n}$ which is generated from P. It is sufficient if the deviation between $P^{(m)}$ and $\bar{P}$ reduces in each loop. In fact, according to the proof of Theorem 5.25, we have

$$
\begin{aligned}
d(l_{ij}^{(m+1)}, \bar{l}_{ij}) &= d(\langle h_{max\{t_{ij}^{(m)}, t_0^{(ij)}\}}, s_{(1-\lambda)\alpha_{ij}^{(m)}+\lambda\alpha_0^{(ij)}} \rangle, \langle h_{t_0^{(ij)}}, s_{\alpha_0^{(ij)}} \rangle) \\
&= \langle h_{max\{t_{ij}^{(m)}, t_0^{(ij)}\}}, s_{|(1-\lambda)\alpha_{ij}^{(m)}+\lambda\alpha_0^{(ij)}-\alpha_0^{(ij)}|} \rangle \\
&= \langle h_{max\{t_{ij}^{(m)}, t_0^{(ij)}\}}, s_{|(1-\lambda)(\alpha_{ij}^{(m)}-\alpha_0^{(ij)}|} \rangle \\
&\simeq (1-\lambda)\langle h_{max\{t_{ij}^{(m)}, t_0^{(ij)}\}}, s_{|(\alpha_{ij}^{(m)}-\alpha_0^{(ij)}|} \rangle \\
&= (1-\lambda) d(l_{ij}^{(m)}, \bar{l}_{ij}) \prec d(l_{ij}^{(m)}, \bar{l}_{ij})
\end{aligned}
$$

Therefore, $d(P^{(m+1)}, \bar{P}) \prec d(P^{(m)}, \bar{P})$. If $m \to +\infty$, then $P^{(m)}$ approaches an additively consistent LHPR. According to (2) of Theorem 5.13, the proof is completed. □

5.2.6.2 Improving the Degree of Additive Consistency

Obviously, Algorithm 12 improve a LHPR by letting it approach to an additively consistent LHPR. In applications, if weak consistency does not meet the requirement of a decision maker, then the concept of the degree of additive consistency can be introduced so that the decision maker can express the threshold of satisfactory consistency. Given P, the degree of additive consistency of a LHPR can be measured by the deviation between each entry in the upper triangular position l_{ij} $(i < j)$ and its ideal value.

Definition 5.27 ([13]) The degree of additive consistency of P is defined as:

$$D(P) = s_g \ominus d(P, \bar{P}) \tag{5.15}$$

where $\bar{P}$ is the LHPR generated by Eq. (5.13) based on P.

The larger $D(P)$ implies the larger degree of additive consistency of P. Linguistically, take the $S^{(4)}$ in Example 2.3 for instance, if $D(P) \simeq s_4$, then we can assert that the degree of additive consistency of P is *extremely good*. Moreover, we have the following theorem:

Theorem 5.28 ([13]) *For any reciprocal LHPR* $P = (l_{ij})_{n\times n}$, $D(P) \simeq s_g$ *if and only if* P *is additively consistent.*

Proof Let $\bar{P} = (\bar{l}_{ij})_{n\times n}$ represent the additively consistent LHPR generated by Eq. (5.13) based on P.

($\Rightarrow$) According to Definition 5.6, $d(l_1, l_2) \succeq s_0$ for any $l_1, l_2 \in \bar{\mathcal{L}}$. Thus $D(P) \simeq s_g$ means $d(l_{ij}, \bar{l}_{ij}) \simeq s_0 (\forall i < j, i, j = 1, 2, \ldots, n)$. Moreover, P is reciprocal, thus $l_{ij} \simeq \bar{l}_{ij} (\forall i, j = 1, 2, \ldots, n)$. Because $\bar{P}$ is additively consistent, P is also additively consistent.

($\Leftarrow$) If P is additively consistent, then according to Theorem 5.22, $P \simeq \bar{P}$. For any $i, j = 1, 2, \ldots, n$, $l_{ij} \simeq \bar{l}_{ij}$, $d(l_{ij}, \bar{l}_{ij}) \simeq s_0$, which means $d(P, \bar{P}) \simeq s_0$. Thus $D(P) \simeq s_\tau$. □

In application, it may be acceptable if the degree of additive consistency of a LHPR is big enough. Given a threshold δ determined by the decision maker, the concept of satisfactory consistency is defined below:

Definition 5.29 ([13]) A LHPR P is said to be of satisfactory consistency if $D(P) \geq \delta$, where $\delta \in \{s_1, s_2, \ldots, s_g\}$.

Given a LHPR, the satisfactory consistency can be achieved automatically by slightly revise Algorithm 12, which is depicted in Algorithm 13.

Algorithm 13 The additive consistency improving algorithm of LHPRs. Input: a reciprocal LHPR $P = (l_{ij})_{n \times n}$, $\lambda \in (0, 1)$, δ; Output: a LHPR $P^{(m)}$ with satisfactory consistency.

1: Let $P^{(0)} = P, m = 0$, generate $\bar{P}$ by using Eq. (5.13);
2: Compute $D(P^{(m)})$ by using Eq. (5.15). If $D(P^{(m)}) \succeq \delta$, go to Step 4; else, go to Step 3;
3: Let $P^{(m+1)} = (1 - \lambda) P^{(m)} \oplus \lambda \bar{P}, m = m + 1$; go to Step 2;
4: Output $P^{(m)}$.

According to the proof of Theorem 5.26, we have

$$\begin{aligned} d(P^{(m+1)}, \bar{P}) &= \tfrac{2}{n(n-1)} \bigoplus_{i<j} d(l_{ij}^{(m+1)}, \bar{l}_{ij}) \simeq \tfrac{2}{n(n-1)} \bigoplus_{i<j} (1 - \lambda) d(l_{ij}^{(m)}, \bar{l}_{ij}) \\ &= (1 - \lambda) d(P^{(m)}, \bar{P}) \end{aligned}$$

Assume that $d(P, \bar{P}) \simeq s_\alpha$, i.e., $D(P) \simeq s_{g-\alpha}$. Then we have $D(P^{(m)}) \simeq s_{g-(1-\lambda)^m \alpha}$. If $\delta = s_\beta (\beta > \alpha)$, then Algorithm 13 will be terminated once $g - (1 - \lambda)^m \alpha \geq \beta$, i.e., $m \geq \log_{1-\lambda} \frac{g-\beta}{\alpha}$.

Example 5.30 Continue with the LHPR P in Example 5.11. According to Eqs. (5.14) and (5.15), $D(P) = \langle h_2, s_{2.98} \rangle$. Assume that the decision maker prefers that the consistent threshold should be *very good*, i.e., $\delta = s_3$. If we let $\lambda = 0.1$, then a new LHPR $P^{(1)}$ can be derived by applying Step 3 of Algorithm 13:

$$P^{(1)} = \begin{pmatrix} \langle h_2, s_0 \rangle & \langle h_2, s_{-2.02} \rangle & \langle h_2, s_{-2.88} \rangle & \langle h_2, s_{-0.96} \rangle & \langle h_2, s_{1.86} \rangle \\ \langle h_2, s_{2.02} \rangle & \langle h_1, s_0 \rangle & \langle h_1, s_{1.84} \rangle & \langle h_1, s_{1.06} \rangle & \langle h_2, s_{2.08} \rangle \\ \langle h_2, s_{2.88} \rangle & \langle h_1, s_{-1.84} \rangle & \langle h_1, s_0 \rangle & \langle h_1, s_{2.82} \rangle & \langle h_2, s_{1.14} \rangle \\ \langle h_2, s_{0.96} \rangle & \langle h_1, s_{-1.06} \rangle & \langle h_1, s_{-2.82} \rangle & \langle h_1, s_0 \rangle & \langle h_2, s_{1.92} \rangle \\ \langle h_2, s_{-1.86} \rangle & \langle h_2, s_{-2.08} \rangle & \langle h_2, s_{-1.14} \rangle & \langle h_2, s_{-1.92} \rangle & \langle h_2, s_0 \rangle \end{pmatrix}$$

and $D(P^{(1)}) = \langle h_2, s_{3.08} \rangle \succ s_3$, thus the algorithm is terminated. Furthermore, if δ is fixed by *very good* (s_3), *middle of very good and extremely good* ($s_{3.5}$), and *extremely good* (s_4), respectively. The numbers of iterations with respect to the values of λ have been illustrated in Fig. 5.5. Note that we use $s_{3.9999}$ to approximate the case $\delta = s_4$.

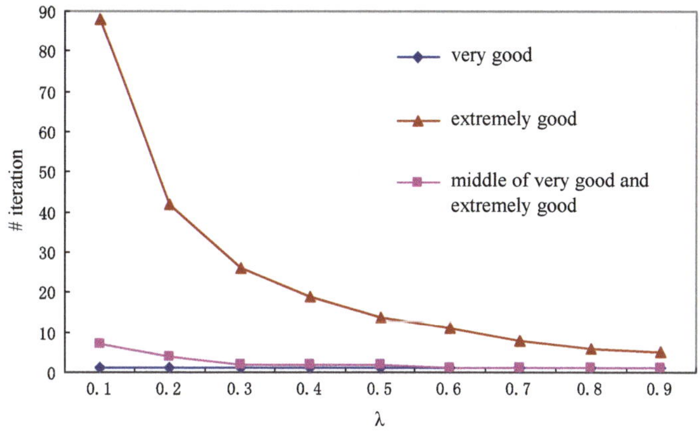

Fig. 5.5 Numbers of iterations with respect to different values of λ based on the LHPR in Example 5.11

Similar to the existing studies, the threshold δ is determined by a decision maker. However, the use of linguistic threshold makes its determination much easier. As can be seen in Example 5.30, the threshold is labelled by interpretable meaning naturally. Moreover, based on the virtual linguistic model, the decision maker could express the threshold within a finer granularity of the given LTS, like $s_{3.5}$ in Example 5.30.

5.3 Conclusions

In this chapter, we have introduced the transformation between multi-granular linguistic hierarchies and LTWHs, presented an approach for MGLDM, and then introduced the concept and consistency measures of LHPRs. Based on fuzzy weighted digraph, some algorithms for consistency checking and improving have also been introduced.

The proposed approach for MGLDM is suitable to the case of linguistic hierarchies. It possesses very good interpretability and acceptable complexity. The algorithm of normalizing multi-granular linguistic information explores the connection between LTWHs and linguistic hierarchies.

Moreover, LTWHs have been introduced to the framework of preference relations. This extended the range of linguistic information which could be employed to express preferences. According to the theoretical developments, the fundamental issues of LHPRs have been resolved.

References

1. Aldlaigan, A.H., Buttle, F.A.: SYSTRA-SQ: a new measure of bank service quality. Int. J. Serv. Ind. Manag. **13**(4), 362–381 (2002)
2. Espinilla, M., Liu, J., Martínez, L.: An extended hierarchical linguistic model for decision-making problems. Comput. Intell. **27**(3), 489–512 (2011)
3. Herrera, F., Martínez, L.: A 2-tuple fuzzy linguistic representation model for computing with words. IEEE Trans. Fuzzy Syst. **8**(6), 746–752 (2000)
4. Herrera, F., Martínez, L.: A model based on linguistic 2-tuples for dealing with multigranular hierarchical linguistic contexts in multi-expert decision-making. IEEE Trans. Syst. Man Cybern. Part B Cybern. **31**(2), 227–234 (2001)
5. Herrera, F., Herrera-Viedma, E., Martínez, L.: A fusion approach for managing multi-granularity linguistic term sets in decision making. Fuzzy Sets Syst. **114**(1), 43–58 (2000)
6. Hussain, M., Gunasekaran, A.: An institutional perspective of non-financial management accounting measures: a review of the financial services industry. Manag. Audit. J. **17**(9), 518–536 (2002)
7. Huynh, V.N., Nakamori, Y.: A satisfactory-oriented approach to multiexpert decision-making with linguistic assessments. IEEE Trans. Syst. Man Cybern. Part B Cybern. **35**(2), 184–196 (2005)
8. Lin, K.C., Chern, M.S.: The fuzzy shortest path problem and its most vital arcs. Fuzzy Sets Syst. **58**(3), 343–353 (1993)
9. Ma, J., Fan, Z.P., Jiang, Y.P., Mao, J.Y., Ma, L.: A method for repairing the inconsistency of fuzzy preference relations. Fuzzy Sets Syst. **157**(1), 20–33 (2006)
10. Morente-Molinera, J.A., Pérez, I.J., Ureña, M.R., Herrera-Viedma, E.: On multi-granular fuzzy linguistic modeling in group decision making problems: a systematic review and future trends. Knowl.-Based Syst. **74**, 49–60 (2015)
11. Saaty, T.L., Ozdemir, M.S.: Why the magic number seven plus or minus two. Math. Comput. Model. **38**(3–4), 233–244 (2003)
12. Seçme, N.Y., Bayrakdaroğlu, A., Kahraman, C.: Fuzzy performance evaluation in Turkish banking sector using analytic hierarchy process and TOPSIS. Expert Syst. Appl. **36**(9), 11699–11709 (2009)
13. Wang, H., Xu, Z.S., Zeng, X.J., Liao, H.C.: Consistency measures of linguistic preference relations with hedges. IEEE Trans. Fuzzy Syst. (2018). https://doi.org/10.1109/TFUZZ.2018.2856107
14. Wang, H., Xu, Z.S., Zeng, X.J.: Linguistic terms with weakened hedges: a model for qualitative decision making under uncertainty. Inf. Sci. **433–434**(3), 37–54 (2018)
15. Xu, Z.S.: A method based on linguistic aggregation operators for group decision making with linguistic preference relations. Inf. Sci. **166**(1), 19–30 (2004)
16. Xu, Z.S.: Deviation measures of linguistic preference relations in group decision making. Omega **33**(3), 249–254 (2005)
17. Xu, Z.S., Wang, H.: Managing multi-granularity linguistic information in qualitative group decision making: an overview. Granul. Comput. **1**(1), 21–35 (2016)
18. Xu, Y.J., Patnayakuni, R., Wang, H.M.: The ordinal consistency of a fuzzy preference relation. Inf. Sci. **224**, 152–164 (2013)

Part IV
Group Decision-Making Based on Multiple Types of Uncertain Linguistic Expressions

Chapter 6
An Aspiration-Based Approach with Multiple Types of Uncertain Linguistic Expressions

As stated in Sect. 1.3.3, decisions are usually made based on not only the performances of alternatives but also how the performances satisfy the decision makers aspiration levels. This chapter introduces a linguistic aspiration-based approach to GDM where the aspiration levels and performances can be expressed by three types of ULEs, i.e., ULTs, HFLTSs, and LTWHs. The approach can deal with complex problems, which involve multiple criteria, multi-groups of experts (in the framework of Sect. 3.1) and multi-granular linguistic information (in the framework of Sect. 5.1). Note that, in the rest of this chapter, a ULE is a linguistic expression taking the form of either ULTs, HFLTSs, or LTWHs. Any other types of linguistic expressions are excluded.

6.1 Utility Functions Based on Linguistic Aspiration Levels

The most significant feature of this chapter is the consideration of aspiration levels. Similar to other aspiration-based solutions in fuzzy circumstance, we consider fuzzy aspiration levels which are expressed by linguistic expressions and refer to them as linguistic aspiration levels. In the introduced approach, aspiration levels and performance values can be represented by all the three mentioned types of ULEs, i.e., ULTs, HFLTSs, and LTWHs. For convenience, a ULE is denoted as ll in the sequel. This section is devoted to defining three types of linguistic aspiration levels, which rely on the similarity measure of two ULEs.

Given LTS $S^{(\tau)} = \{s_\alpha | \alpha = 0, 1, \ldots, \tau\}$, the semantics of the term s_α is a fuzzy set defined in the domain U, usually represented by a trapezoidal fuzzy number (TraFN) (a, b, c, d), where

H. Wang and Z. Xu, *Theory and Approaches of Group Decision-Making with Uncertain Linguistic Expressions*, Uncertainty and Operations Research,
https://doi.org/10.1007/978-981-13-3735-2_6

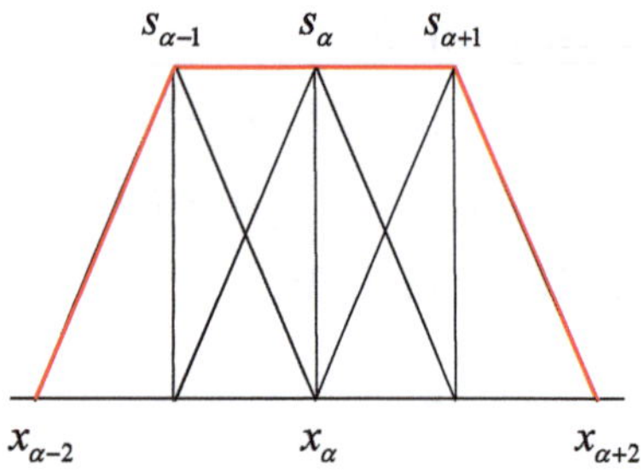

Fig. 6.1 An example of ULTs ($[s_{\alpha-1}, s_{\alpha+1}]$)

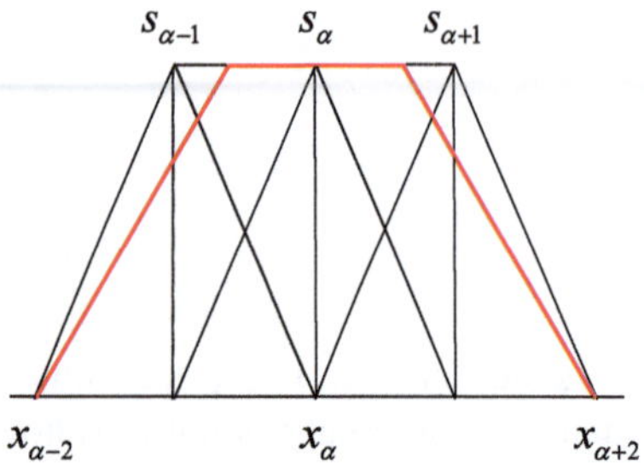

Fig. 6.2 An example of HFLTSs and fuzzy envelopes ($\{s_{\alpha-1}, s_\alpha, s_{\alpha+1}\}$)

$$\mu_{s_\alpha}(x) = (a, b, c, d) = \begin{cases} (x-a)/(b-a), & \max\{L, a\} \le x < b \\ 1, & b \le x \le c \\ (d-x)/(d-c), & c < x \le \min\{d, R\} \\ 0, & otherwise \end{cases} \tag{6.1}$$

If $b = c$, then the TraFN reduces to a TriFN. We assume that, in this chapter, the semantics of terms in $S^{(\tau)}$ is defined by the method in Sect. 2.4.1, that is $s_\alpha = (x_{\alpha-1}, x_\alpha, x_{\alpha+1})(\forall s_\alpha \in S^{(\tau)})$. Given ULT $ll = [s_\alpha, s_\beta]$, where $s_\alpha < s_\beta$ and $s_\alpha, s_\beta \in S^{(\tau)}$, because $s_\alpha = (x_{\alpha-1}, x_\alpha, x_{\alpha+1})$, $s_\beta = (x_{\beta-1}, x_\beta, x_{\beta+1})$, as can be seen in Fig. 6.1, the semantics of $[s_\alpha, s_\beta]$ is:

$$\mu_{[s_\alpha, s_\beta]}(x) = (x_{\alpha-1}, x_\alpha, x_\beta, x_{\beta+1}) \tag{6.2}$$

Although the semantics of a HFLTS has been exploited by Rodríguez et al. [2], it is complicated and not suitable for computing. In this chapter, we make use of the fuzzy envelopes of HFLTSs [1], which are TraFNs. Generally, given a HFLTS $\{s_\alpha, a_{\alpha+1}, \ldots, a_\beta\}$, its fuzzy envelope is denoted by (Fig. 6.2):

$$\mu_{\{s_\alpha, a_{\alpha+1}, \ldots, a_\beta\}}(x) = (x_a, x_b, x_c, x_d) \tag{6.3}$$

where the four parameters can be determined by the method summarized in [1]. An example of the fuzzy envelope can be found in Fig. 5.2.

The semantics of a LTWH $\langle h_1, s_\alpha \rangle$, $\mu_{\langle h_1, s_\alpha \rangle}$, can be found in Sect. 2.4.1.

6.1.1 Similarity Measure of ULEs

To make sure the similarity of two ULEs coincides with our intuition, we revise Eq. (6.1) and express it as the following version:

$$\mu_{s_\alpha}(x) = (a, b, c, d) = \begin{cases} (x-a)/(b-a), & a \le x < b \\ 1, & b \le x \le c \\ (d-x)/(d-c), & c < x \le d \\ 0, & otherwise \end{cases} \tag{6.4}$$

Obviously, some parameters of the TraFN might fall out of the domain. We use this form only for the sake of computing similarity. The similarity measure is determined by the semantics of two ULEs if the domain is uniformly distributed. More specifically, it is measured by the similarity of their semantic functions, as elaborated in the following definition:

Definition 6.1 ([3]) Given two ULEs ll_1 and ll_2 defined in a uniformly distributed domain U, their similarity is defined by

$$Sim(ll_1, ll_2) = \frac{\int_{\Re} \mu_{ll_1}(x) \wedge \mu_{ll_2}(x)dx}{\int_{\Re} \mu_{ll_1}(x) \vee \mu_{ll_2}(x)dx} \tag{6.5}$$

where $\Re$ is the set of real number.

The similarity is defined on $\Re$ (instead of U) because the semantic representations of ULEs may fall out of U.

Example 6.2 Let $S^{(8)}$ be the LTS in Example 2.3 and $\bar{H}^{(2)}$ be the WHS in Eq. (2.47), then $s_0 = (-0.125, 0, 0.125)$, $s_1 = (0, 0.125, 0.25)$, according to Eqs. (6.4) and (6.5), $Sim(ll_1, ll_2) = 1/7$; Furthermore, considering three intuitively similar ULEs, $ll_1 = [s_3, s_5]$, $ll_2 = \{s_3, s_4, s_5\}$, and $ll_3 = \langle h_1, s_4 \rangle$, we have $Sim(ll_1, ll_2) = 0.73$, $Sim(ll_2, ll_3) = 0.91$, $Sim(ll_1, ll_3) = 2/3$.

If a domain is not uniformly distributed but piecewise uniformly distributed, the use of Eq. (6.5) results in $Sim(s_{\alpha-1}, s_\alpha) \neq Sim(s_\alpha, s_{\alpha+1})$, where $s_{\alpha-1}, s_\alpha, s_{\alpha+1} \in S^{(\tau)}$, which is not consistent with our intuition. In this case, the piecewise linear function in Eq. (2.56) is necessary. The function transforms the original domain into a uniformly distributed one. Accordingly, the semantics of ULEs is transformed. Thus, the similarity between two ULEs can be calculated based on the new semantics and Eq. (6.5).

We can draw some properties of the similarity measure in Definition 6.1. The result which has emerged in Example 6.2 can be generalized as follows:

Theorem 6.3 ([3]) *Let $S^{(\tau)}$ be a LTS, $s_\alpha, s_\beta \in S^{(\tau)}$, then*

$$Sim(s_\alpha, s_\beta) = \begin{cases} 1, & \alpha = \beta \\ 1/7, & |\alpha - \beta| = 1 \\ 0, & otherwise \end{cases} \tag{6.6}$$

The proof is trivial. Some general properties are also summarized in the next theorem:

Theorem 6.4 ([3]) *Let ll_1 and ll_2 be two ULEs generated based on the LTS $S^{(\tau)}$ in the domain U, then*
(1) $0 \le Sim(ll_1, ll_2) \le 1$;
(2) $Sim(ll_1, ll_2) = 1 \Leftrightarrow ll_1 = ll_2$.

The proof is omitted. Note that (2) in Theorem 6.4 does not hold if ll_1 and ll_2 are generated from different granularities of LTSs in the domain U.

6.1.2 Linguistic Aspiration Levels and Utility Functions

In the qualitative environment, experts' aspiration levels are usually imprecise and vague, and as such could be expressed by linguistic expressions. In our focused problem, the linguistic aspiration levels, denoted by $ll^{(A)}$, are represented by ULEs. In real world problems, based on a predefined LTS $S^{(\tau)}$ and WHS $H^{(\varsigma)}$, the linguistic aspiration levels could be the three types [3]:

(1) Aspiration levels with benefit form ($ll^{(BA)}$). This type of aspiration levels could be represented by ULT $[s_\beta, s_\tau]$, HFLTS $\{s_\beta, s_{\beta+1}, \ldots, s_\tau\}$ or LTWH $\langle h_t, s_\tau \rangle$, where $s_\beta \le s_\tau$, $s_\beta \in S^{(\tau)}$ and $h_t \in H^{(\varsigma)}$.

(2) Aspiration levels with cost form ($ll^{(CA)}$). This type of aspiration levels could be represented by ULT $[s_0, s_\alpha]$, HFLTS $\{s_0, s_1, \ldots, s_\alpha\}$ or LTWH $\langle h_t, s_0 \rangle$, where $s_0 \le s_\alpha$, $s_\alpha \in S^{(\tau)}$ and $h_t \in H^{(\varsigma)}$.

(3) Aspiration levels with interval form ($ll^{(IA)}$). This type of aspiration levels could be represented by ULT $[s_\alpha, s_\beta]$, HFLTS $\{s_\alpha, s_{\alpha+1}, \ldots, s_\beta\}$ or LTWH $\langle h_t, s_\gamma \rangle$, where $s_0 < s_\alpha \le s_\beta < s_\tau$, $s_\alpha, s_\gamma, s_\beta \in S^{(\tau)}$ and $h_t \in H^{(\varsigma)}$.

It can be observed that we extend the existing concept of fuzzy aspiration by two aspects. On the one hand, experts can express their aspiration levels by means of ULTs, HFLTSs or LTWHs. As will be seen hereinafter, the use of ULEs makes the representation of utilities very easy. On the other hand, the three types of ULEs can be used arbitrarily by experts according to the linguistic expressions in mind.

The utility based on linguistic aspiration levels can be derived intuitively and straightforward. In fact, if the aspiration level is achieved, then the utility is 1; else the utility can be measured by the similarity between the performance value and the aspiration level. This is specified by the following definition:

Definition 6.5 ([3]) Given a performance value ll and its linguistic aspiration level $ll^{(A)}$, the aspiration-based utility of ll is defined by

$$u(ll|ll^{(A)}) = \begin{cases} 1, & ll \subseteq ll^{(A)} \\ Sim(ll, ll^{(A)}), & otherwise \end{cases} \tag{6.7}$$

We now observe that the generalization of linguistic terms results in a generalized definition of utility. For any performance values and any linguistic aspiration levels, both taking the form of ULEs, the computation of utility depends on only Eq. (6.5) and the semantics of ULEs.

6.2 An Approach for Multi-criteria Multi-groups and Multi-granular GDM

6.2.1 *Framework of the Focused Problem*

The traditional MCDM problems refer to the selection among a set of alternatives $A = \{a_i | i = 1, 2, \ldots, I\}$ with respect to the collection of criteria $C = \{c_j | j = 1, 2, \ldots, J\}$, associated with a weighting vector $\boldsymbol{\omega} = (\omega_1, \omega_2, \ldots, \omega_J)^T$ such that $\sum_{j=1}^{J} \omega_j = 1, 0 \leq \omega_j \leq 1$ $(j = 1, 2, \ldots, J)$. However, due to the complexity of the problem, like the outsourcing provider selection of a BDAP in this book, one individual cannot evaluate alternatives with respect to all the criteria. To the contrary, multiple experts are usually considered in order to avoid the arbitrary and biased opinions and enable a way to handle the uncertainty of evaluation (for example, by measuring the group's consensus). Moreover, if the number of experts is large, the group can be divided into several small groups based on the knowledge and expertise of experts. Similar to Sect. 3.1, in this section, multiple groups are necessary due to the complexity of the problem.

A set of experts is divided into M groups, denoted here by $G = \{G_m | m = 1, 2, \ldots, M\}$. The experts in the m-th group are collected by $G_m = \{e_{mn} | n = 1, 2, \ldots, \#G_m\}$, where e_{mn} denotes the n-th expert in the m-th group, $\#G_m$ is number of experts in the group. Experts in the same group are with the similar profession and expertise, and thus can be authorized to evaluate the same subset of criteria. Suppose that each criterion is evaluated by only a single group. Thus, the set C can be divided into M subsets, denoted by $C_m = \{c_{mp} | p = 1, 2, \ldots, \#C_m\}$, where $\#C_m$ is the number of criteria in the set C_m. Especially, the criteria in C_m is supposed to be evaluated by the group G_m. Furthermore, in a qualitative setting, the experts prefer to evaluate different criteria by distinct granularities of LTSs. We assume that a set of Q context-free LTSs defined in the same domain $U = [0, 1]$ are provided for the experts, which are denoted by $\{S^{(\tau_q)} | q = 1, 2, \ldots, Q\}$ with $S^{(\tau_q)} = \{s_\alpha^{(q)} | \alpha = 0, 1, 2, \ldots, \tau_q\}$. The WHS is fixed by the one in Eq. (2.47). The performance values, as well as linguistic aspiration levels, are allowed to be represented by all the three types of ULEs. The framework of the multi-criteria multi-groups and multi-granular GDM (M^3GDM) problem is also illustrated in Fig. 6.3. Assume that the matrix of performance values and the vector of linguistic aspiration levels, with respect to the criteria in C_m provided

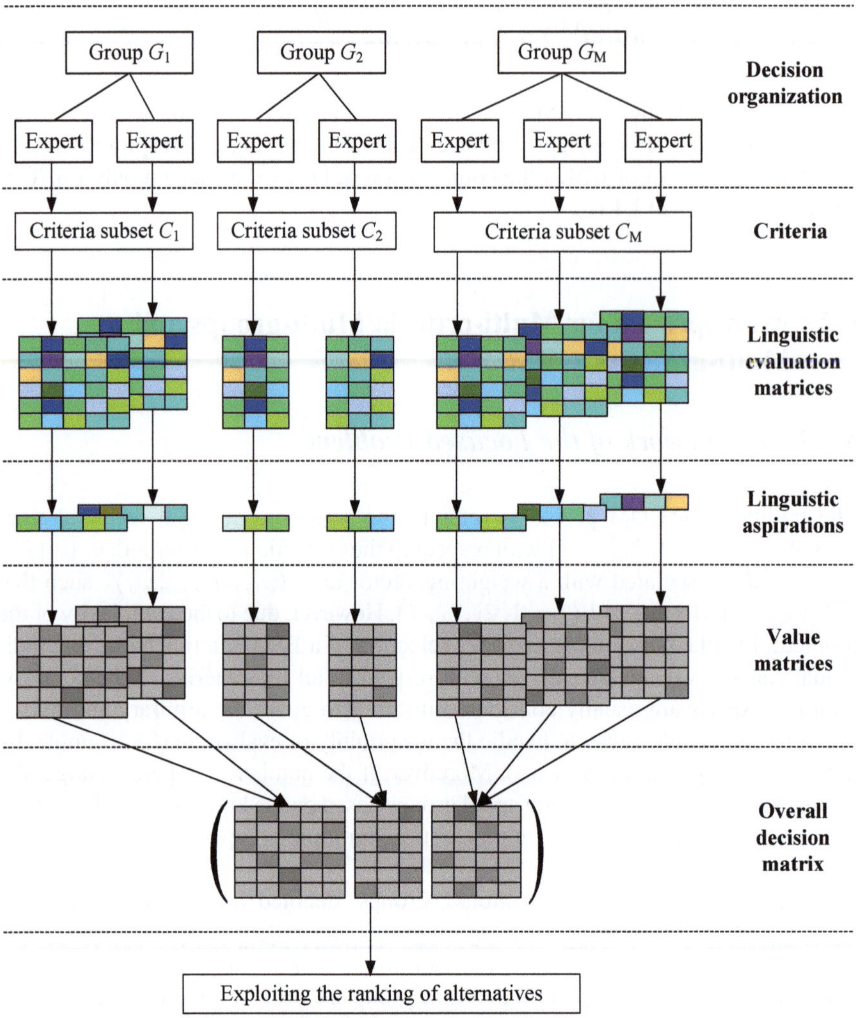

Fig. 6.3 The framework of the proposed M^{3}QDM problem

by the expert e_{mn} is listed in Table 6.1, where $n = 1, 2, \ldots, \#G_m, m = 1, 2, \ldots, M$. The goal of the M^{3}QDM problem is to select the most desirable alternative(s) from A, according to the linguistic information provided by the experts.

6.2.2 *An Approach for M^{3}QDM Problems*

The solution for the M^{3}QDM problem includes three procedures. First of all, the consensus of each group should be acceptable so that the group's opinion is meaningful

Table 6.1 The linguistic aspiration levels and performance values provided by the expert e_{mn}

Criterion	c_{m1}	c_{m2}	$\cdots$	$c_{m,\#C_m}$
Aspiration	$ll^{(A)}_{m,n,1}$	$ll^{(A)}_{m,n,2}$	$\cdots$	$ll^{(A)}_{m,n,\#C_m}$
a_1	$ll^{(m,n)}_{11}$	$ll^{(m,n)}_{12}$	$\cdots$	$ll^{(m,n)}_{1,\#C_m}$
a_2	$ll^{(m,n)}_{21}$	$ll^{(m,n)}_{22}$	$\cdots$	$ll^{(m,n)}_{2,\#C_m}$
$\vdots$	$\vdots$	$\vdots$	$\ddots$	$\vdots$
a_I	$ll^{(m,n)}_{I1}$	$ll^{(m,n)}_{I2}$	$\cdots$	$ll^{(m,n)}_{I,\#C_m}$

for fusion. Then the overall performance can be derived, and finally the ranking of alternatives can be exploited. The aims and tasks are illustrated as follows [3]:

Step 1. Groups' consensus checking. As the aspiration levels are considered, the consensus can be defined and checked by the fact that to what degree the alternatives meet the aspiration levels of experts in a group. Specifically, each group's consensus is measured according to the experts' utilities rather than the performance values. In order that, this step contains two phrases:

(1) The original linguistic information LM_{mn} taking the form of Table 6.1 is transformed to its corresponding utility matrix UM_{mn}, where $n = 1, 2, \ldots, \#G_m$, $m = 1, 2, \ldots, M$.

(2) An optimal model is formed to uncover if $UM_{mn}\{n = 1, 2, \ldots, \#G_m\}$ are acceptable by assigning proper weights to the group's members. Based on which, an interactive algorithm is then developed to improve the group's consensus.

Step 2. Fusion. For each G_m, if the matrices are acceptable, then the m-th block of the overall performance matrix, denoted by UM_m, i.e., the overall performance of the alternative with respect to the criteria in C_m, can be obtained by a weighting averaging operator, where $m = 1, 2, \ldots, M$. Therefore, the overall performance matrix UM is available after all the blocks of the groups are collected.

Step 3. Exploitation. A weighted aggregating operator can be adopted to exploit the ranking of alternatives based on the overall performance matrix.

6.2.2.1 Reaching Groups' Consensus

According to the linguistic aspiration levels provided by e_{mn} and the aspiration-based utility defined by Eq. (6.7), the linguistic matrix $LM_{mn} = (ll^{(m,n)}_{ip})_{I\times\#C_m}$ can be transformed to the corresponding utility matrix $UM_{mn} = (u^{(m,n)}_{ip})_{I\times\#C_m}$, where $u^{(m,n)}_{ip}$ is the utility of a_i with respect to c_{mp} according to e_{mn}, $i = 1, 2, \ldots, I$, $p = 1, 2, \ldots, \#C_m$, $n = 1, 2, \ldots, \#G_m$, $m = 1, 2, \ldots, M$.

Given $m \in \{1, 2, \ldots, M\}$, we consider the consensus of G_m. Suppose that the weighting vector of the experts in G_m is $\mathbf{w} = (w_1, w_2, \ldots, \#G_m)^T$ such that $\sum_{n=1}^{\#G_m} w_n = 1$ and $0 \leq w_n \leq 1$ $(n = 1, 2, \ldots, \#G_m)$. Then the group's utility matrix

$UM_m = (u_{ip}^{(m)})_{I \times \#C_m}$ can be derived by synthesizing the $\#G_m$ utility matrices of the group's members, where

$$u_{ip}^{(m)} = \sum_{n=1}^{\#G_m} w_n \cdot u_{ip}^{(m,n)}, i = 1, 2, \ldots, I, p = 1, 2, \ldots, \#C_m \quad (6.8)$$

Then the deviation $d(UM_{mn}, UM_m)$ between UM_{mn} and UM_m can be derived by

$$d(UM_{mn}, UM_m) = \sum_{i=1}^{I} \sum_{p=1}^{\#C_m} \lambda_p \cdot (u_{ip}^{(m,n)} - u_{ip}^{(m)})^2, n = 1, 2, \ldots, \#G_m \quad (6.9)$$

where λ_p is the weight of c_{mp} which can be obtained by normalizing the weights of criteria in the set C_m, i.e., $\lambda_p = \omega_{mp} \Big/ \sum_{p=1}^{\#C_m} \omega_{mp}$. Consequently, the deviations among all the individual utility matrices and the group's utility matrix can be defined by

$$g(\mathbf{w}) = \sum_{n=1}^{\#G_m} d(UM_{mn}, UM_m) \quad (6.10)$$

Ideally, the deviation in Eq. (6.10) would approach 0 if the group's opinion is highly consensual. In our M^{3}QDM problem, the experts in each group are not assigned weights. To reduce the experts' work as much as possible, we intend to figure out whether there is at least one weighting vector, which results in an acceptable consensus degree of the group. Thus, the following model can be formed:

$$\begin{aligned} &\min g(\mathbf{w}) = \sum_{n=1}^{\#G_m} \sum_{i=1}^{I} \sum_{p=1}^{\#C_m} \lambda_p \cdot (u_{ip}^{(m,n)} - \sum_{n'=1}^{\#G_m} w_{n'} \cdot u_{ip}^{(m,n')})^2 \\ &s.t. \begin{cases} \sum_{n=1}^{\#G_m} w_n = 1 \\ w_n \geq 0, n = 1, 2, \ldots, \#G_m \end{cases} \end{aligned} \quad (6.11)$$

To solve the model, we construct the following Lagrangian function:

$$L(\mathbf{w}, \xi) = \sum_{n=1}^{\#G_m} \sum_{i=1}^{I} \sum_{p=1}^{\#C_m} \lambda_p \cdot (u_{ip}^{(m,n)} - \sum_{n'=1}^{\#G_m} w_{n'} \cdot u_{ip}^{(m,n')})^2 - 2\xi(\sum_{n=1}^{\#G_m} w_n - 1) \quad (6.12)$$

Differentiating Eq. (6.12) with respect to w_n and letting these partial derivatives be equal to 0, we have

$$\frac{\partial L(\mathbf{w}, \xi)}{\partial w_n} = \sum_{i=1}^{I} \sum_{p=1}^{\#C_m} \sum_{n'=1}^{\#G_m} \lambda_p (\#G_m w_{n'} - 1) u_{ip}^{(m,n)} u_{ip}^{(m,n')} - \xi = 0 \quad (6.13)$$

where $n = 1, 2, \ldots, \#G_m$. Then the following tight form can be obtained:

$$G\mathbf{w} - \mathbf{r} - \xi\mathbf{e} = 0 \tag{6.14}$$

where $\mathbf{e} = (1, 1, \ldots, 1)^T$, the $\#G_m \times 1$ vector $\mathbf{r}$ and $\#G_m \times \#G_m$ matrix G are:

$$\mathbf{r} = (r_{n'})_{\#G_m \times 1}, \text{ where } r_{n'} = \sum_{i=1}^{I}\sum_{p=1}^{\#C_m}\sum_{n=1}^{\#G_m} \lambda_p u_{ip}^{(m,n)} u_{ip}^{(m,n')} \tag{6.15}$$

$$G = (G_{n,n'})_{\#G_m \times \#G_m}, \text{ where } G_{n,n'} = \sum_{i=1}^{I}\sum_{p=1}^{\#C_m} \#G_m \lambda_p u_{ip}^{(m,n)} u_{ip}^{(m,n')} \tag{6.16}$$

It is obvious that G is positive definite and G^{-1} is non-negative. Associated with $\mathbf{e}^T\mathbf{w} = 1$, the parameter ξ can be solved at first:

$$\xi = \frac{1 - \mathbf{e}^T G^{-1}\mathbf{r}}{\mathbf{e}^T G^{-1}\mathbf{e}} \tag{6.17}$$

Then the weighting vector $\mathbf{w}$ can be derived by combining Eqs. (6.14) and (6.17):

$$\mathbf{w} = G^{-1}\mathbf{r} + \frac{1 - \mathbf{e}^T G^{-1}\mathbf{r}}{\mathbf{e}^T G^{-1}\mathbf{r}} G^{-1}\mathbf{e} \tag{6.18}$$

Based on Eq. (6.18), the optimal value of $g(\mathbf{w})$, denoted by $g^*(\mathbf{w})$, can be derived. The consensus index of the group G_m can be represented by

$$CI_m = \frac{g^*(\mathbf{w})}{\#G_m I} \tag{6.19}$$

Then, a simple interactive algorithm can be employed to make CI_m reach its satisfactory level CI_m^*. Generally, the value can be assigned by the decision maker or the leader of the group. The smaller value implies the higher level of group consensus. As suggested by Xu [4], we let $CI_m^* = 0.5$ for any $m = 1, 2, \ldots, M$ in this chapter. Given CI_m^* and the max number of interaction N_{max}, the interactive algorithm is depicted in Algorithm 14. The algorithm is terminated once the groups consensus is acceptable or the number of interaction has reached the required limit.

6.2.2.2 Fusion and Exploitation

The overall utility matrix with respect to all the criteria can be formed after the consensus of all groups has been improved by Algorithm 14.

For each $G_m (m = 1, 2, \ldots, M)$, $UM_m = (u_{ip}^{(m)})_{I \times \#C_m}$ can be calculated by Eq. (6.8). The utility matrix UM_m is, actually, the m-th block of the overall utility matrix

Algorithm 14 The interactive algorithm to improve group consensus. Input: the utility matrices $UM_{mn}(n = 1, 2, \ldots, \#G_m), CI_m^*, N_{max}$; Output: the improved utility matrices $UM_{mn}(n = 1, 2, \ldots, \#G_m)$, the optimal weighting vector **w**.

1: Initiate $N = 1$, $UM_{mn}^{(N)} = UM_{mn}(n = 1, 2, \ldots, \#G_m)$;
2: Solve the model in Eq. (6.11), the optimal weight is denoted by $\mathbf{w}^{(N)}$. Calculate $CI_m^{(N)}$ by Eq. (6.19);
3: If $CI_m^{(N)} > CI_m^*$ and $N < N_{max}$, then go to Step 4; else, go to Step 5;
4: Calculate UM_m by Eq. (6.8) return it to the experts in G_m. Let $N = N + 1$. Compute $UM_{mn}^{(N)}$ by using the linguistic information fed back by experts and Eq. (6.7), $n = 1, 2, \ldots, \#G_m$. Go to Step 2;
5: $UM_{mn} = UM_{mn}^{(N)} (n = 1, 2, \ldots, \#G_m)$, $\mathbf{w} = \mathbf{w}^{(N)}$.

UM. Thus, UM is obtained immediately as:

$$UM = (u_{ij})_{I\times J} = \left(UM_1\ UM_2\ \cdots\ UM_M\right)_{1\times M} \tag{6.20}$$

The overall utility of each alternative a_i, denoted by u_i, can be derived by Eq. (6.20) and the weighting vector ω is as follows:

$$u_i = \sum_{j=1}^{J} \omega_j u_{ij} \tag{6.21}$$

where $i = 1, 2, \ldots, I$. Then the alternatives can be ranked by the overall utilities.

6.3 Conclusions

This chapter has introduced a new GDM approach in which the qualitative information takes the form of three types of ULEs, i.e., ULTs, HFLTSs, and LTWHs. The approach could handle the problems where the decision information is evaluated by multi-groups of experts with respect to multi-criteria and then expressed by multi-granular linguistic expressions. Based on the semantics of ULEs, the approach could operate multiple types of expressions. Besides, the approach could incorporate experts' linguistic aspiration levels. The application and analysis of this approach can be found in Chap. 8.

References

1. Liu, H.B., Rodríguez, R.M.: A fuzzy envelope for hesitant fuzzy linguistic term set and its application to multicriteria decision making. Inf. Sci. **258**, 220–238 (2014)
2. Rodríguez, R.M., Martínez, L., Herrera, F.: Hesitant fuzzy linguistic term sets for decision making. IEEE Trans. Fuzzy Syst. **20**(1), 109–119 (2012)

3. Wang, H., Xu, Z.S., Zeng, X.J., Pedrycz, W.: An aspiration-based approach for qualitative decision-making with multiple types of complex linguistic expressions. Technical report, Southeast University (2017)
4. Xu, Z.S.: An automatic approach to reaching consensus in multiple attribute group decision making. Comput. Ind. Eng. **56**(4), 1369–1374 (2009)

Chapter 7
Group Decision-Making with Multiple Types of Uncertain Linguistic Expressions: Stochastic Acceptability Analysis

Uncertain linguistic opinions frequently take the form of ULEs such as ULTs, HFLTSs, EHFLTSs, and probabilistic linguistic term sets (PLTSs) rather than single linguistic terms. A stochastic approach will be introduced to handle GDM problems in which the performance values are expressed by HFLTSs or PLTSs and the weights of experts and criteria are unknown or partially unknown. Based on the involved probabilistic information, the real value of a linguistic variable and the uncertain weights are considered as stochastic variables. Firstly, the threshold of acceptable consensus of a group of linguistic decision matrices is determined by comparing them with randomly generated linguistic matrices. Then the group's consensus degree is measured by either the expected deviation or the consensus acceptability index, where the latter indicates how many different weights support that the group is with acceptable consensus. For consensus improving, a stochastic evolution algorithm is proposed to revise the probabilistic information of the involved linguistic terms. Finally, the alternatives are ranked iteratively based on the possibilities of being not in the last place. Compared with several similar techniques, this approach presents a novel way to handle uncertainties involved in the performance values and the weights, and proposes descriptive measures for decision aiding.

7.1 Motivation of Considering Stochastic Acceptability Analysis

The approach of this chapter is based on the following fact [12]: When a piece of opinion is represented by a HFLTS or a PLTS, the fact is that only one linguistic term in the HFLTS or PLTS, instead of all terms, could be the real value of the opinion. The HFLTS or PLTS is considered just because one can not identify the real one

H. Wang and Z. Xu, *Theory and Approaches of Group Decision-Making with Uncertain Linguistic Expressions*, Uncertainty and Operations Research,
https://doi.org/10.1007/978-981-13-3735-2_7

from the set of possible ones due to the limitation of individual cognition or the lack of information. For instance, if the ability of processing big data of a platform is represented by *between good and very good*, the real opinion is either *good* or *very good*, but not *both good and very good*. From the point of view, if two experts express the same linguistic expressions: *between good and very good*, it seems their opinions are with strict and exact consensus. But if they could collect more evidences, the opinions may be specified in a finer granule and each of the possible terms could possibly and plausibly be the specified value. One may improve his/her opinion to *very good* according to his/her cognition and the new information, whereas the other may specify the opinion by *good*. This is to say, due to the existence of uncertainty involved in the HFLTSs and PLTSs, it is possible and probabilistic that two or more same linguistic expressions are not with exact consensus. It is reasonable to measure the group consensus and rank the alternatives in GDM problems by considering each possible terms in the HFLTSs and PLTSs from a probabilistic, or saying stochastic, point of view. Therefore, the introduced approach measures the consensus degree and the overall performances of alternatives by treating the performance values and the unknown weights as stochastic variables. In this section, the following premises are assumed [12]:

(1) The criteria are independent, and the performance values provided by the group of experts are also independent.
(2) The experts agree to utilize an additive utility function so that the utility of each alternative can obtained by a linear combination of the utilities of performances on each criterion.

The approach is motivated by the stochastic multi-criteria acceptability analysis (SMAA) [4]. Different from other SMAA methods, the approach focuses on two issues: group consensus and derivation of the final ranking of the alternatives. According to the probabilistic distributions implied in HFLTSs and PLTSs, a collection of linguistic decision matrices can be randomly selected from the original performance matrices provided by the experts. Then the consensus degree of the group can be descriptively measured by either the expected consensus degree or how many feasible weight vectors support that the selected linguistic decision matrices are with acceptable consensus. A stochastic evolution approach is also presented to improve the consensus degree of the set of performance matrices if the experts reject to revise them. The ranking exploitation is conducted by computing some traditional measures in the family of the SMAA methods and then selecting compromise alternatives by an iterative process. Similar to SMAA, the involved algorithms are implemented by Monte Carlo simulation.

Compared with other studies of HFLTSs and PLTSs, the advantages of the approach lie in the following aspects:

(1) A stochastic approach is considered to handle each possible term involved in HFLTSs and PLTSs. The defined descriptive measures, such as acceptability indices, can intuitively explain how many weights support an assertion (such as the consensus is acceptable and an alternative ranks the first place). Thus the approach is suitable for decision-making under uncertainties.

(2) The approach allows the weights of experts and criteria could be unknown or partially unknown, and the cases are handled in the same framework. Besides, instead of seeking for an optimal weight vector, the approach computes the averaging weights to support the decision maker to understand how the variety of weights affect the process of decision-making.
(3) A rational approach to determine the threshold of acceptable consensus is provided based on probabilistic theory and simulation. It could be demonstrated that the threshold depends on the granularity of the employed LTS and the risk attitude of decision makers. Moreover, decision makers could determine the threshold by answering a simple question: how many multiples should the consensus degree of the performances matrices provided by the experts be better than randomly generated matrices?

7.2 Probabilistic Representation of ULEs

In some situations, such as GDM problems, a probabilistic distribution of the possible terms might be known or partially known. For instance, 100 customers are asked to take part in a questionnaire. Their responses to a certain question might be a distribution on some options. PLTSs are proposed for this kind of ULEs formed by an artificial language. Given LTS $S^{(\tau)} = \{s_\alpha | \alpha = 0, 1, \ldots, \tau\}$, the definition is as follows:

Definition 7.1 ([7]) Let $S^{(\tau)}$ be a LTS. A PLTS is defined as:

$$l(p) = \{(s_{\alpha_r}, p_r) | s_{\alpha_r} \in S^{(\tau)}, p_r \geq 0, r = 1, 2, \ldots, \#l(p), \sum_{r=1}^{\#l(P)} p_r \leq 1\} \quad (7.1)$$

where p_k is the associated probability of s_{α_k}, $\#l(p)$ is the number of all different linguistic terms in $l(p)$.

The set of all PLTSs based on $S^{(\tau)}$ is denoted as $\mathcal{P}$. Generally, the probabilistic information of a PLTS could be incomplete, the corresponding normalization method has been provided by Pang et al. [7]. In this chapter, all the PLTSs are assumed to be normalized. From a mathematical perspective, it is clear that PLTSs are a general form of HFLTSs and EHFLTSs although their focused linguistic expressions are completely distinct. An EHFLTS $h_S = \{s_{\alpha_1}, s_{\alpha_2}, \ldots, s_{\alpha_n}\}$ could be rewritten as [12]:

$$h_S = \left\{(s_{\alpha_1}, 1/n), (s_{\alpha_2}, 1/n), \ldots, (s_{\alpha_n}, 1/n)\right\} \quad (7.2)$$

Equation (7.2) assumes that all the possible terms in an EHFLTS possess the same probability. This coincides with the semantics of EHFLTSs. The same idea can be found in [13]. In fact, there have been different considerations of the possibilities of the linguistic terms in a HFLTS. A typical strategy is emerged in the definition of fuzzy envelopes of HFLTSs. Liu et al. [5] assumed that the hesitation among several linguistic terms may imply the different importance degrees of them. Take $\{s_\alpha, s_{\alpha+1}, \ldots, s_\beta\}$ $(s_\alpha > s_0, s_\beta < s_\tau)$ for example, the possibilities of the terms in the middle positions being the real values are greater than those of the boundary terms.

According to the definitions in Sect. 2.4, LTWHs can be regarded as special cases of PLTSs. Let $\mathcal{L} = \{l = \langle h_t, s_\alpha \rangle | h_t \in H^{(\varsigma)}, s_\alpha \in S^{(\tau)}\}$ be the set of all LTWHs. Given $l = \langle h_t, s_\alpha \rangle \in \mathcal{L}$, l can be transformed into a fuzzy set on $S^{(\tau)}$ by using Eq. (5.5). Then, the probability of each term can be defined by the derived membership degree. For instance, let $S^{(8)}$ be the LTS in Example 2.3 and $H^{(\varsigma)}$ be the WHS in Eq. (2.47), then $l = \langle h_1, s_4 \rangle$ can be rewritten as $\{(s_2, 1/3), (s_3, 2/3), (s_4, 1), (s_5, 2/3), (s_6, 1/3)\}$, where the numbers in each 2-tuple is a membership degree. Thus when ULE $\langle h_1, s_4 \rangle$ is provided by an expert, the probability of s_4 being the real value can be defined by $1/(1/3 + 2/3 + 1 + 2/3 + 1/3) = 1/3$. Thus $\langle h_1, s_4 \rangle$ can be transformed into PLTS $\{(s_2, 1/9), (s_3, 2/9), (s_4, 1/3), (s_5, 2/9), (s_6, 1/9)\}$.

7.3 Framework of the Stochastic Approach

7.3.1 Problem Description

A set of t experts $\{e_k | k = 1, 2, \ldots, t\}$ are authorized to evaluate the set of m alternatives $\{a_i | i = 1, 2, \ldots, m\}$ with respect to n criteria $\{c_j | j = 1, 2, \ldots, n\}$. The weight vectors of experts and criteria are denoted as $\omega = (\omega_1, \omega_2, \ldots, \omega_t)$ and $w = (w_1, w_2, \ldots, w_n)$, respectively. Due to the nature of some practical problems, the experts utilize HFLTSs, LTWHs or PLTSs to express their subjective opinions, based on LTS $S^{(\tau)}$ whose granularity is fine enough. According to the relationship between HFLTSs, LTWHs and PLTSs, we can use PLTSs for representation without loss of generality. The performances of m alternatives are collected by t probabilistic linguistic decision matrices (PLDMs) $M = (M_1, M_2, \ldots, M_t)$, where $M_k = (l_{ijk})_{m \times n}$ is the PLDM provided by e_k, PLTS $l_{ijk} = \{(s_{\alpha_{ijkr}}, p_{ijkr}) | r = 1, 2, \ldots, \#l_{ijk}\} \in \mathcal{P}$. Especially, if there is only one possible term in each entry of a PLDM, then the PLDM is reduced to a traditional linguistic decision matrix (LDM).

In practice, it is often difficult to obtain exact weights of experts or criteria. Then the set of feasible weights of experts can be defined as:

$$\Omega = \{\omega \in \Re^t | \omega \geq 0, \sum_{k=1}^{t} w_k = 1\} \tag{7.3}$$

In fact, Ω is a $(t - 1)$-dimensional simplex. Similarly, the set of feasible weights of criteria is denoted as W. In addition, it is sometimes possible to obtain partial preference information regarding the weights. The following types of preference information are frequently considered:

(1) weak ranking: $\{\omega_{k_1} \leq \omega_{k_2}\}$;
(2) strict ranking: $\{\omega_{k_1} - \omega_{k_2} \geq \delta_{k_1}\}$;

(3) ranking with multiples: $\{\omega_{k_1} \geq \delta_{k_1}\omega_{k_2}\}$;
(4) interval restriction: $\{\delta_k \leq \omega_k \leq \delta_k + \epsilon_k\}$;
(5) ranking of differences: $\{\omega_{k_1} - \omega_{k_2} \geq \omega_{k_3} - \omega_{k_4}\}$

where $\{\delta_k\}$ and $\{\epsilon_k\}$ are non-negative numbers. Obviously, these five forms can be summarized by an inequality of matrix $A\omega \leq c$. The inequality presents restrictions to the set Ω and results in a limited feasible weight set of experts as follows:

$$\Omega' = \{\omega \in \Omega | A\omega \leq c\} \tag{7.4}$$

Analogously, the set of limited feasible weights of criteria is denoted as W'.

The object of this GDM problem is to select the best alternative(s) or the compromise alternatives from the set of alternatives based on the available information.

7.3.2 Framework of the Stochastic Approach

The stochastic approach includes the following steps [12]:

Step 1: Define the problem in terms of the decision group, alternatives and criteria; Define the LTS $S^{(\tau)}$, the WHS $H^{(\varsigma)}$ and collect the performance information M; Induce the experts' preferences of weights of experts and criteria if possible.

Step 2: Check the group consensus. If the consensus degree of the group is acceptable, then go to Step 4; else, go to Step 3.

Step 3: Improve the set of PLDMs M by either interacting with the experts or using the proposed stochastic evolution algorithm.

Step 4: Select the best alternative. Obtain the group's collective PLDM. Calculate the best alternative by the proposed iterative algorithm and present them to the decision maker. If the decision maker feel confident enough to make a decision, then the approach is complete; else, go to Step 1.

The key points of the proposed approach are as follows:

(1) Group consensus checking and improving. The uncertain performance values (expressed by HFLTSs, LTWHs, and PLTSs) and the uncertain weights of experts are treated as stochastic variables. Then the consensus could be checked by either the expected deviation or how many different weights support that the group is with acceptable consensus. Especially, an easy manner is presented to support the decision maker to determine the threshold of acceptable consensus based on the value of τ and his/her risk attitude. Finally, a stochastic evolution approach is introduced to improve the consensus degree by revising the probabilistic information related to the possible terms.
(2) Ranking alternatives based on the group's PLDM. The group's collective performance matrix is derived by synthesizing the probabilistic information of the possible terms. Similar to the idea of consensus checking, the uncertain performance values and the uncertain weights of criteria are treated as stochastic variables. Based on an ranking function, we could calculate the possibility of

an alternatives being in the best y ranks, $y = 1, 2, \ldots, m$. At last, an iterative approach is introduced to remove the alternative, which is the most possible to be the worst one, from the set of compromise alternatives.

We will specify these two points in the coming two sections.

7.4 Group Consensus

In the stochastic approach, the consensus degree of a group is computed by the consensus degrees of a set of randomly generated LDMs. Therefore, a rational threshold of acceptable consensus should be put forward at first.

7.4.1 *The Threshold of Acceptable Consensus of a Group of LDMs*

Generally, the threshold of acceptable consensus is determined by the decision maker according to the complexity of the problem in hand, the uncertain degree of the available information and his/her risk preference. It is hard to represent the decision maker's preference by a certain threshold. In this subsection, we introduce a kind of thresholds to serve as the benchmark for the decision makers to select their thresholds of acceptable consensus of LDMs, according to their subjective preferences.

Given a set of LDMs, their consensus degree can be measured by the weighted average of any two LDMs. To begin with, we consider two LDMs $M_1 = (s_{\alpha_{ij1}})_{m\times n}$ and $M_2 = (s_{\alpha_{ij2}})_{m\times n}$, where $s_{\alpha_{ijk}}$ $(k = 1, 2)$, are randomly generated from $S^{(\tau)}$ based on a uniform distribution. The deviation between $s_{\alpha_{ij1}}$ and $s_{\alpha_{ij2}}$ is computed by [15]

$$dev(s_{\alpha_{ij1}}, s_{\alpha_{ij2}}) = |\alpha_{ij1} - \alpha_{ij2}|/\tau \tag{7.5}$$

It is rational to assume that $s_{\alpha_{ij1}}$ and $s_{\alpha_{ij2}}$ are independent. Then one can easily prove that the expected value of $dev(s_{\alpha_{ij1}}, s_{\alpha_{ij2}})$ is $(\tau + 2)/3(\tau + 1)$ [12]. The deviation between M_1 and M_2 is usually defined as:

$$dev(M_1, M_2) = \sum_{i=1}^{m}\sum_{j=1}^{n} dev(s_{\alpha_{ij1}}, s_{\alpha_{ij2}}) \tag{7.6}$$

Thus, the expected value of $dev(M_1, M_2)$ is $(\tau + 2)/3(\tau + 1)$, which is irrelevant to the values of m and n. Roughly speaking, the expected deviation of two random LDMs is close to $1/3$.

Then, for a group of t LDMs $M = (M_1, M_2, \ldots, M_t)$ randomly generated from $S^{(\tau)}$ based on a uniform distribution, the consensus degree of the group can be computed by

$$Dev(M,\omega) = \sum_{k_1=1}^{t}\sum_{k_2=1}^{t} \omega_{k_1}\omega_{k_2} dev(M_{k_1}, M_{k_2}) \tag{7.7}$$

where ω is the weight vector of the t LDMs. Because $Dev(M,\omega)$ is a linear function, it is obvious that the expectation is [12]

$$E(Dev(M,\omega)) = (\tau+2)/3(\tau+1) \tag{7.8}$$

which is irrelevant to t. The second row of Table 7.1 shows the consensus degrees of a group of randomly LDMs with respect to some frequently considered LTSs.

Therefore, it is natural to expect that the deviation between a group of given LDMs should be at least less than $(\tau+2)/3(\tau+1)$. But this might not be sufficient for all applications. In practice, one can ask the decision maker the question that how many multiples the deviation between the set of LDMs should be better (less) than the expected deviation of a set of random LDMs. Let σ (≥ 1) be the answer, then the acceptable consensus of a group of LDMs can be defined as follows:

Definition 7.2 ([12]) Let $M = (M_1, M_2, \ldots, M_t)$ be a group of LDMs based on $S^{(\tau)}$. The consensus degree of them is said to be acceptable if

$$E(Dev(M,\omega)) \leq \delta_L(\tau,\sigma) \tag{7.9}$$

where $\delta_L(\tau,\sigma) = (\tau+2)/3\sigma(\tau+1)$ is called the threshold of acceptable consensus.

Obviously, the second row of Table 7.1 serves as the threshold of acceptable consensus of a group of LDMs if $\sigma = 1$. Generally, whether the consensus degree is acceptable or not depends on the risk attitude of a decision maker. However, in applications, it is not good to suggest very big value of σ. Let us feel the influence of σ intuitively by an example:

Example 7.3 Consider two trial LDMs $M_k = (s_{\alpha_{ijk}})_{3\times 3}$, $k = 1, 2$, based on $S^{(2)}$, as follows: $s_{\alpha_{111}} = s_0$, $s_{\alpha_{112}} = s_1$, and $s_{\alpha_{ijk}} = s_0$ for other i, j, k. Then we have $dev(M_1, M_2) = 1/18$. If $\sigma \leq 8$, then M_1 and M_2 are with acceptable consensus. However, if $\sigma \geq 9$, then their consensus degree is unacceptable.

Although only one among 9 pair of values are different, in Example 7.3, the consensus degree is unacceptable if the decision maker let $\sigma \geq 9$. In the classical analytical hierarchy process, Saaty [9] suggested that the consistency index of a given judgement matrix should be 10 times better than that of a random judgement matrix. However, $\sigma = 10$ might lead to an extremely low deviation which may be hard to reach in applications. Associated with Example 7.3, in this chapter, we limit $1 \leq \sigma \leq 10$. Further suggestions about σ will be provided in the sequel.

Table 7.1 The random consensus degrees with respect to the granularity of LTSs

	$\tau = 2$	$\tau = 4$	$\tau = 6$	$\tau = 8$	$\tau = 10$
A set of LDMs	0.4444	0.4000	0.3810	0.3704	0.3636
A set of PLDMs	0.2046	0.1767	0.1653	0.1593	0.1555

7.4.2 *Defining the Consensus Degree and Acceptable Consensus of a Group of PLDMs*

When representing uncertain linguistic information by means of PLTSs, the fact is that only one linguistic term, instead of all, involved in the PLTS is the real value of the linguistic variable. The expert can not decide which one is the real value because of the lack of information, or the coarse knowledge granule. Associated with the probabilistic information of PLTSs, it is quite natural that l_{ijk} represents the known probabilistic distribution of a stochastic variable ξ_{ijk} whose values are linguistic terms in the PLTS and whose density function is denoted as $f_{ijk}(\xi_{ijk})$. Then all the performance information is regarded as a $m \times n \times t$ dimensional stochastic variable ξ with its density function $f_X(\xi) = \prod_{i,j,k} f_{ijk}(\xi_{ijk})$, where $X \subseteq (S^{(\tau)})^{m \times n \times t}$. For convenience, let $\xi = (\xi_1, \xi_2, \ldots, \xi_t)$ be the $m \times n \times t$ dimensional stochastic variable corresponding to the t PLDMs and ξ_k, a $m \times n$ LDM, be the $m \times n$ dimensional stochastic variable corresponding to the PLDM M_k.

Besides, the unknown, or partially known, weights of experts ω can be considered as a t-dimensional stochastic variable uniformly distributed in the set of feasible weights Ω or Ω'. Without loss of generality, we consider Ω' in the sequel. The density function is:

$$f_{\Omega'}(\omega) = 1/vol(\Omega') \tag{7.10}$$

where $vol(\Omega')$ is the volume of Ω'.

The deviation between ξ_{k_1} and ξ_{k_2}, denoted by $dev(\xi_{k_1}, \xi_{k_2})$, can be calculated by using Eq. (7.6) and the deviation between the stochastic LDMs in ξ_k, $Dev(\xi, \omega)$, can be subsequently calculated by using Eq. (7.7). Given a threshold of acceptable consensus $\delta_L(\tau, \sigma)$ determined by the decision maker, if $dev(\xi, \omega) \leq \delta_L(\tau, \sigma)$, then we say the consensus degree of the group of randomly generated LDMs is acceptable.

According to the above analysis, the consensus degree of the group of PLDMs provided by the experts can be defined by the expected deviations as follows:

Definition 7.4 ([12]) The consensus degree of the set of PLDMs $M = (M_1, M_2, \ldots, M_t)$ is:

$$C(M) = E(dev(\xi, \omega)) = \int_X f_X(\xi) \int_{\Omega'} dev(\xi, \omega) f_{\Omega'}(\omega) d\omega d\xi \tag{7.11}$$

The definition is straightforward from the stochastic point of view. However, if the degree of uncertainty is relatively high, it is not very confident to make a decision only by means of expectations. To support stable decision-making, we focus on the favourable weights which support that ξ is with acceptable consensus. The set of favourable weights of experts are denoted as:

$$\Omega'(\xi) = \{\omega \in \Omega' | dev(\xi, \omega) \leq \delta_L(\tau, \sigma)\} \tag{7.12}$$

Ideally, if the consensus degree of M is good enough, then it would be supported by many different weights. Then the consensus acceptability index (CAI) of the group is defined as [12]:

$$CAI = \int_X f_X(\xi) \int_{\Omega'(\omega)} f_{\Omega'}(\omega) d\omega d\xi \tag{7.13}$$

The greater CAI, the more confident one can assert that M is with acceptable consensus. Instead of searching for the optimal weights, we seek for the expected weights for the assertion that the consensus degree of M is acceptable. This results in the following central weight vector [12]:

$$\omega^{(c)} = \left(\int_X f_X(\xi) \int_{\Omega'(\xi)} \omega f_{\Omega'}(\omega) d\omega d\xi \right) / CAI \tag{7.14}$$

The CAI presents a flexible manner of handling uncertain performance values and experts' weights. It indicates to what extent one can believe that M is with acceptable consensus. Given a sufficient small number $\epsilon (\in [0, 1])$, this measure classifies M into two classes: the consensus degree of M is more or less acceptable if $CAI > \epsilon$ and unacceptable if $CAI \leq \epsilon$. The central weight vector could be an intuitive characterization to explore how different weights correspond to the assertions of the consensus of M being acceptable.

7.4.3 Consensus Checking

The consensus degree $C(M)$ and CAI can intuitively measure the degree of consensus of a group. In fact, $C(M)$ is the expected value of the consensus degree of M. The CAI is the probabilities of M being acceptable. The decision maker can decide whether the consensus degree of M is acceptable or not by, for example, defining a threshold value of CAI. Let $\delta_{PL}(\tau, \sigma)$ and CAI_0 be the thresholds of $C(M)$ and CAI, respectively. We suggest the following rules for consensus checking [12]:

Rule 1: If $C(M) \leq \delta_{PL}(\tau, \sigma)$, then the consensus degree of M is acceptable;

Rule 2: If $CAI > CAI_0$, then the consensus degree of M is acceptable;

The decision maker can decide which rule is employed for applications. Accordingly, the consensus checking approach is fixed. The derivation of these measures is the key task of consensus checking no matter which rule is selected. However, it is quite complicated to compute the multidimensional integrals directly although the performance values are independent and only discrete distributions are involved. Therefore, Monte Carlo simulation is considered to conduct the numerical computing of these measures.

To begin with, we address the generation of the weight vector of experts. Similar to the strategy in [11], we could use the rejection technique to randomly generate the weight vector from Ω', as shown in Algorithm 15 [12]. We generate $\omega \in \Omega$ at first, then check if it satisfies the condition $A\omega \leq c$.

Algorithm 1 Randomly generate a uniformly distributed normalized weight vector satisfying $A\omega \leq c$. Input: t, A, c; Output: ω.

1: Randomly generate $t-1$ values q_k $(k = 1, 2, \ldots, t-1)$ by a uniformly distribution on $[0, 1]$;
2: Sort elements in $\{q_k | k = 1, 2, \ldots, t-1\}$ in ascending order; let $q_0 = 0$, $q_t = 1$;
3: For $k = 1, 2, \ldots, t$, do: $\omega_k = q_k - q_{k-1}$;
4: If $A\omega \leq c$, go to Step 5; else, go to Step 1;
5: Output ω.

The algorithm would be inefficient if $vol(\Omega')/vol(\Omega)$ is small. However, according to [11], the complexity would be reduced in some special cases. If only the total order of weights of experts is involved, then the loop in Algorithm 1 could be unnecessary. Moreover, if only the interval restrictions are involved, then the complexity can be reduced by a simple transformation.

Secondly, we concentrate on the computations of $C(M)$, CAI, and $\omega^{(c)}$. This is described in Algorithm 2 [12].

Algorithm 2 Monte Carlo simulation for computing $C(M)$, CAI, and $\omega^{(c)}$ of the group. Input: A, c, $\delta_L(\tau, \sigma)$, $M = (M_1, M_2, \ldots, M_t)$, the number of iterations K_W; Output: $C(M)$, CAI, $\omega^{(c)}$.

1: Initialization. Let $C(M) = 0$, $\omega^{(c)} = (0, 0, \ldots, 0)_{1\times t}$, hit count variable $h = 0$, $r = 1$;
2: If $r \leq K_W$, go to Step 3; else, go to Step 6;
3: Generate ω by Algorithm 1; randomly generate $\xi = (\xi_1, \xi_2, \ldots, \xi_k)$ by M based on the probabilistic distribution of each entry;
4: Compute $dev(\xi, \omega)$ by using Eq. (7.7), $C(M) = C(M) + dev(\xi, \omega)$; If $dev(\xi, \omega) \leq \delta_L(\tau, \sigma)$, let $h = h + 1$ and $\omega^{(c)} = \omega^{(c)} + \omega$;
5: Let $r = r + 1$, go to Step 2;
6: $C(M) = C(M)/K_W$; $CAI = h/K_W$; If $h > 0$, $\omega^{(c)} = \omega^{(c)}/h$.

Accordingly, whether the consensus degree of M is acceptable or not can be checked by either of the above two rules.

In order to facilitate the decision maker to understand and choose the thresholds $\delta_{PL}(\tau, \sigma)$ and CAI_0, one can build a random approach to test the expected values of consensus degrees and CAIs of t randomly generated PLDMs whose entries are PLTSs generated from the LTS $S^{(\tau)}$, which are called the random consensus degrees

Table 7.2 The values of RCAI of a group of PLDMs

σ	$\tau = 2$	$\tau = 4$	$\tau = 6$	$\tau = 8$	$\tau = 10$
1	1	1	1	1	1
2	0.5789	0.6394	0.6653	0.6806	0.6850
3	0.2137	0.2224	0.2267	0.2331	0.2351
4	0.1002	0.1031	0.1077	0.1078	0.1091
5	0.0586	0.0604	0.0610	0.0618	0.0626
6	0.0377	0.0392	0.0398	0.0407	0.0411
8	0.0202	0.0206	0.0213	0.0214	0.0215
10	0.0125	0.0128	0.0130	0.0131	0.0133

(RCDs) and the random consensus acceptability indices (RCAIs), respectively. Obviously, these expected values are independent from m, n, and t. Given $S^{(\tau)}$, a collection of PLDMs are randomly generated at first. Especially, in each PLTS, it is rational to assume that the possible linguistic terms are consecutive in $S^{(\tau)}$ (because non-consecutive linguistic terms do not appear in individual evaluations) and the number of possible terms in a PLTS does not exceed $\tau/2$. Then the consensus degree and CAI can be derived by using Algorithm 2 with $\omega \in \Omega$. Repeating this procedures, we can obtain RCAI and RCF by calculating the averaging values. For the convenience of potential applications, we obtain RCDs and RCAIs when $\tau = 3, 5, 7, 9, 11$. Notice that the computation of RCAI depends on the threshold σ defined in Sect. 7.4.1. After testing the cases $\sigma = 1, 2, 3, 4, 5, 6, 8, 10$, the RCDs are shown in the last row of Table 7.1 and the results of RCAIs are listed in Table 7.2 [12]. For other values of τ and σ, one can run the algorithm to obtain the reference values of RCD and RCAI.

Based on RCDs and RCAIs, such as the data in Table 7.2, the decision maker can determine the thresholds $\delta_{PL}(\tau, \sigma)$ and CAI_0 by answering the question that how many multiples the $C(M)$ or CAI should be better than those of randomly generated PLDMs. Roughly, this answer could be the same as the case in Sect. 7.4.1, which is denoted as σ as well. For instance, if $\sigma = 5$ and $\tau = 6$, then $CAI_0 = 0.0610 \times 5 = 0.305$.

Obviously, the smaller σ would lead to the looser limitation of deviations. If $\sigma = 1$, then the expected consensus degree of randomly generated PLDMs is acceptable. In this sense, σ should be assigned bigger value. However, if $\sigma \geq 8$, then CAI_0 is less than 20%. This means that we have to accept the group of PLDMs even if the CAI is less than 20%. Thus, it is rational to limit $2 \leq \sigma \leq 6$.

7.4.4 Consensus Improving

If the consensus degree of the group is unacceptable, then M should be improved in order that the PLDMs are meaningful for further processing. Generally, this can be achieved by two distinct strategies. Ideally, the decision maker sends the matrices back to the experts and requires improved versions till the consensus degree is acceptable. However, this strategy is sometimes hard to carry out. Thus, an automatic approach which improves the PLDMs based on the original information would be necessary.

To improve the consensus degree of M, one can revise the original linguistic terms in each PLTS, or the probabilistic distribution of the terms in each PLTS, or both. However, there are some differences. If the terms are revised based on specific linguistic computational model, the resultant terms may fall out of $S^{(\tau)}$. See [16] for example. If the probabilistic distributions are revised, then the possible terms are remained. The possible terms which lead to low consensus levels are assigned with relatively low probabilities. A possible drawback is that if the original evaluations are represented by HFLTSs, then the revised results are generally not comparative linguistic expressions but artificial linguistic expressions taking the form of PLTSs. In the sequel, we introduce a stochastic evolution approach which revises the probabilistic distributions of entries in each PLDM. Specifically, we randomly generate t stochastic LDMs form M. If the consensus degree of the set of LDMs are good enough, then we increase the corresponding probability of each entry. Let θ be the increment of probabilities. For each ξ_{ijk} randomly generated from the PLTS $l_{ijk} = \{(s_{\alpha_{ijkr}}, p_{ijkr}) | r = 1, 2, \ldots, \#l_{ijk}\}$, there exists $r_0 \in \{1, 2, \ldots, \#l_{ijk}\}$ such that $\xi_{ijk} = s_{\alpha_{ijkr_0}}$. We replace p_{ijkr_0} by $p_{ijkr_0} + \theta$, and then normalize the probabilistic distribution such that the sum of probabilities is 1. The value of θ can be assigned by the decision maker. The bigger value would result in a smaller number of loops in the algorithm. The small value would help to remain the original information as much as possible. The algorithm is depicted in Algorithm 3 [12].

Algorithm 3 Obtain t PLDMs with acceptable consensus. Input: $M = (M_1, M_2, \ldots, M_t)$, $\delta_L(\tau, \sigma)$, θ; Output: $M^{(1)} = \{M_1^{(1)}, M_2^{(1)}, \ldots, M_t^{(1)}\}$, $\omega^{(c)}$.

1: Compute $C(M)$, CAI, and $\omega^{(c)}$ by using Algorithm 2. If M is with acceptable consensus, go to Step 4; else go to Step 2;
2: Randomly generate $\xi = (\xi_1, \xi_2, \ldots, \xi_k)$ by M based on the probabilistic distribution of each entry;
3: If $Dev(\xi, \omega^{(c)}) \le max\{\delta_L(\tau, \sigma), C(M)\}$, then for each $\xi_{ijk} \in \xi$ revise its corresponding probability p_{ijkr} (in l_{ijk}) by $p_{ijkr} = p_{ijkr} + \theta$; normalize the corresponding probabilistic distribution in l_{ijk}, $i = 1, 2, \ldots, m$, $j = 1, 2, \ldots, n$, $k = 1, 2, \ldots, t$; go to Step 1; else go to Step 2;
4: $M^{(1)} = M$.

In Step 3 of Algorithm 3, the reason of using the derived $\omega^{(c)}$ instead of randomly generated ω is that $\omega^{(c)}$ is the average weight vector which supports that M is with acceptable consensus. Thus it would speed up the convergence. Moreover, we use $max\{\delta_L(\tau, \sigma), C(M)\}$ rather than only $\delta_L(\tau, \sigma)$ because, if the current consensus degree of M is very bad, it would take long time to find such a ξ. In fact, it does not have to find a ξ with acceptable consensus. As can be seen from Table 7.1, the expected consensus degree of a set of PLDMs is much less than that of a set of LDMs.

Thus the ξ satisfying $Dev(\xi, \omega^{(c)}) \leq C(M)$ is good enough, especially in the initial phase of consensus improving. The convergence of Algorithm 3 is depicted in the following theorem:

Theorem 7.5 ([12]) *Given a set of t PLDMs* $M = (M_1, M_2, \ldots, M_t)$*, Algorithm 3 is convergent if* $CAI > 0$.

Proof If $CAI > 0$, then there exist at least one randomly generated ξ and one feasible weight vector $\omega \in \Omega'$ such that $dev(\xi, \omega) < \delta_L(\tau, \sigma)$. As Step 3 increases the probabilities of the entries which could result in acceptable consensus, it is apparent that the probability of $dev(\xi, \omega) < \delta_L(\tau, \sigma)$ grows as well. Therefore, according to Algorithm 2, the loops in Algorithm 3 decrease the expected consensus degree $C(M)$ and increase CAI. For example, if Rule 2 is considered for consensus checking, then the value of hit count variable h in Algorithm 2 would be approaching to K_W, which means $CAI \to 1$. This completes the proof. □

Obviously, the condition of Theorem 7.5 is very loose. In fact, if $CAI = 0$ is derived by the original information, it means that any possibly generated ξ would never be with acceptable consensus when the weight vector varies in the whole feasible weight space Ω'. In this case, the consensus degree of the original information is terrible. Automatic improvement based on this information makes no sense. The decision maker has to ask the experts to re-evaluate the alternatives and resubmit the performance matrices. However, if CAI is extremely low initially, then the speed of convergence of Algorithm 3 is very slow. In practice, it is not meaningful to improve the group's opinions if CAI is very small. In this case, the decision maker could either decrease the value of σ or require the experts to revise their opinions manually.

7.5 Decision-Making with the Collective PLDM

When the t PLDMs are with acceptable consensus, we now focus on selecting or ranking the alternatives based on the group's opinions. First of all, the individual performance matrices should be synthesized so that the collective performance matrix of the group can be derived. Generally, the group's collective performance matrix can be represented by a PLDM $GM = (l_{ij})_{m \times n}$, where the $l_{ij} = \{(s_{\alpha_{ijr}}, p_{ijr}) | r = 1, 2, \ldots, \# l_{ij}\}$ which represents the overall performance of a_i with respect to c_j is derived according to the t PLTS, $l_{ij1}, l_{ij2}, \ldots, l_{ijt}$, provided by the t experts and the central weight vector $\omega^{(c)}$ derived by Algorithm 3. For convenience, a PLTS l_{ijk} is rewritten as [12]:

$$l_{ijk} = \{(s_0, p_{ijk0}), (s_1, p_{ijk1}), \ldots, (s_\tau, p_{ijk\tau}) | \sum\nolimits_{\alpha=0}^{\tau} p_{ijk\alpha} \leq 1\} \tag{7.15}$$

where $p_{ijk\alpha} = 0$ if s_α is not in l_{ijk}, $i = 1, 2, \ldots, m$, $j = 1, 2, \ldots, n$, $k = 1, 2, \ldots, t$. Obviously, we just formalize l_{ijk} by including some linguistic terms whose probabilities are 0 and do not change the probability of each term. Then, given $l_{ij1}, l_{ij2}, \ldots, l_{ijt}$

and $\omega^{(c)}$, l_{ij} can be obtained by a weighted average:

$$l_{ij} = \{(s_\alpha, \sum\nolimits_{k=1}^{t} \omega_k^{(c)} p_{ijk\alpha}) | \alpha = 0, 1, \ldots, \tau\} \quad (7.16)$$

As has been introduced in Sect. 7.3, the weights of criteria are usually known or partially unknown. The set of feasible weights of criteria is denoted as W'. Different from other GDM approaches for HFLTSs and PLTSs, we introduce hereinafter a stochastic approach to present an intuitive view for the decision maker based on the idea of SMAA [4]. Given the collective uncertain performances of alternative represented by the PLDM $GM = (l_{ij})_{m\times n}$, only one linguistic term, rather than all terms, in l_{ij}, could be the real performance value. It is natural to consider the performance value of a_i with respect to c_j as a stochastic variable ξ_{ij} whose probabilistic distribution is depicted in ξ_{ij}. The density function of ξ_{ij} is denoted as $f_{ij}(\xi_{ij})$. Then the performances of the m alternatives with respect to the n criteria can be considered as a $m \times n$-dimensional stochastic variable whose density function is $f_Y(\xi) = \prod\limits_{i,j} f_{ij}(\xi_{ij})$, where $Y \subseteq (S^{(\tau)})^{m\times n}$. Based on the virtual linguistic model, the overall performance of a_i can be simply derived by

$$u(\xi_i, w) = \mathop{\oplus}\limits_{j=1}^{n} w_j \xi_{ij} \quad (7.17)$$

where w is a feasible weight vector of the criteria. Note that, Eq. (7.17) implies an additive utility function $u(s_\alpha) = \alpha/\tau$ is considered by the decision maker. Similar to the discussion in Sect. 7.4, we assume that w is uniformly distribution in W'. Then the density function of w is: $f_{W'}(w) = 1/vol(W')$.

To represent the possible ranks of a_i, the following ranking function is defined [4]:

$$rank(\xi_i, w) = 1 + \sum_{k=1}^{t} \rho(u(\xi_k, w) > u(\xi_i, w)) = x \quad (7.18)$$

where the function ρ is defined by $\rho(true) = 1$ and $\rho(false) = 0$. The set of feasible weights which support a_i ranking x, namely favourable rank weights, are denoted as:

$$W'_{ix}(\xi) = \{w \in W' | rank(\xi_i, w) = x\}, \quad i, x = 1, 2, \ldots, m \quad (7.19)$$

Then the y best ranks acceptability index of a_i, RAI_{iy}, can be calculated by the sum of expected volumes of the set of favourable rank weights that support a_i ranks from 1 to y:

$$RAI_{iy} = \sum_{x=1}^{y} \int_Y f_Y(\xi) \int_{W'_{ix}(\xi)} f_{W'}(w) dw d\xi \quad (7.20)$$

For example, if $y = 1$, then RAI_{i1} indicates the probability of a_i being the best (first) rank. Generally, the y best ranks acceptability index is a measure of the variety of different values that support an alternative being any of the y best ranks and thus can be considered directly in GDM. The assertion that a_i ranks at least y is acceptable if RAI_{iy} is sufficiently high. The Monte Carlo simulation for computing the y best ranks acceptability indices is presented in Algorithm 4:

Algorithm 4 Estimate the y best ranks acceptability indices of alternatives. Input: $GM = (l_{ij})_{m\times n}$, W', the number of iterations K_R; Output: RAI_{iy}, $i, y = 1, 2, \ldots, m$.

1: Initialization. Let $RAI_{iy} = 0$, $h_{ix} = 0$, $i, x, y = 1, 2, \ldots, m$; $r = 1$;
2: If $r < K_R$, then go to Step 2; else go to Step 6;
3: Generate w by Algorithm 1 with input W'; randomly generate $\xi = (\xi_{ij})_{m\times n}$ by GM based on the probabilistic distribution of each entry;
4: For $i = 1, 2, \ldots, m$, compute $x = rank(\xi_i, w)$ by Eq. (7.18); let $h_{ix} = h_{ix} + 1$;
5: Let $r = r + 1$, go to Step 2;
6: For $i = 1, 2, \ldots, m$, $x = 1, 2, \ldots, m$, let $h_{ix} = h_{ix}/K_R$;
7: $i = 1, 2, \ldots, m$, $y = 1, 2, \ldots, m$, $x = 1, 2, \ldots, y$, let $RAI_{iy} = RAI_{iy} + h_{ix}$.

However, the values of the y best ranks acceptability indices of some alternatives might be very close to each other and thus the decision maker are not confident enough to discriminate them because of the presence of uncertainty. To enhance the discrimination, we develop an iterative approach to eliminate weaker alternatives one at a time. Specifically, for m alternatives, we figure out the one that most possibly ranks the last place and remove it from the set of alternatives. If an alternative is eliminated, then we remove all its performance values, re-form the performance matrix, and continue the iteration until only one alternative is left. The approach is specified in Algorithm 5. Obviously, the ranking of alternatives can also be derived by Algorithm 5 according to the order of the alternatives being removed.

Algorithm 5 The iterative approach for MCDM. Input: $GM = (l_{ij})_{m\times n}$; Output: The best alternative.

1: Initialization. Let $A = \{a_1, a_2, \ldots, a_m\}$ be the set of compromising alternatives, performance matrix of compromising alternatives $GM^{(x)} = GM$, current rank $x = m$;
2: If $x > 1$, then go to Step 3; else, go to Step 5;
3: Compute RAI_{iy}, $i, y = 1, 2, \ldots, x$, by using Algorithm 4 with input $GM^{(x)}$;
4: Let $i_x = argmin_{i\in\{1,2,\ldots,x\}}\{RAI_{i,x-1}\}$, $A = A \setminus \{a_{i_x}\}$; remove the i_x-th row from $GM^{(x)}$, denoted as $GM^{(x-1)}$; let $x = x - 1$; go to Step 2;
5: Output A.

7.6 Illustration and Comparisons

7.6.1 An Application of Personnel Selection

As a typical case of GDM problems, personnel selection which refers to identifying an individual from some candidates for a vacant position is one of the most significant activities in human resource management [1]. In general, the complexity of this problem is caused by several facets, such as understanding the criteria and their relationships, identifying criterion measurement, and the ability of making decisions based on imprecise and uncertain information [10]. Frequently, the performances of individuals are evaluated and expressed by the experts' subjective assessments. To facilitate the operation of such information of the MCGDM problem, the fuzzy linguistic approach was frequently considered [3, 13].

We now employ the stochastic approach as a solution for the personnel selection problem. To ease the comparisons, we use the same problem structure and the same linguistic information presented in [13]. Suppose that four candidates $\{a_1, a_2, a_3, a_4\}$ are designated for evaluation with respect to 6 criteria, which are oral communication skills (c_1), past experience (c_2), general aptitude (c_3), willingness (c_4), self-confidence (c_5), and first impression (c_6). The decision organization is formed by four experts $\{e_1, e_2, e_3, e_4\}$. The weights of experts and criteria are unknown. After interview, the performances of four candidates are expressed by HFLTSs based on the following LTS:

$$S^{(6)} = \{s_0 = \textit{very poor}, s_1 = \textit{poor}, s_2 = \textit{slightly poor}, s_3 = \textit{fair}, \\ s_4 = \textit{slightly poor}, s_5 = \textit{good}, s_6 = \textit{very good}\}$$

The performance matrices of the 4 alternatives are listed in Table 7.3.

To illustrate the stochastic approach, we solve the problem according to the framework described in Sect. 7.3.2. Assume that the experts select *Rule 2* for consensus checking and agree with $\sigma = 5$ in consensus checking, $\theta = 0.1$ in consensus improving. Moreover, we assume that no subjective preference of weights is available. In this case, Ω' and W' are reduced to Ω and W, respectively. We also assume that the possible terms in each HFLTS are of equal importance. Thus the possible terms are uniformly distributed in each HFLTS. For simulation, we set $K_W = 30000$ and $K_R = 10000$. The procedures are illustrated as follows:

Step 2: Check the group consensus. According to Algorithm 2, the CAI of the group is: $CAI = 0.0578$, which means that only 5.78% of the feasible weights of experts support that the group is with acceptable consensus. Based on Table 7.2 and $\sigma = 5$, the threshold of CAI is: $CAI_0 = 0.0610 \times 5 = 0.3050$. Thus, the group's consensus is unacceptable.

Step 3: Consensus improving. Assume that the experts reject to revise their opinions. Implementing Algorithm 3, we obtain the set of PLDMs with acceptable consensus after 32 times of revising probabilistic distributions. The resultant CAI is: $CAI = 0.3084$, the central weights are: $\omega^{(c)} = (0.1772, 0.3356, 0.2194, 0.2677)$.

Table 7.3 Linguistic performance matrices provided by the four experts

Expert	Alternative	c_1	c_2	c_3	c_4	c_5	c_6
e_1	a_1	$\{s_5, s_6\}$	$\{s_5, s_6\}$	$\{s_6\}$	$\{s_2, s_3\}$	$\{s_2, s_3, s_4\}$	$\{s_5, s_6\}$
	a_2	$\{s_4, s_5\}$	$\{s_5, s_6\}$	$\{s_5\}$	$\{s_5, s_6\}$	$\{s_4, s_5\}$	$\{s_4, s_5\}$
	a_3	$\{s_3, s_4\}$	$\{s_4, s_5\}$	$\{s_3, s_4\}$	$\{s_4, s_5\}$	$\{s_5, s_6\}$	$\{s_5, s_6\}$
	a_4	$\{s_5, s_6\}$	$\{s_1, s_2\}$	$\{s_3, s_4, s_5\}$	$\{s_6\}$	$\{s_4, s_5, s_6\}$	$\{s_4\}$
e_2	a_1	$\{s_3, s_4\}$	$\{s_5\}$	$\{s_5, s_6\}$	$\{s_4, s_5\}$	$\{s_3, s_4\}$	$\{s_3, s_4\}$
	a_2	$\{s_4, s_5, s_6\}$	$\{s_5\}$	$\{s_4\}$	$\{s_5, s_6\}$	$\{s_4, s_5\}$	$\{s_4\}$
	a_3	$\{s_1, s_2\}$	$\{s_6\}$	$\{s_4, s_5\}$	$\{s_3, s_4\}$	$\{s_5, s_6\}$	$\{s_4\}$
	a_4	$\{s_5, s_6\}$	$\{s_4, s_5\}$	$\{s_3, s_4\}$	$\{s_4\}$	$\{s_5, s_6\}$	$\{s_5\}$
e_3	a_1	$\{s_2, s_3, s_4\}$	$\{s_3, s_4\}$	$\{s_4, s_5\}$	$\{s_4, s_5\}$	$\{s_5, s_6\}$	$\{s_2, s_3\}$
	a_2	$\{s_5, s_6\}$	$\{s_4, s_5\}$	$\{s_4\}$	$\{s_5, s_6\}$	$\{s_4, s_5\}$	$\{s_4, s_5\}$
	a_3	$\{s_4\}$	$\{s_5, s_6\}$	$\{s_4\}$	$\{s_1, s_2\}$	$\{s_5, s_6\}$	$\{s_3\}$
	a_4	$\{s_3, s_4\}$	$\{s_4, s_5\}$	$\{s_2, s_3, s_4\}$	$\{s_3\}$	$\{s_5, s_6\}$	$\{s_5, s_6\}$
e_4	a_1	$\{s_2, s_3\}$	$\{s_4\}$	$\{s_5, s_6\}$	$\{s_3, s_4\}$	$\{s_3\}$	$\{s_4\}$
	a_2	$\{s_3, s_4, s_5\}$	$\{s_6\}$	$\{s_3, s_4\}$	$\{s_4, s_5, s_6\}$	$\{s_3, s_4\}$	$\{s_5\}$
	a_3	$\{s_0, s_1, s_2\}$	$\{s_5, s_6\}$	$\{s_5, s_6\}$	$\{s_5, s_6\}$	$\{s_3, s_4\}$	$\{s_5\}$
	a_4	$\{s_2, s_3, s_4\}$	$\{s_4, s_5\}$	$\{s_4\}$	$\{s_5\}$	$\{s_5, s_6\}$	$\{s_3\}$

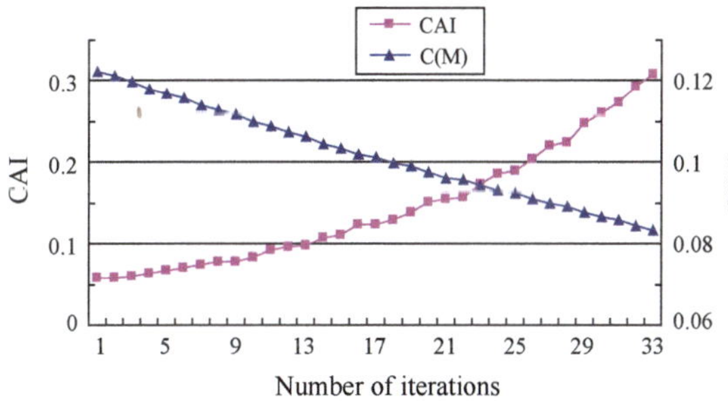

Fig. 7.1 The tendencies of *CAI* and $C(M)$ during the improvement of consensus degrees

For example, the improved PLDM of e_1 is as follows:

$$\begin{pmatrix} \{(s_5, 0.97), (s_6, 0.03)\} & \{(s_5, 0.86), (s_6, 0.14)\} & \{(s_6, 1)\} & \{(s_2, 0.04), (s_3, 0.96)\} & \{(s_2, 0.06), (s_3, 0.70), (s_4, 0.24)\} & \{(s_5, 0.86), (s_6, 0.14)\} \\ \{(s_4, 0.10), (s_5, 0.90)\} & \{(s_5, 0.74), (s_6, 0.26)\} & \{(s_5, 1)\} & \{(s_5, 0.07), (s_6, 0.93)\} & \{(s_4, 0.89), (s_5, 0.11)\} & \{(s_4, 0.60), (s_5, 0.40)\} \\ \{(s_3, 0.70), (s_4, 0.30)\} & \{(s_4, 0.29), (s_5, 0.71)\} & \{(s_3, 0.22), (s_4, 0.78)\} & \{(s_4, 0.43), (s_5, 0.57)\} & \{(s_5, 0.80), (s_6, 0.20)\} & \{(s_5, 0.85,), (s_6, 0.15)\} \\ \{(s_5, 0.77), (s_6, 0.23)\} & \{(s_1, 0.07), (s_2, 0.93)\} & \{(s_3, 0.24), (s_4, 0.67), (s_5, 0.09)\} & \{(s_6, 1)\} & \{(s_4, 0.16), (s_5, 0.13), (s_6, 0.71)\} & \{(s_4, 1)\} \end{pmatrix}$$

To illustrate the improvement process intuitively, the tendency of *CAI* (as well as $C(M)$) is shown in Fig. 7.1.

Step 4: Select the best alternative. Firstly, based on Eqs. (7.15)–(7.16), we obtain the collective performance matrix as follows:

$$\begin{pmatrix}
\{(s_2, 0.02), (s_3, 0.74), (s_4, 0.06), (s_5, 0.17), (s_6, 0.01)\} \\
\{(s_3, 0.01), (s_4, 0.04), (s_5, 0.93), (s_6, 0.02)\} \\
\{(s_1, 0.07), (s_2, 0.53), (s_3, 0.12), (s_4, 0.27)\} \\
\{(s_2, 0.01), (s_3, 0.02), (s_4, 0.46), (s_5, 0.43), (s_6, 0.08)\} \\
\{(s_3, 0.02), (s_4, 0.47), (s_5, 0.49), (s_6, 0.02)\} \\
\{(s_4, 0.02), (s_5, 0.674), (s_6, 0.31)\} \\
\{(s_4, 0.05), (s_5, 0.27), (s_6, 0.68)\} \\
\{(s_1, 0.01), (s_2, 0.16), (s_4, 0.58), (s_5, 0.24)\} \\
\{(s_4, 0.01), (s_5, 0.56), (s_6, 0.43)\} \\
\{(s_3, 0.01), (s_4, 0.81), (s_5, 0.18)\} \\
\{(s_3, 0.04), (s_4, 0.63), (s_5, 0.33), (s_6, 0.01)\} \\
\{(s_2, 0.01), (s_3, 0.15), (s_4, 0.82), (s_5, 0.02)\} \\
\{(s_2, 0.01), (s_3, 0.22), (s_4, 0.74), (s_5, 0.03)\} \\
\{(s_4, 0.01), (s_5, 0.10), (s_6, 0.90)\} \\
\{(s_1, 0.01), (s_2, 0.21), (s_3, 0.12), (s_4, 0.29), (s_5, 0.36), (s_6, 0.01)\} \\
\{(s_3, 0.22), (s_4, 0.34), (s_5, 0.27), (s_6, 0.18)\} \\
\{(s_2, 0.01), (s_3, 0.54), (s_4, 0.23), (s_5, 0.21), (s_6, 0.01)\} \\
\{(s_3, 0.01), (s_4, 0.91), (s_5, 0.07)\} \\
\{(s_3, 0.01), (s_4, 0.26), (s_5, 0.47), (s_6, 0.27)\} \\
\{(s_4, 0.03), (s_5, 0.17), (s_6, 0.80)\} \\
\{(s_2, 0.01), (s_3, 0.22), (s_4, 0.59), (s_5, 0.15), (s_6, 0.03)\} \\
\{(s_4, 0.65), (s_5, 0.35)\} \\
\{(s_3, 0.22), (s_4, 0.34), (s_5, 0.42), (s_6, 0.03)\} \\
\{(s_3, 0.27), (s_4, 0.18), (s_5, 0.54), (s_6, 0.01)\}
\end{pmatrix}$$

According to Algorithm 5, we remove the worst alternatives one at a time. In the first iteration, the derived y best ranks acceptability indices of alternatives are shown in Fig. 7.2. Especially, $RAI_{13} = 0.5429$, $RAI_{23} = 0.9681$, $RAI_{33} = 0.6806$, $RAI_{43} = 0.8084$, which means a_1 is the worst alternative because it is the most possible to rank the last place. We remove a_1 and continue the algorithm. When there are two alternatives (a_2 and a_4) left, their first rank RAIs are 0.7003 and 0.2997, respectively. Apparently, a_2 is the best alternative which is supported by 70.03% of the feasible weights of criteria. The rank of alternatives is $a_2 > a_4 > a_3 > a_1$.

We can see that Algorithm 5 enhances the discrimination. In the first iteration, $RAI_{21} = 0.5439$, $RAI_{41} = 0.2374$. The difference is about 31%. When a_1 and a_3 are removed, we have $RAI_{21} = 0.7003$, $RAI_{41} = 0.2997$. The difference is increased to about 40%. Therefore, the decision maker would be more confident to select a_2 as the best alternative.

Furthermore, let us reconsider the problem by including some subjective preferences of the experts' weights and criterion weights. For the sake of illustration, we only consider the preferences of weights of criteria. Assume that the experts prefer the following total order of the weights:

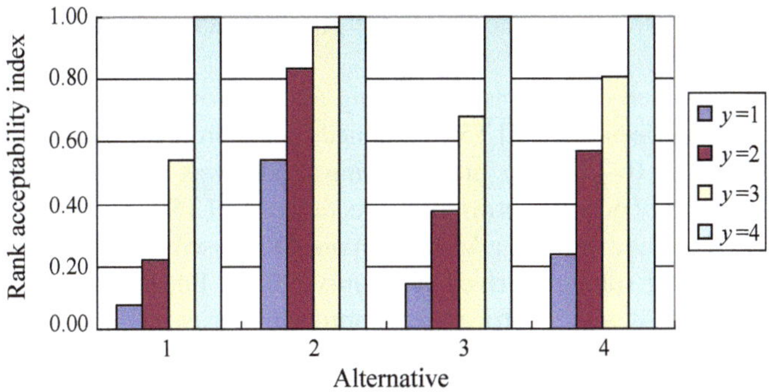

Fig. 7.2 The y best ranks acceptability indices of the four alternatives

$$w_6 \leq w_5 \leq w_4 \leq w_1 \leq w_2 \leq w_3 \tag{7.21}$$

In this case, the rejection technique in Algorithm 1 can be replaced by a simple strategy: generate a weight vector by a uniform distribution on the feasible set by Steps 1–3 of Algorithm 1; reorder the vector according to the order specified hereinabove. The complexity of this strategy is much less than that of Algorithm 1. Then re-executing Step 4, we obtain $RAI_{13} = 0.8731$, $RAI_{23} = 0.9872$, $RAI_{33} = 0.6902$, $RAI_{43} = 0.4495$ in the first iteration. Thus, a_4 is the first one to be removed. The final ranking of alternatives is $a_2 > a_1 > a_3 > a_4$, which is different from the above case.

7.6.2 Comparative Analyses

We analyze the characteristics of the stochastic approach by comparing with some existing approaches regarding group consensus and decision-making, respectively.

7.6.2.1 Regarding Consensus Checking and Improving

Like the case we have specified in Sect. 7.6.1, Wu and Xu [13] assumed that the possible terms in a HFLTS are uniformly distributed. The deviation between two HFLTSs is then computed by the expected labels of them. Based on the deviation, the consensus of the group is defined by three different levels: the attribute level, the alternative level, and the matrix level. The consensus of the matrix level is checked by a threshold which should be fixed by the decision maker's priori knowledge. If the consensus degree is unacceptable, then three rules are developed to identify the entries in the matrices which are with lower consensus degrees, and three other rules are proposed to direct the experts to revise their opinions based on the group's collective matrix. Notice that, to obtain the group's matrix, the weights of experts have to be known.

Another approach of consensus checking and improving was proposed in [2]. The deviation between two HFLTSs is defined by the proportion of the same terms in them. A mixed $0-1$ linear programming model was developed to revise the minimum number of possible terms in a collection of HFLTSs so that they are with an acceptable consensus. Besides, a Manhattan distance based model was employed to further optimize the solution derived by the mixed $0-1$ linear programming model. In the sense of GDM with t matrices, this approach focuses on the consensus degree of t HFLTSs in the corresponding position of the t matrices. Based on the suggested consensus threshold (0.6), the revised matrices can be derived. For example, the revised matrix of e_1 is:

$$\begin{pmatrix} \{s_2,s_3,s_4,s_5,s_6\} & \{s_4,s_5,s_6\} & \{s_5,s_6\} & \{s_2,s_3,s_4,s_5\} & \{s_2,s_3,s_4,s_5\} & \{s_2,s_3,s_4,s_5,s_6\} \\ \{s_4,s_5\} & \{s_5,s_6\} & \{s_4,s_5\} & \{s_5,s_6\} & \{s_4,s_5\} & \{s_4,s_5\} \\ \{s_3,s_4\} & \{s_4,s_5\} & \{s_3,s_4,s_5\} & \{s_4,s_5\} & \{s_5,s_6\} & \{s_4,s_5,s_6\} \\ \{s_5,s_6\} & \{s_1,s_2,s_3,s_4,s_5,s_6\} & \{s_3,s_4,s_5\} & \{s_4,s_5\} & \{s_4,s_5,s_6\} & \{s_4,s_5\} \end{pmatrix}$$

Moreover, their proposed model can obtain the optimal group's matrix as follows:

$$\begin{pmatrix} \{s_2,s_3,s_4\} & \{s_4,s_5\} & \{s_4,s_5,s_6\} & \{s_3,s_4,s_5\} & \{s_3,s_4,s_5\} & \{s_3,s_4,s_5\} \\ \{s_4,s_5,s_6\} & \{s_4,s_5,s_6\} & \{s_3,s_4,s_5\} & \{s_4,s_5,s_6\} & \{s_3,s_4,s_5\} & \{s_4,s_5\} \\ \{s_2,s_3,s_4\} & \{s_4,s_5,s_6\} & \{s_4,s_5\} & \{s_3,s_4,s_5\} & \{s_4,s_5,s_6\} & \{s_4,s_5\} \\ \{s_4,s_5,s_6\} & \{s_3,s_4,s_5\} & \{s_3,s_4\} & \{s_4,s_5\} & \{s_4,s_5,s_6\} & \{s_4,s_5\} \end{pmatrix}$$

which is not a fused result of the 4 matrices, but an optimal case to obtain the desirable consensus degree. Analogously, Li et al. [6] defined another non-linear optimization model to search the best experts' weights which result in the best group consensus. The derived weights are used for fusing the group's performances directly.

The characteristics of the stochastic approach of consensus checking and improving can be summarized as follows:

(1) It presents a rational and simple way to induce the threshold of acceptable consensus. The decision maker just has to think about the relationship between the consensus degree of the group and that of randomly generated matrices. However, other approaches totally leave the determination of thresholds to the decision maker without any guidelines. Moreover, the parameters which affect the expected deviations and the thresholds have also been identified.
(2) The consensus improving approach revises the probabilities of the possible terms instead of revising the possible terms. The advantage of this strategy is that we will never introduce new terms which were not indicated by the experts. However,

if the original information is represented by HFLTSs, the resultant information could only be represented by PLTSs. From this view, the consensus improving approach modifies natural linguistic expressions into artificial linguistic expressions and thus the interpretability is weaker than that of [2].

(3) The stochastic approach can deal with the cases of unknown weights of experts and partially known weights of experts. However, the approach in [13] requires completely known weights for consensus improving, and the approach in [2] can not incorporate the preferences of weights of experts.

(4) The stochastic approach is more general than the comparative approaches. The input information can take the form of not only HFLTSs but also LTWHs and PLTSs. To the best of our knowledge, the approach is the first study of group consensus in the setting of PLTSs.

(5) The main weakness of the stochastic approach is its complexity. Some of the proposed algorithms are time-consuming. This is caused by the Monte Carlo simulation. See Sect. 7.7.1 for more discussions.

7.6.2.2 Regarding the Decision-Making Approach

The first decision-making approach with HFLTSs was developed in [8]. This is based on two operators, i.e., $min - upper$ and $max - lower$, to represent the pessimistic and optimistic attitudes of the decision maker. Then the overall performances of alternatives are represented by linguistic intervals formed by the two aggregation results. Finally, the ranking can be exploited by building a preference relation in which each entry depicts the preference degree of an alternative over another. To make it comparable to the above example, the four individual performance matrices are fused by using the union similar to Definition 2.13 at first. The collective performance matrix is:

$$\begin{pmatrix} \{s_2, s_3, s_4, s_5, s_6\} & \{s_3, s_4, s_5, s_6\} & \{s_4, s_5, s_6\} & \{s_2, s_3, s_4, s_5\} & \{s_2, s_3, s_4, s_5, s_6\} & \{s_2, s_3, s_4, s_5, s_6\} \\ \{s_3, s_4, s_5, s_6\} & \{s_4, s_5, s_6\} & \{s_3, s_4, s_5\} & \{s_4, s_5, s_6\} & \{s_3, s_4, s_5\} & \{s_4, s_5\} \\ \{s_0, s_1, s_2, s_3, s_4\} & \{s_4, s_5, s_6\} & \{s_3, s_4, s_5, s_6\} & \{s_1, s_2, s_3, s_4, s_5, s_6\} & \{s_3, s_4, s_5, s_6\} & \{s_3, s_4, s_5, s_6\} \\ \{s_2, s_3, s_4, s_5, s_6\} & \{s_1, s_2, s_4, s_5\} & \{s_2, s_3, s_4, s_5\} & \{s_3, s_4, s_5\} & \{s_4, s_5, s_6\} & \{s_3, s_4, s_5, s_6\} \end{pmatrix}$$

Note that the second entry of the last row is not a HFLTS but an EHFLTS. Then the overall performances of alternatives are:

$$\left([s_4, s_5] \; [s_4, s_5] \; [s_4, s_4] \; [s_4, s_5] \right)$$

Obviously, there are three non-dominated alternative (a_1, a_2, and a_4) and we can not distinguish them.

The decision-making process in [13] is also constituted by an aggregation phase and an exploitation phase. To obtain the collective performance matrix, a weighted averaging aggregation operator is employed associated with known weights. An ordered weighted averaging operator is used to obtain the overall performances of alternatives. Based on the weight vector of experts $\omega = (0.25, 0.25, 0.25, 0.25)$ and the fuzzy linguistic quantifier "most", the final ranking of alternatives is: $a_2 > a_3 > a_4 > a_1$.

Furthermore, let us consider the GDM approach proposed in [7]. This approach assumes that the individual performances are represented by single terms or HFLTSs. The collective performance matrix is represented by PLTSs which are derived by calculating the frequency of possible terms. In this sense, the collective performance matrix is:

$$\begin{pmatrix} \{(s_2, 2/9), (s_3, 1/3), (s_4, 2/9), (s_5, 1/9), (s_6, 1/9)\} \\ \{(s_3, 1/10), (s_4, 3/10), (s_5, 2/5), (s_6, 1/5)\} \\ \{(s_0, 1/8), (s_1, 1/4), (s_2, 1/4), (s_3, 1/8), (s_4, 1/4)\} \\ \{(s_2, 1/9), (s_3, 2/9), (s_4, 2/9), (s_5, 2/9), (s_6, 2/9)\} \end{pmatrix}$$

Similar to this chapter, Pang et al. [7] assumed the weights of criteria are unknown or partially unknown. A quadratic programming model was developed to search the optimal weights which maximize the deviations of performances of the alternatives. The optimal weight vector is: $\mathbf{w} = (0.1308, 0.1725, 0.1297, 0.1925, 0.1904, 0.1841)$. By defining the distance between an alternative and its positive and negative ideal solutions, an extended TOPSIS process was further proposed to explore the final rank. Besides, an aggregation-based ranking process was also defined. If the extended TOPSIS process is employed, the final rank of alternatives is: $a_2 > a_3 > a_4 > a_1$.

The characteristics of the introduced decision-making approach can be concluded as follows:

(1) The collective performances are derived by means of a weighted average based on the central weights. Compared with the optimal weights which lead to the best group consensus, the central weights are an average of those weights which supports the group consensus is acceptable. Thus the collective performances are more reliable.
(2) The ranks of alternative are calculated by the rank acceptability indices. The indices are an interpretable measure which implies how many percentages of weights support the ranking. However, the rankings derived based on the aggregation operators used in [8, 13] or the distance measure used in [7] highly depend on selected measures and cannot describe how the uncertainties affect the rankings.
(3) The introduced decision-making approach is more suitable for the case when the weights of criteria are unknown or partial unknown, compared with other approaches. The approaches in [7, 13] employ certain weights, pre-assigned or computed, for ranking alternatives. The approach in [8] does not need weights. However, it can not include the preferences of weights if they can be provided by the experts.

(4) The introduced decision-making approach presents the same framework to deal with the problems whose performance information is expressed by HFLTSs, LTWHs and PLTSs.

In summary, the merits of the stochastic approach are as follows:

(1) It presents a new way to handle the uncertainty included in the performance values. In our focused GDM problems, the uncertainty of decision information is represented by ULEs. The stochastic approach highlights the fact that ULEs are caused by uncertainties and only one of the possible terms could be the real value. Each ULE is treated as the probabilistic distribution of a stochastic variable and define several descriptive measures. These measures could support the decision makers to understand better how the uncertainties affect the final decision.
(2) It also presents a new approach to handle the uncertainty of weights of both experts and criteria. Based on the same framework, the approach can deal with unknown or partially unknown weights by treating the uncertain weights as stochastic variables. Especially, if the weights are completely known, then the stochastic approach reduces to an approach which handles the uncertainty included in HFLTSs and PLTSs.

Nevertheless, the weaknesses of the stochastic approach are also clear:

(1) Its complexity is much greater than other comparable approaches. This is because the expected values are defined by multidimensional integrals which can only be estimated by such as the Monte Carlo simulation.
(2) The result of Algorithm 3 is not unique. This is because we randomly select possible terms from the group of matrices. Low deviations exist in two executions of this algorithm. If the value of θ is small, then this deviation is usually acceptable.

7.7 Further Discussions

7.7.1 *Complexity and Accuracy of the Simulation Algorithms*

The complexity of Algorithm 1, denoted as ϕ_Ω, depends on the set of subjective preferences $A\omega \leq c$. If no such preference is provided, then the complexity is mainly caused by Step 2 and thus $\phi_\Omega = O(t \log(t))$. If the preference takes the form of a total order, like Eq. (7.21), then the rejection technique is not necessary and the complexity is not increased. Furthermore, according to [11], if the lower bounds of the weights are given, then the complexity is also $O(t \log(t))$.

The complexity of Algorithm 2 is $O(K_W(\phi_\Omega + mnt^2)$, which is due to the generation of weights (Algorithm 1) and the computation of deviations. If no subjective preference increases the complexity of Algorithm 1, then the complexity is $O(K_W(t\log(t) + mnt^2)$. Similarly, the complexity of Algorithm 4 is due to the generation of weights, the computation of ranks which includes the computation of utilities and a sort operation, and the derivation of final results. Its complexity is $O(K_R(\phi_\Omega + mn + m\log(m)) + m^2 + m^2\log(m))$. In practise, $K_R \gg m$, thus the complexity can be rewritten as $O(K_R(mn + 2m\log(m)))$ if no subjective preference is available.

If K_W and K_R are large enough, according to the central limit theory, then the values of CAI and RAI_{iy} are normally distributed. The number of Monte Carlo iterations (K_W and K_R) should be large enough to achieve a satisfactory accuracy. In fact, the error, denoted as err_0, with 95% confidence for CAI and RAI_{iy} requires the following number of iterations [11]:

$$K_W, K_R = 1.96^2/4err_0^2 \tag{7.22}$$

If we let $err_0 < 0.01\%$, then we have $K_W, K_R \geq 9604$. That is why we set $K_R = 10000$ in Sect. 7.6.1. The accuracy of $\omega^{(c)}$ depends on the number of iterations in which the central weights are accumulated. Thus, in order to approach the same accuracy, K_W should be increased to K_W/CAI. This is why we let $K_W = 30000$ in the case study.

7.7.2 Suggestions About the Parameters

The complexity of Algorithm 3 depends on the two parameters, σ and θ, if *Rule 2* is selected. The former implies the risk attitude of the decision maker. The bigger value of σ indicates the lower deviation expected by the decision maker. The latter represents to what extent the probabilities are revised in each iteration. Theoretically, if we let θ be big enough, then if $CAI > 0$, then the acceptable consensus would be reached after one iteration. However, one would never be interested in such a result. To explore how these parameters affect the procedure of consensus improving. We conduct some additional pieces of experiments based on the data in Sect. 7.6.1. Firstly, we fix $\sigma = 5$ and test the cases of θ varying from 0.1 to 0.9. Figure 7.3 shows the numbers of iterations costed in Algorithm 3. Secondly, we also test the cases of σ varying from 1 to 8 by fixing $\theta = 0.2$. The resultant numbers of iterations are shown in Fig. 7.4. The data in these two figures are based on 10 times of experiments. The maximum numbers, median numbers and minimum numbers are shown in these figures.

The following suggestions are useful and rational for potential applications. Roughly, the bigger θ could result in smaller number of iterations in Algorithm 3. But this phenomenon is not prominent when $\theta \geq 0.6$, as can be seen in Fig. 7.3. Whereas the bigger values could bring about major revisions of the probabilistic information. Therefore, we suggest $0.1 \leq \theta \leq 0.6$. Figure 7.4 demonstrates our initial suggestion in Sect. 7.4.3. In our case, the original linguistic information is with acceptable consensus when $\sigma = 1, 2$. If $\sigma \geq 8$, then the numbers of iterations increase sharply. Moreover, associated with the values of RCAIs in Table 7.2, both

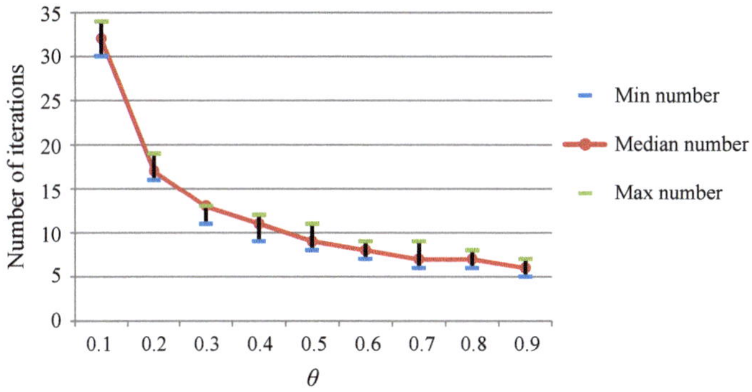

Fig. 7.3 Numbers of iterations of Algorithm 3 with respect to the value of θ based on the data in Sect. 7.6.1

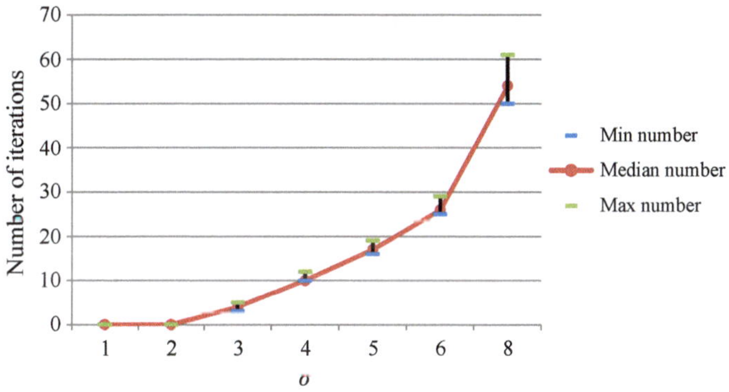

Fig. 7.4 Numbers of iterations of Algorithm 3 with respect to the value of σ based on the data in Sect. 7.6.1

the initial CAI and the threshold CAI_0 are very low and thus not sufficiently admissible. Therefore, we limit $3 \leq \sigma \leq 6$. For the convenience, we suggest $\sigma = 5$ as a compromise value.

7.7.3 Further Extension

When dealing with HFLTSs, LTWHs and PLTSs, the involved probabilistic distributions are discrete. However, this does not mean that the proposed approach can only handle discrete probabilistic distributions. Indeed, it can be directly used in the situations where the uncertain performances vary in any known probabilistic distributions.

In linguistic decision-making, uncertain information is often expressed by ULTs [15]. Given the LTS $S^{(\tau)} = \{s_\alpha | \alpha = 0, 1, \ldots, \tau\}$, an ULT $[s_\alpha, s_\beta]$ indicates that the

Table 7.4 Linguistic performance matrix expressed by ULTs

Criterion	a_1	a_2	a_3	a_4	a_5
c_1	$[s_{5.6}, s_7]$	$[s_{5.7}, s_7]$	$[s_{5.7}, s_{7.1}]$	$[s_5, s_{6.3}]$	$[s_6, s_{7.3}]$
c_2	$[s_{5.3}, s_{6.3}]$	$[s_5, s_7]$	$[s_{5.7}, s_7]$	$[s_{5.7}, s_7]$	$[s_{5.7}, s_{7.3}]$
c_3	$[s_6, s_7]$	$[s_5, s_{6.3}]$	$[s_6, s_7]$	$[s_{5.7}, s_{6.7}]$	$[s_{4.7}, s_6]$

real value is located between s_α and s_β and could be any virtual terms in the interval. It is rational to assume that the real value, considered as a stochastic variable ξ, is uniformly distributed in $[s_\alpha, s_\beta]$. The density function is: $f(\xi) = 1/(\beta - \alpha)$. Then the proposed approach can be employed to solve the GDM problems in which the decision information takes the form of ULTs, associated with the basic operations of the virtual linguistic model. For the purpose of illustration, we consider the problem in [14] and ignore the phase of consensus checking and improving. The collective performances of 5 alternatives with respect to 3 criteria, which are derived by fusing four individual decision matrices, are shown in Table 7.4 (based on $S^{(8)}$). The weights of criteria are unknown.

Using the iterative algorithm in Sect. 7.5, the derived y $(y = 1, 2, 3, 4, 5)$ best ranks acceptability indices of 5 alternatives of the first iteration are as follows:

$$\begin{pmatrix} & y=1 & y=2 & y=3 & y=4 & y=5 \\ a_1 & 0.1738 & 0.4360 & 0.6668 & 0.8707 & 1.0000 \\ a_2 & 0.0719 & 0.2008 & 0.3794 & 0.6463 & 1.0000 \\ a_3 & 0.4565 & 0.7274 & 0.8897 & 0.9746 & 1.0000 \\ a_4 & 0.0777 & 0.2379 & 0.4827 & 0.7167 & 1.0000 \\ a_5 & 0.2201 & 0.3979 & 0.5814 & 0.7917 & 1.0000 \end{pmatrix}$$

Thus a_2 is the one which is the most possible to rank the last place. We remove it and continue the algorithm. When only two alternatives (a_1 and a_3) are left, the first rank acceptability indices are: 0.2935 and 0.7065, respectively. Again, we can see that Algorithm 5 enhances the discrimination. The final ranking is: $a_3 > a_1 > a_5 > a_2 > a_4$.

If we rank the alternatives based on the first rank acceptability indices, then the rank is different from the above one. The possibility of a_1 ranking the first place is less than that of a_5. However, the possibilities of a_1 ranking the first 2, 3, and 4 places are greater than those of a_5. We state that, because of the presence of uncertainty, it is not confident to consider only the possibility of the first rank. Thus, it is not rational to consider that a_5 is better than a_1.

7.8 Conclusions

GDM problems are frequently defined with uncertainties which exist in both the performance information and the weights. In qualitative setting, uncertain performance values could be expressed by HFLTSs, LTWHs and PLTSs elicited by natural or artificial linguistic expressions. Considering the fact that only one, instead of all, possible linguistic term could be the real value, we have introduced a stochastic approach to check and improve the consensus degree of a group and to select the best alternatives. In applications, the weights of experts and criteria might be unknown or partially unknown. the stochastic approach presents some descriptive measures to explore how different weights affect the final decision. The approach has been illustrated by a case study and identified by comparing it with similar techniques.

The stochastic approach presents a new manner to handle uncertainties implied in ULEs. Based on the probabilistic distributions implied in ULTs, HFLTSs, LTWHs and PLTSs, uncertainties are operated by introducing stochastic variables. Compared with other techniques based on the fuzzy linguistic approach, the stochastic approach enables the decision maker a better way to understand how the uncertainties affect the final decision. Moreover, instead of searching for optimal weights, it calculates the central weights. This makes the decision more reliable.

Moreover, this chapter has provided a simple way to support the decision maker to determine the threshold of a set of LDMs rationally, according to his/her risk attitude. Based on this, the decision maker does not have to understand the detail of computation and could stop from selecting arbitrary thresholds.

References

1. Boran, F.E., Genç, S., Akay, D.: Personnel selection based on intuitionistic fuzzy sets. Hum. Factors Ergon. Manuf. Serv. Ind. **21**(5), 493–503 (2011)
2. Dong, Y.C., Chen, X., Herrera, F.: Minimizing adjusted simple terms in the consensus reaching process with hesitant linguistic assessments in group decision making. Inf. Sci. **297**, 95–117 (2015)
3. Kelemenis, A., Askounis, D.: A new topsis-based multi-criteria approach to personnel selection. Expert Syst. Appl. **37**(7), 4999–5008 (2010)
4. Lahdelma, R., Salminen, P.: SMAA-2: stochastic multicriteria acceptability analysis for group decision making. Oper. Res. **49**(3), 444–454 (2001)
5. Liu, H.B., Rodríguez, R.M.: A fuzzy envelope for hesitant fuzzy linguistic term set and its application to multicriteria decision making. Inf. Sci. **258**, 220–238 (2014)
6. Li, Z.M., Xu, J.P., Lev, B., Gang, J.: Multi-criteria group individual research output evaluation based on context-free grammar judgments with assessing attitude. Omega **57**, 282–293 (2015)
7. Pang, Q., Wang, H., Xu, Z.S.: Probabilistic linguistic term sets in multi-attribute group decision making. Inf. Sci. **369**, 128–143 (2016)
8. Rodríguez, R.M., Martínez, L., Herrera, F.: Hesitant fuzzy linguistic term sets for decision making. IEEE Trans. Fuzzy Syst. **20**(1), 109–119 (2012)
9. Saaty, T.L.: Axiomatic foundation of the analytic hierarchy process. Manag. Sci. **32**(7), 841–855 (1986)
10. Sackett, P.R., Lievens, F.: Personnel selection. Ann. Rev. Psychol. **59**, 419–450 (2008)

11. Tervonen, T., Lahdelma, R.: Implementing stochastic multicriteria acceptability analysis. Eur. J. Oper. Res. **178**(2), 500–513 (2007)
12. Wang, H., Xu, Z.S., Zeng, X.J.: A stochastic approach for multi-criteria group decision making with hesitant fuzzy linguistic term sets and probabilistic linguistic term sets. Technical report. Southeast University (2018)
13. Wu, Z.B., Xu, J.P.: Possibility distribution-based approach for MAGDM with hesitant fuzzy linguistic information. IEEE Trans. Cybern. **46**(3), 694–705 (2016)
14. Xu, Z.S.: Uncertain linguistic aggregation operators based approach to multiple attribute group decision making under uncertain linguistic environment. Inf. Sci. **168**(1), 171–184 (2004)
15. Xu, Z.S.: Deviation measures of linguistic preference relations in group decision making. Omega **33**(3), 249–254 (2005)
16. Zhang, G.Q., Dong, Y.C., Xu, Y.F.: Consistency and consensus measures for linguistic preference relations based on distribution assessments. Inf. Fusion **17**, 46–55 (2014)

Part V
Applications

Chapter 8
Provider Selection of Big Data-Based Auditing Platforms with Uncertain Linguistic Expressions

Big data, characterized by an immense volume and high velocity of data with varied and complex structures, have been demonstrated the potential capability of making informative, intelligent and felicitous decisions in various areas. Auditing data share the 5Vs (volume, variety, velocity, veracity and value) of big data [1]. Thus, the profession of audit would benefit from the state-of-the-art big data techniques and technologies as well. Many researchers and auditors are optimistic about introducing big data techniques in audit. Based on an evidentiary requirement perspective, big data could be a valuable complement to traditional audit evidence [10]. Especially, in financial statement audits, big data would benefit to identify and assess the risks of bankruptcy, high-level management fraud, material misstatement of financial statements, and etc [12]. Data consistency, integrity, aggregation, identification and confidentiality are the gaps between big data and the current capabilities of data analysis in continuous auditing.

As an important category of audit, governmental audit has been attached more and more importance by Chinese government. In December 2015, Chinese government issued a new regulation to ensure the implementation of full audit coverage in the big data era. The intention of this regulation is to construct the mode of big data auditing, enhance the capability, efficiency and quality of auditing, and increase the scope and depth of auditing. Towards the targets, some articles of the regulation also pointed out that national auditing systems and platforms (namely big data-based audit platforms, BDAPs) should be built, associated with big data techniques, to enable and/or enhance the capability of analyzing and comparing data from multiple industries and interdisciplinary. One can expect that a series of BDAPs will emerge in a few years. To implement a BDAP, it is essential to evaluate and select from some outsourcing providers. This chapter will construct a hierarchical model of provider section of BDAPs, and implement the selection process by using the approach presented in Chap. 6.

H. Wang and Z. Xu, *Theory and Approaches of Group Decision-Making with Uncertain Linguistic Expressions*, Uncertainty and Operations Research,
https://doi.org/10.1007/978-981-13-3735-2_8

8.1 The Hierarchical Model for BDAP Provider Selection

The drivers of the use of big data in the audit realm include both exogenous forces, which make auditors feel compelled to use them, and endogenous choices, which are caused by the potential benefits of them. The exogenous forces make the audit profession feel that the use of big data is a historical inevitability and a strategic necessity, mainly because big data become an essential component of the business of the clients (auditees) [1]. The endogenous aspect is more optimistic. As big data present the promise of increasing the effectiveness and credibility of work, they are potential to enhance profitability in the case of external auditing and reduce the cost in internal auditing [1]. More importantly, the use of big data techniques could benefit the improvement of audit techniques and capabilities [7, 9, 10, 12].

Proper platforms and infrastructures should be implemented so that big data techniques can be adopted by the audit profession. In the past decade, several auditing platforms were developed, such as ACL[1] and IDEA,[2] for auditing procedures and data of clients' information systems. Similarly, the ubiquity of big data techniques adopted by clients makes auditors to start corresponding platforms so that audit in this new era can be conducted. Especially, the new regulation released by Chinese government also delivered to intensive requirement of designing BDAPs for certain industries.

From the perspective of auditors, or the potential operators, a BDAP should be somewhat like the traditional decision support systems (DSSs). For example, it should be compatible to the operation systems, reliable, and easy to use; the setup and maintain cost should be acceptable; the service quality, including system update and operation training should be satisfactory.

However, the development of a BDAP is very different from that of traditional information systems or DSSs and the differences bring lots of uncertainties of evaluating the outsourcing providers. For instance, when developing an enterprise resource planning systems, most of the necessary techniques are common knowledge for all the potential providers. When facing big data, however, current techniques for almost all aspects of big data processing are far from meeting the ideal requirements. Powerful and state-of-the-art techniques are scattered in some different companies and institutions, maybe preserved by means of patents. This would result in the difficulty regarding assessing the quality of outsourcing providers with respect to big data techniques-related criteria.

Bearing this fact in mind, the selected criteria for evaluating BDAP providers are classified into two parts [8]. The first part focuses on the ability of processing big data and making informative decisions. As can be seen in Table 8.1, two subsets of criteria, namely Data curation and Auditing decision support, are involved and denoted by C_1 and C_2, respectively. Data curation refers to the ability of capturing, cleaning, aggregating, identifying, and protecting data. It prepares high-quality data

[1]http://www.acl.com.

[2]http://www.caseware.com.

Table 8.1 A summary on the hierarchy and criteria of the provider selection model

Criterion in level 1	Criterion in level 2	Weight	Aspiration type
Data curation (C_1)	Data consistency (c_{11})	0.048	Benefit
	Data Integrity (c_{12})	0.037	Benefit
	Data identification (c_{13})	0.043	Benefit
	Data aggregation (c_{14})	0.032	Benefit
	Data confidentiality (c_{15})	0.053	Benefit
Auditing decision support (C_2)	Various data analysis (c_{21})	0.058	Benefit
	Real-time data analysis (c_{22})	0.052	Benefit
	Admissible data analysis (c_{23})	0.058	Benefit
	Data visualization (c_{24})	0.064	Benefit
Service quality (C_3)	System update (c_{31})	0.036	Benefit
	Maintain service (c_{32})	0.037	Benefit
	Training (c_{33})	0.044	Benefit
	System reliability (c_{34})	0.027	Benefit
	Specialization (c_{35})	0.038	Benefit
Integration (C_4)	Compatibility (c_{41})	0.025	Benefit
	Links/Connection (c_{42})	0.023	Benefit
	Flexible (c_{43})	0.021	Benefit
	Customization (c_{44})	0.027	Benefit
Economics (C_5)	Price (c_{51})	0.031	Cost
	Setup cost (c_{52})	0.061	Cost
	Maintain cost (c_{53})	0.042	Cost
Professionalism (C_6)	Reputation (c_{61})	0.053	Interval
	Audit-related experience (c_{62})	0.058	Interval
	Big data-related experience (c_{63})	0.064	Benefit

for data analysis tools. Five criteria are considered to measure the capability of data curation of outsourcing providers.

(1) Data consistency (c_{11}). As data are inevitably generated by different data sources, data conflicts emerge frequently. Three types of inconsistencies, i.e., data format, data synchronization, and data contradiction, might occur in big data [12]. A BDAP should not only supply techniques for the three issues but also offer an effective solution to integrate those techniques in one system.

(2) Data integrity (c_{12}). In big data environment, two issues should be addressed regarding data integrity, i.e., unintentional data modification and incomplete data. It is anticipated to offer highly efficient techniques to audit incomplete information, or alternatively, provide efficient tools to repair the integrity of data.
(3) Data identification (c_{13}). This criterion refers to discover the relationships among several separated pieces of information, generated from distinct data sources, that is related to the same entity. The structures of these pieces might be different. This challenge might be eliminated by some semantics based algorithms or similarity measures based algorithms.
(4) Data aggregation (c_{14}). Aggregating data from different data sources benefits to simplify the structure of big data. In the audit realm, this refers to both the aggregation of raw data and the fusion of exception data. But there is a trade-off regarding this criterion because we may miss detections at the detail level after aggregating.
(5) Data confidentiality (c_{15}). The platform should suffer extremely low risk of data leaking. The security of sensitive data is one of the most urgent goals in a BDAP. Since data can be easily linked with other data in big data, securing confidential data would be much difficult than ever. For example, if data encryption is adopted, then searching and auditing encrypted data would be the resultant challenges.

Auditing decision support focuses on the techniques and technologies involved in the BDAP that are effective enough to support big data-based auditing decisions. According to the characteristics of audit big data, C_2 includes the following four criteria:

(1) Various data analysis (c_{21}). This criterion aims at evaluating the overall capabilities of processing the variety of big data, including the abilities of handling semi-structured, unstructured data, and even incomplete data which take the form of textual natural languages, video, image, audio, and etc.
(2) Real-time data analysis (c_{22}). This is driven by the challenges caused by the volume, variety, and velocity of big data. Informative knowledge should be uncovered from raw data within tolerant time. This consideration would lead to a revolution of the traditional batch processing strategy.
(3) Admissible data analysis (c_{23}). The veracity of big data leads to focus on the credibility of outputs. When big data are involved in audit, the risk of fraud and misstatement in raw data is higher than that in the traditional audit. One of the most important principles of embracing big data is that auditors should get rid of the risk and guarantee the discovered knowledge is admissible.
(4) Data visualization (c_{24}). This criterion is crucial for supporting auditors' judgements. It is acknowledged that the auditors' expertise is very significant no matter how intelligent the algorithms are. Data visualization is a kind of effective tools to interact with users, i.e., auditors.

The criteria in the second part are frequently considered in the provider selection of traditional information systems [2, 4, 6, 11]. These criteria are classified into four subsets, namely, Service quality C_3, Integration C_4, Economics C_5, and Professionalism C_6. Consequently, the hierarchical structure of the proposed model contains 6 groups of 24 criteria, which is shown in Table 8.1. Especially, the Audit-related experience refers to the providers' historical experience of developing auditing information systems or decision support systems. Having such experience would benefit understanding the requirements of auditors in the period of system design. However, too much experience might result in the increase of both negotiation cost and possible obstacle of embracing new idea for auditing. Thus, its aspiration level belongs to the interval form. The big data-related experience focuses on the historical experience of developing big data-based systems and platforms.

The weights of 24 criteria, as shown in Table 8.1, are derived by an extended version of AHP where the entries of each judgement matrix take the form of LTWHs.

8.2 Solving the Model by the M^{3}GDM Approach

As can be seen in the model of Sect. 8.1, many of the selected criteria could only be measured qualitatively. Considering the various types of uncertainties in the evaluations of criteria, we enable the experts to express their opinions by several types of ULEs, including HFLTSs, LTWHs, and LTSs, according to their language conventions. Moreover, the experts are required to express their linguistic aspirations taking the form of CLEs. Thus, the M^{3}QDM approach proposed in Sect. 6.2 can be employed as a solution.

Three groups of experts are invited to evaluate three providers denoted by a_1, a_2, and a_3. The group G_1 is formed by big data experts and data scientists; the group G_2 includes auditors and experts whose specialism is decision support systems; and the experts of the group G_3 are from the financial department. The criteria in C_1 and C_2 are evaluated by the experts in G_1; C_3, C_4 and C_6 are evaluated by G_2; finally C_5 is evaluated by G_3. Moreover, there are three experts in each group.

In the evaluation process, three context-free LTSs, denoted by $S^{(4)}$, $S^{(6)}$ and $S^{(8)}$, are available. The semantics is shown in Fig. 8.1. Associated with the set of linguistic hedges in Eq. (2.47), the experts are allowed to express their aspiration levels and evaluation values by means of ULTs, HFLTS, or LTWHs.

The collected linguistic information with respect to C_1 is listed in Table 8.2 [8]. Then three utility matrices, as shown in Table 8.3, can be derived by using Definition 6.5. To address the group consensus, we obtain the optimal weights of the three experts $\mathbf{w} = (0.33, 0.33, 0.33)$. Accordingly, we have $CI_m = 0.0550$ by using Eq. (6.19). Thus, the group consensus is acceptable.

Associated with the optimal weights, the three utility matrices can be fused to a group utility matrix as follows:

$$\begin{pmatrix} 0.3573 & 0.4013 & 0.4366 & 0.2876 & 0.4250 \\ 0.3210 & 0.7432 & 0.5277 & 0.7215 & 0.1340 \\ 0.2777 & 0.8065 & 0.4284 & 0.4049 & 0.1898 \end{pmatrix} \tag{8.1}$$

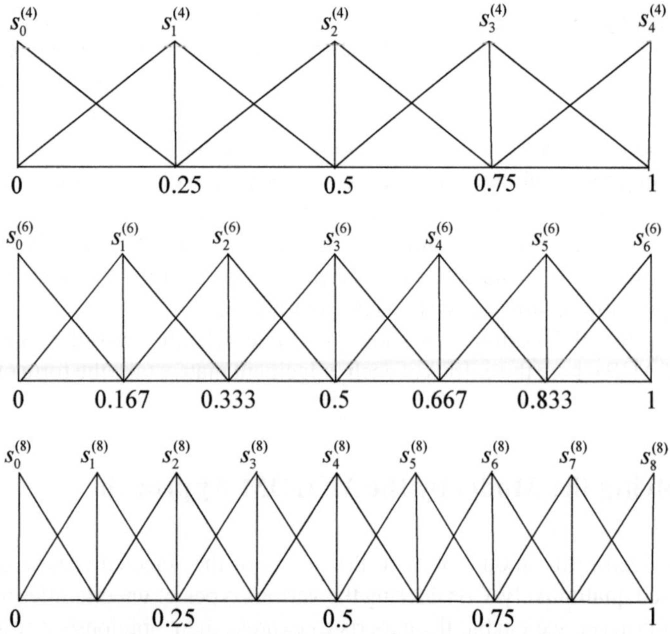

Fig. 8.1 The sets of multi-granularity LTSs for BDAP provider selection

Table 8.2 The evaluation and aspirations of alternatives with respect to C_1

Expert	Criterion	Aspiration	a_1	a_2	a_3
e_{11}	c_{11}	$\{s_3^{(4)}, s_4^{(4)}\}$	$s_3^{(4)}$	$[s_2^{(4)}, s_3^{(4)}]$	$\langle h_1, s_3^{(4)}\rangle$
	c_{12}	$\{s_4^{(6)}, s_5^{(6)}, s_6^{(6)}\}$	$[s_4^{(6)}, s_5^{(6)}]$	$s_4^{(6)}$	$\langle h_1, s_5^{(6)}\rangle$
	c_{13}	$\{s_3^{(6)}, s_4^{(6)}, s_5^{(6)}, s_6^{(6)}\}$	$[s_4^{(6)}, s_5^{(6)}]$	$\langle h_1, s_4^{(6)}\rangle$	$\langle h_2, s_5^{(6)}\rangle$
	c_{14}	$\{s_2^{(4)}, s_3^{(4)}, s_4^{(4)}\}$	$s_3^{(4)}$	$\{s_3^{(4)}, s_4^{(4)}\}$	$s_3^{(4)}$
	c_{15}	$\{s_7^{(8)}, s_8^{(8)}\}$	$\{s_6^{(8)}, s_7^{(8)}\}$	$s_6^{(8)}$	$\langle h_1, s_6^{(8)}\rangle$
e_{12}	c_{11}	$\{s_4^{(6)}, s_5^{(6)}, s_6^{(6)}\}$	$\langle h_1, s_4^{(6)}\rangle$	$s_4^{(6)}$	$[s_3^{(6)}, s_4^{(6)}]$
	c_{12}	$\{s_2^{(4)}, s_3^{(4)}, s_4^{(4)}\}$	$[s_2^{(4)}, s_3^{(4)}]$	$\langle h_1, s_3^{(4)}\rangle$	$s_3^{(4)}$
	c_{13}	$\langle h_1, s_6^{(6)}\rangle$	$s_4^{(6)}$	$\{s_4^{(6)}, s_5^{(6)}\}$	$\langle h_1, s_5^{(6)}\rangle$
	c_{14}	$\{s_4^{(6)}, s_5^{(6)}, s_6^{(6)}\}$	$[s_3^{(6)}, s_4^{(6)}]$	$[s_5^{(6)}, s_6^{(6)}]$	$s_5^{(6)}$
	c_{15}	$\langle h_1, s_4^{(4)}\rangle$	$\langle h_1, s_4^{(4)}\rangle$	$s_3^{(4)}$	$[s_2^{(4)}, s_3^{(4)}]$
e_{13}	c_{11}	$\{s_4^{(6)}, s_5^{(6)}, s_6^{(6)}\}$	$[s_3^{(6)}, s_5^{(6)}]$	$[s_4^{(6)}, s_5^{(6)}]$	$[s_3^{(6)}, s_4^{(6)}]$
	c_{12}	$\{s_3^{(6)}, s_4^{(6)}, s_5^{(6)}, s_6^{(6)}\}$	$s_3^{(6)}$	$\langle h_1, s_4^{(6)}\rangle$	$[s_3^{(6)}, s_5^{(6)}]$
	c_{13}	$\{s_3^{(4)}, s_4^{(4)}\}$	$[s_2^{(4)}, s_3^{(4)}]$	$s_3^{(4)}$	$\langle h_1, s_2^{(4)}\rangle$
	c_{14}	$\{s_2^{(4)}, s_3^{(4)}, s_4^{(4)}\}$	$s_2^{(4)}$	$\langle h_1, s_2^{(4)}\rangle$	$[s_1^{(4)}, s_3^{(4)}]$
	c_{15}	$\langle h_1, s_8^{(8)}\rangle$	$\langle h_1, s_5^{(8)}\rangle$	$[s_5^{(8)}, s_6^{(8)}]$	$[s_6^{(8)}, s_7^{(8)}]$

Table 8.3 The three utility matrices of experts in G_1 with respect to C_1

Expert	Alternative	c_{11}	c_{12}	c_{13}	c_{14}	c_{15}
e_{11}	a_1	0.3618	0.1799	0.2510	0.2510	0.0323
	a_2	0.4825	1	0.3832	0.3504	0.0435
	a_3	0.1691	0.6406	0.1725	0.4062	0.2000
e_{12}	a_1	0.3268	0.5417	0.0588	0.1691	1
	a_2	0.2295	1	0.2000	0.8141	0.2857
	a_3	0.1691	1	0.3913	0.4070	0.2000
e_{13}	a_1	0.3832	0.4825	1	0.3832	0.2427
	a_2	0.2510	0.2295	1	1	0.0728
	a_3	0.4948	0.7788	0.7213	0.4014	0.1694

This matrix serves as the first five columns of the overall utility matrix with respect to all criteria.

Repeating the above process for all six subsets of criteria, the overall utility matrix can be derived. Consequently, the weighted averaging utilities of three alternatives are $u_1 = 0.2863$, $u_2 = 0.2837$ and $u_3 = 0.3158$. Thereafter a_3 is the best alternative.

8.3 Comparisons and Further Discussions

We analyze the M^{3}QDM approach and the hierarchical model by comparing them with some similar techniques in this section. Without loss of generality, we conduct the comparisons by using the linguistic information with respect to the criteria in C_1, i.e., the data in Table 8.2. In this case, $u_1 = 0.3843$, $u_2 = 0.4497$ and $u_3 = 0.3972$. Hence $a_1 < a_3 < a_2$ if only the criteria in C_1 is considered.

8.3.1 Regarding the M^{3}QDM Approach

We begin with comparing the M^{3}QDM approach with two multi-granularity decision-making approaches proposed by Herrera et al. [5] and Fan and Liu [3]. They are comparable because their essential procedures are based on semantics of linguistic terms. Therefore, we transform the original linguistic expressions in Table 8.2 into the corresponding semantics, i.e., trapezoidal fuzzy numbers, before applying the comparable approaches.

In Herrera et al. [5], a basic LTS whose granularity is fine enough is employed. A linguistic expression is then transformed into a fuzzy set on the basic LTS, according to its semantics. Here, the LTS $S^{(8)}$ plays the role of basic LTS. For instance, the ULE $\langle h_1, s_6^{(8)} \rangle$, can be represented as $\{(s_4^{(8)}, 0.33), (s_5^{(8)}, 0.66), (s_6^{(8)}, 1), (s_7^{(8)}, 0.66),$

$(s_8^{(8)}, 0.33)\}$, where the number in each 2-tuple represents the membership degree. To obtain the collective performance of each alternative, an aggregating operator should be relied on. To make the approach comparable, we extend it by aggregating the group's opinion so that it is suitable for GDM. If the weighted averaging operator is considered, then according to their proposed ranking exploitation method, we get $a_1 < a_3 < a_2$.

The approach of Fan and Liu [3] handles both simple linguistic terms and ULTs by means of trapezoidal fuzzy numbers. In order to figure out the collective performance matrix, the traditional trapezoidal fuzzy weighted averaging operator is utilized. Associated with the weighting information, the derived matrix is:

$$\begin{pmatrix} (0.39, 0.64, 0.75, 1.0) & (0.36, 0.56, 0.69, 0.89) & (0.42, 0.61, 0.75, 0.94) & (0.63, 0.58, 0.64, 0.86) & (0.50, 0.79, 0.83, 1.0) \\ (0.42, 0.61, 0.75, 0.94) & (0.36, 0.69, 0.69, 1.0) & (0.44, 0.69, 0.75, 1.0) & (0.39, 0.76, 0.83, 1.0) & (0.54, 0.71, 0.75, 0.92) \\ (0.31, 0.58, 0.69, 0.97) & (0.44, 0.69, 0.81, 1.0) & (0.28, 0.72, 0.72, 1.0) & (0.22, 0.69, 0.86, 1.0) & (0.46, 0.67, 0.79, 1.0) \end{pmatrix}$$

Then the classical TOPSIS is considered, where the positive and negative ideal trapezoidal fuzzy numbers are (1, 1, 1, 1) and (0, 0, 0, 0), respectively, and the Minkowski distance measure between two trapezoidal fuzzy numbers is used and its parameter is fixed by 2. Finally, the ranking of alternatives derived by closeness coefficients is $a_3 < a_1 < a_2$.

It can be seen that the rankings of alternatives with respect to the criteria in C_1 are different. This can be concluded that the consideration of aspiration levels in linguistic setting would greatly influence the final decision. Besides, although it is hard to compare with other techniques through a direct way, we can analyze their characteristics to illustrate the strengths and weaknesses of the M^{3}QDM approach. The strengths are summarized as the following points:

(1) The range of linguistic expressions is extended. Thanks to the proposed M^{3}QDM semantics-based approach, one can deal with three types of ULEs by the same framework. The focused types of ULEs include most of the natural way to express uncertainties in linguistic setting. Experts are permitted to use any type of ULEs to express either linguistic aspirations or evaluation values. Hence, the experts can concentrate on the evaluation rather than stating their opinion by a fixed grammar.

(2) The processing of multi-granularity linguistic information is very easy. For the convenience of evaluation, a set of LTSs are defined on the same domain. During the assessment, the experts can select from the LTSs according to their preference and/or the acquisitus knowledge. When handling this multi-granularity linguistic information, the M^{3}QDM approach defines similarity measures and utilities by means of semantics. This makes the linguistic information be operated as easy as usual.

(3) The M^3QDM approach can handle information provided by several groups of experts. This is meaningful for the complex and complicated GDM problems. Considering the application in this chapter, the M^3QDM approach organizes the groups of experts in a specific manner so that each subset of criteria is evaluated by one group of experts. This manner can be regarded as a special case of the multi-groups decision-making framework defined in Chap. 3.

In sum, the most prominent feature of the M^3QDM approach is that it considers multiple criteria, multiple groups of experts, and multi-granularity linguistic aspiration levels and evaluations simultaneously. The M^3QDM approach suffers some weaknesses which could be improved in the future. Firstly, the group consensus reaching algorithm relies on the interaction with the experts. This might decrease the efficiency of the decision-making process. Moreover, the utility function based on linguistic aspiration levels is adopted to select the most desirable alternatives. This strategy does not follow the traditional way of aspiration-based approaches.

8.3.2 *Regarding the Hierarchical Model*

To the best of our knowledge, the hierarchical model in this chapter is the first one for BDAP evaluation and provider selection. The model is developed based on a similar problem, i.e., information system provider selection. Associated with the critical issues of big data processing, two collections of criteria are included to highlight the significance of data curation and decision support in this circumstance.

According to the linguistic information collected from the groups of experts, as shown in Table 8.2, HFLTs and LTWHs are frequently used to express the aspirations of benefit and cost forms, like *at least good* and *roughly perfect*. ULTs are preferred to represent the aspirations of interval forms, such as *between medium and good*. This phenomenon is natural and can be seen as another evidence of the necessity of enabling all these kinds of linguistic expressions in one decision-making approach.

8.4 Conclusions

This chapter has focused on the model and corresponding solution of the BDAP provider selection. Embracing and employing big data techniques and technologies are inevitable in the audit realm because of both the exogenous forces and the endogenous choices. A BDAP is essential for the auditors to gain the productivity and evolve the profession. The selection of BDAP outsourcing providers motivate to develop the M^3QDM approach because it is quite natural that multiple criteria and multiple groups of experts are involved and multi-granularity linguistic information, taking the form of multiple types of ULEs, is inevitable. Moreover, linguistic aspiration levels have also been considered in the approach. The semantics of ULEs are sufficiently utilized to fuse the linguistic information with distinct granularities and obtain the similarity degrees between evaluation values and aspiration levels. The model and the approach have been identified by a case study. Based on which, we can draw the following conclusions:

(1) The model in Chap. 6 enlarges the range of values that can be assigned to a linguistic variable. Linguistic expressions, taking the form of ULTs, HFLTSs and LTWHs, are available to represent opinions under uncertainties. The use of multiple types of ULEs increases the flexibility of modelling uncertainties.
(2) The consideration of aspiration levels in linguistic setting would greatly influence the final decision. This has been identified by the case study. In real world problems, therefore, it is worthwhile to mine the aspiration levels of the experts.

References

1. Alles, M.G.: Drivers of the use and facilitators and obstacles of the evolution of big data by the audit profession. Account. Horiz. **29**(2), 439–449 (2015)
2. Dibbern, J., Goles, T., Hirschheim, R., Jayatilaka, B.: Information systems outsourcing: a survey and analysis of the literature. ACM Sigmis Database **35**(4), 6–102 (2004)
3. Fan, Z.P., Liu, Y.: A method for group decision-making based on multi-granularity uncertain linguistic information. Expert Syst. Appl. **37**(5), 4000–4008 (2010)
4. Goscinski, A., Brock, M.: Toward dynamic and attribute based publication, discovery and selection for cloud computing. Future Gen. Comput. Syst. **26**(7), 947–970 (2010)
5. Herrera, F., Herrera-Viedma, E., Martínez, L.: A fusion approach for managing multi-granularity linguistic term sets in decision making. Fuzzy Sets Syst. **114**(1), 43–58 (2000)
6. Low, C., Chen, Y.H.: Criteria for the evaluation of a cloud-based hospital information system outsourcing provider. J. Med. Syst. **36**(6), 3543–3553 (2012)
7. Vasarhelyi, M.A., Kogan, A., Tuttle, B.M.: Big data in accounting: an overview. Account. Horiz. **29**(2), 381–396 (2015)
8. Wang, H., Xu, Z.S., Zeng, X.J., Pedrycz, W.: An aspiration-based approach for qualitative decision-making with multiple types of complex linguistic expressions. Technical report, Southeast University (2017)
9. Warren Jr., J.D., Moffitt, K.C., Byrnes, P.: How big data will change accounting. Account. Horiz. **29**(2), 397–407 (2015)
10. Yoon, K., Hoogduin, L., Zhang, L.: Big data as complementary audit evidence. Account. Horiz. **29**(2), 431–438 (2015)
11. Yucel, G., Cebi, S., Hoege, B., Ozok, A.F.: A fuzzy risk assessment model for hospital information system implementation. Expert Syst. Appl. **39**(1), 1211–1218 (2012)
12. Zhang, J., Yang, X.S., Appelbaum, D.: Toward effective big data analysis in continuous auditing. Account. Horiz. **29**(2), 469–476 (2015)

MIX
Papier aus verantwortungsvollen Quellen
Paper from responsible sources
FSC® C105338

If you have any concerns about our products,
you can contact us on
ProductSafety@springernature.com

In case Publisher is established outside the EU,
the EU authorized representative is:
Springer Nature Customer Service Center GmbH
Europaplatz 3, 69115 Heidelberg, Germany

Printed by Libri Plureos GmbH
in Hamburg, Germany